THE GAM / DP THEORY
of Personality and Creativity

Volume III

THE GAM / DP THEORY
of Personality and Creativity

Volume III

William A. Therivel

Kirk House Publishers
Minneapolis, Minnesota

THE GAM / DP THEORY
of Personality and Creativity
Volume III

First Edition

The opinions expressed herein are solely those of the author.

This book is printed on acid-free paper and the binding materials have been chosen for strength and durability.

Library of Congress Cataloging-in-Publication Data
Therivel, William, 1928-
    The GAM/DP theory of personality and creativity / William A. Therivel.
    p.cm.
    Includes bibliographical references and index.
    ISBN 1-886513-52-X
    1. Personality and creative ability. 2. Personality and creative ability–Cross cultural studies. 3. Nature and nurture. I. Title.

    BF698.9.C74 T48 2001
    155.2—dc21
                                                        20011038972

Kirk House Publishers, PO Box 390759, Minneapolis, MN 55439
Manufactured in the United States of America

To Silvia

Contents[i]

---

[i] **G** stands for genetic endowment, **A** for assistances, **M** for misfortunes, **x** for interaction and multiplication, **DP** for division of power, **UP** for unity of power.

Preface

The current volume is a direct continuation of the studies at the base of the previous two volumes. As in volumes 1 and 2, in view of the interdisciplinary nature of the study, I have made use of all the help I could get from the expertise of friends and colleagues. While gratefully acknowledging their assistance, I want to emphasize that any shortcomings are entirely due to myself, and so are all unconventional opinions.

In addition to continued gratitude to my wife Brigitte, I want to extend my thanks to my daughter Silvia for all her help in bringing the first three volumes to completion, and it is to her that this book is dedicated.

As before, references and footnotes follow the system adopted by the American Psychological Associations which separates the references (at the end of the book) from the footnotes (at the bottom of each pertaining page). This separation allows for substantive footnotes that are completely devoted to expanding and clarifying the main text. If at all possible, I would ask the reader not to skip the footnotes.

Quotes are reported verbatim, and not paraphrased, to allow the reader a direct contact with the sources. Whenever possible I have used existing translations of foreign texts, otherwise the translation is mine.

Introduction

This third volume is divided according to the two parts of the theory: Part I includes nine chapters on GAM, and Part II six chapters on DP. All GAM and DP chapters are both an expansion and clarification of the theory and its application,

Part I begins with a long chapter entitled "Gifted Children (High GxA) Will (Should) Become Successful Professionals; Challenged Children (High GxAxM) Will (Should) Become Geniuses". This chapter is offered first to my colleagues in the field of personality and creativity, then to all educators seeking to understand the evolution of their best pupils and all parents of gifted and talented children, and finally to well-educated readers.

Much has been written on gifted and talented children, and on whether or not they become creative. Much of what has been written is of good quality, yet still much remains unclear, and—as reported— even the best experts continue to be unsure on fundamental points and begin their articles or chapters in the form of questions.

What I have done is to consistently apply the GAM theory. This means, basically, to distinguish, point by point, between two groups: the *gifted children* (high GxA), and the *challenged children* (high GxAxM). Once we remember from the previous volumes what it means to be a *challenged personality*, from the additional impact of one or more major misfortunes of youth (and by contrast what it means not to be *challenged*), things quickly fall into place.

The coda of "Appendix 1. Paul Klee: GAM *miner*" is there to back some of the things that I said in the main chapter, and to present evidence that the GAM theory is able to forecast an important aspect of a great creator's personality.

Chapter 2, "GAM's Personality Families Versus Eric Newton's Personality Styles" is a continuation of chapter 9 in volume 1,

"GAM's *Hedgehogs* and GAM *Foxes*", only that this time it is not Isaiah Berlin's classification which is explained, but that by Eric Newton which classifies the personal style of painters into Classic, Romantic, and Realist. At the end, the reader should feel endowed with a triple system with which to understand and appreciate great minds and their works, because the labels Classic, Romantic and Realist apply not only to painters, nor the labels *hedgehog* and *fox* only to writers. By relating the Berlinian and Newtonian classifications to GAM (i.e., to the GxAxM of youth), each classification should acquire an added and fascinating degree of biographical validity.

The next two chapters, "In Praise of *Pruning*; and on the Dangers of Success" and "Thomas Mann's Tragic Lack of *Pruning*" no longer deal with a person's youth but with the continuation of creativity in adulthood.

Chapter 5 "Like Goethe, Calvino was a Berlinian *Fox* by being a GAM *Alchemist*," is a companion piece to chapter 10 of volume 1 "*Maître Renard* James Joyce", only that this time two *maîtres renards* are studied in parallel: Calvino and Goethe. This same subject is then further explored in chapter 7 "Why Berlinian *Fox* or *Hedgehog*?"

The other two chapters, 6 and 8, deal with two GAM personality families: the *trappers* shaped by the misfortune of suffered illegitimate birth (only that here the chapter limits itself to the study of *trappers* who were military commanders, specifically Jephthah and Alexander Hamilton), and the *architects* shaped by early parental death and an aristocratic or business/industrial education.

Part II starts with a long chapter entitled "The Strict *Ritter Personality* of the Japanese", a companion piece of chapter 25 of volume 1 "The *Ritter Personality* of the Germans" and of chapters 5 and 6 of volume 2 on the ethnopsychology of the French and the Spaniards.

All the titles of the remaining chapters are self explanatory with the exception of 11 which should have been longer, i.e., "The liberating civic power of the English Bible under DP, in contrast with the less-liberating civic impact of the German Bible under the partial UP of its princes". While the title of chapter 13 is very simple "DP precursors of Canossa", some of its sections may be an eye opener for some readers and a welcome confirmation for others.

By now, readers are familiar with my deeply felt mantra of "Please do not read this volume before having read volumes 1 and 2," otherwise much will be unclear and seem unjustified. Equally deeply felt, I wish them a most pleasant journey, one chapter after the other.

PART I

1

Gifted/Talented Children (High GxA) Will(Should) Become Successful Professionals; Challenged Children (High GxAxM) Will(Should) Become Geniuses

This chapter is divided into the following sections

1. Introduction: Genius and Giftedness/Talents are Different
2. Definitions
3. Creativity (Definitions and Proposed Classification)
4. Nature and Nurture
5. The Challenged Youth
6. When and Why can the Misfortunes be Creativogenic
7. Intelligence
8. Hard Work
9. Achievement Motivation
10. Qualitatively or Quantitatively Different?
11. Implications for Educational Practice
12. The Relative Importance of Fit
13. Which Kind of Creativity? *Les Demoiselles d'Avignon*?
14. Adolescence, Graveyard of Gifted and Talented Creativity
15. The Stigma of Giftedness
16. The Difficulties of Managing Giftedness in the Peer World
17. Reinventing Oneself, or Being Challenged?
18. Evidence for the GAM Theory: Klee's *Miner Personality*
19. Fruitful Asynchrony?
20. How Important is Creativity in Childhood?
21. Gifted Persons Should Court the Field; Challenged Divide It

1. Introduction: Genius and Giftedness/Talents are Different

Dean Keith Simonton's chapter in the *International Handbook of Giftedness and Talent* (2000) is entitled: "Genius and giftedness: Same or different?" Early in his chapter, Simonton asked: "Does giftedness necessarily transform into genius? If not, why not. And on the other side of the coin, does all genius display giftedness in youth?" (p. 111). Simonton then restated this same problem at the end of his chapter "as two absolutely essential questions:

> (1) Why do so many gifted children fail to realize their potential upon becoming adults? What are the places where the development trajectory is most likely to veer off target? What are the most common blind alleys? This is the problem of the 'nipped bud'.

> (2) Why is it that many highly successful adults managed to display no clear signs of giftedness in their early years? Does the developmental trajectory for these unpromising youths differ in some qualitative manner from that which guides the precocious child to adulthood achievement? This is the problem of the 'late bloomer'" (ib., p. 118).

My answer, as explained in this chapter, is precise:

1. Genius and giftedness are different.
2. Giftedness/talents (high GxA) is not the potential for genius but for professional success.
3. There is no reason why giftedness should transform into genius (i.e., realized high GxAxM); *Challengedness* (high GxAxM) is the potential for genius.

4. Harmonious peer relations are important for the *gifted (➔) success-ful*[1], but not of much importance for the *challenged (➔) genius*.

5. Many gifted suffer of the *Stigma of Giftedness Paradigm* (SGP); practically no *challenged* suffer from of it.

6. We should not talk of buds and nipped buds, nor of early or late bloomers, but of a potential which is realized, or not, in adulthood. A "bud" has in itself everything it needs for blooming; a potential needs much more, for instance long years of focused hard work, pruning, a dynamic DP environment.

7. Without the impact of a major misfortune(s) of youth (the M of GxAxM) on personal script formation, it is nearly impossible to fight an important *war of the scripts* with society, and consequently to develop a new valid vision (the *conditio sine qua non* for sustained high creativity).

8. Finally: gifted/talented children (high GxA) will/should become successful professionals; *challenged* children (high GxAxM) will/should become highly creative (i.e., geniuses).

The above does not exclude the fact that, in a few cases, the same person can be first a gifted child not yet affected by major misfortunes, then a challenged youth, because of major misfortunes of youth, and finally a genius in adulthood. This was the case with Mozart and Picasso.

It is in reference to Picasso's evolution, from gifted to challenged, that we read the following:

> Around this time Pablo [aged 12 to 13] must have realized that, compared with other bourgeois families, his parents were poor and déclassé, and that his beloved father was a pathetically bad teacher and painter. This realization would have dealt Pablo's pride a grievous blow. His response was embodied in a determination to exorcise the stigma of paternal failure by a triumphant display of his own gifts, something that can only have increased his guilt toward his father. (Richardson, 1991, p. 48)

---

[1] I use this little arrow (➔) to indicate the potential.

In parallel, young Pablo—like young Mozart and young Goethe (and all three became *challenged personalities*)—must have realized that in order to exorcise the stigma of the paternal failure, he had to be different from the father in many more things than painting techniques: he had to face life differently, he had to refuse many of the paternal scripts, and, instead, build his own.

Picasso's evolution from gifted to challenged had already begun before (in a process which parallels that of Goethe, and his strong interest for the French language and theater):

> The more the father came to loathe Corunna, the more the son came to love it—so much so that he eventually learned enough dialect to recite poems by Rosalia, the Galician laureate, and to sing songs in Galego. In old age Picasso chided the Galicians for forgetting all about the formative years he had spent in their midst—at the outset such happy years. (ib., p. 41)

The problem was not only the father:

> Although the family was obliged to live on the father's miserable salary as an art teacher, they were never in actual want, thanks to a network of prosperous relatives. However the stigma of being a poor relation permanently bruised Picasso's pride. He remembered charity, above all the niggardly charity of his rich uncle Salvador, the benefactor who stood for the bourgeois hypocrisy and stuffiness that Picasso associated with Málaga. (ib., p. 14)

This same evolution from gifted to challenged can be seen in young Charles Dickens. "His father and mother accepted the offer very willingly, and on a Monday morning only two days after his twelfth birthday Charles started to work. The event left him stunned, sick with despair. [Later he wrote:]

> It is wonderful to me how I could have been so easily cast away at such an age. It is wonderful to me, that, even after my descent into the poor little drudge I had been since we came to London, no one had compassion enough on me - a child of singular abilities, quick, eager, delicate, and soon

hurt, bodily or mentally - to suggest that something might have been spared, as certainly it might have been, to place me at any common school. Our friends, I take it, were tired out. No one made any sign. My father and mother were quite satisfied. They could hardly have been more so, if I had been twenty years of age, distinguished at a grammar-school, and going to Cambridge" (Johnson, 1977, p. 31).

Then, after five months, a small legacy had enabled the father to pay his debts, emerge from prison, and a little later—after a quarrel with the manager of the warehouse—he announced that the boy should cease working and be sent back to school. "[Charles's] mother was appalled. Probably John Dickens's affairs were not yet straightened out. . . . How could they afford to throw away even the seven shillings a week Charles had now been earning?. . . . But John Dickens had taken a stand. Charles, he said, should go back to the blacking warehouse no more, but should go to school. On the boy their divergent positions made a deep impression. He summarized it:

> I do not write resentfully or angrily for I know how all these things have worked together to make me what I am: but I never afterwards forgot, I never shall forget, I never can forget, that my mother was warm for my being sent back. (ib., p. 40)
>
> The time that Charles had spent in the warehouse amounted to no more than five months, but the lonely anguish he endured had made it seem an eternity of suffering. The wound was so deep that its emotional scar remained with Dickens forever. All the remainder of his life he lay under the double shadow of the Marshalsea [where his father had been gaoled for debt] and the workroom dungeon where he had toiled in despair. The experience was crucial for Dickens's entire future course. It is hardly fanciful to say that in the blacking warehouse that unhappy child died, and into his frail body entered the spirit of a man of relentless determination. Deep within him, he resolved that he should never again be so victimized. He would toil, he would fall prey to none of his father's financial imprudence, he would let nothing stand between him and ambition. He would batter his way out of all the gaols that confine the human spirit. (Johnson, 1969, p. 45)

2. Definitions

As will be seen, my own definitions of giftedness/talents and of genius are very short, definitely too short if not presented after several definitions and explanations by others (each dealing with one of the many sides of our field of inquiry):

- Eysenck & Barrett (1993) viewed [correctly] giftedness as a 'fuzzy concept' that can be defined in three major ways: "(1) as synonymous with *general intelligence*; (2) as synonymous with *creativity*; (3) as synonymous with *special (artistic and scientific) ability.*"

- [And that] Renzulli (1982) has asserted that despite efforts throughout the century, "the precise definition of giftedness remains a question with no universally accepted answer". He suggests that the many definitions of gifted range along a continuum from a 'conservative' end represented by Terman's definition of the top 1% in general intellectual ability to the more 'liberal' definition of Witty who recommended that the definition of giftedness be expanded to include any child "whose performance, in a potentially valuable line of human activity, is consistently remarkable". (Mönks, Heller, & Passow, 2000, p.842).

A. Compact, or Simple, Definitions by Others

- **Gifted** "covers all who are naturally endowed with a high degree of mental ability, either general or special" (Burt, 1973, p. 406).

- "Giftedness in a child or adolescent consists of psychological and physical predispositions for superior learning and performance in the formative years and high-level. . . . [Giftedness] includes (a) general intellectual ability, (b) positive self-concept, (c) achievement motivation, and (d) talent" (Feldhusen, 1987, p. 112).

- "Generally, children whose IQ scores are more than two or three standard deviations above the mean are regarded as intellectually gifted. Thus, the minimum IQ score for accelerated programs usually falls somewhere between 130 and 145" (Weiten, 1989, p. 117).

In my readings of the biographies of eminent persons, I have generally been impressed by their high intelligence[2], something in line with the 1926 study, by Catherine Cox: "Her 301 geniuses also displayed a higher degree of intelligence, with IQ scores also averaging around 150 (prior to introducing the correction of data reliability" (Simonton, 2000, p. 112).

Also, in my own words: **Talented children** are those endowed with specific capabilities, for instance for finger coordination, pitch discrimination, memory and handling of tunes and notes or numbers, for running quickly and at length, for directing a ball far away with precision and strength. These are children who, for instance, will be able to draw faithful designs with very little training, will learn to play tennis well with fewer lessons. This definition agrees with the following by Feldhusen and Jarvan (2000): "Talent is a specific ability within a domain of human activity such as art, music, mathematics, political science, drama or literature [and sports]" (p. 274). **Gifted and talented children** are those in which the two types of endowment (intelligence and talents) are present. They are commonly called G/T children.

B. Broader Definitions

American Mensa (the high IQ society) has published, around 1990, a little brochure entitled *Nurturing the Gifted Child: A resource guide for parents*, a list of characteristics of the Gifted Child, based on an original list by The Council of Exceptional Children, of Reston, VA:

> The outstanding abilities of gifted children often enable high-performance in one or a combination of areas including general intellectual ability, specific academic ability, visual or performing arts, creative thinking, leadership, and psychomotor abilities. *Using a broad definition of giftedness, a school system could expect to identify 10% to 15% or more of its student population as gifted and talented.*[my italics, to stress the relatively high prevalence of gifted and talented children]

---

[2] And also impressed by the many with a high (intelligent) sensitivity, i.e., capable of understanding people and situations. Correspondingly, gifted children should not only be those rich in *esprit de géometrie*, but also those rich in *esprit de finesse* (the two minds discussed by Pascal 1647/1976, pp. 315, 345-7).

Characteristics of a gifted child may include:

1. Superior reasoning powers and ability to handle ideas, 2. Persistent intellectual curiosity, 3. Avid reading, 4. Superior written and/or spoken vocabulary, 5. Wide interests, often developing one or more in depth, 6. Ability to learn quickly and easily, and retain what is learned, 7. Insight into arithmetical problems that require careful reasoning and grasp of mathematical concepts, 8. Creative ability and/or imaginative expression in dance, music, art and drama, 9. Sustained concentration for lengthy periods.10. High standards and self-criticism, 11. Initiative and originality in intellectual work, 12. Keen observation and responsiveness to new ideas, 13. Social poise and ability to communicate with adults, 14. Excitement and pleasure from intellectual challenge. (ca. 1990, pp. 10-11)

Many schools have developed all inclusive definitions, for instance a booklet by the Humble Independent School District says that: "Gifted/talented children are those students, identified by professionally qualified persons, who consistently excel or show the potential for excelling. . . . The G/T program is designed as a differentiated curriculum, offering opportunities for growth and enrichment to the academically gifted/talented student. The areas of giftedness to be served include 1. general intellectual ability, 2. specific subject matter aptitude, 3. creative/productive thinking abilities, 4. leadership abilities" (1991, p. 6).

Moving forward in time: "In the year 2000, it would appear that the multi-dimensions of giftedness and the concept of multiple talents will prompt the design and employment of much more authentic and complex identification procedures; less reliance on single tests, particularly IQ tests; more design and dependence on self-identification wherein individuals can demonstrate their talent potential by their performances and products; much more use of enrichment curricular opportunities to provide the basis for manifestation of talent potential and increased efforts to identify talent potential among the many seriously underrepresented populations" (Mönks, Heller, & Passow, 2000, p. 842).

Some talents are labelled *intelligences* by Howard Gardner who identified seven intelligences[3]: 1. logical-mathematical, 2. linguistic, 3. musical, 4. spatial, 5. bodily-kinesthetic, 6. interpersonal (capacity to discern and respond appropriately to moods, temperaments, motivations, and desire of other people), 7. intrapersonal (detailed accurate self-knowledge); (Gardner and Hatch, 1989, p. 6).

Winner and Martino (2000), instead, refer "to children with talent in an art form as gifted" (p. 95), and to their talents as gifts; and "Cropley (1995b) regarded creativity as indispensable for 'true' giftedness,. . . . [while] Hassenstein (1988) argued that a new term is needed to refer to intellectual giftedness, since 'intelligence' is too narrow, and suggested *Klugheit* (cleverness), arguing that this incorporates both intelligence (e.g., factual knowledge, accurate observation, good memory, logical thinking, and speed of information processing) and creativity (e.g. inventiveness, unusual associations, fantasy, and flexibility)" (Cropley & Urban, 2000, p. 485).

In advance of what will be discussed in the next section, the following by Feldhusen and Jarvan (2000) is important: "We argue that giftedness is basically genetic endowment that paves the way to the development of specific abilities, aptitudes, and talents" (pp. 273-74).

Potential: Obviously, people are interested in a child's gifts and talents because they read these gifts and talents as a potential: "Giftedness is an individual potential for exceptional achievement in one or more domains" (Mönks & Mason, 2000, p. 144); and, as reported before, "Giftedness in a child or adolescent consists of psychological and physical predisposition for superior learning and performance in the formative years, and high-level achievement or performance in adulthood " (Feldhusen, 1987, p. 112).

Prodigies are children "who can [very[4]] easily and rapidly master a domain with expertise" (Winner & Martino, 2000, p. 107). Prodigies are "children who perform at an extremely high level within a specific field at a very early age. Genius, on the other hand, implies the transformation of a field of knowledge that is fundamental and irreversible. A prodigy does not transform but rather shows unusual capability within an existing field" (Feldman, 1986, p. 15).

---

[3] Here, "Both cultural and developmental determinants affect which of the intelligences is emphasized, with a biological component determining inclinations and susceptibility to environmental shaping" (Schoon, 2000, p. 213).

[4] I have added "very" to distinguish prodigies from gifted/talented who, also, can easily and rapidly master a domain with expertise.

"A prodigy is a child who, before the age of 10, performs at the level of a highly trained adult in some cognitively demanding domain. . . . Thus, in most cases of prodigiousness, a child of extraordinary native ability is born into a family recognizing, valuing, and fostering that ability when the child's introduction to the culturally available domain reveals its presence. The child is generally exposed to master teachers who instruct the prodigy in a way most likely to engage the interest and sustain the commitment of the child. Invariably, as well, the child demonstrates a combination of inner-directness and passionate commitment to the field of achievement. Prodigious achievement only occurs in domains accessible to children, requiring little prerequisite knowledge and using media and techniques adaptable to a child's use (e.g., a child-sized violin must be available for a 6-year-old prodigy violinist). Most child prodigies are found in chess and music performance. There have been, however, child prodigy visual artists (Pariser, 1987; Goldsmith & Feldman, 1989), infrequently, a child prodigy in mathematics (Bühler, 1981), and occasional writing prodigies (Radford, 1990; Feldman, 1991; Morelock, 1995)" (Morelock & Feldman, 2000, p. 227-28).

Expanding on the above:

We are often astonished by past examples of extremes in human creativity. The list of musical prodigies, for example, is long. Handel played the clavichord 'when but an infant' and was composing by the age of 11. Haydn played and composed at the age of 6. Mozart played the harpsichord at 3, was composing at 4, and was on a tour at age 6. Chopin played in public at the age of 8; Liszt, at 9, Verdi, at 10; Schubert, at 12; and Rossini, at 14. Mendelssohn was playing and composing by the age of 9, Debussy at 11, Dvorak at 12, and Berlioz at 14. . . . As if this information were not oppressive [sic] enough, let me remind you that John Stuart Mill began the study of Greek at age 3, and by the age of 8 he had read Xenophon, Herodotus, and Plato and had begun to study geometry and algebra. At 12 he began logic, reading Aristotle in the original Greek. (McNeil, 1974, p. 264)

Impressive here is the contrast between the first and the second of the above two groups: while for music there is mention of performing first, then of creating (composing), as soon as we move to history and philosophy there is only mention of study. Said simply—and in line with what is said above by Morelock and Feldman—as soon as we move to history and philosophy, there are no creative child prodigies, only studying child prodigies.

Mono-savants (or *idiots savants*, or affected by the *savant syndrome*—see Miller, 1999) are children, or adults, "who present the most striking cases of unevenness, and extreme ability coexists with a subnormal IQ. Savants are retarded, autistic, or both, yet exhibit a strong gift in a particular domain (typically music, visual art, or numerical calculation)" (Winner, 2000, p. 155).

"Prodigious savants occur chiefly within the area of music, mathematics, (lightning and calendar calculating), and memory (Treffert, 1989)" (Morelock & Feldman, 2000, p. 229).

Interestingly, the primary area of the prodigious savant is the same as that of child prodigies: music (with its relations to mathematics), high numerical memory, and chess. The first and third of these domains bring to mind (with no offense to my preferred and most revered composer) the following words of praise for Bach: "One could probably liken [his] task of improvising a six-part fugue to playing of sixty simultaneous blindfold games of chess, and winning them all" (Hofstadter, 1980, p. 7).

Genius, according to Drewer (1962), is "the highest range of mental ability, either general, or in respect of special capacities of a creative order" (p. 107). Then, as reported by Lens and Rand (2000), "Merriam Webster's Collegiate Dictionary (1993, 10th edition, p. 486) defines 'genius' as 'extraordinary intellectual power especially as manifested in creative ability' and 'gifted' as 'having great natural ability'" (p. 193). The last part, on the gifted, seems a valid and well-rounded definition.

C. GAM's Definitions

Finally,

*1. According to the GAM theory, **evident giftedness** (i.e. giftedness and talent) is the normal manifestation of a high GxA.*

This is a most inclusive causal definition because it only excludes what is the result of a high GxAxM. A high GxA may be a high IQ, a high generalized intelligence, evident talents, or one or more of the seven Gardnerian intelligences, or a high level of "normal" creativity, but not revolutionary (which, according to the GAM theory, is the result of a high GxAxM).

A high GxA starts from a high G which is then realized (and magnified) by good assistances. A high GxA (and the same is true for a high GxAxM) is both an actuality (noticeable in the child), and a potential for adult life. Actuality and potential may be less evident in the case of a high GxAxM because the impact of the misfortunes of youth may hide, or even block for a while the presence of a high GxA. Also, the adult creativity of the challenged personality may be unrelated to the giftedness and talents of childhood by being a separate phenomenon (as discussed in volume 1, and hereafter). There are also important cases in which the misfortunes brought with them, or stimulated, quality assistances which would not have been available otherwise.

*2. According to GAM, **genius** is the challenged personality who has realized his/her creative high GxAxM potential.*

Challenged children, are children with a high GxA who have also been affected by one or more major misfortunes of youth (see volume 1). Their personality cannot be understood without taking into account the working of those misfortunes. Challenged children (or youths) have a high GxAxM personality, and a high GxAxM potential. In addition (see chapter 3 of volume 1, on the Fourteen GAM Challenged Personality Families), there are important personality similarities among those affected by the same type of misfortune.

3. Creativity (Definitions and Proposed Classification)

Much of what follows will be clearer if we are able to distinguish among types and levels of creativity. I present hereafter a series of definitions integrated within my proposed classification system, in which creativity is ranked from C1 to C10, C1 meaning little creativity (*little-c*, for Winner and Martino, 2000, p. 95), C10 meaning the highest creativity (the *big-C* of Winner and Martino).[5]

This distinction, in levels of creativity, should hopefully also bring some clarity to the "perennial issue [in] the relation between intelligence and creativity" (Mönks, Heller, & Passow, 2000, p. 853).

Creativity C1 to C2

"Gifted children are creative in the *little-c sense*, meaning that they solve problems in novel ways and make discoveries about their domain on their own" (Winner & Martino, p. 95). This creativity can be labelled C1-C2 .

In children, creativity C1-C2 is the one related to age, (i.e., it refers to acts of creation which are outstanding in comparison to what is done by other children of the same age or even a few years older), but not outstanding per se, (i.e., not outstanding if they were the work of an adult with years of experience).

Here, "A product or response is creative to the extent that appropriate observers independently agree it is creative. Appropriate observers are those familiar with the domain in which the product was created or the response articulated" (Amabile, 1990, p. 65). For instance, qualified kindergarten teachers can independently agree that a given design is creative, and this creative design may not come from the brightest child.

Creativity C1-C2 (and up to C3-C4) is the creativity which is normally expected from a truly intelligent person, as per the following definition by *Webster's New World Dictionary*: "Intelligence is the

---

[5] Strictly speaking, at this stage, my classification is a five point scale (two extremes, a middle point, and two intermediates); however a ten point scale has two important advantages: it is the best known scale, and it allows for future fine-tuning. Five, indeed, is the number of levels of creativity suggested by I. R. Taylor (1959) as discussed by Torrance: 1. Expressive creativity, as in the spontaneous drawings of children; 2. Productive creativity, as in artistic or scientific products where there are restriction and controlled free play; 3. Inventive creativity, where ingenuity is displayed with materials, methods, and techniques; 4. Innovative creativity, where there is improvement through modification involving conceptualizing skills; 5. Emergenative creativity, where there is an entirely new principle or assumption around which new schools, movements, and the like can flourish. Taylor pointed out that many people have the fifth level in mind when they talk about creativity. Because this fifth level is so rare, the lower levels usually have been involved in most investigations regarding creative behavior" (1988, p. 46).

ability to *respond quickly and successfully to a new situation*; use of the faculty of reason in solving problems, directing conduct, etc. effectively" (1988, p. 702, my italics). We can refer the following comments by Sternberg and Lubart to C1-C2 (and up to C3-C4): "We find creativity in everyday life when people see new ways of accomplishing different tasks in their work, when they try daring new ways of relating to one another, and when they strive to turn their lives around" (1995, p. vii).

Creativity C3 to C4

This is the creativity of quality professionals, for instance of the top 10% of architects at any given time and place, or the creativity of the best designers of advertising material. This is the creativity of a Norman Rockwell, and of the higher echelon of researchers in industrial laboratories.

Creativity C3-C4 are the new cadenzas of good quality.[6] For excellent musical performers, with extensive expertise, creating a good new cadenza is natural: a wonderful extrapolation of what they normally do, often with inclusion of stylistic elements from later musical developments, for instance a Lisztian cadenza on Mozart themes.

The following two definitions may apply to C3-C4:

• "Truly creative work is characterized by its distinctness and originality" (McNeil, 1974, p. 265);
• "Creativity is the ability to produce work that is both novel (i.e. original, unexpected) and appropriate (i.e., useful, adaptive concerning task constraints" (Sternberg & Lubart, 1999, p. 3).

Creativity C5 to C6

In science, C5-C6 would be the quality *normal science* discussed by Thomas Kuhn (1970), meaning "research firmly based upon one or

---

[6] "Cadenza is the name given to an unaccompanied bravura passage introduced at or near the close of a movement as a brilliant climax, particularly in solo concertos of a virtuoso character where the element of display is prominent. Until well into the 19th century these interpolated passages were often improvised by the performer, at suitable openings left for the purpose by the composer. They were displays not only of executive power but also of more or less spontaneous imagination and invention" (Donington, 1973, p. 562).

more past scientific achievements, achievements that some particular scientific community acknowledges for a time as supplying the foundation for its further practice. Today such achievements are recounted, though seldom in their original form, by science textbook, elementary and advanced" (p. 10).

Creativity C5-C6 would be the one manifested by the majority of the scientific Nobel laureates, especially those who received a prize in conjunction with one or more colleagues from different laboratories or countries. Basically, theirs is great creativity, but of a kind that is time related: if the discovery or new concept is not made now, it will most probably be made within the next ten years. Usually, the name of these inventors/creators remains known within a relatively small circle, and only for a limited number of years.

Creativity C5-C6 are the dozens of musical compositions that nearly every great conductor writes during a successful career. As with the cadenzas, with so much musical expertise, such compositions, even if of good quality, can be considered "natural", a high quality by-product of their normal work.

Creativity C7 to C8

C7 to C8 is the creativity that borders on the C9-C10 of the giants: it is great creativity. From C7 onward, intelligence in its old general meaning (ability to respond quickly and successfully to a new situation) plays a definite role: without a good intelligence, no C7 to C10 act of creation is possible. Creativity C7-C8 is that of Richard Strauss and Somerset Maugham, as discussed shortly.

Creativity C9 to C10

This is the creativity of the pinnacles, of the undisputable giants. Nearly always, creativity C9-C10 can be labelled *revolutionary*. In science this is the creativity of Galileo, Newton, Darwin, and Einstein; in music this is the creativity of Bach, Handel, Mozart, Beethoven, Wagner and Tchaikovsky; in literature this is the creativity of Dante, Cervantes, Shakespeare, Goethe and Tolstoy. Everybody will have additional names, but practically nobody will deny the highest accolade to those just listed.

Interestingly, even such a great composer as Richard Strauss knew the limits of his art when he said "I may not be a first-class composer, but I *am* a first-class second-rate composer" (quoted by Del

Mar, 1986, *1*, p. xii). And the same is true for Somerset Maugham: "[who] said that he had small power of imagination, that he was a Constable and not a Michelangelo, who had painted easel pictures, not frescoes. 'I know just where I stand,' he wrote. 'In the very first row of the second-raters'" (Morgan, 1980, p. 501).

Finally, looking at the high side of the spectrum, creativity C8 to C10 would be "Big-C creativity, or domain creativity [and] involves changing the domain" (Winner & Martino, 2000, p. 95). It is the long term product of a vision; and it is not teachable (while C1 to C5 can be said to be, in part, teachable). Here we can use the following definitions:

- "Creativity involves the generation of ideas that are original, novel and useful. First and foremost, creativity involves seeing the world in a new and different light" (Weiten, 1989, p. 292).
- A creative individual is "a person who regularly solves problems, fashions products, or defines new questions in a domain in a way that is initially considered novel but that ultimately becomes accepted in a particular cultural setting" (Gardner, 1993, p. 35).
- The most creative ideas have meanings that coalesce over time. In other words, the depth and value of an extremely creative idea often is not apparent at first but becomes more obvious as time passes" (Dworetzky, 1985, p. 386).[7]

---

[7] Caveat: In reality, the above C1-C10 conflates thousands of specialized classifications, one for each domain (e.g. science, sociology, philosophy, psychology, painting, sculpture, music, technology, jurisprudence, military strategy, political and national leadership, sports, industry, commerce), and for each culture, country, epoch. Within the scope of the GAM theory, the problem is not that of finding the ideal classification system, but of uncovering the roots of creativity. One may debate at length if a C10 creativity in jurisprudence or national leadership or industry deserves a C6 or C7 on the overall creativity scale, but less debatable may be the finding by GAM that a C10 in industry, and the founding of a long lived industrial family, is mostly done by a challenged personality.

Albert (1983b) had summarized the results of several surveys on the high prevalence of early parental death among eminent people: presidents, prime ministers, Nobel laureates, and great scientists. For the American Presidents the percent of those having suffered of early parental death was 34%, for British Prime Ministers 35%, for Cox's Historical Geniuses 30%, while for the General British Population it was 8% only (p. 148). In other words, independently of how high or low we rank the creative acts of Presidents and Prime Ministers, such tips of the national pyramids are very often challenged personalities bringing to their job an uncommon vision, drive, and new solutions.

4. Nature and Nurture

Personality first, and then creativity, are, as so much in life, the result of nature interacting with nurture.

Nature for Intelligence

"At the high end a number of researchers maintain the heritability of IQ is about 80%, with only 20% of the variation in intelligence due to environmental factors. A great many researchers characterize the 80% figure as a high estimate. However, even the estimates at the low end of the range suggest that the heritability of intelligence appears to be at least 40%. . . . [Yet], a heritability estimate is a *group statistic* based on studies of trait variability within a specific group, and it cannot be applied meaningfully to individuals. In other words, even if the heritability of intelligence truly is 80%, this does not mean that each individual's intelligence is 80% inherited" (Weiten, 1989, p. 323).[8] Thompson and Plomin (2000), in summarizing "the vast literature on general intelligence across the normal range of ability," concluded that "heritability accounts for roughly 50% of the phenotypic variation, shared environmental influences account for 10-20%, thus leaving 30-40% of the variation to non shared environment and error (Chipeur, Rovine & Plomin, 1990; Plomin & Petrill)" (p. 158).

For the present study it might be helpful to replace "heritability" with "genetic endowment", because heritability brings to mind parents and grandparents and not chromosomes (and their genes) which can

---

[8] Dean Keith Simonton (2000) has reported something important: "Children chosen according to their high IQs tend to have personality profiles rather distinct from those who are selected according to their exceptional scores on tests that have a more direct claim to assess creativity. For example, the latter youths are prone to be more playful and humorous, to be less conventional in their life aspirations, and to be less conforming in their attitude about their education and future careers. . . . I wonder if the tendency for IQ to decline with ordinal positions says more about attitudes than about aptitudes (cf. Zajonc & Mullally, 1997). The later-borns may have less respect for the authorities who unilaterally decide that these measures gauge something significant, and they may even prove too iconoclastic to accept the presumption that the test questions do in fact have a single correct response" (pp. 114, 116).

These comments by Simonton confirm my feeling that not a few challenged youths perform poorly on IQ tests because they find them irrelevant to their lives, asking meaningless questions, asking them to play Q/A when they have far more serious things in mind. On the other hand, I doubt that many challenged youths will be prone to be playful and humorous. Many (but not all) of the misfortunes studied by GAM are not such to cause merriment.

combine in unexpected ways, originating, for instance, a super intelligent child from average parents and grandparents. (See chapters 3 and 4 of volume 1; also Clark, 1971, pp. 7-11, and Fölsing, 1998, pp. 15-16.)

Nature for Temperaments

Buss and Plomin in their *Temperament: Early Developing Personality Traits* of 1984, found that three temperaments were basic: Emotionality, Activity, and Sociability (EAS), and that each of them had a genetic base: "The family data are also consistent with the hypothesis of genetic influence on the EAS traits, though they involve an upper limit of heritability: if all the familial resemblance were due to heredity rather than shared family environment the upper limit is about 40% for Emotionality, 20% for Activity, and 30% for Sociability" (p. 125).[9]

Nature for Talents

"The striking early age of emergence of gifts [talents] in art and music, and the fact that high levels of skill make themselves known prior to formal training, are bothpieces of indirect evidence for an innate component" (Winner & Martino, 2000, p. 106).

In addition, what was just said on the genetic base for intelligence and temperaments confirms the common observation that the gifted children (and the word "gift"—from the gods, the muses, the good fairy, or mother nature—just says it) have been blessed, from conception, with a high genetic endowment (G), be it for intelligence, temperaments, and possibly one or more talents. This also confirms the common observations of many parents that their children can be substantially different from each other from birth, not only in physique.[10]

---

[9] The studies by Buss and Plomin, bring to mind the four temperaments of the Ancient World: *sanguine, melancholic, choleric*, and *phlegmatic*, attributed to the predominance of one of the four humours of the body (blood, black bile, yellow bile, phlegm). This interpretation, clearly, emphasizes physical, constitutional conditions and processes as determinants of temperament.

[10] For instance, in the case of the Marx siblings: "Heinrich, the doting father, may consciously or unconsciously have encouraged Karl's imperiousness and the resulting arrogance which later marked his personality. Very early in Karl's life, his father detected 'splendid natural gifts' in his oldest son and treated him accordingly. At the same time, Heinrich recognized the mediocrity of his other children. Referring to his eighteen-year-old son Hermann, then preparing for a business career in Brussels, Heinrich, in a letter to Karl at the University, wrote: 'Of his diligence I expect a lot, of his intelligence much less. It is a pity that the good-hearted lad doesn't have more brains.'" (Padover, 1978, pp. 27-28).

The above, on the genetic foundations of intelligence(s), temperament, and talents, explains why G (genetic endowment) is the first letter of GAM. G is nature, while A (assistances) and M (misfortunes) are nurture.

Nurture (parents, relatives, friends, other peers, schools, books, television) accounts for the rest, not in simple addition, but in a transactional fashion: "Many studies demonstrated that the child may be strongly involved in determining the nature of his early social relationships. In many situations parental behavior can be seen not to be spontaneously emitted but rather to be elicited by the child's characteristics and behavior. . . . Given parents with similar attitudes and backgrounds, infants with different temperaments elicited different caretaking reactions and as a consequence had differing developmental outcomes" (Sameroff, 1975, pp. 67-8). This was the case with Mozart: "Wolfgang's precocity changed Leopold's life and almost turned his head. He became the servant of his son, utterly devoted to him" (Hutchings, 1976, p. 20); and it is also the case with the *resilient kids*: "More intelligent children may solve problems or protect themselves better; they may attract the interest of teachers" (Masten & Coatsworth, 1998, p. 213).

The genetically brilliant child will, indeed, elicit more assistance, and will use it better. For instance, it will be enough to tell him/her only once, while, to the less genetically brilliant child, things will have to be said several times, at times in vain. Obviously, good assistance is neither pampering nor excessive help, but that which fosters self-development: it is quality first, then quantity.

Specifically on intelligence and assistance, Weiten wrote:

> Heredity unquestionably influences intelligence, but a great deal of evidence indicates that our upbringing also affects our mental ability. . . . What kind of home environment nurtures the development of intelligence? Many factors appear to be involved (Bradley & Caldwell, 1980; Hanson, 1975).
>
> It helps if parents run an orderly household and encourage exploration, experimentation, and independence. In the ideal home, parents are warm, affectionate, and highly involved with their children. . . . A lower-class upbringing tends to carry a number of disadvantages that work against the development of a youngster's full intellectual potential (Blau, 1981).

In comparison to the middle and upper classes, lower-class children tend to be exposed to fewer books, to have fewer learning supplies, to have less privacy for concentrated study, to get less parental assistance in learning, to have poorer role models for language development, to experience less pressure to work hard on intellectual pursuits, and to attend poorer-quality schools (Wolf, 1965).

In light of these disadvantages, it's not surprising that there's a positive correlation between social class and intelligence: children from higher classes tend to get higher IQ scores (Bouchard & Segal, 1985; White, 1982). The average IQ in the lowest social classes runs about 10-20 points lower than the average IQ in the highest social classes. This is true even if race is factored out of the picture by studying whites exclusively. Given the overrepresentation of minorities in the lower classes, many researchers argue that ethnic differences in intelligence are really social-class differences in disguise. (1989, pp. 323-26)

All the positive elements discussed here can be called assistances, which—combined with what was reported erlier by Thompson and Plomin—explains why I say that the gifted children are the result of a high GxA. In turn, the GxA formula immediately says that a very high G will compensate for less A, and vice versa, that a too low G or too low A cannot be compensated, and that the best result will come from the transaction of a high G with a high A.

Clearly, Mozart started with a superior genetic endowment (for intelligence, stamina, pitch discrimination, memory for tones, finger coordination). Alfred Einstein (1946) noted that "In these years [age six to ten] he was very teachable. And whatever his father prescribed he worked at for a time with the greatest industry, so that he seemed to forget everything else, even music, for a certain period. When, for instance, he was learning arithmetic, the table, the chairs, the walls, and even the floor were covered with figures written in chalk" (p. 25). Solomon (1995) related that "Mozart doggedly taught himself to play the violin at the age of six, insinuating himself into a trio rehearsal at home, playing second violin, and then managing the first violin part with wrong and irregular positioning but without ever actually breaking down" (p. 39).

Mozart began his childhood as a gifted child, but then he evolved into a challenged child because of the misfortune of father failure (character and profession)[11] and the addedmisfortune of aristocratic oppression (see chapters 2, 7 and 11 of volume 1). Without these misfortunes, Mozart would have remained a gifted child, a child prodigy, but neither a challenged youth, nor the genius he then grew to be.

The same is true for Einstein, who quite early gave evidence of being a gifted child:

> In 1886, when he was seven years old, his mother, Pauline, wrote to her mother saying, "Yesterday Albert got his school marks. Again he is at the top of his class and got a brilliant record." And a year later his maternal grandfather wrote, "Dear Albert has been back in school a week. I just love that boy, because you cannot imagine how good and intelligent he has become." From these excerpts one might be tempted to conclude that Albert had quickly overcome the handicap of his slow start[12] and had developed into a brilliant pupil, happy at school, and loved by relatives and teachers alike. But Einstein in later life spoke bitterly of his schooling. He disliked particularly the harsh, drill-sergeant methods of rote instruction that then prevailed. This dislike was heightened when, at the age of ten, he left the elementary school to enter the Luitpold Gymnasium.[13] To an inquirer he wrote in 1955, "As a pupil I

---

[11] Parental failure is probably one of the most creativogenic misfortunes, but only if in combination with a high G and a high A, something that, for instance, was evidently lacking in both Biff and Happy, the two sons of Willy Loman the key character of Arthur Miller's play *Death of a Salesman*.

[12] "Nothing in Einstein's early history suggests dormant genius. Quite the contrary. The one feature of his childhood about which there appears no doubt is the lateness with which he learned to speak. Even at the age of nine he was not fluent, while reminiscences of his youth stress hesitancies and the fact that he would reply to questions only after consideration and reflection" (Clark, 1971, pp. 10-11). However, the problem, as seen by the GAM theory, is not the presence of a dormant genius, but the presence of a sufficient high G, which, later, combined with quality assistances and misfortunes will give a high GxAxM, the potential for high and sustained creativity. And, as noted by Talmey, by Hoffmann, and by Fölsing, there was definitely a very high G independent of his lateness in learning to speak.

[13] The German word *Gymnasium* is not to be confused with its athletic English counterpart. It is pronounced with a hard G and a broad a, and it means a secondary school or high school at which students receive a classical education, studying intensively the Latin and Greek classics in the original language.

was neither particularly good nor bad. My principal weakness was a poor memory and especially a poor memory for words and texts." Indeed, his teacher of Greek had said to him, "You will never amount to anything." This hardly makes him seem a dazzling student. But note Einstein's next words: "Only in mathematics and physics was I, through self study, far beyond the school curriculum, and also with regard to philosophy so far as it had to do with the school curriculum." Here at last we have a clearer picture of how the young Einstein was developing. The key phrase is "self study", which was crucially linked with his passionate curiosity and his sense of wonder. (Hoffmann, 1972, pp. 18-20)

In reality, there was a third factor—beside self-study and curiosity, and the most important one: a high intelligence[14] without which there would have been no passionate curiosity, no related sense of wonder, and little self-study.

Even in high school, Einstein did well:

The old story that Einstein was a bad pupil, or even failed altogether at school, has been repeated time and again, presumably to console poor students or their parents. . . . As with so many other fanciful stories about him, he probably let it pass with a smile. Not so, however, a certain Dr. Wieleitner, the principal of the Neues Realgymnasium, the successor of Einstein's school. . . . [who] searched the school records and, in a letter to the editor of a Munich paper, saved the honor of the Luitpold Gymnasium by pointing out that Einstein had "always [received] at least a 2 in Latin, and in the sixth grade even a 1[15]. In Greek he always had a 2 in his school reports. . . Even in the 'secret reports' there is no complaint anywhere of a poor gift for the languages." (Fölsing, 1998, pp. 18-19)

---

[14] Together with a valid temperamental EAS (Emotionality, Activity and Sociability), and good assistances.

[15] In Germany, 1 (*sehr gut*) equals an A in America; and 2 (*gut*) a B.

Einstein, like Mozart, evolved from gifted child to challenged youth under the impact of two misfortunes: father failure, and lack of protection from anti-Semitism (i.e., lacking the protection of a religious faith and of a close and warm Jewish community; unprotected by the lukewarm religiosity of his parents, while being sent to public schools in strongly Catholic Bavaria).

Assistances are all the positive inputs received in life: all the friendly help, the lucky accidents which benefit a person's life. They are those things we wish for ourselves and for our children (misfortunes are the opposite).

Assistance are all kinds of friendly help from mother or father (or parent substitutes), other relatives, friends and teachers, schoolmates and playmates, neighbors, schools, youth organizations, libraries, village or city environment, stimulating jobs, commissions and patrons, and from a lively economic/social/political/cultural environment. Other forms of assistance come from a medium to high cultural-socioeconomic status (e.g., Albert, 1983a; Simonton, 1994), good medical care, and free time to pursue personal interests.

"The importance of a supportive environment and intensive training was demonstrated by Bloom (1985), who found that individuals of world-class status in the arts, mathematics, science, or athletics all reported strong family support and years of training. However, such a finding hardly rules out innate talent: Bloom's subjects also recalled signs of high ability at a very young age, prior to or at the very start of formal training. These memories of early signs of high ability are consistent with parental accounts of child prodigies whose extraordinary abilities seem to emerge from nowhere" (Winner, 2000, p. 154).

Bloom (1982) had also remarked that "in homes where other children were also interested in the talent area, the parents sometimes mentioned that one of the other children had even greater 'gifts' than the individual in the sample, but that the other child was not willing to put in the time and effort that the parents or the teacher expected and required" (pp. 512-13). In turn, also this willingness to work (per se, or to achieve a high standard, in combination or not with a sense of competitiveness and determination to do one's best) is the result of a high GxA given that one of the three basic temperaments (as studied by Buss & Plomin, 1984) is activity (tempo and vigor) with its important genetic roots. Clearly the original genetic level of activity can be magnified or dampened by the kind of assistance received (usually, the more the family is active doing interesting activities, the more the children will be active.

Finally, another essential assistance is that of a dynamic and challenging division of power (DP) environment, the birth place of the *visitor personality*, as discussed in both volumes 1 and 2. There is the challenging assistance of the *big DP* (for instance between emperors and popes, state and church), and that of *smaller DPs*—yet also important—as is living in a lively place, for instance, the London of Shakespeare: "a rapidly expanding city. . . . [whose] playwrights kept a sharp eye on each other's practice; now quarrelling, now collaborating, occasionally cohabiting, constantly appraising and often quietly appropriating elements from each other's work" (Donaldson, 1996, p. 27).[16]

5. The Challenged Youth

The challenged youth is a high GxA[17] child transformed (pruned, distorted, channelled, magnified) by one or more major misfortunes of youth (M).

---

[16] Interestingly, this lively British DP world was prepared by a major state/church DP, viz by "the seizure and distribution of the Catholic monastic lands under Henry VIII [which] put new capital to work in agriculture, industry, and on the high seas. Glastonbury Abbey became a worsted manufactory, Rotherham college a malthouse, and the elimination of saints' days were said to be worth £50,000 each in increased economic activity. . . . The extent to which England's fortune was made by Atlanticization and the opening of America is a Protestant sermon and drumroll in itself. A. L. Rowse, the principal historian of the expansion of Elizabethan England from 1557 to 1603, is unrestrained about 'how much this country owed its future to the Elizabethan drive across the Atlantic to the New World.' Religion was an unmistakable spur. This seafaring and opening-up of the New World, to Rowse, 'was a Protestant activity' [read major DP, and reform, within Christianity], both in commercial spirit and anti-Spanish motivation" (Phillips, 1999, pp. 11-12).

[17] At times it may be useful to split the assistances **A** in **An** (normal assistances) and **Asp** (special assistances). Misfortunes of youth always bring a reduction of normal assistances, e.g. not that of two parents but of only one, probably overwhelmed and overloaded; physical infirmity which reduces schooling through absences from school and a lower level of learning from the interaction with peers. If the missing assistances are not balanced by help from other sources, for instance from grandparents, other relatives, family friends, good schools, high SES, or more high-quality help from the only remaining parent, there will not be a *challenged youth*, but a *different, crushed, pathological youth*, as discussed in chapter 1 of volume 1.

The GxA Part of the Challenged Youth's GxAxM is Giftedness

Through good assistances a high genetic endowment becomes giftedness, and the first and simple manifestation of that high GxA is plain classical intelligence, as shown by the very high IQ estimates AI and AII[18] of Cox's study: Bach 140, 165, Beethoven, 150, 165, Handel 160, 170, Mozart 160, 165.

The same can be said for poets and novelists, for whom Cox also found very high IQ (AI and AII), for instance, for Calderon 175, 170, Cervantes 145, 155, Dickens 160, 180, Goethe 190, 210, Hugo 160, 180, Leopardi 185, 185, Molière 155, 160, Racine 160, 170, Tasso 180, 180. We are reminded of Galton's summary statement that "No man can achieve a very high reputation without being gifted with very high abilities [i.e., very high intelligence]" (quoted by Cox, 1926, p. 12). Clearly, G is much more than the genetic foundation of intelligence: it is alsothe genetic foundation of temperaments, and probably as much to be yet discovered on the making of personality.

Back to intelligence, a high intelligence is the conditio sine qua non for interpreting and making good use of any major misfortune, otherwise the misfortune is nothing but that: a misfortune without contributory value. A high intelligence and/or intelligent sensitivity is needed to process constructively the misfortunes, (i.e., to notice and understand them, to ruminate ceaselessly, and to build personal scripts on them.) Yet, at times, the initial force which draws attention and assistances to a youth, and builds his/her self-confidence and the drive to do more, comes from talent(s), the other manifestation of a high G (and initial high GxA).

In summary, in order to become a challenged personality, (i.e., a potential genius), the child must possess, from conception, a high G,

---

[18] AI refers to the IQ estimate in childhood and early youth; AII refers to the first period of young adulthood. The items studied were, for AI: 1. earliest period of instruction; 2. nature of the earliest learning; 3. earliest production; 4. first reading; 5. first mathematical performance; 6. typical precocious activities; 7. unusually intelligent applications of knowledge; 8. recognition of similarities or differences; 9. amount and character reading; 10. character of interest other than reading; 11. school standing and progress; 12. early maturity of moral attitude or judgement; 13. tendency to discriminate, to generalize, or to theorize; 14. family standing. Both AI and AII are the average of the estimates by three independent raters, who where instructed (a) *to rate objectively on the evidence* recorded for the first 26 years and (b) *not to overrate* (Cox, 1926, p. 64, italics in the original).

Nota bene, these are practical, long-term applied, demonstrated, forms of intelligence, and as such more meaningful than what can be determined by an IQ test.

capable of making good use of available or invited assistances. Then a high GxA will be able to make good utilizationse of the subsequent misfortune(s).

Misfortunes

The most studied of the challenging/creativogenic misfortunes is that of early parental death. Indeed, the GAM theory of personality and creativity (Therivel, 1988, 1990, 1993) was born as an explanation of the high incidence of major misfortunes of youth in the lives of eminent and highly creative personalities, first that of father failure[19], then that of early parental death.

Albert (1983b) summarized the results of several surveys on the high incidence of early parental death among eminent people: presidents, prime ministers, Nobel laureates, and great scientists. Nevertheless, as noted by Albert: "It is not only eminent persons who have a significantly high frequency of such experiences. Compared to the average of 8% general population experiencing early parental deaths, the percentages for adult criminals, adult psychiatric patients (especially depressive), and eminent adults are high and quite close to one another (32%, 27%, 28%)" (p. 147). However, as stressed in my 1993 and 1998 articles, if one eliminates from the study all those who had received little assistances of youth (e.g., because of incapable or uncaring parents of low cultural and socioeconomic status), one would probably eliminate from the comparison the majority of the criminals (Glueck & Glueck 1950, 1968; Konopka, 1966; West, 1967[20]), and probably a fair number of the psychiatric patients (Sameroff & Seifer, 1989). This would leave the eminent people as the recipients of both strong misfortunes and good assistances of youth.

Specifically, on the assistance of a good socioeconomic status (SES), Albert (1983a) wrote: "Although one often hears or reads dramatic stories of the poverty-stricken child who becomes a great person, the evidence regarding the socioeconomic background of eminent persons—evidence from Galton (1869) through Cox (1926) to

---

[19] The first major creativogenic misfortune of youth that drew my attention, back in 1972, was that of father failure, specifically that of the father of Napoleon.

[20] In West's words: "The characteristic social background of persistent delinquents (low class, low income, educational backwardness, broken home, over-large family, child neglect, poor neighborhood) has been described *ad nauseam*. Wherever this cluster of social deprivation is prominent, the delinquency rate is very high" (p. 292).

Roe (1951a, 1951b, 19530, McKinnon (1963), and Oden (1968), up to more recent research of eminent persons (Simonton, 1975b, Zuckerman, 1977)—show that most eminent persons come from middle-or higher-placed families" (pp. 30-31).

The importance of the assistance of a high SES has also been stressed by the medical sociologist Ann Hill Beuf in her book *Beauty is the Beast: Appearance-Impaired Children in America:*

> High socio-economic status is a coping resource. The stigmatized person of means will be afforded more protection than the poorer one. . . . Such a family will be less subject to teasing and discrimination, and thus to the feeling of incompetence. No matter what the physical appearance, the child of a noble, religious leader, or wealthy businessperson has 'borrowed prestige' derived from the parent's position in society and will be treated with the same respect. (1990, p. 22)[21]

On the contrary, a low SES will tragically increase the weight of other misfortunes, as discussed, for instance, by Elsa Ferri in her book *Growing Up in a One-Parent Family: A Long-Term Study of Child Development* (1976), which studied, in Great Britain, a large number of children (selected only by their date of birth) who were fatherless or motherless due to a parent's death by the time they were seven or eleven. By choosing her subjects by their date of birth, Ferri had automatically a majority of low SES people. With these children, the misfortune of early parental death was not only psychological, but financial. And in these conditions, the misfortune of early parental death was just that, a misfortune with no redeeming grace. In Ferri's concluding words:

> The results of the analyses carried out showed that, overall, children in one-parent families had a lower level of attainment in school and were less adjusted than their peers from unbroken homes. . . . Bringing up children singlehanded is an arduous task, both physically and mentally. Help is needed,

---

[21] As noted in chapter 2 of volume 1, there has been so far only one first-class poet who was a hunchback, and only one first-class painter who looked like a dwarf because of accidents to his legs. The first was Count Giacomo Leopardi, the second was Count Henri de Toulouse-Lautrec. Both were much assisted by their very high SES. Nobody in Recanati for Leopardi, or in Albi for Toulouse-Lautrec, would have dared to make fun of their infirmities.

not only in providing for the family's material welfare which is so gravely threatened by the loss of a parent but also in offering guidance, reassurance and moral support to unsupported parents in their lonely role of bringing up children without another adult to share the responsibility. If such is not forthcoming, the strains and pressures on some lone parents may become so intolerable that they are finally forced to relinquish their burden, resulting in perhaps the worst of all possible outcomes—a no-parent family. (pp. 147, 149)

If we then relate the above to the previously reported comments by West (1967), we can well understand why the adult criminals show a significantly high frequency of early parental death, as noted by Albert (1983a).

There are several other equally potent creativogenic misfortunes (together with a high GxA): long-term parental absence, physical infirmity, lack of parental love, parental domination, uprootedness, parental character/professional failure, suffered illegitimate birth, father/mother incompatibility, suffered parental divorce or separation, severe parental sickness, alcoholism or drug addiction, disliked remarriage of one or both parents, negative differential sibling experiences, and strong sibling antagonism.[22]

For instance, as noted by Albert and Runco (1996):

Families of *creative children* generally evidence unusual features (Albert, 1971, 1980a, 1980b). For example, such families tend to experience a high rate of parental loss. Often, the father is much older than the mother and the child an only child, or if he is not, then probably the oldest. The families of *effective children*, on the other hand, tend to fit a more conventional pattern of a nuclear family, with the parents existing together and being close in age: moreover, the child is gener-

---

[22] The GAM theory has moved from the general study of the misfortune of early parental death to the study of the impact on personality and creativity of several types of early parental death (Therivel, 1988, 1990, 1998): 1) with no remarriage, or disliked remarriage of the remaining parent, and no downfall of the family's fortunes; 2) with remarriage disliked by the children, or affairs by the surviving parent; 3) with downfall of the family fortunes (e.g., with move to a poor neighborhood and schools); 4) with a major negative change in the character of the surviving parent, who becomes unloving and uncaring, or incapable.

ally part of a bigger family. The relationship of the effective child to his parents is usually a loving one, in which the process of socialization unfolds in a rather typical manner. This relationship, being harmonious, *allows for a strong binding identification [and adoption of scripts] with the parents*. Father-son relationships are especially tolerable and harmonious, compared with those of the families of creative children (Albert & Runco, 1986, pp. 339-40; my italics and bracketed insert).

Clearly the *creative children* of Albert and Runco are the same as (or simlar to) the *challenged youths* of GAM, and their *effective children* the same as (or similar to) the *dedicated youths* of GAM (see chapter 1 of volume 1).

According to Winner & Martino, "A prodigy is someone who can easily and rapidly master a domain with expertise. A creator is someone who changes the domain. It is likely that personality factors play a major role in becoming a domain creator. Creators are restless, rebellious, and dissatisfied with the status quo (Simonton, 1994; Sulloway, 1996); and they have something new to 'say'" (2000, p. 107). This very last comment—of having something new to say—is of the essence. Being restless, rebellious and dissatisfied with the status quo, may mean something in combination with having something new to say, but by themselves they count little for creativity.

The real question, therefore is the origin of that "something new to 'say'", the originof new good ideas, because novelty, per se, is not sufficient. We are back to the notion that "creativity involves the generation of ideas that are original, novel and useful. First and foremost, creativity involves seeing the world in a new and different light" (Weiten, 1989, p. 292).

However, seeing the world in a new and different light is not something that comes by investing a great deal of energy in mastering a set of skills; on the contrary. It is here that the high G (for intelligence, temperaments, talents) xA of a Mozart and Picasso was important: they could so easily master the skills of their profession that they could also use their brains for much more than strictly music or painting.

As reported in chapter 1 of volume 1, "'the choice of Beaumarchais's comedy *Le marriage de Figaro* as a subject for operatic treatment was deliberately made by Mozart himself' (Jahn,

1900, p. 72)—and proposed to the librettist Lorenzo da Ponte—well knowing that he 'was taking something of a risk [of antagonizing his aristocratic patrons] to set the play to music' (Solomon, 1995, p. 303)." This meant reading something outside of music, but not outside of Mozart's misfortune of aristocratic oppression. Mozart had acquired a new and valid anti-aristocratic vision of himself and of society at large (as proven by his involvement in the Masonic movement, in which he rose rapidly to the highest rank of *Master Mason,* see chapter 11 of volume 1). Here is the source of "having something new to say."

At that time, society was moving from an *insular* to a *visitor* ethnopsychology (see the section of chapter 11 entitled "Mozart, Child of the Division of Power of the Enlightenment"), and Mozart was able to create outside of the standard musical domain. The imperial/ aristocratic musical field did not take it graciously; but that is exactly what happens in every first-class *war of the scripts.*

Vice versa, what are the best ways for both gifted and challenged children *not* to be creative? These are, to list a few: much time devoted to watching television, especially watching professional and para-professional sport events [for sustained high creativity I would recommend not watching television more than four hours per week]; a lot of time given to sports or to playing in the school band; little reading of good books; active participation in low quality peer groups. All this is so obvious that it should not be mentioned at all. I only do it now because I felt that Winner and Martino—and the authors they mentioned—gave the impression that the "something new to 'say'" can be generated by an act of will: "[gifted children] are often unwilling, or even unable, to experiment in the way that one must do in order to be creative" (2000, p. 108).

This, in my opinion, is adding insult to injury. Some of these children are raised very strangely: spending huge amounts of time mastering one skill, and then they are blamed for being unwilling or unable to experiment!

6. When and Why can Misfortunes be Creativogenic

The answer is simple, as soon as we focus on Weiten's definition of creativity: "Creativity involves the generation of ideas that are original, novel, and useful. First and foremost, creativity involves seeing the world in a new and different light" (1989, p. 292).

What the misfortunes of youth do (in combination with a high GxA) is just this: creating that different vision[23] of the world. The misfortunes of youth are a disturbance, like the grain of sand around which the right kind of oyster (capable of secreting large quantities of quality nacre) will build a beautiful pearl.

Major Misfortunes of Youth Reduce Scripts Adoption

This can be seen at work, for instance in young Goethe:

As a result of the Seven Years' War, 7000 French troops took possession of Frankfort in the beginning of 1759 [when Goethe was 9½], and occupied it for more than three years. In the ways of a foreign soldiery at free quarters the Frankforters saw a strange contrast to their own decorous habits of life, but the French occupation was brought more directly home to the Goethe household. To the disgust and indignation of the father, to whom as a worshipper of Frederick [the Great of Prussia] the French were objects of detestation, their chief officer, Count Thoranc, was quartered in his house. Goethe has told in detail the history of this invasion of the quiet household—the never-failing courtesy and considerateness of Thoranc, the abiding ill-humour of the father, the reconciling offices of the mother, exercised in vain to effect a mutual understanding between her husband and his unwelcome guest. As for Goethe himself, devoted to Frederick though he was, the presence of the French introduced him to a new world into which he entered with boyish delight. . . . He threw himself into the pleasures and avocations of the novel society. Thoranc was a connoisseur in art, and gave frequent commissions to the artists of the town; and Goethe, already interested in art through his father's collections, found his opportunity in these tastes of Thoranc, who was struck by the boy's precocity and even took hints from his suggestions. A theatre set up by the

---

[23] "Vision", at first, is too big a word, and no child and few adolescents can be said to have a valid new vision. What the challenged youths have is the seed of the vision in the form of their paucity of common scripts and many personal new scripts developed at the light of their misfortune of youth and the many books chosen and read in accordance. It is from this situation, and resulting *war of the scripts* with society, that a new vision will arise.

French was another source of pleasure and stimulus. The sight of the pieces that were acted prompted him to compose pieces of his own and led him to the study of the French classical drama. . . . A remark which he makes in connection with the French theatre is a significant commentary on his respective relations to his father and mother, *and indicates the atmosphere of evasion which permanently pervaded the household. It was against the will of his father, but with the connivance of his mother, that he paid his visits to the theatre* and cultivated the society of the actors, and it was only by the consideration that his son's knowledge of French was thus improved that the practical father was reconciled to the delinquency. *The direct results of his intercourse with the French soldiery on Goethe's development were at once abiding and of high importance. It extended his knowledge of men and the world, and, more specifically, it gave him that interest in French culture and that insight into the French mind which he possessed in a degree beyond any of his contemporaries.* (Hume Brown, 1920/1971, *1*, pp. 14-16, my italics)

And from Goethe's autobiography:

It was not long before I took up Racine, which I found in my father's library, and declaimed the plays to myself,. . . . I even learned entire passages by rote. . . . .My passion for the French theatre grew with every performance. I did not miss an evening; though on every occasion, when, after the play, I sat down with the family to supper, — often putting up with the remains,—I had to endure my father's constant reproaches, that theaters were useless, and would lead to nothing. In these cases I adduced all and every argument which is at hand for the apologists of the stage when they fall into a difficulty like mine. Vice in prosperity, and virtue in misfortune, are in the end set right by poetical justice. . . . Neither party was convinced; but my father was very soon reconciled to the theatre when he saw that I advanced with incredible rapidity in the French language. . . . I had perseverance enough this time to work through the whole of Racine and Molière and a great part of Corneille. (1811-22/1969, pp. 108, 111)

This case is instructive: Not only did young Goethe not listen to the many normal comments by the reclusIve and despondent father, nor watch him in thousands of normal episodes, but he automatically or deliberately refused thoughts, gestures, habits of the father, which were then labelled by the son as retrograde, surly, cantankerous, ill-mannered. Some of the missing paternal scripts, (i.e., many of the then normal German scripts of his time and SES), were replaced by French literary scripts. However these last did not have the immediacy and strength of the missed paternal scripts, and did not exactly cover the same ground. Literary scripts are not encoded in the brain the same way normal scripts are. Literary loves and hates, honor, pride and prejudice, work differently, on a more cultural plane, but seldom with the totality, the gut feeling, of plain scripts learned unconsciously as absolute truths.

In the end, the challenged youths know enormously more than their peers, yet not with the same assurance. Because of this, they are more curious, more fascinated by what for them is new, while for the others that "new" is unimportant, because they are so instructed by their scripts. In an early article for the *Frankfurter Gelehrte Anzeigen* the young Goethe of 23 stressed an approach to life—he expected to find in others, because he had it so strongly in himself—in which "*alles neu ist*" [everything is new] (1772/1977, *14*, p. 158).

In the absence of common scripts, the challenged personality uncovers much which is new and important because it is truly new, and not prejudged by parents, peers, teachers. While "the [normal] adolescent soon learns that the group can be a dreadful spoilsport if he confesses to liking something that has fallen under a taboo" (Gombrich, 1974, p. 948), the challenged adolescent does not know, or does not care, about the group's taboos. For the challenged youth there are no spoilsports: his own curiosity is the guide.

That same fascination with "*alles was neu ist*" was evident in young Darwin, aged 22—similarly deprived of common scripts even if by a different set of misfortunes (as described in chapter 8 of volume 1 "From shortage of scripts, to enlarged curiosity, to scientific discoveries")—whom his uncle Josiah Wedgewood II described "as a man of enlarged curiosity" (quoted by Brent, 1981, p. 117).

The misfortune of youth may reduce substantially the days at school and foster much personalized reading. Nearly always, the misfortune of youth shortens considerably the interaction with play-mates and schoolmates, it minimizes peer pressure, it minimizes group thinking. Csikszentmihalyi (1991) highlighted the opposite when he noted that "generally, it's very difficult for teenagers who come from well-to-do, healthy, reasonably together families, to do something very different from what other kids do. They are sitting in their environment which is positive, which is supportive, why should they go beyond?" The challenged youth, instead, will go beyond, because he/she is constantly at odds with society[24] in what I have called a *war of the scripts*.

The first battles of the *war of the scripts*, by themselves, will not originate a new vision, "seeing the world in a new and different light" as demanded by Weiten's definition. That will demand several years of fighting which will give them "many knowledge structures, many enterprises, many episodes, many insights. . . . a 'network of enter-prises' as a way of dealing with the continually changing concerns and interests of a purposeful life" (Gruber, 1981, pp. xx-xxi).

Because of this long developmental process, it is nearly always wrong to look for early signs of creativity, especially in the challenged youths who are already "old" in some aspects of their personality, but often immature in others (the penalty of not having been raised normally and not possessing the normal scripts).

That request of not searching too early, say in school, for signs of valid creativity, comes clear in the following contrast, by Siegler and Kotovsky, between *creative-productive giftedness* and *schoolhouse giftedness*:

---

[24]Later, some of them can be called *quality marginal men*: those who find them-selves "striving to live in two diverse cultural groups . . . . living and sharing intimately in the cultural life and traditions of two distinct people; never quite willing to break with his past and his traditions, and not quite accepted, because of racial prejudice" (Park, 1928, P. 881, 892). *Quality marginal men*, indeed, are some of those whom I have called *leadsmen* in my 1998 article. There, I described their formative misfortune as "rootless-ness or uprootedness (e.g., forced conversion or assimilation of parents to religion or ethnic ways of the majority; major changes of abode; major religious or cultural differences between the parents,)" and described the resulting GAM personality as "detached; critical thinkers; relativistic; often showing bold cosmopolitan and pragmatic attitudes" (p. 208). I called them *leadsmen* because their skeptical and critical thinking places them "at the prow, with a lead in their hands, measuring the depth of the waters before deciding where to go". *Leadsmen* like Napoleon, Marx, Freud and Einstein, are quality *marginal men* with a vision, willing and capable of breaking with their past, something, instead, difficult for most *marginal men* (as noted by Park, p. 892).

Creative-productive giftedness is ordinarily manifested in achievements that take months or years. Schoolhouse giftedness typically is manifested in achievements that take hours, days, or, occasionally, in the case of projects, weeks. In part because of these different time frames, creative-productive giftedness seems to require high levels of task commitment. In contrast, people can do well on IQ tests and in many school courses with relatively little commitment to the educational task. Creative-productive contributions are defined by the standard of all contributions that have ever been made in that field. The products of schoolhouse giftedness are judged against more local competition. . . . When we talk about schoolhouse giftedness, we select our population on the basis of childhood achievements. When we talk about creative-productive giftedness, we select our population on the basis of adult achievements. Creative-productive giftedness can involve contributions in extremely narrow domains. Schoolhouse giftedness usually demands reasonable levels of achievement over considerably broader domains. In research on creative-productive giftedness, past achievements are emphasized. In research on schoolhouse giftedness, the emphasis is on what future accomplishments may be possible. (1986, p. 418)

The above was part of an article entitled *Two levels of giftedness: shall ever the twain meet?* The two levels, as indicated above, are: 1. children who are doing well in school and on IQ tests, and 2. adults who have made major contributions in their fields. And clearly the twain shall never (or very rarely) meet, because we are comparing two different and (in most cases unrelated) phenomena. Indeed, the greatest contributions are made by challenged personalities, who often do not do so well in school because they are handicapped by their misfortunes, because they are unwilling to "play the game" as demanded by teachers and peers.[25]

To the challenged personality belong the following comments by Thoreau: "If a man does not keep pace with his companions, perhaps it is because he hears a different drummer. Let him step to the music which he hears, however measured or far away" (*Walden*, 1854/1975, pp. 462-3). Yet, even here, to most of them that special music will

---

[25] It pays to refer to the 1,528 gifted children, with IQs averaging 151, studied by Lewis Terman. These children were surprisingly well rounded and socially well adjusted, and grew up to be successful professionals. However, none made widely recognized intellectual breakthroughs.

sound clear only in adulthood, making it difficult, even at this level, to link youth to adulthood. The high GxAxM of youth is a potential that some (many?) will not transform into steady creativity of adulthood for many reasons, one being, as discussed hereafter, their having done too little homework, another (see chapter 4 in this volume) being the lack of pruning, especially self-pruning.

7. Intelligence

Something more needs to be said on intelligence, hard work and achievement motivation.

Starting with the first, in the words of Mark Runco (1991): "It goes without much argument that most eminent persons are notably talented and cognitively gifted. It also goes without much argument that not all talented and gifted children undergo these transformations [from early giftedness into a long-standing capacity for cognitive exceptionality and noteworthy performance]" (p. 4).

Then, in line with what was said at the beginning, that giftedness alone is not the potential for genius, but for professional success, I quote Winner (2000):

> Systematic study of the gifted began in the 1920s with Terman's (1925) longitudinal study of 1,528 children with IQs averaging 151. These children were surprisingly well rounded and socially well adjusted, and grew up to be successful professionals. However, none made widely recognized intellectual breakthroughs. Thus, even extraordinarily high IQs do not by themselves lead to creative eminence.[26] Whether such IQs predict even professional success could not be determined because Terman did not control for possible effects of socioeconomic background. (p. 153)

---

[26] Probably Terman did not pick any challenged youths (besides the fact that there are few of them: a high GxA is rare, and a high GxAxM very rare), because as Simonton noted: "It is very likely that Terman's sampling procedures are to blame for the dearth of high-grade genius among his Termites [one of the names later given to the gifted persons studied by Terman; a better name is "Terman's children"]. Rather than test the entire student population, Terman relied on teacher nominations to screen those students who their teachers thought had most promise. How many kids were not so named because their teachers thought them more weird than bright? Furthermore, even if a few oddballs somehow got through this first filter, how many of them would have taken the Stanford-Binet with sufficient seriousness to provide answers indicative of their true intelligence? How many future geniuses would have had a diverting time offering humorous or Bohemian responses that would bring their scores down?" (2000, p. 115).

Many of these "well rounded and socially well adjusted, [who] grew up to be successful professionals" can be labelled *dedicated personalities*, as proposed in chapter 1 of volume 1: "These are the model citizen who help society by keeping its institutions running and getting better—from hospitals to schools, justice to academia, based on the accumulated wisdom of the past. They can be creative, they can be great leaders (but not in revolutionary ways)." They are, as said in chapter 3 of volume 1, "Enlightened conservatives; sociable, realistic, mature; have many old and new friends; strong family and community ties; in academe, science, and the arts, they work within the system."

For Simonton,

> IQ is associated not only with increased fame, but also with such assets as superior versatility. The higher the IQ, the more domains in which an individual can succeed. This advantage of versatility is seen in the careers of Leonardo da Vinci, Michelangelo, Descartes, Pascal, Leibniz, Benjamin Franklin, Goethe, and Disraeli—all of whom could have been candidates for the Four Sigma Society. With more intellectual where-withal, they could engage in more enterprises without risking the vitiating dissipation of the dilettante. . . . We can draw some conclusion after all: A high IQ is not irrelevant in understanding who becomes a big success. Although it is not the only factor, the higher a person's ability is, the bigger a person's ability is, the bigger his or her impression on posterity" (1994, pp. 226, 227).

And yet, none of Terman's children left a mark on posterity. Could the missing factor be the absence of major misfortunes of youth?

Going through Simonton's list: Leonardo suffered of illegitimate birth; Michelangelo lost his mother at age 6, and suffered of father failure; Descartes lost his mother at the age of 1; Pascal was affected by severe physical infirmities; Leibniz lost his father at the age of 6; Franklin encountered and provoked strong sibling antagonism[27]; Goethe was much affected by the misfortune of father failure; Disraeli

---

[27] "Continually quarrelling with his overbearing brother, Franklin determined to quit his job, leave the family and Boston, and establish himself by his own efforts unaided. The youthful rebel set forth on his well-publicized journey to Philadelphia, arriving in that bustling town in October 1723, when he was little more that seventeen years of age" (Morris, 1973, p. 9).

suffered of rootlessness. Each of them was a powerful challenged personality. So, indeed, the misfortunes of youth may be the missing element together with a high GxA.

Given that this list has been drawn by Simonton—and not, *ad hoc*, by me—the above can be read as a piece of evidence for the GAM theory of personality and creativity, as one of the *small experiments* I proposed in my 1993 article (pp. 417-18).

There may be another piece of evidence, in the opposite direction, in Thomas Young, who, in the words of Colin Martindale (2001) "did important work in a large variety of scientific disciplines, but that was his downfall. . . . What went wrong? Given his achievements, when we are asked to think of creative genius, why do we think of Newton or Einstein rather than Thomas Young? Sternberg and Lubart (1991) proposed an investment theory of creativity based on an analogy with the stock market. . . . In investing, one wants a diversified portfolio. Thomas Young can be thought of as having a portfolio too diverse" (p. 342).

In the second part of his article, Martindale stressed how intelligent Thomas Young was. Following the method of Catherine Cox (1926), he tried to estimate Young's IQ, and concluded that his IQ could not have been any lower than 180, and most probably was 200 "which is as high, as that of any of the geniuses studied by Cox" (p. 344). Having read this, I went to the four biographies of Young listed by Martindale. In none of them, could I find mention of any major misfortune of youth: not early parental death, not suffered illegitimate birth, not physical infirmity[28], not parental failure, not sibling antagonism, not rootlessness, not father-mother incompatibility. If so, could the absence of a major misfortune of youth explain his too diverse portfolio and corresponding lack of evident major integrated creativity?

This story of Young reminds me, even if on a simpler level, of some luncheons I attended with a group of very intelligent people who met twice a month in a good restaurant. I admired the brilliance of their conversation, and yet was disappointed, and after a few times

---

[28] It is true that "in 1789 [at the age of 16], about the middle of his time with the Barklays, Thomas Young had a severe illness in which he was attended by Dr. Brocklesby and Baron Dimsdale, and from which, with careful nursing, he completely recovered" (Wood & Oldham, 1954, p. 12). However, one severe illness does not bring that shortage of social scripts, those doubts about one's body, that are at the base of the *seeker* and *radiologist* personality (see chapter 3 of volume 1): their physical infirmity was much longer and more severe; we need only to remember the asthma that affected Proust from the age of nine onward.

stopped joining them. I felt that they were more interested in giving evidence of their intelligence and brilliant rhetoric than in discussing a major subject. I felt I was surrounded by beautiful verbal fireworks but not more. They too, at least in those luncheons, and for my taste, were having a too diversified portfolio.

If so, I could expand my interpretation of the creativity of the challenged personality by saying that the misfortunes of youth cut down on diversions and fireworks, bring a more serious attitude to life, lead to concentrated studies, and to creativity in a specialized domain(s).

8. Hard Work

Thomas Alva Edison was right when he said that *There is no substitute for hard work*, and that *Genius is one per cent inspiration and ninety-nine per cent perspiration*. Similar comments where made by Picasso: "I believe in nothing but work" (quoted by Richardson, 1991, p. 48), and Napoleon: "Work is my element. I am born and built for work. I have known the limitations of my legs, I have known the limitations of my eyes; I have never been able to know the limitations of my working capacity" (quoted by Herold, 1961, pp. xx-xxi).

A passion for hard work is a virtue which must be cultivated from childhood onward, and that can be applied to any task. Then there is the hard work that is fostered by quality inspirations, by major goals.

Mark Freeman—having studied some 54 individuals who aspired to become painters and sculptors after having attended the School of the Art Institute of Chicago during the mid-1960s—wrote in his paper *Defying the myth of extraordinary artistic abilities*: "Notice here that those artists who saw their futures as bleak, owing to the ordinariness of their artistic abilities, and those who saw their futures as bright, owing to their 'inherent genius,' faced precisely the same problem: the process of development was brought to a virtual standstill. If you've already got it, they seemed to say, there is nothing more to be done" (1989, p. 12).

Similarly, Robert Bjork (2000) stressed the danger of a shortage of developmental work:

I think the belief that performing well is due to talent or having a "gift" has a number of negative consequences. One consequence is that it can breed an attitude of helplessness: We hope we have the gift to excel in some domain, and we assume there's nothing much we can do if we don't have those gifts. Such beliefs can also function as self-fulfilling prophecies: An early bad experience—on a mathematics or science exam, for example—can lead a young person to label himself or herself as lacking the innate ability to perform well in a given domain. In turn this labelling leads to behaviors that reinforce that conclusion. Educational and occupational activities that might provide evidence to the contrary are avoided, and experiences in some domain of presumed talent are sought out. Over time, these behaviors produce confirming evidence in both directions. (p. 3)

Yet, while indeed there is no substitute for hard work, and hard work can do miracles, the best results will come when hard work is combined with a high G^{29} (i.e., is an integral part of a high GxA, better of a high GxAxM).

As noted by David Raup, "a new idea requires a truly compelling case—intellectual overkill—in order to displace the incumbent. . . . Perhaps the only thing that saves science from invalid conventional wisdom that becomes effectively permanent is the presence of mavericks in every generation—people who keep challenging convention and thinking up new ideas for the sheer hell of it or from an innate contrariness" (1986). So, the truly compelling cases come from people with innate contrariness (read: shortage of common scripts and some grudge against peers and teachers that made fun of them for being different), who will, through years of dogged effort, achieve the needed intellectual overkill.[30] The compelling case will be achieved only thanks to "a sense of special mission, a will to commit enormous

---

[29] "Simonton (1991) showed that the most eminent classical composers began to compose and made lasting contributions after fewer years of formal training than their less eminent peers. The fact that they achieved greater heights with less practice suggests that their success reflected another ingredient besides practice—and a likely candidate is a higher level of inborn musical talent" (Winner, 2000, p. 154).

[30] J. P. Guilford (1970) has correctly remarked how "in her studies of leading artists and of leading scientists in several fields, Anne Roe found only one trait that stood out in common among individuals, this was a willingness to work hard and to work long hours (Roe, 1946, 1953). This is a trait that may contribute to achievement and eminence in any field, however. There is no indication that it has a unique relation to creativity. The trait also merely means a very high level of general motivation, of whose sources we are uncertain. We are thus left with the problem, and the need for more analytical studies is strongly indicated" (1970, p. 175). This problem is solved, according to the GAM theory, by the study of people with innate contrariness (read: shortage of common scripts because of a major misfortune of youth, and derived new and important vision) who backed their contrariness with hard work.

energies and the time necessary, a lifetime to the chosen task" (Gruber, 1986, p. 259).

The need to put long years of work, before something important is created, has been highlighted by Robert Weisberg (1999) in his discussion of the *10-year rule* which says that real valid acts of creation come only after a minimum of ten years of "normal creativity." This, for instance, applies in full to Picasso, Paul Klee, and Toulouse-Lautrec, as discussed by Weisberg, and to Mozart who, in the words of Hutchings, "had he died at 18, his work, though marvelous, would not have aligned him with the [later] enigmatic great artist (1976, 2, p. 3). The 10-year rule becomes evident in his case, as soon as we remember that Mozart's first published composition (four violin sonatas, K. 6-9) is of 1763-64 when he was 7 or 8. Mozart himself was the first to praise hard work, and to dispel ideas that great works came to him from some mysterious gifts and talents: "I have spared neither care nor labor to produce something excellent for Prague. Moreover it is a mistake to think that the practice of my art has become easy to me. I assure you, dear friend, no one has given so much care to the study of composition as I. There is scarcely a famous master in music whose works I have not frequently and diligently studied [A remark to Conductor Kucharz in Prague, who led the rehearsals for *Don Giovanni* in 1787]" (1965, p. 6).

Robert Albert (1978) did not only stress the importance of hard work, but also, very correctly, *"the capacity to work alone"* (p. 207, italics in the original). Thus, Albert, unintentionally, draws attention to the challenged youths who, because of their misfortunes, have far less contacts with playmates, schoolmates, and teachers. Because of this forced loneliness, because of their inevitable difficulties with their peers, the challenged youths tend to work alone at their own things. The others are a disturbance: they know less, are less capable, do not take things seriously or not as seriously as the challenged do. Soon, the challenged youths discover that they must do without the approval of the others; they must be their own judges, and move alone.

All this explains the transformation from curiosity, and the sparks from clashes of the *war of the scripts,* to creativogenic vision(s) and derived "network of enterprises." Also, even if, as reported at the beginning of this chapter, "many highly successful adults managed to display no clear signs of giftedness in their early years," many, instead, displayed a high level of curiosity, from Newton's "insatiable curiosity" (Manuel, 1968, p. 39), to Darwin's "enlarged curiosity" (Brent, 1981, p. 117), to Einstein's "passionate curiosity and sense of wonder" (Hoffmann, 1972, pp. 18-20). It is the hard work of the first ten years or more, the hard work done to win one battle after the other in the *war of the scripts* which will give birth to a vision(s). When least expected things will coalesce, and the challenged personality will shout *Eureka*! Yes, it is so! Without those long years of trial and error that vision would not have arisen. And with a clearer vision—and improved technical proficiency—comes, naturally, creativity of high caliber.

High creativity demands intense concentration, total immersion in the chosen subject, and this is not possible in parallel with other activities. Picasso made this very clear to Françoise Gilot; "Everybody has the same energy potential [not true]. The average person wastes his in a dozen little ways [true]. I bring mine to bear on one thing only; my painting, and everything is sacrificed to it" (Gilot & Lake, 1964, p. 348, my bracketed inserts).

9. Achievement Motivation

Expanding on the studies of Csikszentmihalyi on "flow", I see a fundamental difference in the achievement motivation that leads on one side to gifted/talented people and, on the other, to challenged ones, to creativity.

The first group (high GxA) seems to operate (more than the challenged) "in flow", or in order to achieve "flow": *flow* being the autotelic experience ("rewarding in and of itself"). In the words of Csikszentmihalyi, "artists, athletes, composers, dancers, scientists, and people from all walks of life, when they describe how it feels when they are doing something that is worth doing for its own sake, use terms that are interchangeable in their minutest details. This unanimity suggests that order in consciousness produces a very specific experiential state, so desirable that one wishes to replicate it as often as possible. To this state we have given the name of 'flow', using a term that many respondents used in their interviews to explain what the optimal experience felt like" (1988b, p. 29).

However, when dealing with the pinnacles of creativity, Csikszentmihalyi himself (1991) spoke of *pathological creativity*, not of "flow". He saw those high creators, like Leonardo, as being led by a *defensive overachieving syndrome*, which forced them to invest all their psychic energy, all their attention, in the development of their interests and talents. I agree with Csikszentmihalyi, even if I am not overly fond of the word pathological which distorts the picture by bringing back old and wrong notions of the genius as a mad man, or strangely blessed and cursed by the gods[31].

The way I see it, the challenged personality, besides operating often on flow, is also driven by a desire for recognition after long years of having been considered and treated as "illegitimate" (in the broadest sense of the world, [i.e., not legitimate], negatively marginal, or even pathological) by peers, teachers, employers, colleagues. Said differently, the challenged personality often has a grudge against some sections of society, and a corresponding need for a settling of accounts. Clearly, while these feelings per se cannot contribute to creativity, they can provide those large doses of adrenalin which help the mind to stick with a problem 16 hours a day or more, seven days a week. While these feelings per se cannot contribute to creativity, they can magnify the clashes of the *war of scripts*, they can keep alive old memories of insults and slights received and enlarge them with new ones. In the end, also the creativity of the challenged may be ruled by flow, by the total immersion in the problem and its solution, but by a flow surrounded and backed by strong emotions, by powerful memories. Is this pathological? No. Is this special, in the sense of operating under strong intellectual and emotional forces? Yes. The reader may remember the letter that Empress Maria Theresa wrote in 1772, on the subject of Mozart, to her son the Archduke Ferdinand, at that time Governor of Lombardy:

> "You ask me about taking into your services the young Salzburg musician. I do not know in what capacity, believing that you have no need for a composer or for useless people. If, however, it would give you pleasure, I do not wish to prevent you. What I say is intended only to urge you not to burden yourself with useless people, and not to give such people permission to represent themselves as belonging in your service. It gives one's service a bad name when such people run about like beggars; he has, besides, a large family." The docile Archduke naturally thought no more of engaging Mozart, and did

---

[31] "The pairing of creative genius and insanity goes back at least as far as the ancient Greeks. Plato speaks of divine madness or *enthusiasmos*, and Aristotle believed that 'all extraordinary men . . . . in philosophy, politics, poetry and the arts are evidently melancholic'" (Schuldberg & Sass, 1999, p. 502).

not confer any title upon him. If Leopold [Mozart's father] had had any idea what Maria Theresa, the kindly Queen who had once presented his children with the cast-off clothing of her royal children, really thought about him and Wolfgang ("useless" people—bohemians—bothersome folk!) his loyalty would have suffered a bit. (Einstein, 1946, pp. 32-33)

Probably Mozart did not know of this letter, but his hate of the aristocrats, and his efforts to get even with them, in such operas as *Don Giovanni, Nozze di Figaro,* and *Abduction from the Seraglio,* show that he had understood very well that behind a few polite gestures, as the above mentioned gift of royal clothing, there was nothing but the standard disdain and contempt for servants and others of humble origins. Such an insult had to be washed away, and more than once; and Mozart did it most efficiently, combining flow with bite.[32]

Edward de Bono's definition of thinking expands on the fundamental role of the motivation: "Thinking is the operating skill with which intelligence acts upon experience (for a purpose), because not all thinking has a heavy sense of purpose" (1982, p. 11). Thinking—especially by highly intelligent people—without a heavy sense of purpose, (i.e. without a valid achievement motivation) can lead into what de Bono calls *the intelligence trap*:

Highly intelligent people may turn out to be rather poor thinkers. . . . A highly intelligent person can construct a rational and well-argued case for virtually any point of view. The more coherent this support for a particular point of view the less the thinker sees any need actually to explore the situation. . . . Verbal fluency is often mistaken, in school and after, for thinking. An intelligent person learns this and is tempted to substitute one for the other. . . . The critical use of intelligence is always more immediately satisfying than the constructive use. To prove someone else wrong gives you instant achievement and superiority. . . . The highly intelligent mind seems to

---

[32] The above is in line with the following from Tannenbaum (1983), as quoted by Mönks, Heller & Passow (2000): "Ability alone cannot facilitate great accomplishment. It also requires a confluence of various non-intellective factors such as ego strength, dedication to a chosen field of productivity or performance, willingness to sacrifice short-term satisfactions for the sake of long-term accomplishment and many others. These traits are integral to the achieving personality regardless of the areas in which the talent manifests itself" (p. 851).

prefer-or is encouraged-to place a higher value on cleverness than on wisdom. This may be because cleverness is more demonstrable. . . . There are some other aspects of the intelligence trap. Not all highly intelligent people are caught by the intelligence trap. They may avoid it by chance, upbringing or conscious effort. The danger remains, nevertheless. And the danger cautions us not to accept the automatic assumption that high intelligence means effective thinking. (1982, pp. 11-13)

However, there is another way to avoid being caught in the intelligence trap, and this is by having suffered some major misfortunes of youth which demand focused thinking on the causes of those misfortunes, and on ways to overcome them.[33] The challenged youth has more important things to do than to play intelligence games, than to try to play the smart fellow. In this sense, I always felt that the following two characteristics of the G/T *Gifted Learner*[34] did not apply, or rarely, to the challenged youth: "Has wild, silly ideas", and "Plays around, yet tests well."The child suffering from a major misfortune has other things in mind than having wild, silly ideas, nor does he or she play around, yet tests well.[35]

10. Qualitatively or Quantitatively Different?

"Perhaps the most basic question about giftedness is its relationship to the typical. Do gifted individuals stand out chiefly in terms of the speed with which their abilities develop and with which they process information? O r do they develop and process information in a

---

[33] It may be worth remembering the previous quote:" The experience was crucial for Dickens's entire future course. It is hardly fanciful to say that in the blacking warehouse that unhappy child died, and into his frail body entered the spirit of a man of relentless determination. Deep within him, he resolved that he should never again be so victimized. He would toil, he would fall prey to none of his father's financial imprudence, he would let nothing stand between him and ambition. He would batter his way out of all the gaols that confine the human spirit" (Johnson, 1969, p. 45).

[34] From a table from the *Spice/Wing Parent Handbook* (1991) by the Humble ISD, contrasting the gifted learner with the bright child.

[35] Far be it from me to say that the challenged youth thinks only about his/her misfortune(s); yet they do so often enough to become different from those not so afflicted. For instance, still nine years after the death of his step-father, Newton, while compiling a catalog of his sins, had written: "Threatening my father and mother Smith to burne them and the house over them" (Westfall, 1978, p. 17).

way that is qualitatively different from normal?" (Winner, 2000, p. 153). For me, the question as stated is overly restrictive, and—unwillingly—distorts the search for an answer by directing the attention to either a difference in speed of development and speed in processing information, or different ways of processing information, as if dealing with two types of computers.

The way I see it, the first thing, that distinguishes first class thinkers and creators from lesser ones, is that they are adept practitioners of the maxim "A wise man makes distinctions or says nothing," and this has little to do with speed of processing information, but much with a well indexed memory. Robert Sternberg was on the right track when, in his *The Triarchic Mind — A New Theory of Human Intelligence* (1988), he listed the following three aspects (or subtheories) of intelligence: 1. componential (analytic, computational), 2. experiential (synthetic, creative), and 3. contextual (streetwise, practical).

Sternberg's *experiential creative intelligence* (the one of interest to us now) is the ability to combine disparate experiences in insightful ways. It is the ability to see how existing personal knowledge relates to the new, but not in limited ways: it is making ten different distinctions, it is keeping in mind the essence of the demand by George Kelly (1963) "that a construct is a way in which some things are alike and yet different from others" (p. 111). *Experiential intelligence* is historical in the sense that the new is rapidly compared to the old, and the old to the new: the new is then seen in a new light through comparisons and contrasts, and the old enriched by the new or even radically modified by the new.

Experiential intelligence is creative: "*Barbara* didn't have the best test scores, but she was a superbly creative thinker who could combine disparate experiences in insightful ways. She is an example of the *experiential* subtheory" (from Sternberg, as reported by Trotter, 1986, p. 60). Here, speed of processing helps, obviously, but more important is a large store of personal experiences, related ruminations, and extensive readings, all richly indexed and cross-indexed in memory.

And it is here, at the level of creativity—of the *experiential intelligence*, and of making distinctions—that we encounter, once more, the difference between the gifted and the challenged.

The gifted, especially those with a superb IQ, are the masters of the *componential intelligence*, as exemplified by Sternberg's *Alice* who "had high test scores and was a whiz at test-taking and analytical thinking" (ib., p. 60). Here, indeed, we encounter that high mental processing speed of interest to Ellen Winner.

So, is the difference qualitative or quantitative? My answer is both. Nobody is a gifted person or a challenged person without a high GxA, in other words without a high intelligence capable of processing information at high speed (e.g., a quantitative difference). In addition, especially the *challenged* are masters in *experiential intelligence* based on a huge, well-indexed memory from which to build all kinds of associations and alliances (e.g., a qualitative difference). Also, the *challenged*, with their paucity of normal scripts and a wealth of personal scripts built from their high GxAxM (M in particular), are different persons, and so is their unique *war of the scripts* with society and their final vision and life program (again, a qualitative difference).

On the other hand, as usual, things are not black and white. Many other persons (e.g. the *eccentric* and the *different* of figure 1 in volume 1) did not adopt all the major scripts of society, and developed some unique scripts. They too may harbor some grudge against society. Nor are the *challenged* devoid of all social scripts: they still have some, especially in the areas away from the eddies created by their misfortunes of youth. So, there is continuity. The final answer is the classical "it depends".

It also depends on the level of knowledge, as well summarized by Teres Enix Scott, in her chapter "Knowledge" of *The Encyclopedia of Creativity*:

> Robert Albert's position appears to be 'knowledge is necessary.' Albert conducted longitudinal study on the relationship between giftedness and creativity in male adolescents. Albert believes that self-knowledge and self-directed knowledge are the fundamental source of creativity because knowledge determines decisions and opportunities. Albert assumes that the decisions one makes on the basis of one's knowledge determine the opportunity one has. (1999, 2, p. 128)

However, the best knowledge is the one well indexed and cross-indexed, by focused interests, the one that is alive, constantly used and enriched by powerful passions, by the daily battles of an important *war of the scripts*.

11. Implications for Educational Practice

Knowing whether a child, in particular a gifted and talented child, is *dedicated* or *challenged*—and this can be recognized both by his/her special behavior[36], and by the pertinent set of assistances and misfortunes (if known)—will permit assistances to be tailored.

The *dedicated* child gladly follows instructions and programs as suggested by parents and teachers. He or she derives maximum benefit from such programs and team competitions as the *Academic Decathlon, Academic Enterprises, Odyssey of the Mind,* and *Future Problem Solving* which impose a certain amount of structure and a number of demands and evaluation criteria that are the same for all participants. Here, one does well by playing according to the rules, and by using teamwork. In contrast, the *challenged* youth is unwilling to focus on problems that are foreign to him or her, and objects to being in a competition under uniform, detailed rules. Consequently, the challenged child should not be pushed toward creating or participating in team games, but should be helped to deepen his/her own personal interests, to become his/her own teacher and judge. This is summed up by the remark by the *challenged* Anne Frank, at the age of 13: "I have to be my own mother, I've drawn myself apart from them all; I am my own skipper and later on I shall see where I come to land" (1953, p. 41). This remark highlights the need for a different type of help for *challenged* children: something even less structured than Renzulli's (1986) *Type III Enrichment Program,* less structured than the *Problem-Based Learning* (Stepien, Gallagher & Workman, 1993) with teachers acting as "metacognitive coaches and tutors."

A benign neglect of the *challenged,* on the part of teachers, with the exception of some assistance or friendships outside of class, may be better for adult creativity than participation in enrichment programs. High creativity demands a new, unique vision that is forged in reaction to one's misfortunes. In this sense, it may be best for teachers to allow the youth—within limits—to oppose, refute, and scorn. As Albert and Runco (1986) noted:

A common theme in the achievement of eminence is that "others" have not performed adequately. Implied in a person's

---

[36] For example, the *dedicated individual* is more social, a teammate willing to accept the others' agenda; the *challenged individual* is more of a loner—or a stubborn group leader—following his or her own agenda.

long-term creative behavior is his or her belief that others' efforts were somehow lacking and perhaps not good enough. *Creative behavior is thus in part oppositional and disapproving.* (p. 336, my italics)

To make my point clearer—with few exceptions (and those exceptions are usually evident)—I would recommend not even to mention the word creativity to *challenged youths*. They must grow first, develop according to their own internal logic, with no pressure to produce, to materialize their dreams and passions. The right help was, for instance that given by Baron von Westphalen to young Karl Marx, or that given by Max Talmey to young Einstein:

> Baron Ludwig von Westphalen found in Karl a boy after his own heart. Unlike [his son] Edgar, Karl possessed a formidable intelligence, a fierce determination[37] to know and understand everything that had been said and written. The old man—he was in his sixties—enjoyed taking the boy for walks in the neighborhood of Trier. (Payne, 1968, p. 28)
>
> Eleanor Marx [Karl's daughter] wrote that Baron von Westphalen "filled Karl Marx with enthusiasm for the romantic school and, whereas his father read Voltaire and Racine with him, the Baron read him Homer and Shakespeare—who

---

[37] This determination was stimulated, or strongly reinforced, by the half-forced conversion of his father—and of himself when he was six—from Judaism to Christianity. It was a half-forced conversion, in the sense that the father's (Heschel, later Heinrich) conversion to Christianity was made in order to be able to continue his profession of counsellor-at-law to the High Court of Appeal in Trier, when the Prussian Government decided in 1816 that the Rhineland too should be subject to the laws that had been in force in Prussia since 1812, which, while granting Jews rights equal to those of the Christians, nevertheless made their holding of positions in the service of the state dependent on a royal dispensation, a dispensation that was not given to Heschel Marx. Seen with the eyes of the extended family, and possibly also of Karl, this professional or monetary conversion showed character failure on the part of his father, who was the son of Meier Halevi Marx, rabbi of Saarlouis, later rabbi of Trier. Meier Halevi was then followed in this office by his eldest son Samuel (Karl's uncle). Indeed the Marx family had produced rabbis in unbroken succession for generations. The name Marx is a shortened form of Mordechai, later changed to Markus. Also Karl's mother was the daughter of a rabbi. She consented to the baptism of her children, but asked to defer her own baptism on account of her parents. Her father died one year after, and she was then baptized.

remained his favourite authors all his life." . . . . As well as being a man of culture, the Baron was keen on progressive political ideas and interested Marx in the personality and work of the French utopian socialist Saint-Simon. (McLellan, 1973, p. 15-16)

The influence that initially led Einstein on to his chosen path did not come from the Luitpold Gymnasium but from Max Talmey, a young Jewish medical student who in 1889 matriculated at Munich University. . . . [On young Einstein] Talmey wrote, "He showed a particular inclination toward physics and took pleasure in conversing on physical phenomena. I gave him therefore as reading matter A. Bernstein's *Popular Books on Physical Science* and L. Buchner's *Force and Matter,* two works that were then quite popular in Germany. The boy was profoundly impressed by them. Bernstein's work especially, which describes physical phenomena lucidly and engagingly, had a great influence on Albert, and enhanced considerably his interest in physical science. . . . Thereafter philosophy was often a subject of our conversations. I recommended to him the reading of Kant. At that time he was still a child, only thirteen years old, yet Kant's works, incomprehensible to ordinary mortals, seemed to be clear to him. Kant became Albert's favorite philosopher after he had read through his *Critique of Pure Reason* and the works of other philosophers." (Clark, 1971, pp. 15-16)

Clearly, both Marx and Einstein profited of normal quality assistance in learning substantive matters, not on how to 'bring the process of creativity to bear on a specific subject,' not on how to develop 'originality of thinking and freshness of approaches', nor on 'developing constructive ingenuity.'

With *dedicated youths,* it is just the opposite: they profit from approaches and techniques that will yield measurable creative acts, even if small, one after the other. The dedicated youth, even if unconventional for a few years, is and remains a round peg in a world of round holes, and will easily succeed in life, provided he works hard, avoids stupid mistakes, and has a modicum of normal luck.[38]

The *challenged youths,* instead, are less mature, less integrated and connected, even when they look old and tempered by the adversities of life. Let them mature first. Then creativity will follow most naturally. I would not place a *challenged youth,* for instance, in a special school or special class for gifted and talented children, but plainly leave him or her in the best normal school available. Just because they are special, they will benefit by being surrounded by normal kids and not by other special ones. They are already living in hot houses without the need to further raise the temperature. They do not need to be forced to show that they are smarter than five or ten other very smart fellows. This however should not apply, or less, to after-school and weekend programs on such specific subjects as mathematics and language, which could be the equivalent of the assistance given by Max Talmey to Einstein.

On the subject of help to *challenged youths,* Csikszentmihalyi (1991) is even more radical than I. For him, there is nothing that parents, teachers and other adults can do to foster creativity. I have already shown my disagreement with this approach, by pointing to individual quality assistance. In addition, there is another, more

---

[38] This can be seen in the development of *Terman's children*: "By 1950, at an average age of 40, the men had written and published 67 books, over 1,400 articles, 200 plays and short stories; they had obtained over 150 patents; 78 of them had received a Ph.D., 48 an M.D., and 85 an LL.B.; 74 were university professors, and 47 were listed in *American Men of Science.* As Terman noted, 'the number who became research scientists, engineers, physicians, lawyers, or college teachers, or who were highly successful in business and other fields, is in each case many times the number a random group would have provided' (1954, p. 41)" (Dworetzky, 1985, p.383/384). "Collectively, the gifted children in Terman's sample grew up to be very successful. By mid-life, they had produced 92 books, 235 patents, and nearly 2200 scientific articles (Goleman, 1980)" (Weiten, 1989, p. 312).

However, as reported by Goleman (1980), in a study made by Terman in 1960, "the 100 most successful [among his] men were designated the A group, the 100 least successful, the C group. While the Cs were the 'failures' of the Terman kids, the judgement is relative: most of them equalled or exceeded the national average for job status and income. . . . The A group included 24 university professors, 11 lawyers, 8 research scientists, and 5 physicians. Thirty were business executives, one was a farmer who operated large ranches. Only five men in the C group were professionals, and none was doing well. One, for example, who had done graduate work in mathematics and was employed as an engineer, actually worked at the technician level. The majority worked as clerks, salesmen, or in small businesses" (p. 32). In essence, while the members of the C group were no failures, they seemed not to have been successful either, proof that a high intelligence is not enough even for good normal success in life.

practical way (and an old fashioned method, to boot) to foster the number of highly creative people: with money. Money or educational grants can be an invaluable assistance to *challenged children* and their families. Such financial support, in many cases, can make the difference between adult creativity and an unfulfilled possibility. Often misfortunes bring stringent financial difficulties (see Ferri 1976, discussed above) that force the youth or adult to spend much time and efforts in menial tasks and among uninteresting people. What would have happened to Charles Dickens if he had spent 5 years of manual labor in a paste-blacking factory instead of 5 months? Would he have become a great writer? What saved him, at the age of 12, was money: His grandmother died and left enough money for his father to pay his debts, leave prison, return to work, and free his son from the paste-blacking factory.

Two additional comments: Among the special programs for gifted and talented children, I would always favor those which encourage their achieving excellence also as human beings by nurturing deep moral, social, and civic commitment. Secondly,while constantly demanding, and fostering, the highest school quality, be it general or special for gifted and talented children, I would always stress to each child that he/she is the primary motor of development, not the teachers. Books (and not television) are the greatest help, the greatest mental challenge.[39] It pays to tell the children not to expect much help

---

[39] "As a child Igor [Stravinsky] read omnivorously: Tolstoy, Shakespeare, Dante and translations from the Greek. He was particularly excited by Sophocles' *Oedipus Rex*. His father possessed a large and famous library, with first editions of Gogol, Pushkin and Tolstoy, as well as operatic scores. . . . He came to know the works of Wagner and Rimsky-Korsakov from the piano scores; but generally speaking his adolescence was a period of mounting frustration and bitterness" (Routh, 1975, p.2).

"Igor's first school was the Second St. Petersburg Gymnasium, which he attended until he was fourteen or fifteen. He seems to have hated the classes and to have made very few friends. From there he went on to the Gonrévitch Gymnasium, which he equally loathed. He studied history, mathematics, Latin, Greek, French, German, Russian and Slavonic, and from his own account was an indifferent pupil" (White, 1966, p.4).

Reading helped Stravinsky, and so did—it seems—hating the classes and having very few friends.

Moving to adulthood, it was Michelangelo (in 1509, at the age of 34) who said tersely: "I have no friends of any kind, nor do I wish any, for I have not so much time that I can afford to waste it" (quoted by Clemens, 1978, p. 99). Even Picasso, far more sociable than Michelangelo, automatically kept relations under strict control: "We (he and Françoise Gilot) almost never went to the theater or to the movies. Even our friends were kept within well-defined limits" (Gilot & Lake, 1964, p. 348).

and mental challenge, at school, and—on the contrary—to be happily surprised if a teacher is truly capable, is interested, and provides quality assistance and challenge.

12. The Relative Importance of *Fit*

As noted by Siegler and Kotovsky:

> Whether a child is generally creative may be at best weakly linked to whether he or she as an adult will be extremely creative at any one activity. The predictive problem becomes even more daunting when we realize that there is no guarantee that an adult who could be exceptionally creative at an activity will ever find that activity. Even if the individual does find an activity in which he or she shows exceptional talent, there is no guarantee that he or she will find it sufficiently rewarding to make it a life's work. (1986, p. 420)

Clearly, the moment one speaks of talents, one speaks of something specific, often technical, (e.g., finger coordination, pitch discrimination, memory for tunes), and therefore there will be creativity only if there is a *fit* with the field (e.g., in our case, the figurative arts or the musical world). However, while I completely agree that "Whether a child is generally creative may be at best weakly linked to whether he or she as an adult will be extremely creative at any one activity," I would not confuse the picture by—unintentionally—throwing in a red herring in the form of a fit problem, which in reality, with few exceptions, does not exist.

Shortly before, on this same subject, Siegler and Kotovsky had written that "The fit between the individual and the field is important for both intellectual and motivational reasons. A superior fit allows the individual to learn quickly and deeply the material in the field. It also can motivate the dedication of huge amounts of time and effort that is so critical for even a person of superior intellectual gifts to acquire the knowledge base from which to make eminent contributions" (ib., p. 419). This may be true, if referred to creativity "via flow", when one creates mainly for the pleasure of creating. But this notion of fit has little to do with sustained high creativity, with having a vision, with seeing the world in a new light, with having a sense of mission[40], with being a reformer. What Siegler and Kotovsky are discussing is normal creativity C1 to C6, not high/revolutionary creativity C7 to C10.

To start, there is the factual knowledge that the greatest creators were creative in several fields. Dante, for instance, was great both as a poet (*Divine Comedy*) and as political thinker (*Monarchia*). Did Dante become great because he had been lucky in finding the fields that fitted his talents? It makes no sense to say that Picasso had a "fit" for cubism: he created this visual art style with Braque. Are we going to say that Darwin was creative because he discovered a fit between his talent and an evolutionary theory that did not yet exist, or that Marx was born with a fit for Marxism?

The case of Napoleon is even clearer: "His particular type of brain would seem to have been eminently fitted for the study of the exact sciences, and in a letter he wrote to Laplace, when the Empire was at the height of its glory, he confessed to a certain feeling of sadness in this connection, declaring he was 'sorry that force of circumstances, which had driven him into a different career, had led him so far from that of the scientist'" (Madelin, 1967, p. 30). Said differently, a challenged man of his caliber, would have achieved greatly in many fields; and in each left his mark (see table 2, chapter 3 of volume 1) in function of his complex GAM personality: *alchemist, leadsman, universalist.*

Picasso was also a great poet beside being a great painter: "Rafael Alberti is the only one of Picasso's literary mentors[41] to have had the

---

[40] "Klee assumed importance later than Picasso. . . . Nevertheless, it would be a mistake to view his earlier works as mere preliminaries. We must not be led astray by the small dimensions of his drawings, and the miniature quality of his watercolors. Klee knew perfectly well, from the very start, who he was and what he wanted. It was the difficulties that beset his first attempts, not any doubts as to his mission, that made him reserved toward the world around him. His self-reliance is clearly revealed in his journals and letters; he notes exactly what he thought right and the methods he should employ. At the age of twenty-one he had already realized how hard it is 'to work out a pictorial motif which is the exact equivalent' of a poetic one" (Grohmann, 1954, p. 101).

[41] "Poets exercised an especially formative influence. Max Jacob is the one we associate with Picasso's earliest years in Paris, Guillaume Apollinaire with the Rose period and cubism. Jean Cocteau was the catalyst for the neoclassical period (1918-25)—'*l'époque des duchesses*,' Jacob called it—presided over by the artist's first wife, Olga Kokhlova; André Breton and the surrealists for the 'metamorphic' period when the teenage Marie Thérèse acted as muse; Paul Eluard both for the Dora Maar (1936-45) and Françoise Gilot (1945-53) periods; and Cocteau again (early 1950s until his death in 1963) for the first half of *l'époque Jacqueline*; and, at the very end of his life, the one and only one Spaniard, Rafael Alberti" (Richardson, 1961, p. 5).

prescience to recognize the painter as a major Spanish poet—something that is taken for granted in Spain now that his extensive writings have been published" (Richardson, 1991, p. 8).

What Siegler and Kotovsky said on the importance of *fit* may be true for some people, especially for those with high talents of genetic origin (say for music, mathematics, drawing), but it is not true for the many with high GxAxM, especially when magnified by hard work over a long time.

Freud, for instance, was great in two unrelated fields: physiology and psychology.

Proof for the first is the fact that the Austrian physician Robert Bárány (the 1914 Nobel laureate) had nominated Freud for the 1917 Nobel Prize for his works on physiology of 1877-1883, specifically for his studies of the spinal cord of one of the lowest forms of fish, *Ammacoetes Petroxyon*, while working in Brücke's Physiological Institute from 1877 to 1882 (see Gay, 1988, p. 371). So, what Freud had done, in his early twenties, was of such caliber to bring him close to the Nobel Prize.

There must have been therefore a fit between Freud and the field of physiology. But then the *fit* broke, there was no way for Freud to make a living as a research physiologist, and he had to move to internal medicine and the development of a medical practice[42]. The new development led him to create psychoanalysis. Here too, there was a fit, and this time with a field that did not yet exist, and that he himself created.

Something similar can be said for Piaget, who at the age of 15 was able to have published, "on the sly", a series of articles on the mollusks of Switzerland, Savoy, Brittany and Columbia. "However," as narrated by Piaget in his autobiography, "instead of quietly pursuing the career of a naturalist which seemed so normal and so easy for me after these fortunate circumstances, between the ages of fifteen and twenty I experienced a series of crises due both to family conditions and to the intellectual curiosity characteristic of the productive age.

---

[42] In Ernest Jones's words: "In June 1882, an event took place, which may truly be called one of the great turning points in his life, ... This event was the decision to earn his livelihood as a physician and resign his position in Brücke's Institute. His own account of it, in his *Autobiography* (1923), runs as follows: 'The turning point came in 1882 when my teacher, for whom I had the highest possible esteem, corrected my father's generous improvidence by strongly advising me, in view of my bad financial position, to abandon my theoretical career. I followed his advice, left the physiology laboratory and entered the General Hospital'" (1953, p. 59).

But, I repeat, all those crises I was able to overcome[43], thanks to the mental habits, which I had acquired through early contact with the zoological science" (1952, p. 239).

Again, with Piaget, we encounter a person with a fit for two very different fields: natural science and psychology. Piaget's life confirms what I found in hundreds of biographies of eminent people: they seemed capable of doing wonders in most fields (admittedly not those that demand highly specific talents). In other words, what counts is a high GxAxM potential applied, for many years, under *pruning* (see chapter 3, this volume), to any field not demanding specific talents.

Leonardo da Vinci was a painter, sculptor, scientist, military engineer; Michelangelo was a sculptor, painter, architect, poet; William Blake was a poet, painter, engraver[44], and visionary; Sartre was

---

[43]Before—and this can be read as the M which made a challenged personality out of him—Piaget had written: "My mother was very intelligent, energetic, and fundamentally a very kind person; her rather neurotic temperament, however, made our family life somewhat troublesome. One of the direct consequences of this situation was that I started to forego playing for serious work very early; this I obviously did as much to imitate my father as to take refuge in both a private and non-fictitious world. Indeed, I have always detested any departure from reality, an attitude which I relate to the second important influential factor of my early life, *viz.* my mother's poor mental health; it was the disturbing factor which at the beginning of my studies in psychology made me intensely interested in questions of psychoanalysis and pathological psychology" (ib., pp. 237-38). We have here a compact description of a challenged case of reduced learning of normal scripts (little from the mother, not much from the father who concentrated on his work, little from peers, little from books of fiction), and the building of highly personal scripts from thoughts on the meaning and cause of poor mental health. The whole, obviously, together with a high G and high assistances. On this last point, Piaget wrote that his father had devoted "his writing mostly to medieval literature, and to a lesser extent, to the history of Neuchâtel. He is a man of a painstaking and critical mind, who dislikes hastily improvised generalizations, and is not afraid of starting a fight when he finds historic truth twisted to fit respectable traditions. Among many other things he taught me the value of systematic work, even in small matters" (ib., p. 237).

[44] Both Goethe and Victor Hugo had a talent for drawing. For instance Goethe's beautiful drawing of "Faust and the Spirit of the Earth", hangs now in the Goethe Museum in Weimar, and Victor Hugo's various effective sketches for *Les Miserables*, are in the Maison Victor Hugo in Paris. "The critics of his own day were not mistaken when they wrote that, had he not elected to earn a living writing words, he might have become a great artist" (Edwards, 1971, p. 224). Yet I think that both did well not to follow that talent because, based on the people I have known from boyhood on, I feel that a talent for drawing is not rare— obviously not at the Picasso level. This seems confirmed by the following comments by Leon Miller in his 1999 article on the *Savant Syndrome*: "The most common type of [idiot] savant [or mono-savant] skills are exhibited *in the visual arts, particularly drawing* (Selfe, 1983); musical performance (Miller, 1989); and certain arithmetic skills, including calendar calculating (the ability to give the correct day of the week for a given date) and prime number derivation (Sacks, 1985)" (1999, p. 31, my italics). Teresa Amabile (1990) complained that her evident artistic potential in kindergarten was not fostered: "I haven't done anything even vaguely artistic in the years since; I still draw the way I did in kindergarten" (p. 61). Yet given the relatively high supply of this talent, I am not sure if, even with the best assistances, she would have become a better painter than she is now a psychologist.

eminently creative, practically in parallel, as a philosopher, novelist, and playwright; Simone de Beauvoir was an eminent novelist and essayist; before them, Hildegard von Bingen (1098-1179) was an eminent visionary mystic, the author of the *Book of Compound Medicine*, or *Causes and Cures*, and a composer who expanded Gregorian music. Her songs have been arranged in a cycle under the title *Symphony of the Harmony* or *Celestial Revelation* (now available on records).

Marx could easily have become a first class philosopher or novelist; and Einstein a C10 philosopher, if we remember that when "he was still a child, only thirteen years old, yet Kant's works, incomprehensible to ordinary mortals, seemed to be clear to him. Kant became Albert's favorite philosopher after he had read through his *Critique of Pure Reason* and the works of other philosophers" (Talmey as quoted above). But if so, why did Einstein pursue the study of physics and not philosophy. In all probability, because his father had become a partner of the electrical engineering factory J. Einstein & Cie in which the J. stood for Jacob, his younger brother who had attended the Polytechnic in Stuttgart, and graduated as an engineer. Such an environment fostered an interested in scientific tools, and, indeed, Einstein related how he experienced great wonder when, as a child of 4 or 5, his father showed him a compass (Fölsing, 1998, p. 13). "The story [of the compass] is simply that when the boy was five, ill in bed, his father showed him a pocket compass. What impressed the child was that since the iron needle always pointed in the same direction whichever way the case was turned, it must be acted upon by something that existed in space—the space that had always been considered empty" (Clark, 1971, p. 11).

In no way do I say that that sense of wonder is the result of a high GxAxM. No, the sense of wonder can be found in many non-challenged gifted children: it reflects their high intelligence and related high curiosity. However, I will say that the M of the misfortunes (better said the GxAxM) is needed to have these gifted children overcome adolescence (as discussed hereafter) while keeping intact their sense of wonder, their infinite curiosity. Adolescence, with its strong peer pressure for conformity is the graveyard of much non-challenged curiosity, of much non-challenged sense of wonder.

The challenged Einstein emerged intact from this leveling process: "Not giving a damn about accepted beliefs was an attitude which [Einstein] certainly developed at the Gymnasium. . . . It taught him the virtues of skepticism. It encouraged him to question and doubt, always valuable qualities in a scientist" (ib., p. 13). Part of Einstein's skepti-cal-challenged personality evolved at a conflicting border between poorly defended Jewish religiosity, and science. As reported in chapter 3 of volume 1, his parents were lax Jews who "sent Albert and his sister, Maja, two and half years his junior, to the nearby Catholic elementary school[45], where the two children learned the traditions and tenets of the Catholic faith" (Hoffmann, 1972, p. 16). The subsequent developments are interesting: "Their education in Judaism was not, however, neglected. Young Albert quickly became intensely religious, both spiritually and ritualistically. For years he refused to eat pork, for example, and he took it amiss that his parents were lax in their Jewish observances. . . . [But then came adolescence, and the help he received from Max Talmey, as discussed above] One striking effect of the science books on the impressionable Albert was to make him suddenly antireligious. He could not fail to see that the scientific story con-flicted with the biblical. Hitherto he had found the solace of certainty in religion as it had been taught him. Now he felt he had to give it up, at least in part, and this he could not do without an intense emotional struggle. For a while he became not just a nonbeliever but a fanatical skeptic, profoundly suspicious of authority" (ib., pp. 16, 24).

Back to Einstein's sense of wonder for physical phenomena—like that for the compass—this is the sense of wonder which could be crushed neither by his peers at school, nor by his teachers who were all shown naked under the light of his challenged skepticism. Sure, at one point, every challenged youth must make a choice, after a number of trials and errors, and specialize; but his/her creativity has less to do with a fit with the field than with other conditions, for instance politi-cal defeat. We would never have had the *Divine Comedy* if Dante had not been exiled from Florence and, instead, had continued to grow in the administration and politics of his city. It is only after his resound-ing defeat at the polls in 1945 that Winston Churchill busied himself with writing his great history of *The Second World War* in six vol-umes, becoming therefore the great historian who was honored in 1953 with a Nobel Prize. Once more, a challenged personality proved perfectly fit in two different domains.

---

[45] "The choice of a Catholic school was not as strange as it seems. Elementary education in Bavaria was run on a denominational basis. The nearest Jewish school was some distance from the Einstein home and its fees were high. To a family of little religious feeling the dangers of Catholic orientation were outweighed by the sound general instruction which the school gave" (Clark, 1971, p. 10).

For Siegler and Kotovsky, "Within the domain of writing, creative writers of historical novels would not necessarily be creative writers of short stories" (ib., p. 420). This may be true, but only by stressing technical specialization at the expense of vision. Writers like Dante, Cervantes, Shakespeare, Goethe, Schiller, Pirandello, to name only a few, wrote masterpieces in different literary genres; they wrote marvelous historical plays (see Shakespeare's *Julius Caesar*, Goethe's *Götz von Berlichigen*, Schiller's *William Tell*), as well as more intimate and individualistic ones (*Romeo and Juliet, Faust, The Robbers*). Also, as reported by Siegler and Kotovsky:

Albert and Runco, Csikszentmihalyi and Robinson, Feldman, Gruber, and Tannenbaum have presented compelling arguments for the importance of the *fit* between eminent contributors and the field of their contribution. As these contributors indicate, creative innovations require a meshing of an individual's talents, personality, and institutional resources with the issues of the time and the larger cultural context. The requirements for eminent contributions may differ at different times, even within a single field. In the second half of the 19th century, scientists without superior mathematical ability could make fundamental contributions to the understanding of genetics and evolution. Scientists with similar abilities might not be able to make comparable contributions today. (1986, p. 419)

Strictly speaking this may be true, and yet it leads into error as soon as one tries to derive some valid conclusions. Indeed, already Einstein, while reasonably good at mathematics was no mathematical genius, as Robert Albert himself had correctly reported: "Even Einstein for years had a number of post-Ph.D.s mathematicians to help him at his mathematics as apparently his mathematics was sometimes not equal to his grasp of theoretical physics" (1978, p. 206). Fölsing (1998) had even stronger comments: "As a student Einstein had not been particularly fond of mathematics and had shown interest in it only to the extent necessary. Nothing about this attitude had changed by the time he went to Prague. At the Solvay conference in the fall of 1911 he had surprised his colleagues by his statement that he had only a slight knowledge of mathematics. . . . In Prague, however, he realized that his mathematical knowledge needed broadening. Quite often he would run down the stairs to the Mathematical Institute to confront Professor Georg Pick with his problems and to get Pick to recommend books to him" (p. 311). The mathematical fit may have been there, but it was not great. What Einstein had in abundance, however, was curiosity, like Darwin: "'I have no particular talent. I am merely extremely inquisitive.' Einstein remarked one day to a friend who asked him to speculate on the source of genius that had led him to be hailed as one of the immortal scientists of all times" (Barnett, 1972, p. 431).

"I have no particular talent. I am merely extremely inquisitive," this and not a problem of fit, is what characterizes so many challenged personalities (even if some, like Mozart and Leonardo, had undeniable talents). Even in our days, little mathematics is needed in most scientific fields, be they biology, physiology, medicine, chemistry, psychology, or sociology. So, the idea, that the lack of adult creativity by some highly creative children could be due to a lack of fit, demands many corrections. The person with a vision will always find a domain in which to operate, and if not found, he/she will create it.

In essence, the idea of fit evaporates as soon as we remember Wayne Weiten's definition of creativity: "Creativity involves the generation of ideas that are original, novel and useful. First and foremost, creativity involves seeing the world in a new and different light" (1989, p. 292). Such a new sight will always find a way, it will always find a fit, in one established domain or another, or in a brand new one.

Sure, if one is a round peg, one has the interest of looking for round holes; but creativity is different: it is taking an ax and carving a new type of hole. This is what David Raup did, and this is what he recommended: "It is clear, therefore, that the new theory is guilty until proven innocent, and the pre-existing theory is innocent until proven guilty. . . . The practical effect is that a new idea requires a truly compelling case—intellectual overkill—in order to displace the incumbent" (1986, pp. 195-96). What Raup described is the work of a *visitor personality* "revolutionary and creative" (table 5 of volume 1), and not of an *insular personality* "dependent, knowing one's place, being controlled or controlling others, conservative and less creative." Under these conditions, clearly, the *visitor* does not fit, and the *insular* fits.

In a *visitor society,* the challenged personalities will always find a fit thanks to the inherent division of power at the basis of a *visitor* world; in an *insular society*, instead, very few challenged personalities can create: its unitary field accepts only the old or new praises for the *supremo.*

Back to Siegler and Kotovsky, Galileo would have achieved little to nothing, if he had followed the opinion of the best professors of his time as to what to do. None of them would have advised him to learn how to polish lenses and build telescopes, yet this is what led him to his greatest discoveries. But also for less substantial creativity, I would stress vision and drive and not fit. Vision and drive will naturally discover a fit, while fit will not bring vision and drive.

Basically, it is wrong to speak of fit, or not, early in life: it is putting the cart before the horse. The real suggestion is the one given in 1851 by John Soule: "Go west, young man", which, translated for this chapter, becomes "Go where few are, and work hard. At the end of many years you will realize that you had a vision, and a perfect fit for what you created."[46]

As for those with high talents, they, and their parents, usually, know perfectly what to do, as was the case with Mozart and Picasso. With them the fit is automatic, as it was with Martha Graham who wrote: "People have asked me why I chose to be a dancer. I did not choose, I was chosen to be a dancer, and with that, you live all your life. When any young student asks me, 'Do you think I should be a dancer?' I always say, 'If you have to ask, then the answer is no'" (1991, p. 5).

13. Which Kind of Creativity? *Les Demoiselles d'Avignon?*

There is another difficulty with the way Siegler and Kotovsky see the *fit* problem: it leaves out too much creativity, particularly some of the highest. In particular, it omits the creativity in moral and social domains, where the problem of *fit* is irrelevant. I am referring to such acts of creation as St.Paul's letters, St. Francis of Assisi's *Canticle of*

---

[46] A different story is the relation of personality to the nature/style of the act of creation, as discussed in chapter 3 of volume1, and highlighted in its table 2 "Four GAM Rows and Four Professional Columns".

the Creatures (also known as *Canticle of the Sun*) and his "invention" of Lady Poverty; Martin Luther's *Ninety-five Theses*; Henry Dunant's foundation of the Red Cross. I am referring to the Magna Carta, the US Declaration of Independence, the US Constitution (especially its First Amendment on the separation of state and church). I am referring to the Marshall Plan, and the creation of the United Nations. I am referring to modern philanthropic foundations, like the Ford Foundation, the Rockefeller Foundation, the Duke Endowment, and the Carnegie Corporation.

Indeed, "although charitable endowments existed in antiquity, the modern foundation is predominantly a 20th-century American phenomenon. . . . Foundations are exempt from federal and state income taxes on their investment income. They are also usually exempt from local property taxes. Gifts of property to foundations are not subject to gift taxes and bequests are exempt from estate and inheritance taxes. Charitable contributions to them are deductible within limits in determining taxable income for a person or corporation" (Hill, 1973, pp. 654, 656). This last, too, is revolutionary DP creativity of the first order which leaves the money and then the initiative of what to do, when and where, to the individuals, and not to the State! Also, some foundations award annual grants for such activities as "enhancing local quality of life," for artists who "benefit humanity," for individuals who "enhance the human conditions"or "who further water quality" (Ferguson, 2000, p. 81).

In an article which was part of a special issue of *Creativity Research Journal* devoted to "Creativity in the Moral Domain", edited by Howard Gruber and Doris Wallace, Helen Haste wrote that there are three components to moral creativity: "Vision, efficacy, and responsibility. *Vision* means the ability to take a wide view, to see beyond the conventional constraints of the situation. This may derive from a sophisticated philosophical perspective, or from more complex levels of moral reasoning—as for example reflected in Kohlberg's stages—or simply from having a different perspective. . . .*Efficacy* is the sense that one can act alone or with others. This requires knowledge of how to act, and belief that one has the strength and resources to act. Further, it includes the belief that one's actions are necessary and right. *Responsibility* is in a sense the outcome of vision and efficacy" (1993, p. 154). As discussed before, vision is the first thing.

On the other hand, "something is rotten in the state of our culture" if so much praise is piled on Picasso's *Demoiselles d'Avignon*[47], and so little on Henri Dunant's *Red Cross*[48] whose great importance does not only rest in actual generous deeds, but in having revolutionized the world's mentalities. One must read how soldiers and prisoners of war were considered and treated, before and after the creation and growth of the *Red Cross*, in order to appreciate the huge change. There is a radical improvement from seeing people as dispensable cannon fodder, and from total disregard for the wounded of the other camp, to an appreciation of the positive fundamental values and liberty of every human being. After Henri Dunant, no army general could think for a moment what Napoleon said to Prince Kourakin: *"Votre maitre a-t-il comme mois vingt-cinq mille hommes à dépenser par mois?* (Does your master [the Tsar] have, as I have, 25,000 men to expend each month?) (quoted by Chaptal, 1962, p. 182). Henri Dunant has made each of us more civilized: more just, fair, and generous.

---

[47] *"Demoiselles* was an attack on all previous ideas of art. Like *Elektra* [by Richard Strauss] and *Erwartung* [by Arnold Schoenberg], it was modernistic in that it was intended to be as destructive as it was creative, shocking, deliberately ugly, and undeniably crude. Picasso's brilliance lay in also making the painting irresistible. The five women are naked, heavily made up, completely brazen about what they are: prostitutes in a brothel. They stare back at the viewer, unflinching, confrontational rather than seductive" (Watson, 2000, p. 61). "'*Les Demoiselles d'Avignon*—how that name annoys me, Picasso said. 'It was Salmon who invented it. As you well know it was originally called *Le Bordel d'Avignon*'" (quoted by Richardson, 1996, p. 18), in relation to "a brothel in the carrer d'Avinyó (Avignon Street) in Barcelona" (Penrose, 1981, p. 132).

[48] *"Red Cross and Red Crescent,* in full The International Movement of the Red Cross and Red Crescent, formerly (until 1986) International Red Cross, humanitarian agency with national affiliates in almost every country in the world, first established to care for victims of battle in times of war but later aiding in the prevention and relief of human suffering generally. Its peacetime programss include first aid courses, accident prevention, water safety, training of nurses' aides and mothers' assistants, and maintenance of maternal and child welfare centers and medical clinics, blood banks, and numerous other services. . . . The Red Cross arose out of the work of Jean Henri Dunant, a Swiss humanitarian, who, at the Battle of Solferino, in June 1859, organized emergency aid services for Austrian and French wounded. In his book *Un Souvenir de Solferino* (1862; "A Memory of Solferino") he proposed the foundation in all countries of voluntary relief societies, and in 1864 the first societies came into being. . . . During wartime the [Red Cross International] committee acts as intermediary among belligerents and also among national Red Cross societies. It also visits prisoners in war camps and provides relief supplies, mail and information for their relatives" (*Encyclopaedia Britannica*, 1993, *9*, p. 982).

With all due respect to Picasso and his *Demoiselles d'Avignon,* can anything so positive be said about him and his painting? Even a fraction so praiseworthy? And yet, for instance, the 847-page book *A Terrible Beauty: A History of the People & Ideas that Shaped the Modern Mind* by Peter Watson (2000), while devoting five pages to Picasso, plus many references to him and his work elsewhere, does not mention once the names Dunant and Red Cross.

The same is true for the 1,169 pages of *Cities in Civilization* by Peter Hall (1998), in which Picasso's "revolutionary art" is discussed at pages 201, 204, 222-23, 237, 287, as well as in several other places, but not once are Dunant and his Red Cross mentioned. The same is true of the 877 pages *From Dawn to Decadence 1500 to Present: 500 Years of Western Cultural Life* (2000) by Jacques Barzun, who discusses Picasso at pages 193, 512, 647, 649, 721, 724-5, 745, 790, but does not know, or does not appreciate, Henri Dunant and the Red Cross.[49]

Truly, "something is rotten in our civilization" if this is our scale of values; and Jacques Barzun is right in speaking of the decadence of our times, if our values are so corrupt that we count for nothing honesty and generosity[50], and praise instead to the skies the prostitutes *d'Avignon.*

14. Adolescence, Graveyard of G/T Creativity

"Highly gifted children often face a crisis at adolescence. Bamberger (1982) points out that prodigies in music experience a midlife crises at adolescence, when they become increasingly critical of their playing, and this crisis often results in dropping out of music. . . .

---

[49] Also totally neglected by Barzun, Hall, and Watson—each of whom has long discussions about the United States in their books—are all other generous organizations,in sharp contrast with Tocqueville who had written: "I have come across several types of associations in America of which, I confess, I had not previously the slightest conception, and I have often admired the extreme skill they show in proposing a common object for the exertion of very many and in inducing them voluntarily to pursuit it" (1835-40/1988, p. 514). The difference, among many, is that Tocqueville was not mesmerized by the visual arts, but was interested in *visitor* social virtues, in *visitor* social progress.

[50] Kudos, instead, to the Gulf Coast Mensa who recently (early 2001) invited me to their 1st International Charity Gala "to benefit the Houston American Red Cross."

When discussing artistically gifted children, the art historian Hartlaub commented that *the promise of these 'over-potential years of childhood is almost never fulfilled in adulthood'"* (Winner & Martino, p. 107, my italics).

On a broader basis, in the words of George Betts and Maureen Neihart, in their "Profiles of the Gifted and Talented" in *Gifted Child Quarterly*:

> *Perhaps as many as 90% of identified gifted students in school programs are Type 1's.* Children who demonstrate the behavior, feelings, and needs classified as Type 1's have learned the system. They have listened closely to their parents and teachers. After discovering what 'sells' at home and at school, they begin to display appropriate behavior. They learn well and are able to score high on achievement tests and tests of intelligence. As a result, they are usually identified for placement in programs for the gifted. Rarely do they exhibit behavior problems because they are eager for approval from teachers, parents and other adults. These are the children many believe will 'make it on their own.' However, Type 1's often become bored with school and learn to use the system in order to get by with as little effort as possible. Rather than pursue their own interests and goals in school, they tend to go through the motions of schooling, seeking structure and direction from instructors. They are dependent upon parents and teachers. They fail to learn needed skills and attitudes for autonomy, but they do achieve. Overall, these children may appear to have positive self-concepts because they have been affirmed for their achievements. *They are liked by peers and are included in social groups.* They are dependent on the system but are not aware that they have deficiencies because of the reinforcement they receive from adults who are pleased with them and their achievement. However, Goertzel and Goertzel (1962) concluded that the brightest children in the classroom may become competent but unimaginative adults who do not fully develop their gifts and talents. *It seems that these children have lost both their creativity and autonomy.* Gifted young adults who may underachieve in college and later adulthood come

from this group. They do not possess the necessary skills, concepts, and attitudes necessary for lifelong learning. *They are well adjusted to society but are not well prepared for the ever-changing challenges of life.*[51] (1988, p. 249, my italics)

Adolescence has traditionally been considered a more difficult period in development than the middle-childhood years, for both adolescents and their parents. . . . Adolescence is a challenging and sometimes difficult stage of life. Why should this be so? The first and most obvious answer is that adolescence, and particularly early adolescence, is above all a period of change - physical, sexual, psychological, and cognitive changes as well as changes in social demands. It seems almost unfair that so many socialization demands - for independence, changing relationships with peers and adults, sexual adjustment, educational and vocational preparation - are made at the same time that individuals are experiencing an almost unprecedented rate of biological maturation. Besides coping with all these developmental changes, adolescents are struggling to achieve an identity of their own - a personal answer to the age-old question "Who am I?" . . . . Most studies indicate a rather rapid rise in conformity needs and behavior during the pre-adolescent and early adolescent years (9 or 10 to 13 or 14) followed by a gradual but steady decline from middle through late adolescence (14 or 15 on). However, the strength of the need to conform, and to a lesser extent the age at which conformity peaks, may vary with sex, socioeconomic level, pa-

---

[51] This "they are well adjusted to society" may establish a bridge between this study and the good results of "Terman's children" who, as reported, "were surprisingly well rounded and socially well adjusted, and grew up to be successful professionals,. . . . [even if] none made widely recognized intellectual breakthroughs" (Winner, 2000, p. 153).

rental relationships, and personality factors[52]. . . . *Adolescents with high self-esteem and strong feelings of competence are less conforming than their peers*[53]. . . . *A few individualists, confident of their own goals and interests and possessed of a strong sense of ego identity, may neither need nor seek peer approval. But most adolescents, still judging their own worth to a considerable extent in terms of others' reactions to them, are dependent on the approval of respected peers.* (Mussen, Conger, Kagan, & Huston, 1984, pp. 461, 495, 498, my italics)

So, it is not surprising if many gifted children decide to give priority to becoming capable and successful adults, and neglect talented-activities and derived creativity which they now regard as

---

[52] "Peer relationships, along with family and school, are major settings in which adolescents develop the personal and social characteristics they will need as adults. . . . Adolescents spend more time with people of their own age than children do. Although children interact with peers, of course, they do so less often and in less mature ways than adolescents do. . . . Peer influences may be of two types: informational influence and normative influence. In *informational influence* peers serve as sources of knowledge about behavioral patterns, attitudes, and values and their consequences in different situations. In *normative influence* peers exert social pressure on adolescents to behave as others around them behave. Two social psychological processes seem especially important for understanding the influence of peers on adolescents: social comparison and conformity.

Peers provide opportunities for adolescents to compare their own behavior and skills with those of others of similar age and social standing. This process is called social comparison: using others' behavior and skills as a standard against which to evaluate oneself. Social comparison is a fundamental social psychological process; adults and quite young children, as well as adolescents, engage in social comparison. But social comparison seems to have an especially powerful impact in adolescence. *Perhaps the most commonly noticed result of the information derived from social comparison processes is conformity, the process of adopting the same behavior or attitudes others have adopted. . . . young adolescents' sense of others' attention to their behavior may have caused them to conform to the erroneous judgments of others to avoid standing out*" (Sprinthall & Collins, 1984, pp. 259-74, my italics).

[53] And yet, "The literature on the highly gifted suggests that the majority of extremely gifted students deliberately moderate or conceal their exceptional abilities in the regular classroom in attempts to win social acceptance by peers (Hollingworth, 1926, 1942; Pringle, 1970; Silverman, 1993; Morelock, 1995). Gross found that 70% of the early readers in her study deliberately stopped reading, or significantly moderated their in-class reading, within the first few weeks to conform to peer expectations (Gross, 1993a)" (Gross, 2000, p. 186).

childhood activities with little or no relation to the process of becoming an adult. Some may even feel that the pressure they endured, to be a gifted child or child prodigy, was detrimental to their becoming successful, well-rounded adults, and that they had wasted too much time away from friends, games, sports, and normal studies.

15. The Stigma of Giftedness

[Lawrence] Coleman (1985) articulated a stigma of giftedness paradigm [SGP] based on Goffman's stigma construct (1963), which asserted that being tainted (in this case, identified as gifted) makes apparent to other people a set of variables which influence the tainted person to alter the way he or she typically interacts with others. The SGP has three tenets: (1) gifted students desire normal social interactions; (2) they learn that others will treat them differently when they learn of their giftedness; and (3) they learn to manage information about themselves in order to maintain normal social interactions. Implicit in this theory is the existence of social cognition in gifted students. There is another important idea underpinning this paradigm. That is, unlike certain stigmatizing qualities, i.e., visible differences one might have from a group of others, giftedness is only potentially stigmatizing; it can be masked or hidden. (Coleman & Cross, 2000, p. 209)

The above is in line with findings by Miraca Gross (2000), that "the literature on the highly gifted suggests that the majority of extremely gifted students deliberately moderate or conceal their exceptional abilities in the regular classroom in attempts to win social acceptance by peers" (p. 186).

In contrast, in my studies of hundreds of biographies of eminent challenged personalities, I have never encountered one single case of SGP. For one reason or another (but probably because of their internal compass)—peers seem to play a small role with them; they had no reason to hide their gifts and talents, nor to push them to attention.

At school, Karl Marx "seems to have made no permanent friendship among his fellow-students, although several of them were of a calibre to achieve some distinction. . . . Karl's fellow students had mixed feelings about him [who at that time wanted to be a poet], for he already showed the trait of intellectual intolerance and sarcasm that were to characterize him as a man. His class-mates liked his exuberance but dreaded his mockery" (Padover, 1978, p. 38).

Einstein, had "made great progress in mathematics at school but was backward in most of the other subjects. There was nothing to draw attention to him. It was significant that even at the moment of his swift rise to glory, none of his school companions boasted of a friendship with him; no teacher claimed to have molded the mind of a genius. His former teachers, in fact, did not even remember having had him in their classes" (Vallentin, 1954, p. 22). On the other hand, Einstein had no reason to participate more actively in class or to make friends. His intellectual and emotional life was elsewhere: "Einstein in later life spoke bitterly of his schooling. He disliked particularly the harsh, drill-sergeant methods of rote instruction that then prevailed" (Hoffmann, 1972, pp. 19-20).

In the case of Proust it was his severe asthma which forced him to be very often absent from school and school mates. Hayman (1990) indeed entitled a long chapter of his biography of Proust "Absentee Schoolboy."

Another cause for peer separation was language difficulties and a lower SES. Young Napoleon was sent at the age of nine from Corsica to military academies in France. When he set foot on French soil, he found himself among people whose language he did not understand. "Napoleon's first task was to learn French. . . . He found it difficult. He was not good at memorizing and reproducing sounds, nor did he have the flexible temperament of the born linguist. . . . Most [boys] were his social superiors. Some boys had names famous in history, others had fathers or uncles who hunted with the King, mothers who attended Court balls. In Corsica he had been near the top socially; now he suddenly found himself near the bottom" (Cronin, 1972, pp. 30-32). Once again, we have a situation which places the peers outside of their normal role; there was nothing that Napoleon could have done to ingratiate himself to them. Besides he hated them because they were French, those French who had deprived his Corsica of her liberty.

"It seems clear that Newton [about twelve] did not get along with the boys. . . . As far as we know, Newton had grown up in relative isolation with his grandmother. He was different from other boys, and it is not surprising if he was unable to get along with them easily. As they came to recognize his intellectual superiority, the boys in the school apparently hated him. . . . Early in Newton's stay in Grantham, a crisis occurred which burned deeply into his memory. He had not even had time to assert his intellectual prowess. Whether because he was ill-prepared by the village schools, or because he was alone again and frightened, he had been placed in the lowest form, and even there he stood next to the bottom. On the way to school one morning, the boy next above him kicked him in the belly, hard. . . . [There followed a battle which Newton won; [then] Not content with beating him physically, he insisted on worsting him academically as well; once on his way, he rose to be first in the school. As he rose, he left this trail behind him, his name carved on every bench he occupied. The benches do not survive, but a stone windowsill still bears one of his signatures. By the time Stukeley was collecting anecdotes, Newton's genius was taken for granted" (Westfall, 1980, pp. 58-60).

The following on Goethe deals with three major points: 1. his self-directed development, 2. the continuity of personality from youth to adulthood, and 3. his "superior" relations with his peers:

> His other confession is a still more significant illustration of the vital lack of sympathy between father and son. He left Frankfort [at the age of 16], he says, with the deliberate intention of following his own predilections and of disregarding the express wish of his father that he should apply himself specifically to the study of law. Only his sister Cornelia was the confidant of his secret intention, and apparently no attempt was made to effect even a compromise between the aims of the father and those of the son. . . . We have it on Goethe's own word that with his departure for Leipzig begins that self-directed development which he was to pursue with the undeviating purpose and the wonderful result which make him the unique figure he is in the history of the human spirit. . . . In his case, we can say with certainty, was fully verified by the adage, that the boy is father of the man. Alike in internal and in external traits we note in him as a boy characteristics which were equally marked in the mature man. In his demeanour, he himself tells us, there was a certain stiff dignity which excited the ridicule of his companions. It was in his nature even as a boy, he also tells us, to assume airs of command: one of his own acquaintance and of his own years said of him, 'We were all his lacqueys'. (Hume Brown, 1920/1971, pp. 18-19)

Then, there are the cases of obvious talents (much helped to flourish by an expert parent, as was the case with Mozart and Picasso) which again separate the challenged youths from their peers, thereby eliminating peer pressure and any possible trace of the stigma of giftedness. For instance, Picasso aged 13, having followed his father in his move from La Coruña [Corunna] to Barcelona, entered the local art school. There, the boys "although they tended to be chauvinistic toward southerners, they welcomed Pablo. He was after all only thirteen years old when he enrolled: five or six years younger than most of them. Instead of feeling threatened by his gifts, fellow students soon succumbed to his mercurial charm and physical magnetism—the huge, all devouring eyes, the small wiry frame, the cool Andalusian swagger—and accepted him as one of themselves, just as they would come to accept him as a paragon. Pablo never had trouble attracting friends. The first day he attended Tiberi Avila's anatomy class, he found himself sitting next to a second year student, Manuel Pallarès y Grau, a farmer's son from a remote village in the mountains of southern Catalonia. Although Pallarès was nineteen—almost six years older than Pablo—the two students became instant friends" (Richardson, 1991, p. 65).

Each of these *challenged* cases is different, from total neglect from the peers to total acceptance, yet with no trace of *Stigma of Giftedness Paradigm*. All these youths, thanks to their high GxAxM, went on their way without much looking left or right, as if the peers did not exist, or they asserted themselves in ways that pushed the peers into a secondary role.

16. The Difficulties of Managing Giftedness in the Peer World

Laurence Coleman discussed in *Schooling the Gifted* how many gifted try to avoid getting in trouble with their peers through "invisibility"[54]:

The strategies gifted children use to be 'invisible' attempt to hide or minimize differences. Invisibility strategies, or as-

---

[54] Another strategy is *high visibility*, of which being obnoxious, or being the class clown are two variants.

pects of them, are used more often than other strategies, especially as the child enters the secondary school years. A common theme of these strategies is to cover up or to camouflage high abilities and advanced interests in order to appear to conform and to 'pass for normal' (Freeman, 1979, p. 252). . . . The following are some of the examples obtained from conversations with students: don't carry a calculator, miss a few answers on a test, wear contact lenses, don't volunteer answers, don't admit a test was easy. . . . be seen with people who are not gifted, ask silly or crazy questions" (1985, pp. 181-82).

Nothing of this is needed by the *challenged* because their gifts are often invisible. For instance—in reference to what was reported before—at no moment would Einstein have tried to discuss with others what he was learning with the help of Max Talmey, or Marx what he was discussing with Baron von Westphalen, or Goethe what he knew of Racine, Corneille, or Molière. In each case it would have been like speaking Chinese. In each of these cases, the giftedness was already of a type so advanced and specialized that it had nothing to do with doing well in class, with passing tests, or with volunteering answers. In each case, there was probably some plain contempt for school, teachers, and peers. This contempt, together with their own strong interests, often led to a shortage of regular study, could lead to doing poorly in class, thereby eliminating one of the major causes of trouble.

Some invisibility was very natural, so natural that some challenged youths, like Einstein, were later thought to have been mentally slow, not gifted at all! And the very first who thought so were some teachers, and most peers. Unwillingly, but very successfully, Einstein had managed to be *invisible*. The great advantage of this invisibly was a lack of peer pressure, and a totally independent mental development, as reported by Coleman (1985):

Being different is problematic in that differentness prevents, or, at least interferes with, full social acceptance and personal development. . . .[As reported in the American Association for Gifted Children's book by gifted children, *On Being Gifted*, 1978] "Probably the only single thing all twenty of us agreed on . . . . in our lives—was that we hate the word 'gifted.' It is flattering, it's pleasing, but it alienates us from friends (p. 4)". . . .

It is in adolescence that the gifted child is faced with the conflict of developing abilities in opposition to demands for socially acceptable behavior. In a study that asked special-program graduates to reflect on their past, Bachtold reported that secondary school years were "the worst of school" with intellectual starvation and alienation from peers being primary problems of that time. . . . Ziv has described the dilemma for the gifted child in these terms: "He can adopt the same perception and interests as his peers and probably abandon his intellectual interests and scholarly achievements, or he may ignore his peers' preferences and continue as he is" (p. 34). (pp. 163-67)

The following are some of the strategies used [by a group of gifted college women]: Modifying one's language so that ideas were seen as contributing to the group; making constructive criticism; showing belief in something the group could respect; listening to others and not invoking feelings of personal threat; earning credit with the group over time by good service" (ib., pp. 184-85).

In the above we clearly notice a desire for peer acceptance, for having friends, and the adoption, by many, of one of various coping strategies, chiefly being invisible, often abandoning intellectual interests and scholarly achievement. Seen from the point of view of the challenged, this is kowtowing to the group, but it may be needed by the non-challenged.

Friends, often, speak of their families. But would Newton have spoken of his mother and step-father, he who—as mentioned—at the age of twenty, while compiling a catalog of sins, had written: "Threatening my father and mother Smith to burne them and the house over them" (Westfall, 1978, p. 17)? Would Leonardo da Vinci have spoken of his father? "Father and son apparently were not close; many years later when the old man died Leonardo made only the briefest mention of the fact in one of his notebooks, commingled with observations on scientific matters. 'On the 9th of July, 1504, Wednesday at 7 o'clock, died Ser Piero da Vinci, notary at the palace of the Podestà [governor], my father, at 7 o'clock. He was 80 years old, left ten sons and two daughters.' The impersonality of the notice has an added chill because Leonardo appears to have jotted it down absentmindedly—he repeats '7 o'clock' and overstates his father's age by three years" (Wallace, 1967, p. 11). The list is long, indeed, of geniuses who would not have liked to speak of their fathers: Beethoven, Cervantes, Cezanne, Goethe, Klee, Michelangelo, Napoleon, Picasso, Rubens. Long, also, is the list of those who would not have liked to speak of their mothers: Balzac, Baudelaire, de Kooning, Sartre.

Further in his book, Coleman reported another comment by a gifted child who had suffered from the combined lack of understanding of her teachers and the annoying muttering from her classmates ('She thinks she knows everything'): "So in a futile effort to conform and satisfy them, I sink down in my seat just a little and let the rest of the questions slide by. The teacher becomes angry that no one has read the assignment and feels he must repeat the chapter. And another day is wasted. So goes it, and unfortunately, too often. As a result, I do not feel challenged" (1985, p. 168).

However, the *challenged* children feel no need to be challenged in class. It is not that they do not want to go to good schools, but that their intellectual and emotional challenges come from outside the school: from their misfortune(s), from books, or from family friends like Max Talmey and Baron Von Westphalen. Of all this their teachers and peers know little or nothing, the less the better.

Basically, *challenged* children have few or no peer problems because they have no peers.[55] Some of them, on an exceptional basis, may have one friend, but probably one they dominate, as Picasso did with Manuel Pallarès.

---

[55] In fairness to the peers, some challenged children—because of their misfortunes of youth—may lack those social skills which are learned normally from peers, and, correspondingly, they behave awkwardly, for instance oscillating from too little to too much involvement, as well described by Koestler in the first part of his autobiography: "The first minute or so after meeting the other child, I felt petrified with timidity. . . . However, as soon as the adults had settled at the *jour* table and we children were left alone in the nursery, my timidity wore off and I changed into a frenzied little maniac. The ingenious games I had devised in my daydreams all had to be tried out during those infinitely precious moments, ... The other child, whether younger or older, would usually be swept off his feet by this torrent of new games and ideas, and within a quarter of an hour I would become transformed from a tongue-tied puppet into a fierce bully who had to have it all his own way" (1961, p. 42).

As reported above, "Ziv (1977) has described the dilemma for the gifted child in these terms: "He can adopt the same perception and interests as his peers and probably abandon his intellectual interests and scholarly achievements, or he may ignore his peers' preferences and continue as he is". But what does it really mean to "continue as one is"? Can the gifted child continue to be a child? No, he has to change, he must become an adult, he must manage many of the *developmental tasks* which will transform him into a successful adult such as: 1. breaking-up childish personality structures, 2. achieving adult inner controls, 3. experimenting with new roles, 4. developing new ideas of self, 5. reorienting to the peer group, 6. developing new skills, 7. living with sex, 8. achieving emancipation, 9. establishing economic independence or vocational competence (Wattenberg, 1973, pp. 6-7).

The real approach, then, is not "in continuing as one is" which is impossible, but in becoming a "quality new person" capable of by-passing the peers, for instance through knowledge, that knowledge which would have saved the young Spaniard discussed by Gombrich:

What wonder, therefore, that there are few areas where 'social testing' plays a greater part than in aesthetic judgments? The adolescent soon learns that the group can be a dreadful spoilsport if he confesses to liking something that has fallen under taboo. Imagine a young Spaniard in the first decade of the seventeenth century meeting his friends after a longish absence abroad and mentioning casually that Romances of Chivalry are his favourite reading. Suddenly he finds himself the center of mocking attention; he is called Don Quixote, or the Knight of the Sorry Countenance, and may never live this down. It would need a strong character indeed in a similar situation to stick for Amadis of Gaul and to discourse on its artistic merits which, after all, had been apparent to everyone. Even if our imaginary victim would try, the defense would die on his lips. He would find in his heart that maybe Amadis was all a lot of nonsense and that he was silly to have been taken in by that bombast. The more seriously art is taken by any group, the more adept will it be in such brainwashing; for to enjoy the wrong thing in such a circle is like worshipping false gods; you fail in the test of admission to the group if your taste is found wanting. (1974, p. 948-49)

Now imagine that same young Spaniard knowing well not only *Don Quixote*, but Marlowe's *Doctor Faustus*, Montaigne's *Essais*, Shakespeare's *Julius Caesar* and *Hamlet*, Quevedo's *La vida del buscón*, Ben Jonson's *Volpone*—and yet also loving old *Amadís de Gaul*—and immediately the tables are turned. Now it is the group who is ridiculously backward and limited.

Goethe's peers, and probably his teachers too, knew little of Racine, Corneille, Molière, particularly in the original French. Einstein's peers knew a fraction of what he knew of physics and philosophy, and so Marx's peers of history and political science. Under such conditions the separation is natural, and peer pressure evaporates.

17. Reinventing Oneself, or Being Challenged?

"Adolescence is the time when prodigies must make the transition from technical perfection to innovation and big-C, domain creativity. Only those who can reinvent themselves will make the leap between childhood giftedness and adult creativity (Gardner, 1993)" (Winner & Martino, 2000, p. 107). The problem is that every child is already reinventing him/herself during adolescence; and this is a difficult process. To change so much and also make the transition from technical perfection to innovation and big-C, domain creativity, is a most difficult task.

"But of course a few prodigies do go on to change their respective domains. These are the ones who earn the epithet 'creative' or 'creative genius'. These are the individuals who, at adolescence or early adulthood, take a new stance. They begin to take risks; they challenge the establishment (Gardner, 1992, 1993). . . . [However] as Hurwitz (1983) points out, gifted children have invested a great deal of energy in mastering a set of skills, and are often unwilling, or even unable, to experiment in the way that one must do in order to be creative" (ib., p. 107-08).

But, taking a new valid stance is practically impossible if one has not in oneself new ideas or different scripts. Anyone who decides to challenge the establishment must do so for some clear reason, not simply to be original, not *la différence pour la différence* [difference for the sake of being different]. Without a new vision, without a valid *war of the scripts*, any attempt to be substantially creative will fail. In order to experiment, one must have an idea of what to try and why.

Having courage is not enough. Courage must be the consequence of a direction clearly indicated by one's inner compass, something which comes naturally to the challenged child but is difficult for the non-challenged.

"Take the case of Alexandra Nechita. She is famous now as a child for painting in the style of Picasso. But will anyone take notice of her as an adult if she continues only to paint in the style of Picasso? Rostan, et al. (1998) found that the childhood drawings of great artists (*Picasso, Klee, Lautrec*) were not distinguishable from drawings of contemporary gifted child artists. Yet surely few if any of this contemporary group will become great artists. Clearly, while high ability is necessary, it is not sufficient. Degree of skill in childhood cannot by itself predict later creative eminence; nor can early detection or the best and most rigorous courses of training (Scripp & Davidson, 1994)" (Winner & Martino, p. 107, my italics).

Picasso, Klee, and Lautrec? These three names give evidence for the validity of the GAM theory of creativity because all three were challenged personalities with a high GxAxM. In other words, it was not only their talent for drawing—not distinguishable from the drawing of contemporary gifted child artists—which made them great artists, but a paucity of normal scripts, a *war of the scripts* with society, and a derived new vision.

Picasso and Toulouse-Lautrec were discussed in detail in chapter 3 in volume 1; Klee is even more interesting now, because—in further studying him for this chapter—I stumbled on a fascinating piece of evidence, as described hereafter, of the capability of the GAM Theory for making valid personality forecasts.

18. Evidence for the GAM Theory: Klee's *Miner Personality*

I had discussed Klee as a GAM *miner personality* in a first draft of *The GAM Theory of Personality*. That first version of my book was never published because I felt it needed more research. I now report it as Appendix 1 to this chapter.

As a caveat, let me say, up front, that Klee keeps company with Leonardo da Vinci in being poorly known. Many have been led to see Klee as a friendly "fairy-tale" artist, the creator of such evocative paintings as: *Battle scene from the comic fantastic opera "The Seafarer"* (1923), *Landscape with yellow birds* (1923), *The big dome* (1927), *Floating town* (1930), and *Park near Lu(cerne)* (1938). But there is a darker, *miner*, side to Klee's work: bitter, sarcastic, cynic, misogynistic as discussed in Appendix 1.

The *miner* in him is, for instance, the creator of the *Twittering Machine* of 1922 in which "with a few simple lines, he had created a ghostly mechanism that imitates the sound of birds, simultaneously mocking our faith in the miracles of the machine age and our sentimental appreciation of bird songs. The little contraption (which is not without sinister aspect; the heads of the four sham birds look like fishermen's lures, as if they might entrap real birds) thus condenses into one striking invention a complex of ideas about present-day civilization" (Janson, 1991, pp. 732-3).

Klee also wrote high quality poetry. Indeed, the main chapter of Robert Fisher's 1966 book *Klee* is entitled "Klee, the poet-painter," and Anselm Hollo (1962) wrote in his introduction to his selection and translation of a number of Klee's poems: "Apart from the interest these texts have as commentaries and sidelights on Klee's painting, they have considerable influence on post-war German poetry; Rainer M. Gerhardt, a very fine poet and critic of the post-45 generation, wrote of them in 1951: 'I do not know what German poet has written comparable lines during the last fifteen years.'" (p. 30). In turn, this poetic side of his creativity can be linked to a discovery I made, already in the 80s—and now reported in chapter 3 of volume 1—that "Many great poets are *miners*."

New is that, in re-reading the part of Appendix 1 on Klee's misogynism, it came to mind that if Baudelaire had been a painter he would have drawn such misogynistic works as Klee's *Pandora Box* (1920) and *Concerning the Fate of Two Girls* (1921). My next task, then, was to see if somebody else had come up with the idea of relating Klee to Baudelaire. What I found was better: I found a comment by Klee himself which concurred with my discussion of "Affinity" in chapter 9 of volume 2, where I wrote that "Nobody appreciates the work of a *miner* better than another *miner*. . . . Not only did Baudelaire translate Poe,. . . . Block loved Poe and Baudelaire; Rimbaud and Trakl were influenced by Baudelaire; and Yevtuschenko appreciated Rimbaud." What I found is the following:

"Klee's favorite authors were E.T.A. Hoffmann, Poe, Gogol, and Baudelaire, whom he felt to be kindred spirits" (Grohmann, 1954, p. 42). So Klee not only appreciated Baudelaire, but Baudelaire was one of his favorite authors, a kindred spirit.

Finding—very quickly—what the theory says should be there, is the kind of evidence that I am trying to provide for GAM/DP.

19. Fruitful Asynchrony?

In chapter 4 of volume 1, I reported how, in 1988, Gardner and Wolf had concluded that "Asynchrony is too easy to find. Given a complex life, and even a minimally competent biographer, one can dredge up multiple instances of asynchrony. What is needed are definite objective ways in which to assess asynchrony, to ascertain whether there are certain kinds of asynchronies that stand out and which are particularly likely to mark the lives of creative individuals. . . . Coming up with a metric of synchrony, asynchrony, and (perhaps) productive and unproductive asynchrony is by no means a straightforward task" (pp. 113-14). I then presented my case that the misfortunes of youth (combined with a high GxA) were the origin of a series of important asynchronies, only that I felt it better to label them, not asynchronies, but the consequences of the lack of normal script, of the creation of new scripts at the light of one's specific misfortunes, of a *war of the scripts* with society, and of intuitions from the sparks generated by the clashes of the *war of the scripts.*

When I read in Winner and Martino (2000) that "Gardner's (1992) notion of asynchrony is compatible with Getzel and Csikszentmihalyi's (1976) notion of problem finding" (p. 108), I realized that the creativogenic asynchrony had been sighted once more. I remembered that it was Howard Gardner who had resurrected the asynchrony in the form, this time, of *fruitful asynchrony*:

> Naturally, some asynchrony will mark any productivity, whether highly creative or not. My claim is based on two other propositions: First, there can be cases of asynchrony that are too modest or too pronounced; neither proves productive for creativity. An intermediate amount of tension or asynchrony, here termed *fruitful asynchrony*, is desirable. Second, the more instances of fruitful asynchrony that surround a case, the more likely that genuinely creative work will emerge. However, an excess of asynchrony may prove nonproductive: what is desirable is to have substantial asynchrony, without being overwhelmed by it. (Gardner, 1993, p. 41)

Those in search of asynchronies can feel rewarded by these case studies [Freud, Einstein, Picasso, Stravinsky, Eliot, Graham, Gandhi] which document considerable initial asynchrony as well as a decided taste for creating more. In this way, the creative individual certainly differs from the individual who does not seek to stand out in any way. . . . My own hunch is that our seven model creators are different, and that the degree and type of asynchrony they represent is somehow more fruitful—more fruitful, say, than Wilhelm Fliess's scheme, which was too bizarre, or Pierre Janet's scheme, which was less sharply delineated and less expertly disseminated. But in the absence of convincing methods for evaluating both asynchrony and fruitfulness, this must remain a speculation. (ib., p. 383)

However, I still feel that we have not solved the problem, and that, as before: "given a complex life, and even a minimally competent biographer, one can dredge up multiple instances of [fruitful] asynchronies. What is needed are definite objective ways in which to assess [fruitful] asynchrony. Coming up with a metric of [fruitful] asynchrony is by no means a straightforward task" (Gardner & Wolf).

But what is this asynchrony?

- For Gardner and Wolf (1988) "Creative efforts are more likely to arise when there is a certain tension or asynchrony among the principal factors that underlie human behavior. It is this tension that ultimately gives rise to the creative work (p. 101).
So asynchrony is a tension;

- For Gardner (1993) "In using the term *asynchrony*, I refer to a lack of fit, an unusual pattern, or irregularity within the creativity triangle [Csikszentmihalyi's locus of creativity of Individual Talent, Domain/Discipline, Field (judges, institutions)]" (p. 41, 38).
So asynchrony is a lack of fit;

- For Policastro and Gardner (1999) "Creative individuals stand out not on account of their 'asynchrony' from the society per se, but rather in light of the ways in which they deal with these deviations. Rather than becoming despondent or shifting to another line of work, creative individuals are characterized by their disposition to convert differences into advantages. Gardner and

Wolf (1988) have referred to the capacity of certain individuals to exploit their differences from the norm as fruitful asynchrony. A few examples from our own case studies can convey a flavor of this phenomenon. Freud, an ambitious Jew from a relatively impoverished family, decided to pursue a career in science. When he failed to achieve status as a world-class researcher, he exploited his particular strengths in the linguistic and interpersonal areas to create a new quasi-scientific domain called psychoanalysis. Einstein, an indifferent student in several respects, stood out from other scientists in his combination of mathematical and spatial gifts; these became the foundation of his most important discoveries about relativity. (p. 223)

So asynchrony is the capacity to exploit a personal difference from the norm.

However, as discussed previously, Freud was not failing to achieve status as a world-class researcher in his physiological research; on the contrary he had already been nominated for the Nobel prize[56]. It was lack of money that forced him to change direction. Nor was Einstein an indifferent student, just the opposite as reported before in sections 4 and 11. Both would have done asynchronically well in a dozen different situations, because of their strong asynchronic (*challenged*) personality.

The difference with GAM is that the major misfortunes of youth of the pinnacles of creativity are clearly identifiable, and should never be called asynchronies. The severe asthma which afflicted Proust from age 9 onward is not an asynchrony. The shortened legs of Toulouse-Lautrec, the hunchback of Leopardi, the illegitimate birth of Leonardo are not asynchronies, neither are the failure of the *Electrotechnische Fabrik J. Einstein & Cie.*, nor the imprisonment for debt of John Dickens, nor the conversion to Christianity of Hirshel ha-Levi Marx. These are major misfortunes. And so was Bertrand Russell's loss of his mother at the age of two and his father (Viscount Amberley) at the age of four: "The Amberleys had very advanced views and had intended to place Bertrand and his brother Frank (then aged ten) under

---

[56] In 1917 Freud complained in his calendar, "No Nobel Prize 1917." He had been nominated for his studies of the spinal cord of one of the lowest forms of fish, *Ammacoetes Petroxyon*, while working in Brücke's Physiological Institute from 1877 to 1882. What Freud had done in his early twenties was of such caliber to bring him close to the Nobel Prize.

the guardianship of friends who were atheists. But the children's grandparents had no difficulty, given the feeling of the time, in upsetting the will and getting the two boys made wards in Chancery, so that they were brought up by their Russell grandmother, a strict yet politically liberal-minded Puritan with a rigid personal conscience and exacting standards. Bertrand Russell was educated privately, *had little contact with other children, and developed an intense inner life, full of idealistic feeling and metaphysical profundities* (partly a product, he later theorized, of sublimated sexual desires), all imbued with a passionate desire for certainty in knowledge. At the age of 11 he had already begun to have religious doubts, and, eventually, the skeptical cast of his intelligence prevailed over his upbringing. He came to disagree with his family on everything except politics" (Crawshay-Williams, 1978, p. 35, my italics). Later, "there is no doubt that Russell made himself and many other people close to him extraordinarily unhappy; there is no doubt that he was frequently cruel and thoughtless in ways that a less self-engrossed person would not have been; and no doubt that he was casually dismissive of less talented people than himself, and that the reverse of the coin was a painful degree of self-loathing" (Ryan, 2000, p. 3).

Those early losses, of both father and mother, coupled with that unbalanced—to say the least—education, could not but produce major distortions one after the other: some highly creative (as logician and philosopher) and some not (in social relations, family in particular). Being an orphan, so early in life, is a misfortune, not an asynchrony.

In addition, the prevalence of certain misfortunes can be calculated and related to eminence, as has been the case—as discussed in chapter 1 of volume 1—with the misfortune of early parental death: 28% for eminent adults versus 8% for the general population (Albert, 1983, p. 147). With some efforts the same could be done with other misfortunes, and then related to IQ, and various forms of assistance.

Definitely, the challenged personality lacks fit with society, is often under tension, and has the capacity to exploit a personal difference from the norm, but it makes more sense to interpret these three aspects of personality as the result of the M of a high GxAxM, and derived paucity of normal scripts and a *war of the scripts*, rather than to an optimal asynchrony, neither bizarre nor less sharply delineated and less expertly disseminated.

20. How Important is Creativity in Childhood?

"What if, however, creativity in childhood is unrelated to creativity in adulthood?" asked Siegler and Kotovsky (1986, p. 420). "As Feldhusen notes, 'creativity or divergent thinking tests offer no compelling evidence of validity links to creative production of adulthood.' This lack of linkage may be due to adequate tests of creativity not yet having been developed. Another possibility, however, is that the linkages simply do not exist" (ib., p. 420).

My position is clear; creativity in youth is related to creativity in adulthood if the youth has a high GxAxM in which the G includes evident talents, (e.g. talents for music, or for drawing/painting/sculpting). Both Mozart and Mendelssohn were born with musical talents; Leonardo, Michelangelo[57], and Picasso with drawing/painting/sculpting talents. In the absence of obvious talents, there may indeed be no link between creativity in childhood and creativity in adulthood, and this applies both to challenged and non-challenged persons.

Creativity tests and divergent thinking tests are basically giftedness tests, only tapping another side of g (Spearman's general factor in intelligence); and, as said before, a certain amount of creativity is expected from every truly intelligent person. So, doing well on these tests may only say, or confirm, that one is intelligent.

Both Leonardo and Mendelssohn are worth discussing in detail not only because of the evident continuity in creativity from youth to adulthood, but because their creativity of youth may already have been stimulated and imprinted by their misfortune of youth. Leonardo da Vinci (1452-1519), must have suffered quite early in life, of the worst

---

[57] Michelangelo was affected early by two major misfortunes, the first being the death of his mother when he was only six years old; the second, in the words of Csikszentmihalyi (1991): "Michelangelo's father was a businessman who became poorer and poorer and more and more depressed as Michelangelo grew up, and at the age of 13 he was apprenticed to work outside the family." In the words of Howard Hibbard: "The Buonarroti had been fairly prominent and successful up to the mid-Quattrocento, when Michelangelo's grandfather lost money. The family business had been small-scale money-changing —really, disguised lending at interest. . . . Michelangelo's father was a mediocre man—too proud to work for a living, too poor to live well" (1974, p. 16). In terms of creativity, his first reported sculpture, and one already of great quality, is the head of the faun he sculpted, for Lorenzo de Medici, when he was fifteen.

of all insults: that of being a *bastard*,[58] besides the pain of being separated from his mother when he was about four. As noted by Csikszentmihalyi (1991) "He was taken away from his mother and brought up in his father's household, as an illegitimate child without the mother's support." Moving to creativity, Robert Wallace reports an episode—from Vasari's (1550) *Lives of the Most Eminent Painters*— on young Leonardo in which his earliest recorded painting can be related, on one side, to the pains of his misfortune of youth, and on the other to some of his fearful military inventions of adulthood as discussed in chapter 3 of volume 1:

> In the story, Leonardo's father is approached by a peasant of his estate who has cut a round shield from the wood of a fig tree and who asks Ser Piero to take it to Florence so that an artist may paint something on it. Ser Piero was indebted to the peasant for his skill in catching bird and fish, and so agreed.[59] But instead of giving the shield to an established craftsman he gave it to Leonardo, who thereupon "began to think what he should paint on it, and resolved to do the head of Medusa to terrify all beholders. To a room to which he alone had access, Leonardo took lizards, newts, maggots, snakes, moths, locusts, bats and other animals of the kind out of which

---

[58] Leonardo was neither the illegitimate son of a king or prince, nor the illegitimate son of a pope or *condottiere* or humble peasant, for whom bastardy carried small stigma in those days. He was the son of a notary—in the little Tuscan town of Vinci—whose "forebears for four generations had been notaries, thrifty and shrewd to become upper-middle landholders bearing the title of *Ser*, which fell also to Leonardo's father. . . . [Ser Piero] must also have been a capable notary—when, in his thirties, he moved a short distance down through the hills and established himself in Florence, his services were much in demand by the aristocrats of the city" (Wallace, 1967, p. 6). Leonardo therefore belonged to those children—neither very high in social status, nor very low—who could be the target of insults by other children; and some children can be cruel, especially in these matters. Even Jacob Bronowsky—who praised the importance in the Renaissance of the self-made man, independent of his origins—felt forced to say: "Nevertheless, we get the feeling that Leonardo never walked easily in the houses of the great, and that his wariness goes back to his childhood" (1972, p. 12).

[59] Fascinating! In the middle of the 15th century a peasant goes to his master and asks him to bring to the main town a nice piece of wood which he had cut from a tree, so that an artist may paint something on it! *Se non è vero, è molto ben trovato* (If not true, it is well invented). On the other hand, this story fits nicely with similar visitor stories by Boccaccio and Sacchetti, as discussed in chapter 24 of volume 1.

he composed a horrible and terrible monster, of poisonous breath, issuing from a dark and broken rock, belching poison from its open throat, fire from its eyes and smoke from its nostrils. . . . He was so engrossed with the work that he did not notice the terrible stench of the dead animals, being absorbed in his love for art." (1967. p. 11)

In time Ser Piero forgot about the shield, but when Leonardo had finished his painting he showed it suddenly, without warning, to his father who was so startled that he began to run out of the room. "Leonardo detained him," says the story, "and said, 'This work is as I wanted it to be; take it away, then, as it is producing the effect intended.'" (ib., 1967, p.11) Obviously, this can also be interpreted as nothing more than a juvenile prank, even though of a special quality.

Felix Mendelssohn (1809-1846) was an extremely precocious musical composer. He wrote numerous compositions during his boyhood, among them five operas, eleven symphonies for string orchestra, concerti, sonatas, and fugues. Some of his works, composed when he was only fourteen, can be heard from time to time on radio, and are of very high quality. Mendelssohn's misfortune of youth was unprotected anti-Semitism, unprotected—as is not rarely the case—by some paternal failure of character. His father was Abraham Mendelssohn the son of Moses Mendelssohn, the eminent German-Jewish philosopher, critic, and Bible translator and commentator. His mother was Leah Salomon (from whom he took his first piano lessons) whose brother had converted to Protestantism in 1805 and changed his name from Salomon to Bartholdy, from the name of a piece of property he owned on the River Spree, which had belonged in former times to a Mayor Bartholdy. Bartholdy's influence on his sister was considerable: he never ceased adjuring her and her husband to become Christians, if not for their own sake then for their children. So much so that "On March 21, 1816, Abraham took his children to the New Church in Berlin and had them baptized. Fanny was ten; Felix seven; Rebecca, four; and Paul, two. It was all done very quietly;. . . . Among other things, Leah was not anxious for her mother to know about it; old Madame Salomon had cut off her son Bartholdy and might just as readily do the same to her daughter. However, six years later, on October 4, 1822, both Leah and Abraham took advantage of a trip to Frankfurt to undergo baptism themselves; to be Jewish parents of Christian children was an obvious impossibility. [However]

Abraham Mendelssohn appears never to have been altogether comfortable about his conversion. . . .Along with his new religious affiliation, Abraham also accepted Bartholdy's offer of his name. Henceforth, he became known as Abraham Mendelssohn Bartholdy and passed the double name along to his children, whether they wanted it or not" (Kupferberg, 1972, pp. 99-101).

However the baptism did not save Felix and his siblings from attacks: "Felix's first recorded encounter with overt anti-Semitism came in 1819, the year of the *Judensturm* in Germany, a widespread wave of looting and violence aimed at the newly 'emancipated' Jewish citizenry and a distant forerunner of the Nazi's *Kristallnacht* of 1938. The war cry for the Judensturm outburst was "hep, hep!"—an exclamation concocted by university students from the initials of the Latin words *Hierosolyma est perdita* ("Jerusalem is destroyed"). While the demonstrations were going on, Felix happened to meet in the street one of the Prussian royal princes with whom he had a slight acquaintance; the boy marched up to him, spat at his feet, and exclaimed: 'Hep, hep, *Judenjung.*' Considering the physical violence inflicted on many Jews that year, Felix got off easily, but the experience was one he remembered" (ib., pp. 115-16).

"Another incident occurred in 1824, when Felix was fifteen. The family spent its vacation in Dobberan, a then much frequented watering place on the Baltic. This time both Felix and his beloved sister Fanny were insulted by street urchins, who shouted 'Jew-boy' and similar epithets and finally threw stones at them. Felix defended his sister vigorously and staunchly, but seems to have collapsed afterwards. His tutor J. L. Heyse writes tersely after the incident: 'Felix behaved like a man, but after he had returned home could not conceal his fury about the humiliation, which in the evening broke out in a flood of tears and wild accusations'" (Werner, 1963, p. 40).

"Such incidents seemed to nurture Felix's feelings for his Judaic origins. A strong streak of stubbornness was one of his characteristics; so was his innate feeling of respect for and obedience to his parents" (Kupferberg, 1972, pp. 115-16). Still, that sense of obedience was not sufficient to make him accept that incongruous name of Bartholdy and the implicit betrayal of the ancestral name of Mendelssohn. When Felix was sixteen years old, his father "had a set of calling cards engraved for him. Deliberately, he had them printed: 'Felix M. Bartholdy.' Equally deliberately, Felix refused to accept them. His name, he said, was not Bartholdy but Mendelssohn, although if his father insisted, out of respect for him he would agree to be called Felix Mendelssohn Bartholdy" (ib., p. 116). Four years later, on his first visit to London, the young composer had his name listed on the programs, as well as in newspaper announcements, as Felix Mendelssohn. His father wrote him angrily from Berlin. "Nevertheless, Felix continued to use the name Mendelssohn through his life." (ib., p. 117).

"His mental equilibrium was shattered [again] in 1832 [at the age of 23], when his family, very much against his will, persuaded him to be a candidate for the position of director of the Berlin *Singakademie*. He suffered a sever rebuff; the *Singakademie* would not elect a 'Jewboy,' brilliant as he might be. It preferred a mild mediocrity, Herrn Rungenhagen, whose directorship was to a great extent responsible for the stagnation of Berlin musical life during the years 1830 to 1850" (Werner, 1963, p. 40).

Sadly, but music does not speak as do written texts, painting and sculpture. There is no way for us to feel bitterness and resentment in the music of young Mendelssohn. However it would be strange if his total immersion in musical creativity was not a constructive reaction to his tears of rage and humiliation, in an impossible situation: his parents had made him Christian, like those who were spitting at his feet and chanting "Hep, hep, Judenjung." Given the times, and the minimal Jewish scripts he had adsorbed in his youth, a conversion back to Judaism was out of the question. The misfortune of youth could not but continue to hurt him all his life.

In the end, Siegler and Kotovsky are correct in saying that "whether a child is generally creative may be at best weakly linked to whether he or she as an adult will be extremely creative at any one activity" (1986, p. 420), provided that this observation refers to nonchallenged children. When discussing challenged children the link may exist, especially if born with recognizable talents.

On the other hand, we must remember that the link between youth creativity and adult creativity was easier to develop in the past when children had all the interest of following their fathers or uncles in their profession, otherwise they would have become nothing more than servants or soldiers. Bach, Mozart, and Beethoven did well in becoming musicians like their fathers. On the other hand, already Leonardo and Michelangelo did not follow the paternal profession, but both came from families with a higher SES than those of Bach, Mozart, and Beethoven. Nowadays, the first thing a challenged youth will do (with the exception of the early misfortune of parental death) will be to avoid anything that has to do with the parental profession. This, in turn, reduces the possibility of receiving, quite early, professional assistance of good quality. So, the absence of "the link", discussed by Siegler and Kotovsky, is definitely stronger now than it was in the past. Similar considerations explain the present smaller number of artistic families, especially of creative families.

21. Gifted Persons Should Court the Field; Challenged Should Divide It

According to Csikszentmihalyi and Wolfe (2000): "Finally, the ability to convince the field about the virtue of the novelty one has produced is an important aspect of personal creativity. One must seize the opportunities to get access to the field and develop a network of contacts" (p. 85). This is a perfect piece of advice for the non-challenged gifted and talented persons and his/her normal creativity (C1 to C6); but it may be a dangerous piece of advice for the challenged and his/her revolutionary creativity (C7 to C10). Too much networking by the challenged will bring them to accept the ideas of the field and thereby, to commit creative suicide. The challenged personalities, instead, should pray that—in their adult years, when they are ready to present the results of their intuitions and work to the educated public—*the field be divided or divisible.*

What saved Luther was not a networks of contacts with the Curia in Rome, but the fact that the field was divided: on one side Emperor Charles V and Pope Leo X Medici, and on the other the Elector Frederick III the Wise who in 1521-1522 gave Luther refuge at the Wartburg.

The challenged personality should always remember that "one difference between East and West, heavily emphasized in the writing of economic historians, was that the West was politically fragmented between more or less autonomous units that competed for survival, wealth, and power. . . . The possibilities of migration within Europe allowed creative and original thinkers to find a haven if their place of birth was insufficiently tolerant, so that in the long run, reactionary societies lost out in the competition for wealth and power" (Mokyr, 1990, pp. 206, 233). So, challenged youth, pray, that when it is your turn, the situation is similar, and you are not forced to kowtow to the *field.*

22. A Funnel Problem?

According to Winner and Martino "one reason why only a few artistically and musically gifted children and prodigies make the transition to become domain creators as adults is that the funnel is small: there is simply not enough room at the top for all prodigies to become creators; and so there is an inevitable weeding out. Any domain would be in chaos if there were as many creative adult innovators as there are child prodigies" (2000, p. 107).

Winner and Martino would have been right if they had spoken, for instance, of the transition from gifted musical performer to first class adult performer. Here, yes, there is a limited number of places for first violins in great orchestras, and even less room for world class players. But it is the same in every human activity, there is room for only one person at the top of any pyramid, and for very few one step down: it is the nature of the pyramid.

When we move to creativity, it is a different story: so much rests in the person, in what that person can create. In music, to stay with this domain chosen by Winner and Martino, there is a scarcity of good composers. Every great orchestra would welcome compositions of creators of the caliber of Samuel Barber, Prokofiev, Shostakovich, Stravinsky, or for the past (and leaving aside the giants) of the caliber of Leclair, Marin Marais, Monteverdi, Schütz, Zelenka. Similarly, there is plenty of room for creators in every other domain; and Winner and Martino's fear of chaos, because of too many creative adult innovators, is a dialectical joke with no reference to reality.

There may be a small variant of the funnel problem imbedded in the *10-year rule*: people may need the opportunity to create works of average quality for about ten years before coming with truly innovative and valid works. However, even this may be a false problem. A young composer may work for a while at less glamorous assignments: music for videos, commercials, medium quality films, and then gradually move to more significant assignments. Many great composers of the past did similar things, accepting small assignments, even humiliating ones, for quite a while, as Bach was willing to accept, in 1742, at the age of 57, to compose some music for Count Kaiserling who suffered from insomnia! The Count's pianist was Johann Gottlieb Goldberg, a former student of Bach, a very accomplished player on the piano, but without any marked talent for composition, "so one day the Count asked Bach to write for Goldberg some clavier music, of a soothing and cheerful character, that would relieve the tedium of sleepless nights. . . . [The masterful results was later named*Goldberg Variations*] Perhaps Bach was never so well rewarded for any composition as for this. The Count gave him a golden goblet containing one hundred louis d'ors" (Forkel 1802/1974, pp. 119-120). Who among today's musicians would compose to relieve the tedium of a single sleepless person? And yet, as in many other similar instances, a masterpiece was created by commission, *under purely extrinsic motivation.*

23. Creativity Versus Eminence

Catherine Cox was right when she said that "a painter whose creation is destroyed before it is seen, or an author whose work is lost before it has been read, may be great but he can scarcely be eminent" (1926, p. 20). One valid approach, in the case of lack of recognition for one reason or another, is to believe in the existence, somewhere, of a *superior field* ["Heaven is above all yet; there sits a judge that no king can corrupt," *Henry VIII, iii. i. 99*]: a small group of highly intelligent, knowledgeable and wise persons who would have no problem in understanding, appreciating and praising what was not presented to the normal field (as in the above case of destroyed paintings and lost texts) or what was refused by a sclerotic field.

Eminence is a different matter, and many have become eminent without being truly creative. Up to a point, history continually weeds out undeserved eminence and—from time to time—gives it posthumously to deserving ones.[60]

The *field* is famous for wrong judgments. For quite a while the field refused, for instance, to accept Newton's discoveries of the composite nature of solar light, and made his life miserable, with great losses for science by diverting his interest to alchemy:

Among the most important dissenters to Newton's paper was Robert Hooke, one of the leaders of the Royal Society who considered himself the master in optics and hence he wrote

---

[60] Inevitable, on the other hand, is the problem of major cultural changes. Poems, novels, plays, which were clear and beautiful to past generations, may become obscure and meaningless to the present one. In such a case, the present generation will hardly be able to redress past errors of judgment.

a condescending critique of the unknown parvenu. One can understand how the critique would have annoyed a normal man. . . . Less than a year after submitting the paper, he was so unsettled by the give and take of honest discussion that he began to cut his ties, and he withdrew into virtual isolation. . . . Newton was also engaged in another exchange on his theory of colours with a circle of English Jesuits in Liège, perhaps the most revealing exchange of all. Although their objections were shallow, their contention that his experiments were mistaken lashed him into a fury. The correspondence dragged on until 1678, when a final shriek of rage from Newton, apparently accompanied by a complete nervous breakdown, was followed by silence. The death of his mother the following year completed his isolation. For six years he withdrew from intellectual commerce except when others initiated a correspondence, which he always broke off as quickly as possible. *During his time of isolation, Newton was greatly influenced by the Hermetic tradition with which he had been familiar since his undergraduate days. Newton, always somewhat interested in alchemy, now immersed himself in it, copying by hand treatise after treatise and collating them to interpret their arcane imagery.* (Westfall, 1978, p.18, my italics)

The failure of both Hooke and Huygens [the eminent Dutch mathematician, astronomer, and physicist] to understand the nature of Newton's objectives in the letter [to Henry Oldenburg, subsequently published in the *Philosophical Transactions*], never mind the question of whether or not he had attained them, is by no means unique in the history of science. *It is perhaps the rule rather than otherwise that the point or thrust of major innovations has been at first ignored or misconceived. In this case, despite their eminence in other parts of optics,* neither of Newton's critics possessed his extensive familiarity with prism experiments and the phenomena of the spectrum, therefore, like others . . . . both Hooke and Huygens failed to attend to the experimental character of Newton's investigation. His first question, as posed in the letter—why is the spectrum long rather than circular?—was too simple for them. (Hall, 1992, pp. 126-127, my italics)

24. Are Gifted Children Pulling the Short Straw?

At this point, it might seem that the challenged personality is the great winner in life, and the gifted, in comparison, the loser. But it is not so. On the contrary, gifted children are, by far, in the winning position. Indeed, "systematic study of the gifted began in the 1920s with Terman's (1925) longitudinal study of 1,528 children with IQs averaging 151. These children were surprisingly well rounded and socially well adjusted, and grew up to be successful professionals" (Winner, 2000, p. 153).

Indeed, many gifted children—as noted in volume 1—become well rounded and socially well adjusted, [growing] up to be successful professionals; many become model citizens who help society by keeping its institutions running and getting better—from hospitals to schools, justice to academia, based on the accumulated wisdom of the past; many become enlightened conservatives; sociable, realistic, mature; have many old and new friends; strong family and community ties; in academia, science, and the arts, they work within the system. And in Lewis Terman's words: "In physical growth and in general health the gifted group unquestionably rates on the whole somewhat above par. There is no shred of evidence to support the widespread opinion that typically the intellectually precocious child is weak, undersized, or nervously unstable" (1926, p. 634).

Nobody should begrudge the challenged personalities their high creativity, they paid dearly for it: Proust with his severe asthma from age 9, Toulouse-Lautrec with his short legs, Leopardi with his hunchback, Leonardo with the stigma of illegitimacy, Newton with the death of his father and hated remarriage of his mother. And these are the small shiny tip of the iceberg: many challenged never manage to be creative for one reason or another: poor health, family problems, lack of money, exhausting menial jobs, inability to practice normal creativity for more than ten years and so reach intellectual overkill, consistent neglect by the field. The list could continue. On average it is the challenged personality who has drawn the short straw, not the gifted and talented.

25. Are Chance Encounters Important?

According to Albert Bandura "chance encounters play a prominent role in shaping the course of human life" (1982, p. 747). To prove his point, Bandura wrote in detail on the case of Paul Watkins:

For purposes of the present discussion a chance encounter is defined as an unintended meeting of persons unfamiliar to each other. Consider, by way of example, the following fortuitous encounter that profoundly altered a person's life. Paul Watkins was a talented teenager headed on a promising course of personal development—He enjoyed a close family life, was well liked by his peers, excelled in academic activities, and served as student-body president of his high school, hardly the omens of a disordered destiny (Watkins & Soledad, 1979). One day he decided to visit a friend who lived in a cabin in Topanga Canyon in Los Angeles. Unbeknown to Watkins, the friend had since moved elsewhere and the Manson "family" now lived there. This fortuitous visit led to a deep entanglement in the Manson gang in the period before they embarked on their "helter skelter" killings. To an impressionable youth the free flow of communal love, group sex, drugs, spellbinding revelations of divine matters, and isolation from the outside world provided a heady counterforce that launched him on a divergent life path requiring years to turn his life around. In the preceding case the initial meeting was entirely due to happenstance. Human encounters involve degrees of fortuitiveness. People often intentionally seek certain types of experiences, but the persons who thereby enter their lives are determined by a large element of chance. (p. 748)

However, it is here that we encounter a major difference with challenged youths: Watkins "was well liked by his peers" something which is not often the case with challenged youths. Being well liked by his peers meant behaving in ways that peers approved and liked. Then, in Topanga Canyon, Watkins met a new peer group—the Manson "family"—he liked them, and behaved in ways to be liked by the group. Lacking an internal stabilizing-gyroscope, lacking an internal directing-compass, he was impressed by the family's free life style, flow of communal love, group sex, drugs, etc. The new peer group easily replaced the old one. Here, yes, a chance encounter determined a life path. Further in his article, Bandura wrote that:

Analyses of the power of chance encounters to inaugurate enduring change generally emphasize personal susceptibilities to social influence. These are usually treated as personal vulnerabilities in influences judged to be negative and as personal competencies in influences that lead toward beneficial futures. Personal attributes certainly play a significant role in determining what changes, if any, fortuitous influences may produce. However, the attributes of social environments into which persons are fortuitously inducted also operate as highly influential determiners of the degree and course of personal change. Indeed, closed social systems wielding strong coercive and rewarding power can work profound irreversible changes even in the seemingly invulnerable. *As the Watkins case cited earlier illustrates, even the best laid personal foundations can be undermined by powerful group influence.* (pp. 749-50, my italics)

Here, while I fully agree with the first section in italics which stresses the danger of a person's susceptibility to social influence, I have my doubts about the second: Are we sure that Watkins had the best laid personal foundations, and was not, instead, highly susceptible to social influences? As reported by Bandura "Paul Watkins was a talented teenager headed on a promising course of personal development—he enjoyed a close family life, was well liked by his peers, excelled in academic activities, and served as student-body president of his high school, hardly the omens of a disordered destiny" (ib., p. 748). The problem is not in having or not omens of a disordered destiny, but in having a sound character, in having clear values, something which may or may not be predicated by the above list of features and accomplishments which sounds too good, in contradiction to La Fontaine's dictum that "It is impossible to please all the world and one's father." I suspect that teenagers trained in contrarianism would have applied this attitude to the Manson gang, and come away unscathed.

This said, do I consider chance encounters unimportant? No, but not in the way of Bandura, especially for challenged personalities. Not that the challenged personality does not make use of chance encounters, only that out of a hundred of chance encounters, he pays attention to the one that fits his life program, and follows it only as long as it makes sense with his *war of the scripts*, with his vision, with his chosen tasks.

In 1775, at the age of 26, Goethe had a chance encounter with Major von Knebel, the tutor of Prince Constantin of Weimar, which then led to an encounter with Constantin and his elder brother Karl

August, Duke of Saxe-Weimar. On the basis of this second encounter[61], Goethe entered into the service of Karl-August, as indispensable minister of the little state, inspecting mines, superintending irrigation schemes, even organizing the issue of uniforms to its tiny army. And in parallel, there was much major artistic creativity.

However, this new life "was not as surprising as it might seem. Goethe's interests were too diverse and his opinion of his abilities too generous for him to regard himself simply as a professional writer, and he would almost certainly have entered the public service of his native city had he not gone to Weimar. He was after all a member of one of Frankfurt's first families and a trained jurist and solicitor, and he must always have regarded a political career as the most likely means of providing him with the security and material resources necessary for the development of his genius" (Craig, 2000, p. 54). In other words, even without the chance visit by von Knebel, Goethe would have entered the public service, and made a political career in parallel to his artistic career. What counted was the direction he was giving to his life, not the chance encounter with Duke Karl August.

26. The Importance of Character

Ingrid Schoon asked at the beginning of her chapter "A life span approach to talent development": "How is budding talent transformed into adult achievement?" (Schoon, 2000, p. 213). One partial answer is the above by Bandura: Chance encounters have an impact, therefore much may depend on chance. On the other hand, Bandura himself felt that also character played an important role:

> The scholastically gifted are more likely than are school truants to enter the ranks of eminent scientists. Metamorphoses of social isolates into vivacious personalities or aggressors into passive personalities are not all that common. There are two psychological processes by which the products of early development can foster continuities in behavioral patterns. One process operates through selection of environments, the sec-

---

[61] In reality those two were not totally chance encounters, because Von Knebel was keenly interested in literature, was a poet himself and an ardent admirer of Goethe; and the two princes had expressed the desire to meet the author of the recently published, and highly successful *Werther*. In other words, even life's chance encounters may be determined by the direction of one's interests and works, provided these are substantial and coherent.

ond through production of environments. After people acquire certain preferences and standards of behavior, they tend to select activities and associates who share similar value systems, thereby mutually reinforcing preexisting bents (Bandura & Walters, 1959; Bullock & Merrill, 1980; Alkin & Westley, 1955; Mischel, 1968). Through their actions people create as well as select environments. By constructing their own circumstances they achieve some regularity in behavior (Bandura, 1977; Raush, Berry, Hertel, & Swain, 1974). (1982, p. 747)

For a different or sharper answer to Schoon, we may refer to the challenged Thomas Mann who studied carefully a series of eminent personalities in his *Adel des Geistes* (*The Aristocracy of the Mind*; 1945/1955). In his essay on Richard Wagner, he said: "Destiny is nothing more than the unfolding of character" (1945/1955, p. 392). This, in turn, agrees with Howard Gruber who said in "The self-construction of the extraordinary" (and already this title says the essential: *self-construction*) that "The development of a self-concept adequate for creative work must include: . . . . 2. A sense of special mission; a will to commit enormous energies and all the time necessary, a lifetime, to the chosen task" (1986, p. 259).

But what is character?

Character is

   a gyroscope for stability[62]

   a compass for direction

   a map for location

   a telescope for long view

   a microscope for in depth sight

   a dynamo for drive

---

[62] For this, and the following points, one may refer to my definition of personality: *Personality is that which permits a prediction and explanation of what a person will do differently, in a given situation, in comparison with specified others; and permits a prediction and explanation of which situation a person will select given a choice.* And the first three items (gyroscope, compass, and map) were probably missing in Paul Watkins's make-up.

In all these aspects of character, the challenged have an advantage because they built the above (compass, map, etc.) themselves, because they did not inherit them from parents, school, society at large. "The style is the man himself", said Buffon, and every challenged person has his or her unique style shaped by a unique GxAxM. Paraphrasing Tolstoy (1876): Happy families are all alike; all unhappy challenged youths are unhappy in their own way, and this profoundly marks their character.

In the section "Passion, drive, self-confidence" of chapter 1 of volume 1, I wrote: "Misfortunes, like physical infirmity or rootlessness, separate the challenged youths from their peers, and often force on them periods of solitude that are spent reading, dreaming, and thinking of their misfortunes and ways to redress matters. Through their lives, the challenged personalities know that they do not belong to the pack, and that other people call them into question. Challenged personalities must prove themselves through creativity and leadership. Only through their work can they justify, to themselves and the others, their being different and their independence." All this homework develops character: the gyroscope, the compass, the map, the dynamo. And because they have been the builders of their own character, they are capable of flexibility where needed: not the terrible flexibility of a Paul Watkins, but the flexibility of a Newton or a Darwin (as discussed in chapter 8 of ovlume 1).

Said differently, character is the set of scripts that a person has, when applied to a given situation, through intelligence(s) and temperaments. Because the scripts of the challenged are his/her own—tested, tempered, expanded through a long *war of the scripts* with society— these scripts are strongly felt, and yet flexible because when a change is made it will not infringe on deeply ingrained taboos, and only reflect additional thoughts.

Caveat: For clarity, I have overstressed the character strength of the challenged. However the dedicated personality family—and many gifted and talented youths belong to this group—also includes wonderful, admirable people who have a strong character. The world would, indeed, be an impossible place to live in, if left only to the challenged. So I ask the readers to do the needed adjustments to what I said in function of their knowledge and interests, rendering to each group its due.

27. In the End

In answer to Simonton's questions (reported in Section 1):

- Most gifted children do *not* fail to realize their potential upon becoming adults. What many may fail is the wrong expectations of their parents and teachers who are mesmerized by the creative lives of Mozart and Picasso.
- Being intelligent (and with some talents) is *not* the same as being a "bud" that will naturally evolve into a beautiful flower or a mighty tree, provided that an accident does not come that either freezes, burns, or dries it out.
- Being intelligent and having some talents—in GAM parlance, having a high GxA—is *not* a potential for creativity but for becoming a successful professional.

This last can be seen best in the studies of Benjamin Bloom and associates. Indeed their (1985) book is entitled *Developing Talent in Young People*, where we can read on the back cover: "Olympic swimmers. World-class tennis players. Concert pianists. Sculptors. Research mathematicians. Research neurologists. One hundred and twenty young men and women who had reached the highest levels of accomplishment in their chosen fields were interviewed by a University of Chicago research team to determine how and why they were able to develop such exceptional talent. The result of the study indicates that talent development requires a minimum of a dozen years of commitment to learning. Central to this process is the amount and quality of support and instruction that children receive from their parents and teachers."[63]

Bloom focused, very correctly, on professional success (not creativity): those "who had reached the highest level of accomplishment in their chosen field." Accordingly, Bloom stressed the assistances from parents and teachers, going so far as to say that the successful sibling was not the more talented but the one willing to

---

[63] Bloom speaks of talents, but clearly, when dealing with research neurologist, and also with mathematicians and sculptors, he must refer to giftedness, i.e., to high intelligence. To be ecumenical, and in line will everything said in this chapter, I would say that all his subjects were G/T youths with above-average intelligence and above-average talents. (One does not become an Olympic swimmer, world-class tennis player, or concert pianist without high intelligence).

follow the dictates of parents and teachers. In the formula GxA, he stressed (up to a point) more the A (asisstances) than the G (genetic endowment). So, for Bloom there is no "bud," but good parents, good teachers, a desire to work hard, and a valid initial gift and talent.[64]

Back to Simonton's interpretation, being a G/T youth, and having good parents and good schools, is not a potential for high creativity, but for becoming a first class physician, architect, engineer, historian, politician, and for being happy to boot. Correspondingly, there are no "common blind alleys" if they are not those created by over-zealous parents and teachers in the desire to attain creativity of the highest magnitude. Correspondingly, with few rare exceptions, there are no "nipped buds" the way Simonton sees them. For the G/T individuals there will be creativity in adulthood, plenty of it, but of the C1-C2, the C3-C4 and even some C5-C6 type; but not much higher. If there is some creativity during childhood, even as high as C3-C4, that should not come at the expense of a regular youth, normal education and professional growth. As for courses in creativity for G/T youths, such courses will do plenty of good provided they do not hinder normal education.

However, when we move to the challenged youths, the developmental rules change radically. For them, what is often needed is plain financial assistance: direct money or educational grants. As said before, such financial help, in many cases, can make the difference between adult creativity and unfulfilled possibilities (remember Charles Dickens).

Simonton saw things differently than Bloom, but probably with reference to different types of youths (challenged, at least in part?):

---

[64] Very interesting, when reading the results of the interviews that Bloom's associates had with the sculptors, I noticed, here and there, that the basic Bloomian rule for success had been infringed (the rule which demands full agreement with parents and teachers), and I sensed the presence of some elements of the M (and derived challenged personality) at the base of high creativity. I read, for instance that "The sculptors were evenly divided between those whose parents were noticeably helpful to their artistic development during this period [adolescence] and those whose parents provided little if any assistance. . . . A few parents do seem to have become very angry at their child's decision to work toward being a professional artist, and they made their displeasure clear to the aspiring artist for several years" (Sloane & Sosniak, 1985, pp. 112, 133). This in turn brings to mind the above quoted remarks by Albert and Runco that "the parents [of creative children] themselves often do not get along, and this, too, affects the level of conflict experienced. The creative child typically had more hostility to contend with than the equally bright but less creative child" (1986, p. 340). So, when moving to creativity, it would seem that Bloom and associates encountered GxAxM, and not only the GxA at the base of professional success.

"Mentors can have a detrimental effect on talent development if they are motivated to clone themselves through their students. In part, it is for this cause that it is usually more advantageous to experience multiple mentors rather than lean heavily on just one" (2000, p. 117). This may not be true for Olympic swimmers, world-class tennis players, and concert pianists (and possibly also for research mathematicians, research neurologists), where it is often better to stay with one great master and not change style. I remember the pains my mother went through when she decided to have a better cello teacher: the great player she went to demanded so many changes, starting with hand positions, and she had to painfully unlearn before finally beginning to learn anew.

So, we constantly need to make important distinctions: normal child, G/T child, challenged child, remedial child (without forgetting all the intermediate cases). We must also remember that there is no reason why highly creative adults should display clear signs of giftedness in their early years (with the exception of a good intelligence which is always there, as in the case of Einstein). A high GxAxM is a potential for high creativity; and there will be creativity after many years of hard work.

The title of this chapter is "Gifted Children (High GxA) Will/Should Become Successful Professionals; Challenged Children (High GxAxM) Will/Should Become Geniuses." In each case the word "will" is followed by the word "should" to highlight the fact that things do not always evolve successfully, especially for the challenged. What is important to remember is the fact that we are dealing with two different sets of people, and that we should act accordingly.

Appendix 1

Paul Klee: GAM *Miner*

Miners

- Causes: Lack of love, (e.g., lack of love from the remaining parent after one died, divorced, or was put aside).
- Results: Skeptics with a tendency toward pessimism and satire; sharp eye for hypocrisy. Many great poets are miners. (From table 1 of volume 1)

Father

At the source of the *miner* in Paul Klee are his father's "almost legendary powers of sarcasm" (San Lazzaro, 1957, p. 21) which undermined his paternal love and pedagogical talents. This sarcasm built a barrier between him and his son which was all the more powerful because it consisted less of what the father said than of what he could have said if the son had not been careful. In his diaries, Klee wrote: "For a long time, I trusted my Papa implicitly and regarded his words (Papa can do anything) as pure truth. The only thing I couldn't bear was the old man's teasing. On one occasion, thinking I was alone, I indulged in some playful mummery. A sudden amused 'pf!' interrupted and wounded me. Even in later life, this 'pf!' was heard occasionally" (1965, p. 4).

"Intellectually his father was above average, but his career was not crowned with the success for which he had hoped; disappointment probably showed itself in a sarcastic tongue which was often turned against his son"[65] (Grohmann, 1954, p. 26)[66]. The sarcasm was reciprocated, when the eighteen-year-old Klee in a postcard to his father, said:

> Dear Hans, I write you on a postcard, whose address I wrote already three years ago; at that time I was making that five day tour with professor Tobler, and I had taken with me five addressed postcards. Of those five, three remained in my papers, and I use them now from time to time. The good thing is that the address forces me, at least once to write you a few words. I know that you neither demand it, nor expect it. . . . You, at least, in my position, would not write at all. . . . but it will nonetheless please you. . . ." (reported by Felix Klee, 1960, p. 32).

Five years later, "During his Italian trip he [Klee] had already shown traces of considerable pessimism and a tendency toward satire. From Rome in 1902 he had written to his father: "Classical art is a sort of paradise for me. Culturally speaking, our art is very unimportant. That does not matter; we were born that way and must accept the situation. In order not to be laughed at, however, one must make others laugh, even at an image of themselves. That is one of the motives behind my present experiment" (Grohmann, 1954, p. 46).[67]

Misogyny

Klee's relations with his mother were far from warm, probably the results of the humiliations she may have had to swallow: the paternal sarcasm can hardly have been aimed only at the son. In Klee's diaries we read: "#28. One night my mother returned at night from a

---

[65] "Failure makes people cruel and bitter" said Somerset Maugham (quoted by Peter, 192, p. 196).

[66] Something similar, even if in a milder form, seems to have happened to the father of Picasso: "Failure would give an increasingly sardonic edge to José's fabled irony—a trait that he passed on in good measure to his son" (Richardson, 1991, p. 18).

[67] "No matter whom he happened to be with, Klee was always reserved; not deliberately, but because he could not be otherwise. Although intensely perceptive, he seemed to live in another world. Even on the occasion of festivities arranged in his honor, Klee remained his usual self. His withdrawal was so compellingly apparent that no one dared to trespass upon his private world. This was all the more remarkable as Klee's outward behavior was so modest and unassuming" (Grohmann, 1954, p. 25).

bed and was supposed to be asleep. I pretended to be, and her home-coming was only celebrated the next morning (eight years)" (1965, p. 8). Strange, that after an absence of three weeks, her son pretends to be asleep, and does not rush to kiss his mother.

Things were even stranger in Klee's behavior to the opposite sex, possibly—again—the result of how the father treated his wife. In "Diary 1—Memories of Childhood", Klee wrote: "#14. From time to time, I played tricks on a little girl who was not pretty and who wore braces to correct her crooked legs. I regarded her whole family, and in particular the mother, as very inferior people. . . . At the right moment I'd give my protegée a slight push. The poor thing would fall, and I'd bring it back in tears to its mother, explaining with an innocent air: 'It tumbled.' I played this trick more than once, without Frau Enger's ever suspecting the truth. I must have gauged her correctly (five or six years)" (ib., p. 5).

One complementary interpretation would raise the suspicion that the paternal sarcasm may have also dealt on sexual matters, and that the intelligent and sensitive son may have detected it, and quite early. There is a pen drawing, entitled *Four Nudes: Mother and Children Afraid of Father's Return*, of 1908 (reproduced by Lynton, 1964, p. 35), in which Klee shows us the (or a) paternal attack. It is a picture charged with sexual overtones, where the mother is too busy with herself, protecting her genitalia, and too dignified to be able to protect her children. More than anything, mother and children are afraid of the inquisitive eye of the 'phallic' father (phallic for the shape given to his whole body).

The mother—in relation to a poem by Klee, to be discussed shortly—does not have sufficient 'individuality': "A mother is planning her entrance - Shushhh! you don't belong here. You are divisible." You belong to the "heavy father", and you come to life only when he wants you.

Misogynous is Klee's famous drawing of 1903 entitled *Jungfrau im Baum* [Virgin in a tree] (reproduced, for instance, in Grohmann, 1954, p. 106). Here woman is a spider, waiting at the center of her web to catch a curious fly. To be twice sure that his message was clear, Klee painted on a side branch two birds, half peacock, half vulture, the two sides of his vision of woman.

Even more misogynous are two drawings of 1920 and 1921, reproduced and commented by Margaret Plant, 1978. That of 1921, is entitled *Concerning the Fate of Two Girls* (fig. 11, p. 26):

These girls in the grip of fate are vulnerable figures with insignificant eyes and carefully embroidered hair, and they stand with gesticulating, welcoming arms and transparent, high-lifted skirts, displaying themselves before their audience. On the right of one figure her 'fate' is drawn as a line from the base of her skirt. It sharply declines to bear the weight of another toppled figure, the same girl later in the time-sequence. One upward-turned skirt is in fact a giant vaginal symbol of lips marked with a fine hairline. (p. 26)

The second drawing, of 1920, entitled *Pandora's Box* (fig. 79, p. 130) was "described[68] as an 'ominous receptacle. . . . emitting evil vapours from an opening clearly suggestive of the female genitals'" (p. 130).

These last comments by Plant are part of her discussion of another work by Klee: *Ceramic/Erotic/Religious* of 1921 (figure xv, p. 96), in which "the figure appears to have two sets of legs, increasing the effect of lewd prancing. The background is squared, and out of the squares two vases emerge: the symbols of Aphrodite. . . . It is clear that the 'vessels of Aphrodite' are the containers of evil fumes . . . . This work, with its unambiguous image and its precise reference both to a traditional theme and to its modern theatrical incarnation, is among Klee's most specific satirical work. In that process of visual condensation of which Klee is a master, the female body of Aphrodite takes on the shape of the vase" (pp. 130-31).

Poetry

In 1900, Klee had written in his diary: "Twenty-one years old! I never doubted my vital force. But how is it to fare with my chosen art? The recognition that at bottom I am a poet, after all, should be no hindrance in the plastic arts! And should I really have to be a poet, Lord knows what else I should desire. Certainly, a sea swells within me, for I feel. It is a hopeless state, to feel in such a way that the storm rages on all sides at once and that nowhere is a lord who commands the chaos" (1965, p. 42).

---

[68] By Dora and Erwing Panowsky, in their 1956 book *Pandora's Box, the Changing Aspects of a Mythical Symbol*; London: Routledge and Kegan Paul, pp. 111-13.

Klee, indeed, was both painter and poet. His poems, even if less known, have been highly praised. "Rainer M. Gerhardt, a very fine poet and critic of the post-45 generation, wrote of them in 1951: 'I do not know what German poet has written comparable lines during the last fifteen years.'" (Hollo, 1962, p. 5)

Klee wrote poems with a painter's mind, and painted with a poet's mind. In his painting, Klee "sought to take the viewer beyond the concepts of language, beyond the idea that the real world is what we see, and to remind those who looked at his works that life is full of mysteries. The real, for him, was the universe of self-expression through art, and the signs and symbols he painted were adumbrations of what he felt to be true but hidden nature of the world" (Fisher, 1966, p. 3).

The following two samples of Klee's poems—from the 1960 collection edited by his son—are vivid clues to his *miner personality*. The first is a self-portrait, in which I was tempted to highlight every word starting with "admonishes pedantically Papa" (especially that "And I, watching it all, astonishment in my eyes, with a sharpened pencil in my left hand.") The second poem is a descent into his *miner's inner sanctum*:

Individuality

Individuality is not divisible,
It is a living organism.
It is composed of elementary objects
of various kinds
living inseparably together
Try to divide it and
the parts will die.

Take myself for example:
I am a whole dramatic ensemble.
Enter a prophetic ancestor,
Roar a brutal hero,
An alcoholic bonvivant argues with
a learned professor.
Swoons a chronically lovesick singer
Admonishes pedantically Papa
An indulgent uncle arbitrates

Aunt Chichat gossips
Giggles lewdly the maid

And I, watching it all,
astonishment in my eyes.
with a sharpened pencil
in my left hand.
Try to enter a pregnant mother
Shushhh! I stop her.
You don't belong here.
You are divisible!
She fades.
(1905)

Last Things

In the heart's depths
Only one prayer:
Receding steps.
   (undated)

  The solution, indeed, is that of the *miner painter-poet*: "The only prayers - are steps receding."

2

GAM's Personality Families Versus Eric Newton's Personality Styles

In chapter 9 of volume 1, I explained why, according to GAM, a person becomes a Berlinian *hedgehog* or *fox*.[69] At the same time, I compared Berlin (and my explanation) to a similar division by George Kennedy (1963) between thinkers who emphasized goals and absolute standards and talked much about truth [in essence, *hedgehogs*], and those for whom these concepts seemed shadowy or imaginary, and who found certainty only in the process of life and the present moment [in essence, *foxes*].

Here, I would like to present a similar causal explanation for the three "Newtonian" families of *personal artistic styles*: *Classic, Romantic* and *Realist*. The art critic Eric Newton, former Slade Professor of fine arts at Oxford, is the author of several books, among these: *European Painting and Sculpture* (1956), *The Arts of Man* (1960), *The Meaning of Beauty* (1962), *The Romantic Rebellion* (1964). In 1957, Newton gave five talks for the British Broadcasting Corporation on "Style and Vision in Art". In these talks, he discussed three major families of personal style (*Classic, Romantic*, and *Realist*) each the expression of a basic temperament. These personal styles or 'personal visions' are then integrated with or superimposed upon the *vision of the period* in which they lived, be it Renaissance or Baroque.

---

[69] *Hedgehogs* are those thinkers who relate everything to a single central vision, one system, in terms of which they understand, think and feel. *Foxes,* on the other side, are those who pursue many ends, often unrelated and even contradictory; connected, if at all, in some de facto way. Accordingly, Berlin classified Dante, Plato, Hegel, Nietzsche and Proust as *hedgehogs;* Shakespere, Aristotle, Montaigne, Moliere, Goethe and Joyce as *foxes.*

In his analysis of the ***Classic*** painters, Newton said: "They see their world as something imperfect but also as something that is always aiming at a perfection which they themselves undertake to find. . . . The Classic artist always seems to say: 'This is the world as it would be if I could redesign it." (1957, p. 552).

This definition by Newton could be used verbatim for the GAM *universalists*. I did not use the word "classic" for this *challenged family* because of its formality and link to the art of the Greeks and the Romans. *Universalist* seemed to me to better express the universal vision that the members of this personality family have: their search for ultimate principles, for a higher order of things, a universal brotherhood, a supreme law, a supreme deity. Yet, Classic could have been my next choice.

For Newton, Raphael is the epitome of the Classic painter. It so happens, and not by coincidence, that Raphael's mother died when the boy was eight, and his father when he was eleven, thereby causing him to develop into a GAM *universalist*. Other Classic artists mentioned by Newton are David, Canova, and Seurat: David lost his father at the age of nine, Canova his father at the age of four, and Seurat encountered much paternal absence in his youth. Claude Lorrain is not among Newton's examples, but he is as Classic as Raphael and Canova. He is "the best known and one of the greatest masters of ideal-landscape painting, an art form that seeks to present a view of nature more beautiful and harmonious than nature itself" (Kitson, 1978, p.694). Claude Lorrain lost both parents when he was twelve years old. It seems therefore that the same cause (early parental death, category A[70]) gives origin to a GAM *universalist*, and to persons—in particular painters or sculptors—with a Classic personal style. Said differently, a GAM *universalist* painter will paint in a Newtonian Classic personal style.

Newton mentioned in his article only two non-painter Classic personalities: Plato and Racine. On the first, he wrote: "Plato, like Seurat, brooding on the quintessence of beauty, decided that its secret

---

[70] Parental death category A is the one which causes a parental vacuum, but with no additional misfortunes. Parental death category B is the one followed by problems (mainly lack of love for the children) when, for instance the remaining parent soon remarries (for personal reasons, not to provide a substitute father or mother for the children) or has an affair; or is overwhelmed by his/her difficulties and unable to give love and attention to the children. Parental death category C is the one which starts a painful socioeconomic downfall of the family. Parental death category B is at the source of many *miners*, while parental death category C is a the source of many *critical jesters*.

lay not in copying the beautiful but in pure mathematics. That its true symbols were 'straight lines and circles or solid forms produced by lathes and rulers'" (1957, p. 554).

We don't know much about the youth of Plato, but it would seem that his father died early: "[Plato] was the son of Ariston and Perictione. . . . Perictione apparently married as her second husband her uncle Pyrilampes[71], a prominent supporter of Pericles; and Plato was probably chiefly brought up in his house" (Taylor & Merlan, 1973, p. 20). In turn, Racine lost his mother at the age of one, and his father at the age of three.

Moving to persons closer to us in time, we detect that same fundamental *universalist* approach in the contemporary English philosopher Richard Hare, who lost his father at the age of ten and his mother at the age of fifteen. In him, we once again find top priority given to an all encompassing high, and true, orderly vision. Hare's own words are revealing: "The moral concepts have two properties which, together, suffice to produce a logic for moral argument. The first is the one which the philosophers call 'universality', which means, roughly, that any moral judgement I make about a case, I must make about any precisely similar case. The second property which I think moral judgements have is the one called 'prescriptivity'. . . ." (1978, p. 331). Hare, in this, epitomizes the attitude of the *universalist*. His is not the transient, the humorous, the romantic, the day-to-day attitude. Instead, the absolute validity and importance of his discoveries lead to 'prescriptivity', to clear moral rules and laws. In this we are reminded that, for Plato, the legislator is at the pinnacle of society.

In the same direction "despite the enduring impact of his theory of knowledge, Hume [who lost his father at the age of 3] seems to have considered himself chiefly as a moralist" (Jessop, 1978, p. 1192).This, essentially, is what every *universalist* is: a *moralist*. Knowledge or art are never for their own sake; they are part of a higher scheme of salvation.

Newton's second personal artistic style is ***Romanticism***, about which he wrote:

---

[71] An uncle as stepfather, especially if old, especially in ancient times less interested in the child as child, may not cause in the boy or girl those pains of lack of love by the surviving and remarried parent (parental death category B), which often give origin to a *miner* personality (see Baudelaire and Sartre, as discussed in chapter 10 of volume 2).

In art, three qualities seem to me at the heart of it: first, mystery (e.g., the mystery of moonlight as opposed to the clarity of sunlight); secondly, heightened personal emotion (e.g., all forms of intense human love and all forms of terror-fear of thunderstorms, or of crags and precipices); thirdly, a refusal to conform to law (e.g., elopements, abnormalities, the whole realm of the unfamiliar or the rebellious). I am aware that this is a rather ramshackle way of conducting a serious enquiry into Romantic style or modes of expression, but there is something in romanticism itself that tempts one to be rather slipshod. Classicism is a central position, and therefore a reliable and definable one. Romanticism is, literally, eccentric and can crop up anywhere and in any form. (1957, p. 593)

Finally, Newton's third personal artistic style is *Realism*: "The Realist is content with life as it is, accepting it gladly without wanting to idealize it [Classicism]or to emotionalize it [Romanticism]" (1957, p. 468). For Newton, Velázquez is the exemplar Realist:

In the portraits of Philip IV in the National Gallery there is no feeling that an important sitter is challenging the insight of a serious artist. The king is seen as only a great painter could see him, without a trace of exaggeration and with no thought of flattery. Yet it is not photography. Velázquez has a comment to make. Not only "I accept the world as I see it" but "I am supremely interested in the world as I find it. I have no wish to improve it or to penetrate beneath the surface, for that surface is sufficiently exciting in its own right to occupy the whole of my considerable attention". (1957, p. 629)[72]

---

[72] Similar comments on Velázquez were made by Joseph-Emile Muller: "Neither his themes nor the emotions he expresses nor (usually) his vision are in any way astonishing. One might say that he sees the world through the eyes of the ordinary man, except that he regards it with an attention and a gravity of which few men are capable. Many painters are bent on communicating ideas or conveying their dreams or emotions, whether exaltation, fears or inward rebellion, but he is most true to himself when he represents the evidence of his remorselessly observant eyes. Velázquez is the painter of visible reality—which is not at all the same as saying that he creates merely a duplicate of that reality. . . . In his personal life too Velázquez differed from Rembrandt. For him there was no period of decline, no heartbreak, no old age clouded by poverty, no repeated bereavement. Instead he enjoyed an uninterrupted rise to a position of eminence, and honours in more than sufficient quantity to satisfy his aspirations as a man, even if they did not always come to him as the result of his activities as an artist [but as court chamberlain in charge of the royal apartments and of the King's journeys]" (1976, p. 7).

From all the books I read on Velázquez, I would classify him as GAM *dedicated*: those who—as discussed in chapter 3 of volume 1— have been shaped by good parental assistances and no major misfortunes, and are "enlightened conservatives; sociable, realistic, mature; have many old and new friends; strong family and community ties; in academe, and the arts, they work within the system."

In his articles, Newton mentioned the following *Romantic* artists: Brueghel, Rowlandson, Bosch, Turner, Rembrandt, Blake, Rubens, Michelangelo, El Greco, Piero di Cosimo, Bellini, Giorgione, Titian, Grünewald, Altdorfer, Francis Bacon, Sutherland, Watteau, Delacroix, Géricault, Van Gogh, Edward Munch, Soutine, Kokotschka, Derain, Dufy, Vlaminck, Matisse, Pollock, Hartung, Soulages, Mathieu, Caravaggio, Picasso. Such a long list (and it could have easily been longer) was to be expected, given the fact that there are few Classic painters, and even fewer Realist.

Seen from the point of view of the GAM theory, once we exclude the *dedicated* (Realist) painters, and the *universalist* and *architect* (Classic), all the others, from GAM 3 (*seeker*) to GAM 14 (*trapper*) must be (and are) Newtonian Romantics.

In the above list of Romantic painters, all the giants—that I have been able to study, thanks to the availability of sufficient information on their youth—are *challenged personalities*, as discussed in this and previous volumes: Rubens (*alchemist*), Michelangelo (*universalist & alchemist*); Francis Bacon (*radiologist*); Edward Munch (*miner*); Picasso (*alchemist*).

Sadly, for many others, there is not sufficient information on their youth, for instance on Brueghel, Bosch, Rembrandt, El Greco[73], Grünewald; yet enough is known on them and their art to see them as challenged personalities from #3 *seeker* to # 14 *trapper*.

In summary, the following table of correspondence can be drawn:

Newton's Personality Style		GAM Personality Family
Classic	~	Universalist and Architect
Romantic	~	Seeker to Trapper
Realist	~	Dedicated

---

[73] Purely based on his art, I would classify El Greco as GAM *seeker*.

Understandably, the correspondence of Newton's personality styles with the Berlinian classification of thinkers is only partial, because not all hedgehogs are Classic: indeed many Berlinian hedgehogs (according to GAM) would not be Newtonian Classic but Romantic (the *seekers*, the *reformers*, and many *leadsmen*). Clearly the two, Berlin and Newton, had different interests and different classification criteria, as do I.

What is important, is to use these classification for an added layer of understanding, and not for pidgeon-holing people. In the case of Berlin, he used the hedgehog/fox classification for his discussion of Tolstoy who, in Berlin's mind was a fox who believed he was a hedgehog[74]. In the case of Newton, his labels of *personal artistic style* (Classic, Romantic, Realist), in addition to a *period vision* label (e.g., High Renaissance, Baroque, Mannerism, Impressionism, Cubism, Surrealism) can definitely sharpen the discourse on, as well as a final understanding and love for the artists under study.

In my case, I hope that by linking the GAM classification to those of Berlin or Newton, one can establish a vivid bridge between the creative works on one side and personality and biography on the other (personality in its broader sense, and biography as an explanation of the personality and creativity potential and drive). This bridge can be crossed in both directions, from GAM to a better understanding of works and their creator, and from these back to an improved understanding of the GAM theory of personality and creativity.

---

[74] Something with which I disagree (as explained in chapter 9 of volume 1, for me, Tolstoy was a hedgehog).

3

In Praise of *Pruning* and on the Dangers of Success

In chapter 3 of volume 1, I wrote that *pruning* refers to all kinds of limitations (imposed from the outside, or deliberately chosen through self-discipline) which eliminate or forbid diversions, lateral careers, non-essential promotions, distracting successes. *Shortage of pruning is probably one of the main causes for the lack of sustained creativity by both challenged and dedicated persons. Similarly, prolonged success, which nearly always negates pruning, is one of the main causes for the end of sustained creativity.*

Basically, as pruning in agriculture is the practice of cutting living parts from a plant in order to increase fruit or flower production, so it is with human creativity. There are two types of pruning: self-pruning (done deliberately by the individual), and enforced pruning (involuntary, suffered unwillingly).

1. Self-Pruning

One good example of successful self-pruning is Hans Adolf Krebs, 1953 Nobel prize for physiology:

> *How did Krebs evade the more standard trajectory of declining productivity? His own answer would be that he avoided the temptations that befall most eminent senior scientists to divert their energies in other directions.* Although, like other Nobel laureates, Krebs too responded to some of the demands made on him by that accolade, he refused to allow himself to be drawn away from his laboratory. All the way until the final illness that preempted the last few days of his life, Krebs con-

tinued to show up at his laboratory every morning at the same early hour. (Holmes, 1999, p. 137, my italics)

Under self-pruning, I would also report the following observations by Policastro and Gardner:

> Talented individuals generate creative work in the context of prolonged, meaningful, and intrinsically motivating pursuits, which demand total immersion. The other side of the coin is that they must leave many of the delights of personal and avocational pursuits aside for the sake of their mission. Einstein, for instance, conceded that much had to be given up to become the kind of scientist he wished for. Only monomaniacs, he confessed to his friend Besso, made scientific discoveries. (1999, p. 215)

Before moving to the next type, let me add that, in general (see volume 1), *hedgehogs* self-prune more than *foxes*, so much so that pruning is often a litmus test, which separates the two groups. Self-pruning, indeed, comes easier to those who have a defined high, long range goal, and work actively in their pursuit. Yet, this is not the whole story, because self-pruning is also a classical virtue, a good habit, a script that can be learned like many other scripts from parents, teachers, religious leaders, psychologists, and books.

2. Enforced Pruning

As a consolation to those who dislike self-pruning, enforced pruning is the most efficient form of the two for creativity, but also the most painful: poor jobs, exile, prison, sickness, poverty, lack of success, neglect, unlucky relations, and are but a small sample.

Lewis Carrol's Stammer

Stammering pruned Lewis Carrol (alias Charles Dodgson) during all his life. To this misfortune of youth (among other factors, including his high G [genetic endowment], and first class A [assistances of youth]), and consequent pruning of adulthood, we owe his *Alice's Adventures in Wonderland*, and *Through the Looking-Glass*. In the words of Derek Hudson:

> Dodgson's ordeal as a stammerer may provide at least a partial explanation of his attitude. Those who have suffered similarly will testify that during childhood their stammering,

such as it was, did not worry them (and hence they have tended to look back to their childhood, as Dodgson did, with a somewhat exaggerated and nostalgic affection). In the unsympathetic atmosphere of a public school, the situation is different. As the stammerer begins to make his way into adult society the barrier between him and the rest of the world becomes increasingly formidable. He tends to withdraw into himself and to avoid any situation that might provoke embarrassment. It is a curious fact that he is often at his happiest in the company of children. He can talk to them, he finds, quite naturally and freely probably because they expect less of him and are ready to take him as he comes. (1977, p. 87)

This stammering was, indeed, treated with gentle fun by Charles himself, in the fist of the Croft Rectory magazines which appeared when Charles was thirteen. "There was a typical touch of tribal ruthlessness [he and his younger four brothers and seven sisters] in the poem called 'Rules and Regulations'. First the couplet:

Learn well your grammar
And never stammer . . . .
And later:
Eat bread with butter,
Once more, don't stutter.

[Not only] Charles himself was afflicted with a stammer which, except in the presence of his child friends, never left him or responded to treatment. Several of his brothers and sisters also suffered" (Pudney, 1976, pp. 33-34). So, these rules on stammer and stutter applied to several of the siblings making them part of normal life in handling a shared difficulty. But, as said, things soon became serious, and caused real hurt and pruning, as soon as Charles left the enchanted world of his protected home.

Dante's Exile

Dante wrote his *Divine Comedy*, from 1308 to 1321, while he was exiled from his beloved Florence, and harshly persecuted.[75] He

---

[75] Because of their opposition to the *Blacks* "'faithful devotees to the Roman Church [i.e. to Pope Boniface VIII],'" on 10 March 1302, "he and fourteen other former priors were condemned to be burnt to death. . . . [In addition] by a decree of 1303 his sons had been sentenced to the same banishment as himself when they reached the age of fourteen" (Anderson, 1980, pp. 157, 160).

commented on his pain, in the third part of his poem, in the form of a prediction by his ancestor Cacciaguida:

Thou shalt abandon everything beloved
Most tenderly, and this arrow is
Which first the bow of banishment shoots forth.
Thou shalt have proof how savoreth of salt
The bread of others, and how hard a road
The going down and up another's stairs.
(Paradise, xvii, 55-60)

Without this exile, without this persecution—and instead a good political career in Florence—we would not have the *Divine Comedy*.

Machiavelli's Enforced Seclusion

As discussed in chapter 20 of volume 1, it was during his enforced seclusion in his little estate of San Casciano, hounded by poverty and unhappiness, after having been tortured and imprisoned by the Medici, that Machiavelli, between spring and autumn 1513, wrote his two most famous works: *Il principe* ("The Prince") and a large part of the *Discorsi sopra la prima deca di Tito Livio* ("Discourses on the First Decade of Tito Livy").

Mozart's Humiliations by the Royalty

In April 1789, Mozart left for the royal Castle of Potsdam, having told his wife Constanze that "he had received confirmation that King Friedrich Wilhem II of Prussia not only would welcome him but was anxiously awaiting his arrival in Potsdam. . . . [However] a court document dated 26 April, shows that, far from the King eagerly awaiting him, Mozart's arrival at court was wholly unexpected:

> One named Mozart (who at his ingress declared himself to be a Kapellmeister from Vienna) reports that he was brought hither in the company of Prince Lichnowsky, that he desired to lay his talents before Your Sovereign Majesty's feet and waited the command whether he may hope that Your Sovereign Majesty will receive him.

The king supposedly so impatient for Mozart's arrival did not grant him an audience; instead, he wrote on the document the words,

'Directeur du Port,' meaning that Mozart was to be referred to the director of chamber music at the Prussian court, the cellist Jean Pierre Duport" (Solomon, 1995, pp. 438-39).

One year later, Mozart tried to set in motion his stalled application for the post of second Kapellmeister in Vienna. In a letter to the Archduke Franz, he wrote:

> I make so bold as to beg your Royal Highness very respectfully to use your most gracious influence with His Majesty the King with regards to my most humble petition to His Majesty...., I venture to apply for the post of second Kapellmeister, particularly as Salieri, that very gifted Kapellmeister, has never devoted himself to church music, whereas from my youth up I have made myself completely familiar with this style. . . .

Alfred Einstein who reported this letter, commented as follows: "What a humble and humiliating letter, even including an obeisance before Salieri" (1946, p. 59). Notwithstanding this, even this second class appointment was not given to him. And yet, Mozart continued to create, till his death in December of 1791, masterworks like his operas *Cosi fan tutte* (1790), *The Magic Flute* (1791), *La Clemenza di Tito* (1791), and his *Requiem Mass* (left incomplete).

Beethoven's Approaching Deafness

The first symptoms had appeared before 1800.

> But by 1802 he could no longer be in doubt that his malady was both permanent and progressive. . . . He was tempted to take his own life. 'But only Art held back: for, ah, it seemed unthinkable for me to leave the world forever before I had produced all that I felt called to produce. . . .' More significant, perhaps, are his words in a letter to his friend Franz Wegeler: 'I will seize fate by the throat. . . .' Elsewhere he remarks, 'If only I were rid of my affliction I would embrace the whole world.' He was to do both, though the condition he hoped for was not fulfilled. . . .[From 1815] Beethoven's creative life entered its third and final phase. Because of his deafness he became more of a recluse than ever. His rate of composition, too, began to decrease. The works written between 1815 and 1827 comprise a mere fraction of his output after

1792; but they have a density of musical thought far surpass-
ing anything that he had composed before. (Buddess, 1993,
pp. 739-40)

Einstein's Years as an Employee of the Swiss Patent Office

Einstein's very best discoveries were made during his humiliating
years as an expert for the Swiss Federal Patent Office, from June 1902
to October 1909. "'I must confess to you that I was amazed to read
that you have to sit in an office for eight hours a day! But history is
full of bad jokes.' This is how Johann Jakob Laub, Wilhelm Wien's
collaborator in Würzburg, reacted to the news that the 'Esteemed Herr
Doctor,' from whom, at the beginning of 1908, he had requested an
offprint and for whose sake he was willing to come to Bern for three
months, was not to be found at the university but at the Patent Office"
(Fölsing, 1998, p. 235).

3. Not all Annoyances Prune

But, isn't everybody constantly pruned by the world around us?
That may well be, but not every annoyance, not every pain, is pruning
in the sense used in this book: only those difficulties which force a
person to begin and continue with a major creative task; the others are
dispersions. The worries of buying a new house, of having an affair or
a divorce, are—in most instances—distractions from the creative task.

Expanding on what said above on Einstein: "He searched in vain
for an academic position and finally took a post with the patent office
in Berne, where his main duty was the preliminary examination of
patent applications. His job left him with ample time to contemplate
the fundamental problems in physics" (Balazs, 1973, p. 95). That was
an ideal situation: a humiliating pruning which demanded vindication
through a great scientific discovery—and ample time to think about it.

4. The Dangers of Success

Rossini

In 1823, at the age of 31, rich and much applauded for his many
operas, Rossini moved to Paris where he was enthusiastically welcomed. The Academy in Paris received him; all the town fawned upon

him. There, even if at a much reduced scale, he continued to compose operas up to 1829. "Then he decided, at the age of 37, not to write again for the theatre. . . . [And he did not, for 39 years, up to his death at the age of 76. His only compositions, in all these years were two religious works, and a few songs and piano pieces.] The reasons for his musical silence remain only suppositions. Some cite his legendary laziness as the cause, while others point to the Parisian hostility to his work and Rossini's resulting sulkiness. Another cause might have been his jealousy over the Parisian success of the opera composer Giacomo Meyerbeer" (Causson, 1978, p. 1161).

However, Rossini had not always been lazy, on the contrary. In the six years from 1810 to 1815, he had composed 17 operas, among those such jewels as *La scala di seta, Il Signor Bruschino, L'italiana in Algeri,* and *Il barbiere di Siviglia.* He composed another 17 operas in the following seven years, among those *La Cenerentola, Mosé,* and *Semiramide.* Sulkiness and jealousy might be better explanations, but only as byproducts of something different, which may be plain lack of pruning: "[In Paris] Rossini gave way to the sweetness of life and to being a wise man who permitted himself to shine in society with a few clever expressions and witticisms. His bon mots, in fact, are legendary, as was his caustic wit and low humour. At his Paris home and later at his villa in Passy, Rossini gave superb gourmet dinners attended by many of the greats of the musical and literary world of the mid-19th century" (ib., p. 1161).

Picasso

As discussed by John Berger in his *The Success & Failure of Picasso*[76]: "In recent years all accounts of Picasso as a personality have become absurd. He has surrounded himself with a court, and he is king. The effects of the consequent flattery and insulation have been devastating, not only on the judgement of all those who know him, but on his own work. A special kind of sickening poeticizing has been invented for the homages. Thus Georges Besson wrote in 1952:

"I almost forgot to tell you—or have I told you already?— that this man, whose tastes are not extravagant, has a weakness for black diamonds. He owns two superb ones and he

---

[76] In turn discussed by McCully (2002, p. 863).

will never part with them. They weigh a good hundred carats each. He wears them where other people have eyes. It's as I tell you. And I assure you that those women on whom these diamonds turn their fire are utterly bowled over". (Berger, 1965/1980, p. 14)

Picasso is the king. Everything and everybody revolves round him. His whim is law. No word of criticism is ever heard. There is a great deal of talk but very little serious discussion. Picasso behaves and is treated like a child who has to be protected. It is perfectly in order to like one picture better than another. But it is inconceivable that anybody should suggest that any painting is a total failure. There is no sense whatsoever of a struggle towards an aim; only a sense of Picasso struggling blindly within himself, and everybody else struggling to keep him amused and happy. Manners are informal but the degree of self-abnegation byzantine. (ib., p. 180).

The negative consequences were inevitable:

However favourably one judges Picasso's work since 1945 it cannot be said to show any advance on what he created before. To me it represents a decline: a retreat, as I have tried to show, into an idealized and sentimental pantheism. But even if this judgement is mistaken, the extraordinary fact remains that the majority of Picasso's important late works are variations on themes borrowed from other painters. However interesting they may be, they are no more than exercises in painting—such as one might expect a serious young man to carry out, but not an old man who has gained the freedom to be himself.

It is sometimes claimed that Picasso only takes Delacroix or Velazquez as a starting point. In formal terms this is true, for Picasso often reconstruct the whole picture. But in terms of content the original painting is even less than a starting point. Picasso empties it of its own content and then is unable to find any of his own. It remains a technical exercise. If there is any fury or passion implied at all, it is that of the artist condemned to paint with nothing to say. . . .Why has nobody pointed this out? Why has nobody considered Picasso's likely desperation? Apparently it is not only in his own household that nobody dares to mention the word failure. Apparently we need to believe in Picasso's success more than he does himself. (ib., pp. 183-86)

Businessmen

Charmont (1970) commented on the fact that prolonged years of success in business can lead one to unrealism: *"Le succès entraîne le caprice et, comme le dit Octave Gélinier, pour beaucoup le luxe suprême de ceux qui ont réussi est de pouvoir enfin mépriser les faits* [Success brings whim, and as Octave Gélinier said, for many who prospered, brings the supreme luxury of being able to finally despise the facts]" (p. 119).

5. Creative Self-Pruning from Self-Control

Prince Metternich, the eminent Austrian statesman who opposed Napoleon for so long, later still praised him not for his military know-how or audacity but for his self-control:

> My opinion of Napoleon has never varied. I have seen and studied him in the moments of his greatest success; I have seen him and followed him in those of his decline. . . . Master of himself, he soon became master of men and events. . . . Surrounded by individuals who, in the midst of a world in ruins, walked at random without any fixed guidance, given up to all kinds of ambition and greed, he alone was able to form a plan, hold it fast, and conduct it to its conclusion. . . . The prodigious successes of which his life was full had doubtless ended by blinding him; but up to the time of the campaign of 1812, when he for the first time succumbed under the weight of illusions, he never lost sight of the profound calculations by which he so often conquered. (quoted by Hutt, 1972, pp. 112, 117)

6. The Extended Formula for Sustained Creativity Power

If the beginning of high creativity is rooted in a high GxAxM (and, optimally, a DP in the surrounding society), then its realization, year after year, demands an additional *personal GxAxP*, in which P (pruning) of adulthood replaces the M of youth. In youth, the M (misfortune) reduces script adoption from society; in adulthood the P reduces accommodation to the scripts of society. Both in youth and adulthood, high creativity is paid for dearly.

7. Pruning in the Form of Pain and Patience

- "Genius is nothing but a greater aptitude for patience." (attributed to Buffon by Hérault de Séchelles)
- "Mais le génie n'est le plus souvent qu'une longue patience.[77] - Général André Beaufre (*Introduction a la Stratégie*, 1965, p. 16)[78]
- "Genius is an infinite capacity for taking pains" - Ellice Hopkins (*Work Amongst Working Men*, 1883, p. 52)
- "Genius is patience."- Popular proverb.

Clearly, per se, each of these statements is wrong. Genius is not patience, genius is not an infinite capacity for taking pains. However, if these statements are read as proof of a long continuation of the working of GxAxM—especially when the new act of creation is repeatedly refused because of its novelty, and because it upsets the apple cart—then these statements show validity and strength.

Said differently, that capacity for taking pains, that long patience, is nothing but the acceptance of pruning: the pruning which eliminates distractions, and provides instead long hours of focused work. Within the bare walls of the creative cell, the key ideas will be sharpened, expanded, further tested, further applied and interrelated. Only in this painful way will the acts of creation acquire solidity and beauty.

Among the sources of quality pruning, one must list the *field*[79] (critics, public), with its habit of rejecting the truly new and important (it is easy to accept the new, right or wrong, if unimportant). In turn, this pruning, if not drastic or permanent, will stimulate creativity:

"A new idea requires a truly compelling case—intellectual overkill—in order to displace the incumbent" (David M. Raup, *The Nemesis Affair,* 1986, p. 196). However, a truly compelling case, an intellectual overkill, is not built in a few days, not even in a few years; that demands patience, and an infinite capacity for taking the pains of refusals, denials, and ridicule by the *field.* In such a case, there are no

---

[77] "But genius is most often nothing more than immense patience."

[78] This seems a direct translation of the subsequent quote, but I doubt that General Beaufre knew of Ellice Hopkins. Beaufre made his comment so that people would not overestimate the divine spark of genius (he was referring to Napoleon). I reported both quotes, even if nearly identical, coming from different sources, and yet praising pruning so clearly.

[79] See Csikszentmihalyi (1988a).

short-cuts. I may go so far as to suspect that if Einstein had had less success—from 1921 onwards, the year he was awarded the Nobel prize—he would have continued to be creative for many more years. His last twenty years—one may even say his last thirty years from 1925 to 1955—were devoid of major creativity: "Pursuing his own line of theoretical research [which turned fruitless] outside the mainstream of physics, he took an air of fixed serenity. 'Among my European friends, I am now called *Der grosse Schweiger* ("The great Stone Face"), a title I well deserve,' he said" (Michelmore, 1978, p. 513).

The opposite happened to Newton. In 1672, seven years after his great discovery of the nature of light and colors, he volunteered a paper on it. He awaited acclaim. Instead, to his dismay, he found himself in the most exasperating of disputes. "Discussions about his paper were still going on in 1675. In December of that year he wrote, 'I was so persecuted with discussions arising out of my theory of light that I blamed my own imprudence for parting with so substantial a blessing as my quiet to run after a shadow.' *One effect of the controversy was that Newton was led to investigate other effects of colour, to inquire how light was produced and to develop the emission or corpuscular theory of light, according to which light is the product of emission by a luminous body of a host of tiny particles traveling in empty space . . . ."* (Glazebrook & Cohen, 1973, p. 419, my italics).

Obviously, patience does not mean not being upset, not feeling insulted, not suffering for being unjustly neglected or misunderstood; it means, instead, continuing to work ceaselessly; it means doing more not less, and working hard at preparing "a truly compelling case, an intellectual overkill."

4

Thomas Mann's
Tragic Lack of Self-Pruning

[Thomas Mann] positively hungered for praise, thirsted
for appreciation. He wanted no critical comment on his work;
he preferred to have his publishers, his secretary and the members of his family hide such articles from him. He took even
mild criticism as a personal affront. Even to feel that he had
been slighted infuriated him. (Reich-Ranicki, 1989, p. 37)

A sincere interest in the opinion of others, especially if critical,
especially from competent readers, is mandatory for clear thinking.
Such an interest is also a most effective self-pruning tool because the
criticisms deflate wrong and exaggerated ideas we have of ourselves.
The danger of madness from hubris is ever present, particularly in a
more intelligent and competent person. *Quos vult Jupiter perdere,
dementat prius*[80]. The Gods take pleasure in the fall of great men, not
of small ones. Self-pruning is one of the least painful, and one of the
most efficient means to avoid hubris, and to remain highly creative.

Why was Thomas Mann's lack of self-pruning tragic? His uncontrolled hunger for praise and hatred of criticism first blinded him, then
poisoned his relations with his family (in particular, his children) and
lastly, his creative work. Furthermore; his unpruned passion for irony

---

[80] "Those whom Jupiter wishes to destroy, he first makes mad," Euripides, fragment.

vitiated some of his best writings. In his *Recollections* of 1986, Golo Mann—the third child of Thomas[81] who became the most successful German historian of his time—wrote: "[In the years of the First World War] he still managed to radiate kindness, but more often it was silence, severity, irritation or anger. I remember scenes at the table only too well, outburst of temper and brutality" (quoted by Reich-Ranicki, 1989, p. 178). Then, "in a phone conversation, in which the subject was his relation to his father, he told me: 'I wished his death.' This scared me, and I asked him, quite excited: 'Do you know what you just said?' To this, Golo: 'Yes it is so. I wished his death. It was inevitable'" (Reich-Ranicki, 1999, p. 514).

Also, "It remains one of the ironic aspects of Thomas's genius that given the love he lavished on his works, he should sometimes have failed to show it in real life. Konrad Hellen, his secretary for several years, has remarked on his curious relationship with his children, his 'impersonal manner in dealing with them,' the way he wrote about 'their books or articles as though he were criticizing the work of some author entirely unknown to him'"[82] (Hamilton, 1978, p. 354).

As to irony, through it the speaker or writer is in control of listeners or readers.[83] And in many occasions this approach is fine, appropriate to the task at hand. But uncontrolled irony, used too often, especially at the wrong time and place, can ruin the best work of art, as it happened to Thomas Mann, at the crowning episode of his opus magnum *Joseph and his Brothers*[84]: the encounter of Joseph with Pharaoh.

---

[81] Erika, born in 1905; Klaus, 1906; Golo, 1908; Monika, 1909; Elizabeth, 1918; Michael Thomas, 1919.

[82] His first son, Klaus, the novelist, committed suicide in 1949.

[83] We are reminded of the mother of D. H. Lawrence: "Usually the father's physical blustering was no match for the mother's tongue. 'I'llmake you tremble at the sound of my footstep,' he would shout. 'Which boots will you wear?' she replied. 'Never mind which boots I shall wear.' But she had made him ridiculous and taken the wind out of his sails. Young Bert [i.e., DHL] soon learnt to use his tongue to defend himself against physically superior boys at school" (Sagar, 1980, p. 16).

[84] The publication dates of the four volumes in the original German are: 1933, 1934, 1936, 1943.

Possibly taking a lead from Sigmund Freud, Thomas Mann decided, in a brilliant move, that the pharaoh of Joseph was the famous Akhenaton (Amenhotep IV)[85], whom Sigmund Freud saw as the founder of monotheism, a monotheism which an Egyptian Moses[86] then passed on to the Jews.In Mann's novel, Joseph explains the famous dreams of the seven fat and seven lean cows to a most eminent religious reformer and possibly the first monotheist in recorded history, Akhenaton, thereby bringing together two extremely fine minds from different high religious backgrounds: the Jewish and the Egyptian.

Here was a wonderful opportunity for writing a magnificent dialogue on the meaning of life, on destiny and free will, on the nature of God, on good and evil, on the relative merits of two great civilizations—the first with a great past, the second with a great future. But no, Thomas Mann, could not free himself of his irony, he had to make fun of Akhenaton. From the beginning, Mann tells us that Akhenaton is a 17 year-old adolescent, who "looked like an aristocratic young Englishman of somewhat decadent stock,. . . . [whose] legs were not only too short but otherwise out of proportion, the thighs being dis-

---

[85] "Akhenaton (sometimes written Ikhnaton, also known as Amenhotep IV or Amenophis IV), one of the world's great religious reformers, was king of Egypt in the 14th century BC. He reigned for 17 years (1379-1362 BC), during the age of Egypt's imperial power....The religion of the Aton is not completely understood. Akhenaton and Nefertiti worshipped only this sun-god. For them he was 'the sole god'. . . . The king addressed a beautiful hymn to his god, expressing gratitude for the benefits of life. The Aton, says the hymn, gave these blessings not only to the Egyptians but also to 'Syria and Nubia' and to 'all distant foreign countries,' to 'all men, cattle, and wild beasts,' to the lion coming from his den, the fish in the river, and the chick within the egg. Men live when the sun has risen, but at night the dark land is as if dead. It has often been pointed out that this hymn has a remarkable similarity to Psalm 104 in the Bible. Both the hymn and the psalm reflect a common family of ideas, according to which God or the god is praised for his bounties" (Wilson, 1978, pp. 401-02).

[86] For Freud, in his *Moses and Monotheism* of 1937-39: "Among the intimates of Ikhnaton was a man who was perhaps called Thothmes, as many others were at that time; the name does not matter, but its second part must have been '-mose.' He held a high rank and was a convinced adherent of the [new] Aton religion, ..." (1967, pp. 73-74).

tinctly too big while the legs looked almost as thin as a chicken's" (1933-43/1978[87], pp. 932-33).[88]

In addition, Mann decided that the great encounter between Pharaoh and Joseph would take place in front of Akhenaton's mother, Tiy. That in itself would not have been bad, on the contrary, because the experts say that the monotheism of Akhenaton was initiated by his father Amenhotep III, and was shared by his capable wife Tiy who ruled Egypt for several years after her husband death. However, Mann's addiction to irony felt the need to downgrade both Akhenaton's speech to his mother, as if he was a ten years old, and his mother's answers to him, as if she was nothing better than an impatient, nagging and petty housewife. So, for instance, we read the following exchanges between son and mother (my italics):

> Amenhotep worked himself out of the hollow of his chair and sprang to his feet. He strode to his mother's seat, *moving swiftly on those odd limbs of his—the heavy thighs and thin lower parts* showed plainly through the batiste garment. "Mama," he said, "now we have it! My king-dreams are now interpreted to me and I know the truth." Queen Tiy: "Memi, Your Majesty is incorrigible,. . . . you forget the meaning even as you utter it, to get lost in the most remote and impossible speculations. Is that like a mother? I could not even call it fatherly; and *I can scarcely wait until this man here has gone*

---

[87] This is the translation by Helen Lowe-Porter which Thomas Mann labelled an "admirable translation—an achievement of loyalty and devotion" (ib., p. xiii).

[88] It is true that "when artistic inventiveness was encouraged, forms were exaggerated to the point of caricature. Since the young king had a drooping jaw, a scrawny neck, sloping shoulders, a pot belly, and thick thighs, these features were carved in a grotesque way. The shape of the King became the flattering pattern for his followers, so that they also were shown with thin necks and round bellies" (Wilson, 1978, p. 402). Yet, thick thighs do not imply legs which "looked almost as thin as a chicken's." All the representations we have of Akhenaton show him as grown-up man, often together with his wife and his children (he had six of them) praying to the Sun-God who, in turn, blesses him and his family with rays ending in little hands. These are most impressive, highly religious bas-reliefs (e.g. Schlögel, 1986, pp. 58, 96, 160), in which the form of the legs of pharaoh, and of the others with him, totally lose importance in relation to the mystical union of the Pharaonic family with Aton. It takes therefore a most ironic spirit to transform this "world's great religious reformer" into a ridiculous adolescent, as if Mann wanted to give an example of Orace's bon mot *Parturient montes: nascetur ridiculus mus* (Mountains will be in labor, and a ridiculous mouse will be born).

back where he came from and we are alone, to admonish you
indignantly from my maternal throne. . . . You excite yourself,
Memi, and it is not good for Your Majesty's health. You should
rest, after the interpretation [of the dreams]". . . . . But the
King was unwilling. "Mama, You talk like the nurses in my
childhood; when I felt my liveliest, then they said: 'You are
overtired, Lord of the Two Lands, you must go to bed.'*It could*
only make me savage, I could have kicked with rage. . . . . I do
not believe in the realms of fear and the demons and Usiri
with his frightfully named ones and the devourer down there
below. I don't believe in it! Don't believe, don't believe."*Pha-*
raoh sang and trilled, skipping on his misshapen legs, whirling
round with arms outstretched and snapping the fingers of both
hands. After that he was out of breath (pp. 936-957; my italics).

It is funny, no doubt. It is brilliantly ironic in deflating any
grandiose idea we might have harbored about the mighty, revolutionary pharaoh Akhenaton. But, does it correspond to the stated aim of
the author of creating the first "mythical epic in the German language"
(Reich-Ranicki, 1989, p. 38)? Is this really the *grosse Gespräch mit*
Pharao [great conversation with Pharaoh], as Mann wrote in his
Joseph und seine Brüder: Ein Vortrag, 1948, p. 178?

That conversation could have been great, indeed, considering that
"in essence [Akhenaton's] doctrine rejected the universal concept of
idolatry. . . . He proclaimed a new god, unique mysterious, whose
forms could not be known and which were not fashioned by human
hands. The single-minded zealotry with which Akhenaten promoted
the worship of a spirit, self-created daily, and transcendental, in place
of a tangible repository of numinous power, reveal a self-assurance
which has provoked modern critics to class him, and his chief queen
Nefertiti, as religious fanatics; just as their subjects in their day
recognized their exceptional charisma with backs bent low in adora-
tion" (Aldred, 1988, p. 7). Now, instead, the great encounter has been
reduced to funny petty talk, and the great pharaoh to a young spoiled
brat who will soon be admonished by an indignant mother.

A few pages further Thomas Mann applied his irony to beautiful
Nefertiti. Called by Pharaoh, she comes, and for a short while Mann's
description of her dispels the unpleasantness of the previous dialogue.
But, already mid-way in the page describing her beauty and beautiful
dress, everything is turned ugly by Mann's putting thoughts of vomit
in Pharaoh's words to her:

"Was my summons a burden to thee? Art thou at the moment not suffering from thy present sacred condition? My majesty does wrong, perhaps, even to ask; for I might thereby rouse and recall thy nausea with my words. You see how the King has understanding of all. I would have been so grateful to the Father if you had today been able to keep our excellent breakfast by you" (p. 963). Pharaoh may have an "understanding of all," but not Thomas Mann who could have saved the reader from relating the great new god of Akhenaton, the Father [sic], to Nefertiti's keeping in that excellent breakfast.

It is not forbidden to blend the highest ideas with humor. Goethe did it very well in the "Prologue in Heaven" of *Faust*, when he has Mephistopheles say, on departing:

Von Zeit zu Zeit seh ich den Alte gern
Und hüte mich, mit ihm zu brechen.
Es ist gar hübsch von einem grossen Herrn,
So menschlich mit dem Teufel selbst zu sprechen.

[I like to see the Old Man, now and then,
And take good care not to brake off relations.
It's very pleasant of such a great Lord,
to speak so friendly, even with the Devil.]

However Akhenaton is neither a devil, nor a ridiculous mouse. That conversation between Pharaoh and Joseph is a tragedy not only because Thomas Mann missed an extraordinary opportunity to have his characters compare and contrast the best in the Jewish and Egyptian religions, but also because that conversation cast a sense of childishness and futility on the whole book. Why then read the 1200 pages of *Joseph and his Brothers*, if it comes to this?

There was already much irony before, but the reader could still accept and enjoy it. However, in the *"grosse Gespräch mit Pharao"* Thomas Mann went overboard, at a place where he could have easily avoided irony if he had learned to accept, here and there, the pruning of the criticism from relatives, friends and literary experts (especially the latter ones). Any of them could have told him that here he was ruining what could have become his *Divine Comedy*.

However, later in life, also Goethe, before Mann, suffered for lack of self-pruning, as discussed in chapter 5 of volume 1:

As an old man he could still say to his *famulus*, Riemer: "Above all no professionalism. That is against my nature. I want to do everything I can as though it were a game, just as it occurs to me and for as long as the inclination lasts" . . . . This is a somewhat dangerous principle to follow when one is trying to establish a scientific theory of colour, and is abusing all physicists as fools [first of all Newton], which is precisely what Goethe was doing at the time he said this. (Friedenthal, 1965, p. 24).

In that key episode of *Joseph and his Brothers* Thomas Mann seems to have done just that: doing things as though they were a game; only as long as the inclination lasted.

On the subject of Mann's irony, R. J. Hollingdale has written a long chapter, which he began by relating the conclusions that Arthur Koestler drew from his 1937 interview with Thomas Mann:

[The interview seemed to offer] an explanation for a certain aspect of Mann's art which has always puzzled me: I mean the absence of charity. In Mann's universe 'charity is replaced by irony'. Certain episodes in his life—such as his support for the German war of 1914, the alleged tardiness of his break with the Nazi regime, his acceptance of the Goethe Prize from the East German government—were, according to Mr. Koestler, 'symptoms of a bluntness of moral perception, of a defect in ethical sensibility caused by the absence of charitas'.[89] All readers of Mann are struck by his famous 'ironical style' and the distancing effect—the 'absence of charity'—it produces. . . .In the present case: if Mann had suffered from a 'defect in ethical sensitivity' he would have been incapable of treating ethical subjects ironically—irony being, according to the *Concise Oxford Dictionary*, the 'expression of one's meaning by language of opposite or different tendency'. Perhaps one is even justified in concluding that habitual or obsessive employment of irony would be evidence of extreme, even morbidly exaggerated, sensitivity in respect of that about which one is habitually ironical. (p. 76)

If so, does this mean, in the case of Akhenaton, that Mann's habitual employment of irony is evidence of an extreme, even mor-

[89] *The Invisible Writing* (1954), pp. 373-74.

bidly exaggerated, sensitivity? Why not call spade a spade, and speak instead of a bad habit?Also Joseph Brennan, in his *Thomas Mann's World*, dealt with Mann's irony:

> Like so many other concepts which absorb Thomas Mann, irony to him has two aspects. It is at once literary and metaphysical. As a literary device, irony is the principle of objectivity. It is that delicate self-skepticism by which a literary creator prevents himself from taking his own convictions overseriously, thereby alienating the reader by too passionate a subjectivism. It is that which enables a writer to smile down on his own masterpiece, and even to poke kindly fun at his own characters. The *Magic Mountain* is a playground for this stylistic aspect of irony. (p. 171)

However, neither Joseph nor Akhenaton are Mann's characters: they belong to the Bible, to ancient Egypt, to universal culture. A serious writer cannot decide to write a novel on the *Genesis*, assume that the great pharaoh of the dreams is the well known historical figure of Akhenaton, and then proceed with all kinds of meaningless deformations with the help of a nagging Mama, and least so when intending to write Joseph's *grosses Gespräch mit Pharao*.

In Thomas Mann's honor, I have to say that he was unrepentent till the last. At the very end of *Joseph and his Brothers*, when it was the moment to conclude the opus magnum with a page which would summarize his interpretation of that marvelous sequence of significant events, we still encounter his belittling of Pharaoh. Joseph, addressing his brothers, says: "You talk as though you were and want me to forgive you! Am I then as God? Down in Egypt they say I am as Pharaoh and he is called god; but really he is just a sweet pathetic thing" (ib., p. 1207).

A sweet pathetic thing? And this about Akhenaton? What is gained by belittling Pharaoh so much? With my strong love for the division of power, I am definitely on the side of Joseph, and against Pharaoh and his UP, but not in this manner. Instead of a mighty fight between two great thinkers—between the best of two mighty civilizations—we get some fun at the expense of "a sweet pathetic thing."

Having so belittled his opponent, Joseph is left with nothing important to say, and the book ends with not more than this: "Thus he [Joseph] spoke to them and they laughed and wept together and stretched out their hands as he stood among them and touched him, and he too caressed them with his hand. And so endeth the beautiful story and God-invention of JOSEPH AND HIS BROTHERS" (ib., p. 1207). Charming, no doubt, but not inspiring: the penalty for Thomas Mann's lack of self-pruning.

5

Calvino, like Goethe, was a Berlinian *Fox* by being a GAM *Alchemist*[90]

1. Introduction

While reading *Mr. Palomar*, Italo Calvino's last narrative text, of 1983 (he died in 1985), it became evident to me that its protagonist, Mr. Palomar, was as strong a Berlinian *fox* as was Goethe's Faust. Both these stories of Berlinian foxes are the masterwork of *foxes* (and GAM *alchemists)*: Goethe and Calvino, shaped by the same misfortune of father failure, and by a similar assistance (*detours abroad*, as discussed in chapter 6 of volume 1): the French theater for Goethe, and American films for Calvino. The *alchemist* Goethe was discussed in chapter 3 of volume 1. In turn, the present chapter is devoted to the *alchemist* Calvino.

To establish the link between an author and his work, let me say that the experts on Calvino have stressed the strong autobiographical nature of *Mr. Palomar*, for instance, Giulio Ferroni in his *Storia della letteratura italiana—Il Novecento* (1991, p. 586). In turn, Maria Antonietta Morettini-Bura, in her *Linee di storia della letteratura italiana—Il Novecento* went so far as to coin the term "Palomar-Calvino" in her discussion of Calvino (1993, pp. 77, 78).

---

[90] As discussed in chapter 9 of volume 1, while all GAM *alchemists* are Berlinian *foxes*, not all *foxes* are *alchemists*; for instance, GAM *miners* and *trappers* are also *foxes*.

This said, we can move to Calvino's high GxAxM of youth, in which the main M came from his father's failure of character (at least according to his son).

2. Father Failure

The intensity of young Calvino's opposition to his father is evident in his explicit autobiographical text *The Road to San Giovanni* of 1962. Very early in the book he writes:

> The way my father saw things, it was from here up [from their house up to the fields, vineyards, woods] that the world began, while the other part of the world below the house [that of the city of San Remo, on the Ligurian coast] was a mere appendix, necessary sometimes when there were things to be done, but alien and insignificant, to be crossed in great strides, as though in flight, without looking right or left. *But I didn't agree, in fact quite the opposite*: as I saw it, the world, the map of planet, began on the other side of our house and went downwards, everything else being a blank space, with no marks and no meaning; it was down in the town that the signs of the future were to be read, from those streets, those nighttime lights that were not just the streets and lights of our small secluded town, but the town, a glimpse of all possible towns, as its harbour likewise was all the harbours of the continent. . . . The only thing [my father] saw in the world were plants and what ever had to do with plants,. . . . his main passion [was] in farming our San Giovanni estate (1993, pp. 4, 7; my italics)

"Italo Calvino was born on 15 October 1923 in Santiago de Las Vegas, a suburb of Havana, Cuba, where his parents were conducting scientific experiments. His father, Mario, a tropical agronomist and botanist, had spent a number of years in Mexico and other Central American countries. His mother, Eva Mameli-Calvino, a native of the island of Sardinia, was a botanist and also a university professor. . . . Less than two years after their son's birth, the Calvinos returned to Italy and settled permanently in San Remo, Mario's native town. Thus Italo grew up on the Italian Riviera in the midst of nature, dividing his time between his family's Villa Meridiana in San Remo, where his father directed an experimental floriculture station, and their country house in the hills, a small working farm where the elder Calvino pioneered in the growing of grapefruit and avocados" (Weiss, 1993, p. 2). However, from what Calvino reported himself, most of his time, definitely all the time he was allowed to be himself, was neither spent in the Villa nor working in the paternal farm at San Giovanni, but down at San Remo, especially in its cinemas.

3. Father and Son

Talking to each other was difficult. Both verbose by nature, possessed of an ocean of words, in each other's presence we became mute, would walk in silence side by side along the road to San Giovanni. . . . This [paternal] impatience, this intolerance at finding himself anywhere but on his own land, would sometimes seize him halfway through the day,. . . . The nearer we go to San Giovanni, the more my father would be overcome by a new tension. . . . His urgency to cancel out everything in his life that was not San Giovanni, and at the same time a feeling that since San Giovanni was not the whole world but merely a corner of the world besieged by the rest, it would always spell despair for him. . . . He would immediately be oppressed again by reminders that all was precarious and beset by dangers and once more the fury was upon him. And one of these reminders was myself, the fact that I belonged to that other world, the painful awareness that he couldn't count on his children to consolidate this ideal San Giovanni civilization of his, which thus had no future. . . *And me? I imagined my mind was elsewhere. What was nature? Grass, plants, green places, animals. I lived in the midst of it and wanted to be elsewhere.* (Calvino, ib.,pp. 10, 18, 24-25, 32-33; my italics)

Many things went wrong between the two. How much of it was fault of the father? A lot, from the way Calvino remembered it; and the same applies to Goethe's recollections of his father. However at times, there are unsurmountable differences of personality rooted in biology (the G of genetic endowment) or in birth order.[91]

---

[91] Italo was the first of two boys, four years older than his brother Florio. This condition is reflected in Calvino's novel *The Baron in the Trees*, where the main character, the young Baron Cosimo, is four years older than his brother Biagio. As discussed in chapter 5 of volume 1, the eldest child, in general, reacts more strongly than the other siblings against any form of paternal domination. Similarly, Goethe was a first born, followed, one year later, by his sister Cornelia.

Calvino's mother also played a role; not in opposition to the father as was the case with Goethe, but as his ally, thereby reinforcing the oppression (real or perceived):

> But immediately my mother came to wake us [Italo and his brother] up again. "Get up, get up, it's late. Dad went ages ago!" and she would open the window onto the palm trees rustling in the morning wind, pull the bedclothes off us, "Get up, get up. Dad's waiting for you to carry the baskets!". . . .She never left the garden where every plant was labelled, the house swathe in bougainvilleas, the study with its herbariums and the microscope under the glass dome. Always sure of herself, methodical, she transformed passion into duties and lived on those. (ib., pp. 14-16)

Those "duties" extended to restricting the boy in his greatest passion: the cinema.

4. Calvino's Fascination with the Cinema

> There were years when I went to the cinema almost every day and maybe twice a day, and those were the years between '36 and the war, the years of my adolescence. It was a time when the cinema became the world for me. A different world from the one around me, but my feeling was that only what I saw on the screen possessed the properties required of a world, the fullness, the necessity, the coherence, while away from the screen were only heterogeneous elements lumped together at random, the materials of a life, mine, which seemed to me utterly formless. . . . I would go to the cinema in the afternoon, slipping out of the house on the sly, or with the excuse that I was going to study with some friend or other. . . . The proof of my passion was my determination to get into the theater as soon as it opened, at two. . . . I'm talking about the films I saw between, let's say, between thirteen and eighteen years old, when the cinema engrossed me to an extent far beyond anything that came before or after. (ib., pp. 37-39, 41)[92]

---

[92]Also, "my memories are those of one who discovered the cinema in adolescence: I had been kept under tight rein as a child; for as long as she could, my mother tried to keep me from any dealings with the world that didn't have a planned and obvious purpose; when I was a small boy she rarely took me to the cinemas, and then only for films that she felt were 'suitable' or 'instructive.'" (ib., p. 41).

5. Creative Detours Abroad

First Calvino, then Goethe:

> The Italian films of the time, might just as well not have been. And if I don't mention them here, despite having seen and still remembering almost all there were, it's because, for better or worse, they made so little impression, and hence there is simply no place for them in an essay presenting the cinema as another dimension of the world. In my determination to see as many American films as I could, there was more than a little of the collector's doggedness, so that every role played by an actor or actress was like a postage stamp in some series I was gradually sticking down in the album of my memory, painstakingly filling in the gaps. (ib., pp. 54-55)

In Goethe's equivalent recollections:

> My passion for the French theater grew with every performance. I did not miss an evening; though on every occasion, when after the play, I sat down with the family to supper— often putting up with the remains—I had to endure my father's constant reproaches, that theatres were useless, and would lead to nothing. . . . I had soon exhausted the whole range of the French stage; several plays were performed for the third and fourth time; and all had passed before my eyes and mind, from the stateliest tragedy to the most frivolous afterpiece; and as when a child I had presumed to imitate Terence, I did not fail now as a boy, on a much more inciting occasion, to copy the French forms to the best of my ability and want of ability. . . . [Shortly after he was reading the texts:] I had perseverance enough this time to work through the whole of Racine and Molière and a great part of Corneille. (1811-22/1971, pp. 108, 111)

However, Calvino's detour abroad was abruptly brought to an end, not by his parents, but by the UP of the Mussolini regime:

> Of course, when compared with all the other prohibitions and obligations that fascism had imposed, and the even tougher ones it was now imposing in those prewar years and would later impose during the war, the banning of American films

[around 1938] was a minor, even minimal deprivation, and I was not so foolish as not to appreciate this: but it was the first to strike directly at me, who knew no other regime than fascism, nor had felt any needs other than those that the world I lived in had been able to prompt and satisfy. It was the first time that a right I enjoyed had been taken away from me: more than a right, a dimension, a world, a mental space; and I experienced this loss as a cruel oppression, one which contained within it all the forms of oppression that I knew about only from hearsay or from having seen others suffer. (ib., p. 58)

This too was a misfortune of youth, and an important one, which contributed to the making of the *challenged personality* of Calvino.

6. Chameleon Calvino, Chameleon Goethe

In her discussion of Calvino, Morettini-Bura wrote: *"Ma la sua natura camaleontica, scoiattolesca spinge Calvino a nuove sperimentazioni."* [Yet, Calvino's chameleonic, squirrelly, nature pushes him to new experimentations] (1993, p. 75).

Frau Herder had said the same of Goethe (as reported in chapter 9 of volume 1): "He is almost like a chameleon, sometimes I quite like him, sometimes only half" (quoted by Hume Brown, 1920/1971, p. 396). To this, Hume Brown had added in a footnote "Goethe more than once applies this expression to himself." And I would add: A fox is not a chameleon, yet its successful search for many things is predicated on forms of disguise and adaptation to many environment which can be called chameleonic.

Fascinating, too, that in an interview given to Giulio Nascinbeni a few months before his death, Calvino said: "I do not know, in the end, if there is a unitary sense in all that I have done" (quoted by Morettini-Bura, 1993, p. 75). This comment applies to most foxes, probably even to Goethe.

7. Maître Renard Goethe

Expanding on the above, and in addition to what I said in volume 1, let me report three *fox* aspects of Goethe, *Maître Renard des Renards*.

- During the [1793] campaign in France he came, by what he calls a "strange dispensation," on a copy of a book which had interested him since his early youth. It was the well-known beast-fable of the Middle Ages, *Reineke Fuchs [Reynard the Fox]*, which recounts how the fox by his inexhaustible wiles triumphed over his enemies and became chief minister at the Court of King Lion. . . . [Goethe translated the fable anew]. His rendering was something between a "translation and a recasting," and was executed with a gusto which we do not feel in his original work of the same period. . . .[93] The translation of *Reineke Fuchs* had immediate and permanent success. . . . By Goethe himself, too, it was always regarded with special satisfaction , and there is none of his writings which he was more frequently in the habit of quoting. (Hume Brown, 1920/1971, pp. 436-37).[94]

---

[93] "The fable had been fashioned by medieval monks, with their own cause secretly in mind: the head, the intelligence, is what matters, not brute force. Reynard with his cunning proves himself the master, superior to all heraldic and noble beasts, to the wolf, the bear and the noble but foolish lion, their king. He triumphs even in combat and solemn ordeal with his enemy Isegrim, who relies solely on the weapon of his teeth, and he triumphs through cunning: he shaves himself and rubs grease on to make himself more slippery, uses his tail to beat dust into his enemy's face and blind him, seizes him from below by his genitals and tugs at him until the wolf rolls bleeding in his own excrement. Reynard has triumphed and all his many crimes are forgotten" (Friedenthal, 1965, p. 318).

[94] Not only *Similia similibus curantur* ("The like cures the same" as discussed in chapter 10 of volume 2, where I said that nobody appreciates the work of a *miner* better than another *miner*), but *Similia similibus amantur* ("The like loves the like"). This is particularly evident in Goethe, not only for his fascination with the old story of *Reynard the Fox*, but for his great love of the works of the *Berlinian fox* Shakespeare (mentioned in chapter 6 of volume 1). To this, let me add the nearly fifty pages in Goethe's *Wilhelm Meister's Apprenticeship* devoted to the staging of *Hamlet*. There we can read for instance that "In deference to Wilhelm's love for Shakespeare, their conversation soon turned to that author. He assured Serlo that he looked with the fondest hopes to the epoch which would arise in Germany from his incomparable productions, and he soon introduced the character of Hamlet, with which he had been much occupied of late" (1795-96/1898, p. 225). Wilhelm not only played the role of Hamlet, but before "had been for some time engaged in the translation of *Hamlet*. . . . As soon as he had completed his task, he read it over to Serlo and the other members of the company. They expressed themselves delighted, and Serlo indulged in many complimentary observations. . . . The curtain fell; and tumults of applause resounded from all parts of the house. The four royal corpses sprang up and joyfully embraced each other.... The audience would not permit any other play to be spoken of, but loudly required that the present piece to be repeated" (ib., pp. 276-77, 300).

- Goethe's lovely home at the Frauenplan in Weimar houses his art collection consisting of 26,511 pieces (from Schuchardt's inventory). In addition there are about 22,000 items in the science collection, of which more than 18,000 are mineral and rock specimens. Already in 1803 he owned a collection of over 1,400 casts of ancient coins which, together with an original set of Papal coins and medals of the Renaissance, formed the basis of a new numismatic collection of his own, purchased specifically as a "talisman to transport me comfortably and attractively, to remote places and times". (Boyle, 2000, p. 736)

Only a master fox could lovingly assemble so much first class material. [95]

- Until the very last days of his life he maintains an active interest in every part of his universe, in natural science, mineralogy, even in astronomy, with which, hitherto, he has hardly concerned himself. He sends a note to the observatory in Jena telling them to make preparations for observing the comet that is expected in 1834. (Friedenthal, 1965, p. 525)

However, so many *fox* activities came at a price. This is true, for instance, of *Wilhelm Meisters Lehrjahre* which Goethe was developing "into a kind of last will and testament, with the same mixture of wisdom and disorder as the *Works* [the first forty volumes of his writings]. [However] The colourful and varied life, which made the first Meister novel so rich, is completely excluded from the *Wanderjahre* that the novel becomes deliberately grey, colourless and, in many parts, dark and sombre. With the 'wandering' of its title the book has little to do, or at any rate not in the romantic sense extolled in the *Wanderlieder* of the day. Goethe's characters move about and the scene changes, but all trace of naturalness, of high spirits, of freedom to roam from place to place is denied them. . . . Maxims, reflections, and poems are scattered throughout the book. Goethe has lost all interest in his earlier characters" (Friedenthal,1965, pp. 486-87).

---

[95] A visit to the Frauenplan, now the "Goethe National Museum", is fascinating and impressive. For those unable to go in person, I recommend either the small *Goethe und sein Haus am Frauenplan* by Jericke (1964), or the rich and impressive *Goethe-Museum* (715 pages, large format; 52 plates in color, and 505 black and white) by Holtzhauer (1969).

Hume Brown had similar comments: *Wilhelm Meisters Lehrjahre* "is not a work of art, in which the parts are organically connected and rightly proportioned in view of a finished whole. . . . We read on and have not even clearly borne in upon us in what Wilhelm's apprenticeship consists. . . . In making Wilhelm the characterless figure he is, however seriously marred the interest of the tale. Wilhelm von Humboldt called him 'an insignificant and senseless creature', and he has the general opinion with him. . . . From its first appearance the book has failed to find wide acceptance either in Germany or elsewhere" (1920/1971, pp. 685-88, 691).

8. Maître Renard Calvino

In the words of Beno Weiss,

> Palomar observes his lawn, the stars, lizards, turtles, a topless bather on the beach, visits a Parisian cheese shop, goes to the zoo. But, similar to ever-changing waves which seem to come either from shore or from the sea, like Calvino he too typically continues to provide suggestions without arriving at definite answers. . . . Indeed, when from the vantage point of his Roman terrace Mr. Palomar tries to conceive the world as it is seen by birds, he arrives at the conclusion that "*it is only after you have come to know the surface of things,. . . . that you can venture to seek what is underneath. But the surface of things is inexhaustible.*" (1993, pp. 211-12)

There is an almost deliberate absence of psychological elements in Calvino's writings, as the author has stated, he was "not attracted to psychology, to the analysis of feelings, or to introspection": what interested him more was *the "whole mosaic in which man is set,* the interplay of relationships." (ib., p. 205)

"The idea of infinite contemporary universes in which *all possibilities are realized in all possible combinations*" is one of the bases of what Calvino calls the "hypernovel" and which he put into practice when he wrote *If on a Winter's Night a Traveller* in 1979. (ib., p. 167; my italics).

We have here, in a nut shell, the Decalogue of the "*fox* novelist." Clearly, the two, Calvino and Goethe, are different. Yet, the similarities, for causes and results, can be both instructive and fascinating because *foxes* are fascinating beings, more so (*sed magis amica veritas [but dearer still is truth]*) than the *hedgehogs.*

6

GAM *Trappers* Military Commanders

1. Introduction

Back in the early 1980s, I had written that "The *trapper* [high GxAxM, in which the M is the misfortune of insulting illegitimate birth[96]] has had the insulting glove thrown in his face, asking him to prove his identity. He is supposed to have none, none valid. He is supposed to be vile as his birth was. But many *trappers* will catch the glove and hurl it back with tremendous force and cunning. War, politics, and the arts are activities favored by *trappers,* and in which they often succeed."

Focusing on eminent, illegitimately-born military commanders, I listed: David Beatty, Cesare Borgia, the two Don Juan of Austria (the first the son of Emperor Charles V, the second the son of King Philip IV), Alexander Hamilton, Jephthah, Lawrence of Arabia, Federico da Montefeltro, Francisco Pizarro, Shaka, Francesco Sforza, William the Conqueror. Later I added the names of James Fitzjames duke of Berwick, Vladimir I, Thutmoses III, and—with two grains of salt— Leonardo da Vinci: *inventor of war engines and military engineer.*

---

[96] Obviously, an illegitimate child raised where nobody knows of his unfortunate birth, or nobody cares, will not become a *trapper*, or only within the limits that this knowledge bothers him in his vision of himself or for fear that his condition will be discovered (for instance for an important public position, or by the parents of the girl he wants to marry). However, most often in the past, the insults were there from stepsiblings and other relatives, from schoolmates and playmates, and from laws, rules and scripts, which penalize the bastard.

In a biography of the last shogun, Tokugawa Yoshinobu, I found him criticized for lacking the military virtues of the bastards, proof that the same misfortunes evoke similar personality results all over the world. In what follows, from Ryotaro Shiba, Yoshinobu is called Keiki, the name he hadbefore becoming shogun:

"I want no part of it," [Keiki] announced. Surprised, Hiraoka understood in a flash of insight that Keiki was disabled by an utter lack of ambition, the result perhaps of his aristocratic upbringing. *Men of similar background who were the illegitimate offspring of a powerful man's concubine tended to harbor strong [military and political] ambition*, but Keiki had been born to his father's official wife. As an aristocrat of impeccable standing, he had always been accorded certain privileges, which he took for granted, so he had none of the common man's desire for self-betterment, nor any apparent need for it either. (1998, pp. 41-42; my italics)

After this Japanese introduction we can move to two *trappers* about whom we know a little more: Jephthah, the Israelite and Alexander Hamilton, the American.

2. Jephthah

In Judges 11 of the *Authorized (King James) Version* of the Bible we read:

Now Jephthah the Gileadite was a mighty man of valour, and he was the son of an harlot: and Gilead begat Jephthah. And Gilead's wife bare him sons; and his wife's sons grew up, and they thrust out Jephthah, and said unto him, Thou shalt not inherit in our father's house; for thou art the son of a strange woman. Then Jephthah fled from his brethren, and dwelt in the land of Tob: and there were gathered vain men to Jephthah, and went out with him.

And it came to pass in process of time, that the children of Ammon made war against Israel. And it was so, that when the children of Ammon made war against Israel, the elders of Gilead went to fetch Jephthah out of the land of Tob: and they said unto Jephthah, Come, and be our captain, that we may fight with the children of Ammon. And Jephthah said unto the elders of Gilead, Did not ye hate me, and expel me out of my father's house? and why are ye come unto me now when ye are in distress? And the elders of Gilead said unto Jephthah, Therefore we turn again to thee now, that thou mayest go with us, and fight against the children of Ammon, and be our head over all the inhabitants of Gilead. And Jephthah said unto the elders of Gilead, If ye bring me home again to fight against the children of Ammon, and the LORD deliver them before me, shall I be your head? And the elders of Gilead said unto Jephthah, The LORD be witness between us, if we do not so according to thy words. Then Jephthah went with the elders of Gilead, and the people made him head and captain over them: and Jephthah uttered all his words before the LORD in Mizpeh. . . .

And Jephthah vowed a vow unto the LORD, and said, If thou shalt without fail deliver the children of Ammon into mine hands, then it shall be, that whatsoever cometh forth of the doors of my house to meet me, when I return in peace from the children of Ammon, shall surely be the LORD's, and I will offer it up for a burnt offering. So Jephthah passed over unto the children of Ammon to fight against them; and the LORD delivered them into his hands. And he mote them from Aroer, even till thou come to Minnith, even twenty cities, and unto the plain of the vineyards, with a very great slaughter. Thus the children of Ammon were subdued before the children of Israel. . . .

And Jephthah came to Mizpeh unto his house, and, behold, his daughter came out to meet him with timbrels and with dances: and she was his only child; beside her he had neither son nor daughter. And it came to pass, when he saw her, that he rent his clothes, and said, Alas, my daughter! thou hast brought me very low, and thou art one of them that trouble me: for I have opened my mouth unto the LORD, and I cannot go back. And she said unto him, My father, if thou hast opened thy mouth unto the LORD, do to me according to that which hath proceeded out of they mouth; forasmuch as the LORD hath taken vengeance for thee of thine enemies, even of the children of Ammon. And she said unto her father, Let this thing be done for me: let me alone two months, that I may go up and down upon the mountains, and bewail my virginity, I and my fellows. And he said, Go. (v. 1-38)

No doubt, Jephthah knew reasonably well what he was doing when he promised that "whatsoever cometh forth of the doors of my house to meet me, when I return in peace from the children of Ammon, shall surely be the LORD's, and I will offer it up for a burnt offering." Would the Lord have given him victory in exchange for a cat or dog, or a lowly servant? Probably not. Jephthah wanted victory, at any cost, not because of the children of Ammon who did not disturb him, but because of his half-brothers. So he knew that there was a price to be paid for getting his vengeance. He may have hoped to trick the Lord in sending him, forth of the doors, something of low value upon his return, but he cannot have truly believed in such a piece of luck.[97]

There is also no doubt, that the elders of Gilead asked Jephthah to lead them in war against the children of Ammon because he had given ample proof of his military talents, the result of having had to fend for himself when his brothers had thrown him out. Alone in the wilderness, he had to learn its harsh laws. He could not be a refined Keiki: that luxury was not permitted to him.

Yes, the *trapper* can avenge himself through the arts or science; however, he will be applauded only if the public, patrons or critics do so voluntarily. The military commander, instead, has the ultimate power. His is the sort of victory nobody can deny. Through the power of arms, the *trapper* can say, as Brennus did in 390 B.C.: *Vae victis*, (Woe to the vanquished). The victor in battle has shown courage and talent, he cannot be vile.

Most trappers will not be thrown out of the family, as happened to Jephthah, yet they know that the people around them would like them dead, the sooner the better. If that is so, if life has been rendered so dirty by the insults of "bastard," then life is not so much an absolute value, but something dispensable. War, indeed, is the game in which life is dispensable at any moment: a game at which the clever ones

---

[97] We are reminded of poor Iphigenia, the eldest daughter of Agamemnon and Clytemnestra, who was sacrificed by her father in order to gain favorable winds for the Greek fleet on its way to Troy. Those were difficult times for women, daughters in particular.

come out alive and victorious. In addition, war is the game where one can avenge oneself against mankind, and yet be applauded for winning. Not romantic, with no illusions, *trappers* can wage war efficiently and cold-bloodedly.

3. Alexander Hamilton

The following short text on Hamilton, by Alexander De Conde, tells of the important place he holds in the history of the United States, of his misfortune of illegitimate birth, and of his personality which was so different from that of the other Founding Fathers:[98]

> Alexander Hamilton, publicist, politician, and first secretary of the treasury of the United States under George Washington, the first president, was the foremost champion of a strong central government for the newly united former colonies. As treasury secretary, he created the Bank of the United States, secured the nation's credit both at home and abroad, and established a national currency. . . . Although he came from good stock, Alexander Hamilton from his earliest years was sensitive to the fact that he was illegitimate. . . . Unlike Benjamin Franklin or Thomas Jefferson, he did not have a broad inquisitive mind nor was he speculative in his thinking in the philosophical sense of seeking intangible truths. He was ambitious, purposeful, a hard worker, and one of America's administrative geniuses. In foreign policy had was a realist, believing that self-interest should be the nation's polestar; questions of gratitude, benevolence, and moral principle, he held, were irrelevant. (1978, pp. 584, 588).

Moving further in our understanding of his misfortune of youth, and its "military consequences":

> John Adams called him "the bastard brat of a Scots peddlar." Uncharitable as one might expect of an Adams, but a charac-

---

[98] Richard Morris (1973) lists Hamilton among the seven founding fathers of the USA in his *Seven who Shaped our Destiny: The Founding Fathers as Revolutionaries*; the other six were: Benjamin Franklin, George Washington, John Adams, Thomas Jefferson, John Jay, and James Madison.

terization aimed right at the jugular. Alexander Hamilton's illegitimacy was not a matter of spurious conjecture; its ugly truth was embalmed in the court record. The humiliating circumstances of his origins, childhood, and early poverty left galling memories[99], memories effaced only by romanticizing the past[100], establishing respectable credentials in the present, and feeding one's cyclonic ambitions for the future. . . .

The real debt Hamilton owed his father he never could have acknowledged. *The stain of illegitimacy and poverty that James Hamilton had left on the family name could be effaced only by illustrious achievement, and Hamilton from boyhood was an overachiever,* one who found it necessary to more than compensate for his feelings of inadequacy. A dreamer, irked at the unglamorous clerkship that was his lot, he became competitive, audacious, and exceedingly ambitious. Anxiety over family and money, combined with resentment over the stigma of bastardy that he was forced to bear, made him enormously concerned about his reputation above all else, a concern which was to prove his ultimate undoing. . . .

It was characteristic of Hamilton that throughout his life he was wont to prefer military solutions to political ones in times of emergency, whether it was to satisfy the officers and public creditors in 1783, or to put down the wretched whiskey insurrectionaries a decade later, or to settle differences with France arising during President Adams's administration. In fact,

---

[99] "Writers have contended that, in the licentious society of the Leeward Islands, the Hamilton-Rachel liaison was so completely regarded as a matter of course that Alexander had no reason to be sensitive about his illegitimacy. This is contradicted by every piece of legal evidence that survives. The court records of St. Croix, indeed, reveal what seems today an almost unbelievably brutal attitude towards Rachel and her 'obscene' children. Considering the standard cruelty of small boys to each other, it follows that little Alexander was on the streets an object of public mockery. That this was indeed so is copiously testified to by Hamilton's behavior after he grew up" (Flexner, 1978, pp. 27, 29).

[100] "Had his statement been factual, had Hamilton possessed an adoring and admirable mother, his character and career would certainly have been very different. A mother's betrayal is the worst blow a child can receive. 'You know,' Hamilton wrote his friend John Laurens in 1788, 'the opinion I entertain of mankind . . . .' Hamilton's low opinion of mankind, his aloofness, his inability to feel with his fellowmen, was to be the great statesman's Achilles' heel" (Flexner, 1978, p. 27).

his admiration for Julius Caesar continued throughout his life. (Morris, 1973, pp. 221-224; my italics to highlight the kind of drive that must also have been behind those illegitimate off-spring of a powerful man's concubine discussed by Ryotaro Shiba, 1998)

Expanding on the military side:

Hamilton's delight in military action became the driving passion of his life. In time this was to frighten many of his adversaries: John Adams, in a slighting reference to his size, his appearance and his unabashed hunger for battlefield glory, referred to him as "The Bloody Buoy." Some historians agreed with Thomas Jefferson, who saw in him a Caesar manqué, too eager for combat, with a hidden urge to govern by the sword. . . . Not only were his manners martial—he always moved and stood just like a soldier—so were the patterns of his mind. Military standards were in part his standards, by which he judged other people and himself. (Emery, 1982, p. 33)

On Friday, July 13, 1804, "the following paragraph appeared in James Cheetham's *American Citizen*: 'Death has sealed the eloquent lips of GENERAL HAMILTON! . . . . As soon as our feelings will permit, we shall notice this deplorable event, this national loss [the duel in which Burr cut Hamilton down with his first shot]'" (Fleming, 1999, p. 336). "In 1804 everyone called Alexander Hamilton 'General.' He was even accorded the title in the New York City directory. A lieutenant colonel in the American Revolution, Hamilton had achieved this new rank in America's first undeclared war, the nasty brawl with revolutionary France that lasted from 1798 to 1800. All the shooting had been done at sea; General Hamilton's army never fought a battle. But he was extremely proud of achieving this rank and virtually insisted on preserving it as a civilian" (ib., pp. 2-3).

4. Conclusion

Similar misfortunes seem indeed to stimulate the development of similar personalities, across historical and cultural lines. This said, each case is different on many aspect, and must be studied separately.

Not all *trappers* will become military commanders; and, obviously, not every military commander is a *trapper*. Yet there is something special about the misfortune of suffered illegitimacy.[101]

---

[101] For lack of A (possibly also a limited G, but we will never really know), Timofey, the illegitimate son of Tolstoy by Aksinya Bazykina remained an illiterate serf (*). Also, for lack of insult, illegitimacy did not affect badly the composer Aleksandr Borodin, as discussed by Serge Dianin (1963).

As usual it depends, but a "depends" that can be understood, and forecast should the opportunity arise.

(*) "It is worth remembering that while Tolstoy attacked Turgenev for the faulty upbringing of his daughter—his illegitimate daughter, whom he acknowledged to all the world and on whom he lavished infinite care—he Tolstoy, had at Yasnaya a three-year-old son *by his peasant mistress Aksinya whom he did not acknowledge publicly and on whom he lavished no care at all: a little boy who was to grow up to be a coachman* on the Tolstoy estate" (Crankshaw, 1974/1986, p. 120; my italics).

7

Why Berlinian *Fox* or *Hedgehog*?

This chapter is a complement to chapter 9 of volume 1 "GAM's *Hedghogs* and GAM's *Foxes*" in which the difference between the two, and those that are neither one nor the other, is discussed in terms of script formation. There are indeed several versions of scripts formation of youth, the principal ones being: A. regular, B. independent-refusal, and C. independent-vacuum.

A. Regular, in which the child accepts and adopts parental scripts.

With capable and loving parents, the child has no reason to refuse what parents say on a long list of subjects, such as truth, honesty, love, religion, science, sexual relations, morality, work ethic, and so on. This does not mean that the child will evolve into a mirror image of his parents; there still remain the results of inevitable differences in intelligence, temperament, SES (higher or lower), culture, and sibling interaction. However, when compared with challenged personalities, there is a definite continuity of scripts, so much so that we can often say that the resulting personality is either a *mild hedgehog* (giving priority to the strongest adopted scripts), or a *mild fox* (in search of new experiences but never too far away from received scripts). Accordingly, most GAM *dedicated personalities* are *mild hedgehogs* or—in rare cases—*very mild foxes* (they will definitely not evolve into Berlinian *hedgehogs* or *foxes*).

Dedicated personalities (mild hedgehogs) can be great scientists in all areas, whose explorations will not raise problems with their received scripts. Two examples are Louis Pasteur and Max Planck. Pasteur was a chemist and microbiologist who proved that microorganisms cause fermentation and disease; among other notable achievements, he originated the process known as pasteurization. Max Planck was a theoretical physicist who originated quantum theory. He formulated the correct mathematical description of thermal radiation from a perfect absorber (blackbody) and showed that the formulation required a discontinuous process of emission or absorption involving discrete quantities of energy. Both Pasteur and Plank were *mild hedgehogs*.

B. Independent-Refusal, in which the child rejects/refuses to adopt parental scripts, and is guided by misfortune in the build-up of new scripts.

There is a long list of misfortunes of youth that will lead a child to reject many parental scrips as false, wrong, or even evil. In this category we have the personalities discussed in chapter 9 who became *foxes*: for instance *alchemists* (from father or mother failure), *brewers* (from father/mother incompatibility), *miners* (from lack of parental love), and *trappers* (from suffered illegitimate birth).

If we focus for a moment on the youth of Leonardo da Vinci, what respect should he have had for the scripts of his father, and his father's wives?

The enigma of Leonardo begins with his birth. He was the illegitimate child of a woman about whom almost nothing is known—neither her surname nor her age, appearance, intelligence or education. As a rule biographers call her a peasant girl and let it go at that; in Vinci the tradition is that she was a barmaid. She is known only as Caterina. . . . Leonardo was duly acknowledged by his father, even baptized in his presence and that of several other members of the family. He was not, however, taken immediately into the household. Soon after his birth he was sent with Caterina, to a peasant's home in the nearby village of Anchiano. He remained there for perhaps four years, during which Ser Piero married the first of his series of wives, a 16-year-old girl of higher social standing than Leonardo's mother. The young wife was barren. Possibly for that reason Leonardo was admitted to the Vinci house, to live with his grandparents, uncle, father and stepmother, at some time before he was five. The tax records for 1457 [when Leonardo was five] locate him there as *figlio di Piero illegitimo*. (Wallace, 1967, pp. 9-10)

Under these conditions, what would Leonardo think when his father or stepmother spoke of fatherhood and motherhood, of marriage, of baptism, of God, of the Ten Commandments? He had enough personal reasons not to believe them. Among others, he may have felt that if his stepmother(s) had borne a child, he would have remained illiterate, a poor farm hand, not called to live with Ser Piero and receive an education. And his mother? Who took care of her? Was she only a body for Ser Piero's pleasure? And he, Leonardo, who was he? *Figlio di Piero illegitimo* was the official answer. Is there any honesty in this?

The consequence is a steady refusal of parental scripts and of many societal scripts, together with doubts on the pertaining epistemology and ontology. All those highfaluting notions were tainted. What remained was "the reality in the process of life and the present moment" (Kennedy, 1963, p. 15). What remained was the rich life unrestricted by abstractions, and this may even include the design of non-conventional buildings:

In nonchurch architecture, Leonardo's fastidious nature, although not his interest in the activity itself, led him to design the most secular of buildings: a bawdyhouse. His constant wandering in search of beautiful, grotesque or corrupt faces evidently led him into Milan's red-light district, where he observed that the customary, haphazard plans of bordellos left much to be desired. In consequence, he designed a house with right-angled corridors and three separate entrances, so that the clientele could come and go with smaller risk of embarrassing meetings. (Wallace, 1967, p. 79)

Leonardo was a Berlinian *fox* with all the plusses and all the minuses of the *foxes*:

[His] name has become legendary, a synonym for greatness and for universal genius. And no wonder, for the man who bore it was proficient in almost every area of intellectual and cultural endeavor—in mathematics and geometry; in physics, engineering, anatomy, geology, botany, and geography; in music, sculpture, architecture, and not the least in painting....[However] he was called 'capricious and fickle,' and complaints about his unreliability and dilatoriness were commonplace in his own day. Lodovico Sforza, duke of Milan, who hired Leonardo to cast a bronze equestrian statue, wrote to Lorenzo de' Medici in Florence asking that Lorenzo send him one or two masters to execute the work, because it did not seem to him that Leonardo would ever finish it. And, years later in Rome, Pope Leo X became so exasperated with Leonardo that he was moved to say: 'Alas, this man will do nothing; he starts by thinking of the end of the work before its beginning'" (Wasserman, 1984, p. 7).

Yes, the fox has so many things that interest him, that the completion of existing tasks is unimportant, boring and useless.

C. Independent-Vacuum, for lack of parental input, yet guided by the misfortune of youth.

In the case of parental death or extended parental absence, by one or both parents, the child is not provided with the constant, cumulative, and natural presentation of parental scripts. The child does not hear the parent's comments, admonitions, criticisms or plain information about everything under the sun.

From the moment of birth, parents are the "normal", "fully authorized" source of all norms. Even Klee, discussed in the Appendix of chapter 1 of this volume, said: "For a long time, I trusted my Papa implicitly and regarded his words (Papa can do anything) as pure truth" (Klee, 1965, p. 4). Annemarie, the daughter of General Colin Powell wrote in a book on fathers and daughters by the photographer Mariana Cook: "Dad is the smartest person I have ever known. He always wins at Trivial Pursuit. He's always been frank with me when it was necessary. He looks great in a tux or his dress blues. His successes never surprise me; they just make me proud" (Powell, 1995, pp. 217-218).

Nothing can replace a father and mother for script transmission. All other sources are weak in comparison. Eliminate one or both, and the transmission of scripts is much reduced, particularly in children with high GxA.[102] These children can quickly detect what is not genuine in other people's scripts, especially teachers and ministers.

In the absence of the steady learning of scripts from both parents, the challenged youth will build his/her own from the sources available to him/her: books, other relatives, family friends, priests/pastors/rabbis other religious teachers, friends, etc. This learning, contrary to that of the *foxes*, will be guided (obviously up to a point) by the nature of the misfortune which caused the death or long parental absence, as discussed in chapter 9 of volume 1. Basically, the high GxAxM youth so affected has constantly his misfortune in mind. Why did father or mother or both die so early?

It is this kind of question which will guide the choice of books to read, which will make some important and others not. It is this kind of questions which will guide the selection of friends (few of them) and the build-up of a special style of friendship. Gradually things will crystallize, they will specialize, and give birth to the Archilochian "*hedgehog* who knows one big thing."

Jean Piaget[103]

The case of the *hedgehog* GAM *universalist* Piaget is important on two accounts, first he did not suffer of the misfortune of early parental death but of "indirect parental (mother and father) absence", second he told us (as reported in chapter 1) the essential lines of his personality development. Hereafter I report once more what he said:

---

[102] Let me repeat, that everything here refers to youth with a high GxA. An average GxA would be insufficient. In the case of Leonardo, Catherine Cox reported IQs AI of 155, and AII of 180 (*), and the assistance he received in Ser Piero's house must have been of good quality. Left as an illiterate peasant his high IQ would still have been very useful but in a very limited domain; similarly the good assistance in Ser Piero's house would have given limited results if his IQ had been around 100.

(*) AI refers to the IQ estimate in childhood and early youth; AII refers to the first period of young adulthood.

[103] Swiss psychologist (1896-1980) "who was the first to make a systematic study of the acquisition of understanding in children. He is thought by many to have been the major figure in 20th-century developmental psychology" (*Encyclopaedia Britannica*, 2002, p. 416).

My mother was very intelligent, energetic, and fundamentally a very kind person; her rather neurotic temperament, however, made our family life somewhat troublesome. One of the direct consequences of this situation was that I started to forego playing for serious work very early; this I obviously did as much to imitate my father as to take refuge in both a private and non-fictitious world. Indeed, I have always detested any departure from reality, an attitude which I relate to the second important influential factor of my early life, viz., my mother's poor mental health; it was the disturbing factor which at the beginning of my studies in psychology made me intensely interested in questions of psychoanalysis and pathological psychology. (1952, pp. 237-8).

Besides an obvious high G, there were first class assistances. As said above, his mother was very intelligent, energetic, and fundamentally a very kind person. On his father: "[He] has devoted his writing mostly to medieval literature, and to a lesser extent, to the history of Neuchâtel. He is a man of a painstaking and critical mind, who dislikes hastily improvised generalizations, and is not afraid of starting a fight when he finds historic truth twisted to fit respectable traditions. Among many other things he taught me the value of systematic work, even in small matters" (ib., p. 237).

At no moment is there mention of a lack of parental love, but there is a clear statement about foregoing play for serious work, very early, which implies little peer interaction, besides the fact that his peers would not have been able to follow him in his scientific interests. Indeed, from seven to ten years of age he became successively interested in mechanics, birds, in fossils of secondary and tertiary layers and in sea shells. Then it was malacology, which he knew so well at the age of 15 that he was able to get published, "on the sly", a series of articles on the mollusks of Switzerland, Savoy, Brittany and Columbia. "However," as narrated by Piaget, "instead of quietly pursuing the career of a naturalist which seemed so normal and so easy for me after these fortunate circumstances, between the ages of fifteen and twenty I experienced a series of crises due both to family conditions and to the intellectual curiosity characteristic of the productive age. But, I repeat, all those crises I was able to overcome, thanks to the mental habits, which I had acquired through early contact with the zoological science" (ib., p. 239).

The "indirect parental (mother and father) absence" prevented the adoption of many common scripts, and fostered the development of his own, under the guidance of his misfortunes of youth, mainly his mother's poor mental health which made him, at the age of 22, "intensely interested in questions of psychoanalysis and pathological psychology" (ib., p. 238). However, the intelligent boy must have begun long before, to think about the reasons for his mother's poor mental health, and from there, about the meaning of life and death, of health and sickness. Accordingly, between 1914 and 1918 "I began to read everything which came to my hands after my unfortunate contact with the philosophy of Bergson: some Kant, Spencer, Auguste Comte, Fouillé and Guyau, Lachellier, Boutroux, Lalande, Durkheim, Tarde, La Dantec; and in psychology, W. James, Th. Ribot, and Janet" (ib., p. 241). He read everything which came to his hands, yet all these were very serious, very theoretical, very *hedgehog* readings.

Fascinating, therefore,are the following comments by Piaget which show him as a pure-bred *hedgehog*:

On re-reading some old documents dating from my years of adolescence,. . . . [I see] that, in spite of their immaturity they anticipated in a striking manner what I have been trying to do for about thirty years. There is therefore probably some truth in the statement by Bergson that a philosophic mind is generally dominated by a single personal idea which he strives to express in many ways in the course of his life, without ever succeeding fully. . . . My one idea, developed under various aspects in (alas!) twenty-two volumes, has been the intellectual operations proceed in terms of structure-of-the-whole. (ib., pp. 237, 256)

8

GAM *Architects*

1. Introduction

The *architects* are a fascinating GAM personality family. *Architects*, in GAM terminology (see chapter 3 of volume1), are those who have been shaped by the same misfortune as *universalists* (early parental death or much parental absence coupled with love and good assistance from the remaining parent or relatives; good assistance from school and a stable socioeconomic status) but have been raised (or involved from an early age on) in an aristocratic, upper class, military, professional, or business environment. *They show vision and great enterprise, give priority to the institution they are part of or have created.* Many great statesmen, and many founders of long lived family enterprises were *architects*.

The most important status/professional assistances at the origin of the *architects*, coupled with the misfortune of early parental death are: 1. the aristocratic environment surrounding the children of kings, princes, and chieftains; 2. military academies, or other forms of military training; 3. professional schools (law, medicine, physics, chemistry, engineering); 4. business environment, especially when assuming early responsibility in the family business; 5. other professional environment.[104]

---

[104] Originally, I had called this personality type *semi-universalist* because of the directions or limitations imposed on what would have become otherwise a *universalist* personality. I then called them *architects* because they build their *enterprise* the way an architect designs and follows the construction of a church or palace or hospital with attention to both, the whole (function and beauty) and to all details. The new building must work on all planes, and its cost must be affordable.

On occasion one feels in *architects* what would have been otherwise a *universalist* vision, but one which was bent down by state or professional demands. In the end their view of the world approaches the detachment of the universalist in that the State or the Enterprise has priority over everything else: family, friends, happiness.

2. *Architect* Professions

There are several fields of human endeavor in which we encounter the strong presence of GAM *architects*: national leadership and the foundation of important industrial enterprises with familial involvement. GAM *architects* are *hedgehogs* shaped by early parental death or much parental absence, and therefore they "know one big thing" be it the State, or their newly founded enterprise.

State Leaders

To begin with something concrete, below is a list of eminent *architect* state leaders (DMo refers to death of the mother, DFa to death of the father, and the number following is the age at the time of parental death).

There is no need to stress the assistances given to young aristocrats, particularly members of royalty, in terms of teachers and other learning opportunities. They are usually surrounded by capable persons who are willing to answer questions or be of help. Even if given as hostage to an enemy, royal children will usually be treated with deference, and equally importantly, they know their importance and high destiny. If they succeed their fathers at an early age, they will have capable counselors during their minority. On the other hand, the early death of the father eliminates one of the strongest abrasive forces on earth: a father king, with the combined power of both. This in turn explains the paucity of good *dedicated* kings.

From the above one can see that whereas the *universalist* is strongly 'self-made', the *architect* is less so. Basically *architects* know less solitude and are given more specific assistances. They often receive a goal-oriented professional education and specific training. Many know early on what is expected of them, what their position in life in life will be, their precise task. All have specific ambitions, plans, goals, with aims and methods that are worldlier than those of *universalists.*

England	Elizabeth I	DFa 14	DMo 3
	Cromwell	DFa 16	
France	Cardinal de Richelieu	DFa 5	
	Louis XIV	DFa 4	
	Napoleon	complete parental absence from age 9[105]	
Japan	Oda Nobunaga	DFa 17	
	Toyotomo Hideyoshi	DFa 8	
	Tokugawa Ieyasu	DFa 7	
Mexico	Benito Juarez	DFa 3	DMo 3
Russia	Peter I the Great	DFa 4	
Rome	Caesar	DFa 16	
	Augustus	DFa 5	
South America	Simón Bolívar	DFa 3	DMo9
Spain	Isabel I of Castille	DFa 3	
Turkey	Kemal Atatürk	DFa 10	
United States	George Washington	DFa 11	
	Thomas Jefferson	DFa 14	
	Abraham Lincoln		DMo 9
Vietnam	Ho Chi Minh	DFa 10[106]	

The *architect* has some of the moral and religious dreams of the *universalist,* but with his feet planted firmly on the ground: he is applied science, while the *universalist* is theoretical science. The *architect* looks high and has a sense of history, but within the context of his company or family. Still, like *universalists, architects* have an interest in broad plans. For instance, of the three rulers to whom Columbus presented his plans to reach the Indies by going westward through the Atlantic—John II of Portugal (DFa 26), Ferdinand of Aragon (DFa 27), and Isabel I of Castile (DFa 3), it was the *architect* Isabel who was most interested in his plans and who helped him.

---

[105] Strong uprootedness from his Corsican foundations, father character failure, and DFa 15.

[106] The reader will remember, from chapter 1 of volume 1, my discussion of Robert Albert's (1983b) review of several statistical studies on the early parental death of eminent and highly creative personalities, among them of American presidents and British prime ministers.

Each *architect* has a strong will and a high vision of him/herself and his/her destiny. Each has great courage, drive, and a superb capacity for hard work. Most excel in getting themselves first-class collaborators. Usually not the smallest detail escapes their attention; they are interested in everything. They want to know and control everything. Of Elizabeth I, "the judgement made on her by the French ambassador in 1597 said that, 'she is a very great Princess, who knows everything' reflected a general verdict" (Jenkins, 1978, p. 729). And as an efficient *architect* "During her reign England was transformed from a poor country into an imperial power; The Spanish rival was defeated or contained; London became a wealthy city; the arts flourished" (Kermode, 2001, p. 68).

Cardinal de Richelieu[107] is said to have relished governing the lives of others. This applies to many *architects*. Very *architectic* are the following comments by O'Connell: "In the ecclesiastical as in the secular sphere he is an enigma only to those who fail to understand that he was at one and the same time the supreme theorist and the supreme pragmatist—a proclaimer of goals, but an adroit practitioner who forever tried to take the middle way, an autocrat imperious by instinct who was often moderate in his methods and liberal in his achievement" (1968, p. x).

In line with the above on Richelieu, as much as the *universalist* is interested in the *Civitas Dei,* the ideal city of perfect aims and perfect methods, the *architect* is interested in the State, in politics, in conquests, in the glory of this world, or in his/her enterprise.

Of the three *architects* who brought the unification of Japan—Oda Nobunaga (b. 1534), Toyotomo Hideyoshi (b. 1538), Tokugawa Ieyasu (b. 1542)—it is the last, who was shaped by the strongest misfortunes of youth. Not only did he lose his father at the youngest age—seven—but he was permanently separated from his mother from the age of two because of a change of political alliances, and he had to spend eleven years—from age six to seventeen—as a hostage of the Imagawa family. Of the three, it is he who was able to pass intact his power to his descendants: the Tokugawa shoguns, who ruled Japan from 1603 to 1867.

The *architect* is on the side of Caesar: he knows whose face is stamped on the coins. Like Caesar, not many *architects* are lovable:

---

[107] Third son of François du Plessis, seigneur de Richelieu.

"Yet, though not lovable, Caesar was and is attractive, indeed fascinating. His political achievement required ability, in effect amounting to genius, in several different fields, including administration, and generalship besides the minor arts of wire pulling and propaganda" (Toynbee, 1978, p. 579). Similar things apply to the *architect*-founders of industrial or professional enterprises.

Enterprise Founders/Leaders

Already in my first unpublished version of the *GAM Theory of Personality and Creativity* (1980s), I pointed to the fact that many founders of major professional and industrial enterprises (as well as founders of great families, in which many members were active in the family business) were *architects* shaped by the misfortune of early parental death. This is true, for instance, for the Rothschild (banking), DuPont de Nemour (chemicals), Krupp (steel), Mayo (medicine and surgery), Ford (automobiles), Agnelli/FIAT (automobiles), and Olivetti (typewriters and calculators), whose founders were:

Name	DFa	DMo
Mayer Amshel Rothschild	DFa 11	DMo 11
Pierre Samuel DuPont de Nemour		DMo 16
Alfred Krupp	DFa 14	
William Worral Mayo	DFa 7	
Henry Ford		DMo 13
Giovanni Agnelli	DFa 5	
Camillo Olivetti	DFa 1	

In some instances, the enterprise, as left by the founder, loomed larger than the descendants themselves; the enterprise sustained them with top jobs which they would probably not have had otherwise. In other instances, sons and grandsons greatly expanded the founder's nucleus and assured the financial greatness and fame of the family.

The high-aimed vision of the *architects* can be seen in Henry Ford:

He kept talking about the Ford Motor Company as the institution. Price reduction and plant expansion were the growth of the institution. . . . the company was an institution in the sense that it existed not to make money, but jobs and goods, and it was to continue for generations. . . . His own life had been hard working and in general ascetic. 'I have never known what to do with money after my expenses were paid. I can't squander it on myself without hurting myself, and nobody wants to do that.'His personal profits were tremendous - but they were nearly all reserved for plant expansion, 'to build more and more factories, to give as many people as I can a chance to be prosperous.' (Nevins, 1954, pp. 575-76)

The *architect*, like the *universalist*, can be a reasonably good father who rarely fosters rebellion in his children. This explains why his family prospers, and why his children and grandchildren are willing to remain with his enterprise, career considerations aside. Oftentimes, first-class dedicated sons and possibly grandsons follow first-class *architect* family founders, as did the five Rothschild brothers, the two Mayo brothers and Charles William Mayo of the third generation, and Adriano Olivetti, Camillo's son.

The creativity of the great founders is different from the creativity of novelists and poets, painters and sculptors, composers, philosophers and scientists, in that the act of creation is now the whole enterprise from innovation to realization through planning, financing, organizing, staffing, directing, producing, marketing, control and representation. Each piece must work well[108] and in a relatively new field: cars for Ford, typewriters for Olivetti

The biography of Camillo Olivetti by Bruno Caizzi (1962) is fascinating in this respect. We encounter Camillo at the drafting board in 1908, designing his first typewriter. He is training his workforce, building job satisfaction and morale, creating a corporate conscience, integrating production-marketing-publicity, training his son, Adriano, for the succession, giving him responsibilities and power.

Being the founder of what became the world's largest clinic is somewhat different yet it demanded the vision and drive of an *architect* as noted in the following comment by his grandson Charles W. Mayo:

---

[108] In the words of Peter Drucker: "'The bottle neck is at the head of the bottle,' goes an old saw. No business is likely to be better than its top management, have a broader vision than its top people, or perform better than they do" (1965, p. 68).

In 1892, when Grandfather was seventy-three and his sons [William James and Charles Horace] were well established in his office, he developed a master plan. First he taught Edith Graham, his office nurse and later my mother, to administer anaesthesia, all about chloroform and the other anaesthesia less frequently used, how to watch blood pressure, pulse, moisture or dryness of the skin, the eyes and other reflexes. She became an expert. Next he took in a partner, Dr. Augustus W. Stinchfield, a capable and courtly man said to be the best doctor in Rochester, next to the Mayos. Having satisfied his conscience that his patients wouldn't suffer, Grandfather retired. . . . My grandfather's place in medical history is secure: he launched the Mayo Clinic. When I retired from active surgery in 1963, the Clinic was a world model of integrated group practice of medicine triumphing over the early years of opposition within the profession against group practice in any form. Here 360 doctors were working together on a unique basis. . . . Six hundred Fellows from all the world were working on their postgraduate degrees and that year 190,000 patients streamed through our examining rooms. (1970, pp. 20-21)

What fascinates me is that the creativogenicity of the misfortune of early parental death does not limit itself to the classical domains of creativity discussed in volumes 1 and 2, extends itself not only to state leaders, but also to the more mundane—yet very important—world of business. Here too we encounter first class *architects* who are highly creative; their creativity deserves equal study.

5. Fascinated by the West: Peter I, Atatürk, and Bolivar

The three political giants of Russia, Turkey, and South America, were all GAM *architects*. In addition, much of their greatness, especially for the first two, rested in having brought many features of the West to their countries.

Peter I (1672-1725)

Peter I the Great, tsar of Russia from 1682 and emperor from 1721, was one of his country's greatest statesmen, organizers, and reformers. . . . Having already sent some young nobles abroad to study nautical matters, Peter, in 1697, went with the so-called Grand Embassy [of about 250 people] to western Europe. . . . Its chief purposes were to examine the international situation and to strengthen the anti-Turkish coalition, but it was also intended to gather information on the economic and cultural life of Europe. Travelling incognito, Peter familiarized himself with conditions in the advanced countries of the West. For four months he studied shipbuilding, working as a ship's carpenter in the yard of the Dutch East India Company at Saardam; after that he went to Great Britain, where he continued his study of shipbuilding, working in the Royal Navy's dockyard at Deptford, and he also visited factories, arsenals, schools, and museums and even attended a session of Parliament. Meanwhile, the services of foreign experts were engaged for work in Russia. . . .At the beginning of Peter's reign, Russia was backward by comparison with the countries of western Europe. This backwardness inhibited foreign policy and even put Russia's national independence in danger. Peter's aim, therefore, was to overtake the developed countries of western Europe as soon as possible, in order both to promote the national economy and to ensure victory in his wars for access to the seas. Breaking the resistance of the boyars, or members of the ancient landed aristocracy, and of the clergy and severely punishing all other opposition to his projects, he initiated a series of reforms that affected, in the course of 25 years, every field of the national life - administration, industry, commerce, technology, and culture. . . . He did not completely bridge the gulf between Russia and the Western countries, but achieved considerable progress in development of the national economy and trade, education, science and culture, and foreign policy. (Nikiforov, 1978, pp. 157-61)

Atatürk (1881-1938)

In 1913 he was sent to Sofia as military attaché, and during his stay there he acquired a good knowledge of the Western standards in taste, the arts, and the relations between men and women in polite society. He made good use of this knowledge later when he set about reforming social life in his country. . . . [In 1917 he] fell ill, and for treatment he went to Vienna and Carlsbad where he had a further opportunity to observe European civilization. . . . [Later, when he was in power he carried out his program of reform]: he closed down all institutions based on the Muslim canon law, all monasteries, and religious orders. 'Science is the most reliable guide in life,' he remarked, and abolishing the traditional system of education, which was mainly religious, he established secular schools of the modern type. The whole Ottoman legal system was modernized, and a new civil and penal code was adopted. The Oriental forms of dress that carried a religious significance were discarded in favour of European dress. Dances, balls, and other forms of entertainment involving both men and women were encouraged, and the enlightened classes adopted the European way of life. . . . Setting aside all the old laws and traditions that held women inferior to men, he established complete equality between the sexes, including the right of electing and being elected. In 1928 he substituted Roman characters for the Arabic that had been used in Turkey for centuries. He endeavored to popularize Western classical music and the theatre in Turkey. . . . In 1930 he made a second attempt at introducing a multiparty regime, by allowing the creation of the Free Republican Party; but, as this party soon became a centre for antireformist ideas and activities, it met the same fate as the Progressive Republican Party. (Akdag, 1978, pp. 255-57)

Bolívar (1783-1830)

"Simón Bolívar, soldier-statesman to whom six Latin-American republics owe their freedom from Spanish rule, is regarded by many as the greatest genius the Hispanic-American world has produced. A man of international renown in his own day, his reputation has steadily increased since his death" (Masur, 1978, p. 1205).

In 1826 Bolívar was considering the formation of a Federation of the Andes, from Mexico to Cape Horn: "'Mexico, Guatemala, Columbia, Peru, Chile, Bolivia might form a glorious Federation. . . . Such a Federation would have the advantage of being homogeneous, solid, and closed'. . . . . He suggests that this Federation of the Andes be placed under the protection of Great Britain, 'the Mistress of the Nations,' as he called her. . . . England was for him the liberal country par excellence; its constitution had become Bolivar's model because its government was founded on freedom. Bolivar had no fear that England, even in the role of protector, would concern herself with the internal problems of South America" (Masur, 1969, p. 412). "[However] Bolívar was aware that his plans for hemispheric organization had met with only limited acceptance. His contemporaries thought in terms of individual nation-states, Bolívar in continents" (Masur, 1978, pp. 1205-1208).

But, how did Bolívar conceive this idea? In 1810, he had gone on a mission to London: "Although he failed in his negotiations on all counts, his English sojourn was in other respects a fruitful one. It gave him an opportunity to study the institutions of the United Kingdom, which remained for him models of political wisdom and stability" (Masur, 1978, p. 1206).

Basically, all three of these *architects*—Peter The Great, Kemal Atatürk and Simon Bolivar—were open-minded thanks to their shortage oflocal scripts: they had no difficulties in seeing that other people had made much progress in many fields, and that it was no dishonor to learn from them. Their detours abroad brought rich fruit. Yet, great as their results were, they remained incomplete because they were UP endeavors, because they were UP impositions from above and not a DP development from below.

What makes in my eyes Canossa, Legnano, Runnymede, Philadelphia so important is that all subsequent developments were the result of the ideas and actions of a large number of people acting on their own and not because they were prodded, or forced, by the high vision of the supremo. Some or even much insularity remained in Russia, Turkey, and South America. Atatürk wanted a democratic country, but democracy will not arise by the fiat of a leader, even a great one.

PART II

9

The *Strict Ritter*[109] Personality of the Japanese

This chapter is divided into the following sections:

---

[109]See chapter 25 of volume 1 for a description of the ritter, particularly Table 6 on p. 339.

7. Flexible Immutability
    -   Koestler's and Patrick Smith's Comments
    -   Know-how, but not Assimilated Knowledge
8. What if Japan had not been United, but had Evolved into a Confederation?
9. A Critique of Arima Tatsuo's *The Failure of Freedom: A Portrait of Modern Japanese Intellectuals*
    -   Arima's Main Thoughts
    -   Critique of Arima's Thoughts on Japan
    -   Critique of Arima's Thoughts on the West
    -   Ikegami's Correct Thoughts on Japan versus the West
    -   Nishida Kitaro
    -   Uchimura Kanzo
10. "Japan as Swamp" Revisited
11. Behind the Smiling Mask
12. Conclusion and Recommendation
13. From *strict-Ritter* to *Insular* and *Skeptic*?
    -   *Okami*; in Particular that of the Educational System
    -   Those Cute Japanese Women
14. More on the Recommendation

Appendix I
   A *non-Ritter,* but *strict-Ritter* Passion for Apologies
    -   The Profuse Apologies
    -   The System is at Fault, not the Individual
Appendix II
   Cui bono the Japanese Virtues of Dependence and Self-effacement?

1. Introduction

When writing chapter 25 of volume 1 "The Ritter (Knight/ Warrior) Personality of the Germans", I knew that I had to have an equivalent chapter on the Japanese *strict Ritter*. I also knew that I should begin my additional studies on Japan with Endo Shusaku's[110] understanding of Japan as *swamp* in his historical novel *Silence*: "Father, you were not defeated by me, you were defeated by this swamp of Japan." However, *Ritter* do not live in swamps. Therefore, this chapter starts with my critique of Endo, and continues with a new understanding of many key aspects of the Japanese ethnopsychology derived from a wide range of important texts, and personal experiences.

Strictly speaking, I should have spoken of the *Samurai personality*, and not of the *strict Ritter personality of the Japanese*, but in so doing I would have lost the immediacy of many parallels with the German *Ritter* for both causes and results.

Even more than my other ethnopsychological chapters this one is addressed first to the Japanese people themselves, then to those who already have a good knowledge and love for Japan. Others too can read this chapter, but they need to integrate it with other readings, for instance Marainis' *Meeting with Japan*.

I would ask the reader to follow me through this chapter as if on a journey of discovery, each section being a stage of the trip, up to the last one of conclusion and recommendation.

2. No, Endo, Japan is Not a Swamp but the Land of the *Strict Ritter*

"Father [Rodrigues], you were not defeated by me, you were defeated by this swamp of Japan." With these words from Inoue Lord of Chikugo to Father Rodrigues, Endo Shusaku summarized, at the end of *Silence*, his views on Japan in relation to the West.

---

[110] Endo Shusaku (b. 1923, Tokyo), [is] one of the major contemporary Japanese novelists, notable for his examination of the relationship between East and West through a unique Christian perspective. Endo became a Roman Catholic at age 11 with the encouragement of his mother and aunt. . . . One of Endo most powerful novels, *Chimmoku* (1966; *Silence*), is a fictionalized account of Portuguese priests who traveled to Japan and the subsequent slaughter of their Japanese converts" (*Encyclopedia Britannica*, 1993, *4*, p. 490).

As described on the back cover of the book: "Silence is the story of foreign missionaries attempting to convert seventeenth-century Japan to Christianity in the face of relentless persecution by the authorities. Under torture the missionaries give in—they are defeated not only by men, but also by Japan itself" (1966/1978).

Then, as explained by the translator William Johnston,

> finally in 1614 the edict of expulsion was promulgated declaring that "the Kirishitan band have come to Japan . . . . longing to disseminate an evil law, to overthrow true doctrine, so that they may change the government of the country, and obtain possession of the land. This is the germ of a great disaster, and must be crushed." This was the death blow. It came at a time when there were about 300,000 Christians in Japan (whose total population was about twenty million) in addition to colleges, seminaries, hospitals and a growing local clergy. "It would be difficult", writes Boxer [1951], "if not impossible, to find another highly civilized pagan country where Christianity had made such a mark, not merely in numbers but in influence".
>
> Especially savage was the third Tokugawa, the neurotic Iemitsu—"neither the infamous brutality of the methods which he used to exterminate the Christians, nor the heroic constancy of the sufferers has ever been surpassed in the long and painful history of martyrdom." At first the most common form of execution was burning; and the Englishman, Richard Cocks, describes how he saw "fifty-five persons of all ages and both sexes burnt alive on the dry bed of the Kamo River in Kyoto (October 1619) and among them little children of five or six years old in their mothers' arms, crying out, 'Jesus receive their souls!'".
>
> But the Tokugawa Bakufu[111] was not slow to see that such 'glorious martyrdoms' were not serving the desired purpose; and bit by bit death was preceded by torture in a tremendous effort to make the martyrs apostatize. Among these tortures was the "ana-tsurushi" or hanging in the pit, which quickly became the most effective means of inducing apostasy.

---

[111] *Bakufu* is the Japanese word for shogunate; in this context one can simply read "government".

The victim was tightly bound around the body as high as the breast (one hand being left free to give the signal of recantation) and then hung downwards from a gallows into a pit which usually contained excreta and other filth, the top of the pit being level with his knees. In order to give the blood some vent, the forehead was lightly slashed with a knife. Some of the stronger martyrs lived for more than a week in this position, but the majority did not survive more than a day or two.

A Dutch resident in Japan declared that "some of those who had hung for two or three days assured me that the pains they endured were wholly insufferable, nor fire nor torture equalling their languor and violence." Yet one young woman endured this for fourteen days before she expired.

From the beginning of the mission until the year 1632, in spite of crucifixions, burning, water-torture and the rest, no missionary had apostatized. But such a record could not last; and finally the blow fell. Christovao Ferreira, the Portuguese Provincial, after six hours of agony in the pit gave the signal of apostasy. . . .

Nevertheless some missionaries tried to enter. There was Marcello Mastrilli who came partly to make amends for Ferreira and of whom Inoue, the Lord of Chikugo, boasted that he died 'an agonizing death, yammering and screaming in the pit.' And finally in 1643 came a group of ten (European, Chinese and Japanese) among whom was Giuseppe Chiara - Mr. Endo's Sebastian Rodrigues. Quickly captured, they all apostatized after long and terrible tortures; though most, perhaps all, later revoked their apostasy. . . .

The two foreign apostates [Ferreira and Chiara] were immediately taken as symbols of a Christianity which has failed in Japan because it is so stubbornly Western. "Father, you were not defeated by me," says the victorious Inoue. "You were defeated by this swamp of Japan." It is precisely the swamp of Japan that cannot absorb the type of Christianity that has been propagated in these islands. (1978, pp. 6-12)

Moving to the actual text of the novel, at its end, when the by then apostate Ferreira gradually convinces Rodrigues to abjure:

"I, too, heard those voices, I heard the groaning of men hanging in the pit. . . . When I spent the night here five people were suspended in the pit. Five voices were carried to my ears on the wind. The official said: 'If you apostatize, those people will immediately be taken out of the pit, their bonds will be loosed, and we will put medicine on their wounds.' I answered: 'Why do these people not apostatize?' and the official laughed as he answered me: 'They have already apostatize many times. But as long as you don't apostatize these peasants cannot be saved.'" (pp. 264, 267)

Finally, Father Rodrigues apostatizes in similar circumstances to put an end to the atrocious pains and cries of three unfortunate Christians hanging in the pit.

This was the most devilish form of torture for the two priests. Each of them might have withstood torture on their own bodies, but not when inflicted on those who, through their missionary message, had converted to Christianity. How could the priests of a religion of love refuse to step upon the *fumie*[112] if this could spare horrible pains to others? They may have done it for love, for a high religious sense, or for lack of nerves in an extremely difficult situation, even if this was, for everybody else who was not intimately acquainted with the situation, pure betrayal, full apostatizing. Some time after the event just described, as further narrated by Endo, Inoue summoned Rodrigues:

---

[112] The bronze image of Christ used by the Shogunate officials to test suspect Christians and to formalize apostasy.

The Jesuit Father Mathy, in his introduction to Endo's *The Golden Country* said that he could not understand how a man of Ferreira's high caliber could apostatize after only five hours in the pit, while other priests had endured the pit until death, which came after two, four, or six days. I have no problem understanding this—leaving aside the fact that Ferreira was "aged and ailing" (Boxer, 1951, p. 390)—because people differ widely in their resistance to pain. Already in common life some can easily endure pain, others not. For these last, it may be that their brains simply cannot endure pain, or that the same physical impact—e.g. a piece of red iron at the same temperature—will produce in them far more pain than in others. No, Father Mathy: when dealing with torture one must never pass judgment on those who fail. I greatly admire those who do not give up, but totally abstain from negative comments on those who fail. Inoue-Endo knew very well that torture could break the spirit, and for the rest of the life. Some men never recover from torture, and Ferreira was one of them. Basically all the blame must go to the torturers, and none to the tortured!

"I've told you. This country of Japan is not suited to the teaching of Christianity. Christianity simply cannot put down roots here. . . ..Father, you were not defeated by me." The Lord of Chikugo looked straight into the ashes of the brazier as he spoke. "You were defeated by this swamp of Japan." (1966/1978, p. 292)

As to my critique: **No, Endo**: Swamps do not burn people, do not torture them in the pit, do not torture their leaders by having their followers in the pit suffer terribly and scream in their presence. Lord Inoue was lying when he said: "Father, you were not defeated by me. You were defeated by this swamp of Japan." He, Inoue, and not Japan, is the one who defeated Sebastian Rodrigues, and Father Ferreira, and countless Japanese Christians.

How could Endo forget that he himself, early in the book, had reported how Inoue "had become for all practical purposes the architect of the Christian persecution. Quite unlike his predecessor Takenaka, he was cunning as a serpent so that the Christians who until now had not flinched at threats and tortures succumbed one by one to his cunning wiles" (p. 36)? And now comes the lie from the mouth of this cunning serpent that the Christians have not been defeated by him but by the swamp![113]

William Johnston then concluded that "Japan is a swamp because it sucks up all sorts of ideologies, transforming them into itself and distorting them in the process. It is the spider's web that destroys the butterfly, leaving only the ugly skeleton" (pp. 13-14).

No Johnston: There was and there is no swamp, no spider, but a land ruled by *strict Ritter*, i.e. by human beings shaped by the partial strict unity of power of shogun, emperor, daimyo.

David Landes said it correctly: "The Japanese went about eradicating Christianity with characteristic ferocity. Nero would have been ashamed for his softness. Christians were compelled publicly to

---

[113] In *The Golden Country* of 1970, Endo himself put the following words in the mouth of Inoue when speaking to Father Ferreira: "I'll wait for the torture to rob you of all discernment and wit and to derange your spirit. Do you understand? Through the torture of the pit, by tomorrow you'll have lost all discretion and understanding. You'll have lost your freedom to oppose my words. What I call left, you will call left. What I call right, you will call right. When I say 'Apostatize,' you will apostatize'" (1989, p. 94). So there is somebody who knows the dreadful power of torture.

abjure. Those who refused or backslid were tortured and burned or beheaded. Those who helped missionaries, the same. The third Tokugawa shogun, Iemitsu, continuing the policy of his grandfather and father, often attended the torture sessions himself. Those who resisted were killed to the last babe in arms" (1998, p. 355). This, for sure, is not the description of an ontological swamp, but of the loathsome ferocity of *strict Ritter*.

3. The Land of the *Strict Ritter*

Endo is not the only writer to highlight the harsh thinking and behavior of the Japanese *strict Ritter* (to use my terminology), and this before, during and after the Tokugawa era of 1603 to 1867. My first quote, hereafter, is from a recent book by Patrick Smith and deals with the Tokugawa era; the second quote is also from a recent book, of 1997, by Kagawa Hiroshi devoted, this time, to contemporary *Inscrutable Japanese*. After that I will move back in history with my next three sections. Basically there is continuity between past and present, even if clearly the present generations are not as strict as the previous ones.

Patrick Smith's Recent Comments

There was a sort of federalist settlement between the shoguns and the daimyo, but otherwise the [Tokugawa] era was marked by merciless exploitation, purposeful deprivation, paranoic police controls, coercion, more or less constant official violence—and more or less constant popular resistance to all of these things. In its terror and totality, its nightmarish bureaucracy and manipulation of knowledge, Edo Japan is usefully compared with the later Soviet Union. In its violent dream of Oriental agrarianism it suggests the Cambodia of the Khmer Rouge. (Smith, 1998, p. 49)

Forty-seven Ronin was immensely popular among commoners. The tale, as famous as *The Three Musketeers* in the West, remains a national legend. Yet it is a narrative of tragic senselessness. It suggests a society dedicated to the complete eradication of individual judgment in the name of spirit. The extent of such a society's malevolence could be limited only by the instruments of violence available to it. (ib., pp. 191-92)

Avoiding Eye Contact

Why do Japanese avoid eye contact? One answer may lie in Japan's feudal history. Until just 130 years ago, when it opened its doors to the outside world and began to modernize, Japan had a strict class system. Every aspect of Japanese society was affected by this system, which reached its height during the Edo period (1600-1867). Commoners were forbidden to speak or have contact with the samurai warrior class, and inter-marriage was quite unthinkable. Not only was eye contact with a person of higher social status considered very rude, *it could cost the offender his life.* Although this system ended with the Edo Period itself, its psychological and emotional impact on the Japanese psyche remains. Japanese still unconsciously avoid making eye contact as a way of being polite. What about Americans? American children are raised in a society with democratic ideals, where individual opinions are greatly valued. Direct eye contact is seen as proof of self-confidence and trustworthiness, and has traditionally been a good thing. (Kagawa, 1997, pp. 19-21; my italics to stress the constant dangers that commoners had to face in the past with every samurai)

Indeed, the samurai, "was always ready to disembowel himself because of a slight done to his lord, but claimed the right to test the sharpness of his sword on the first beggar he met in the street. Valignani, an Italian Jesuit, wrote in the sixteenth century: 'They are ready to kill those subject to them on the slightest of pretexts, and think no more of cutting a man in half than of doing so to a dog; many of them, chancing to meet some unfortunate, will cut him in half solely to test the edge of their *katana*'" (Maraini, 1960, p. 124).

Squeezing the Farmer to the Utmost, and Brutally Punishing Every Protest

The social disruption caused by economic change, plus the pressure of taxation, as feudal lords tried to maintain or increase their revenues, brought unrest to the countryside. Though never absent altogether, rebellions averaged fewer than two a year in the seventeenth century. In the next fifty years, the number doubled; in the hundred years after 1750, it doubled again. A few of the outbreaks were on a major scale, especially after 1800, involving large bodies of peasants from many villages. Others, though little more than protest marches, were nevertheless put down with the same severity. At the local level, rioters usually directed their anger against the nearest targets: village headmen and other non-samurai officials, or well-to-do farmers, who had taken up money-lending as a supplementary source of income. (Beasley, 1999, pp. 163-64)

One of the attempts to obtain temporary relief evolved into an Edo-era legend:

It concerns a village headman named Sogoro, who lived near Narita, north of the capital, in the early 1600s [1645?]. The daimyo raised the rice tribute so high that Sogoro's village faced starvation. When appeals to the local official failed, Sogoro took the dangerous step of leaving the village to confront the daimyo himself at his alternative residence in Edo. He was rebuffed again. It remained only to approach the shogun—a move certain to end in execution, for in the order of things Sogoro's right of appeal began and ended with those directly above him. The narrative continues:

His heart contained only the thought that by sacrificing his own life, he would take upon himself the entire responsibility for the peasants' sufferings and save the masses from their hardships. How firmly resolved was he to act, and how incomparable was his courage!

Sogoro prevailed after planting his petition in the shogun's rubbish bin. It was discovered and taken to the shogun, who ordered the excessive tributes withdrawn. Then Sogoro was crucified with his wife and four sons because he had 'treated public authority lightly'. (Smith, 1998, p. 197)[114]

---

[114] For an illustration of the Japanese crucifixion—different from the Roman one—see Boxer, 1951, p. 256/xiii.

The story so impressed the people that it was rendered in one of the famous Kabuki works:

> When the play of Sakura Sogoro is to be performed, the actors repair to Sogoro's village, not far away from Tokyo, where stands a shrine sacred to the martyred village head who presented a direct appeal to the Shogun to lessen the heavy burden of taxes imposed upon the farmers, and in consequence forfeited his life. There the actors address his spirit, and during the run of the play a temporary shrine is erected within the theatre before which daily offerings of fruit, vegetables, and wine are made. (Kincaid, 1965, p. 46)

Loathsome Ferocity also at the Top of the Pyramid of Power

"During 1595, despite the protestations of [Tokugawa] Ieyasu and other advisors, Toyotomo Hideyoshi slaughtered his adopted heir, Hidetsugu, and Hidetsugu's wife, consorts, and children, a total of thirty people. He did this so that his two-year-old son Hideyori could become his unrivaled heir" (Totman, 1983, p. 6).

Earlier, around 1576, Tokugawa Nobuyasu, the first son of Ieyasu, "began leading military forces and fought fiercely. He was a violent, unpredictable young man, who abused his wife [a daughter of Oda Nobunaga] and embittered many of Ieyasu's vassals by treating them badly. Then he became entangled in an anti-Oda political intrigue. [His mother] Lady Tsukiyama, who got along poorly with her daughter-in-law, and who probably had never forgiven Ieyasu for throwing over her relatives in favor of Nobunaga, was centrally involved. Nobunaga learned of the intrigue in July 1579, when his daughter wrote him a letter denouncing her husband and mother-in-law on twelve counts of anti-Oda plotting and abuse. He was enraged and demanded that Ieyasu have the young man commit suicide. . . . It was a hideous predicament for Ieyasu, and worse yet for Nobuyasu and his mother. . . . He procrastinated for nearly a month and a half, trying to find a way out of his dilemma. He finally sent a vassal named Okamoto to assassinate the boy's mother. . . . On September 15, 1579, at Ieyasu's order, his eldest son disemboweled himself" (ib., pp. 41-42).

In May 1615, Tokugawa Ieyasu resumed the siege of the castle of Osaka. "Ieyasu had promised safety to Hideyori [the son of

Hideyoshi], but naturally his word was not believed after his previous falsehoods. . . . [On June 3] the Tokugawa forces entered the inner defence zone of the castle. That evening Hideyori's wife (who was Hidetada's daughter) sent a message asking Hidetada and Ieyasu to spare her husband and his mother, Yodogimi. No reply came. On June 4 Hideyori committed suicide and Yodogimi was killed by a retainer to save her from capture. On moral grounds the conduct of Ieyasu was unforgivable, for he had basely broken oath after oath; but he had destroyed the house of Toyotomi, and was supreme in Japan. In contrast to the fleeting dominance of Nobunaga and Hideyoshi, the Tokugawa family was to govern the country for two hundred and fifty years" (Sansom, 1961, p. 398).

"Hideyori had a son, Kunimatsu, and a daughter, Chiyomine, by a consort. Both children survived the fall of Osaka Castle and fled with a nurse to Fushimi. There they were captured, and at Ieyasu's orders the boy was slain, along with his attendants, and the little girl placed in a nunnery in Kamakura. Ieyasu was determined that no one could ever claim to be a legitimate successor to the great Hideyoshi. In the same ruthless spirit, surviving *ronin* were rounded up, executed, and their heads posted along the Fushimi highway" (Totman, 1993, p. 179).

Entrusting the Lord with Matters of Good and Evil

As stressed by Yamamoto[115], "if one were to say in a word what the condition of being a samurai is, its basis lies first in seriously devoting one's body and soul to his master. . . . Being a retainer is nothing other than being a supporter of one's lord, *entrusting matters of good and evil to him*, and renouncing self-interest. . . . Nakano Jin'emon constantly said, 'A person who serves when treated kindly by the master is not a retainer. But one who serves when the master is being heartless and unreasonable is a retainer. You should understand this principle well'" (ca. 1700/1985, pp. 66, 20, 132; my italics to

---

[115] "Yamamoto Tsunetomo (1659-1719) was a samurai retainer of the Nabeshima Clan, Lords of Hizen province, who became a Buddhist monk in 1700 after the Shogunal government prohibited the practice of *tsuifuku*: suicide of a retainer on the death of his lord. The book was dictated to a younger samurai during the author's seclusion over a seven year period" (Wilson, 1979, back cover).

highlight the similarity with the *cortigiano*'s devotion to his *signore*[116]).

First we have the complete devotion to the lord—leaving matters of good and evil to the one most corrupted by Acton's Law of Power—then we have this same rule elevated to total absurdity: the more heartless and unreasonable the lord is, the better. Not even the samurai is entitled to be treated kindly.

4. The Making of the *Strict Ritter* Personality

The Early Making of the German *Ritter*

Karin Grossmann, Klaus E. Grossmann, Gottfried Spangler, Gerhard Suess, and Lothar Unzner, of the University of Regensburg, in a 1985 paper entitled "Maternal Sensitivity and Newborns' Orientation Responses as Related to Quality of Attachment in Northern Germany" contrasted the way northern German mothers raised their children, with how American mothers raised theirs:

Although Baltimore and Bielefeld mothers had almost the same amount of close bodily contact with their 10-month-old infants, the quality of holding differed: the Bielefeld mothers were generally less tender and affectionate, their holding episodes were shorter, and their pickups were more frequently interfering as compared to the Baltimore mothers. The Bielefeld infants also seemed to communicate less with their mothers.

In the Strange Situation a much higher percentage of the Bielefeld sample was classified as group A (avoidant) than in the Baltimore sample (49% versus 26%). We interpret this part of our findings with respect to the cultural values that we be-

---

[116] "It is true that many things which seem evil are good. Thus it is sometimes allowable, in the service of one's master, to kill not just one man but ten thousand, and do many things which on superficial view would appear evil though they ar not" (Castiglione, c. 1510/1976, p. 131). And who knows what is truly good or evil? Only the master. And don't ask him: "The essence of a courtier's prudence consists in a willingness to accept an inferior status and in an unquestioning obedience. 'It is often improper for him to inquire into the reasons behind the orders he receives,' warns the Neapolitan Stranger; a courtier 'must not want to know too much' (Tasso, 1586/1973, p. 31)" (Trafton, 1973, p. 8).

lieve to be dominant in North Germany, where people tend to keep a larger interpersonal distance. As soon as infants become mobile, most mothers feel that they should now be weaned from close bodily contact. To carry a baby who can move on its own or to respond to its every cry by picking it up would be considered as spoiling. *The ideal is an independent, nonclinging infant who does not make demands on the parents but rather unquestioningly obeys their commands.* One is reminded of [Kurt] Lewin's observations on the social-psychological differences between the United States and Germany:

> For someone who comes from Germany the degree of freedom and independence of children and adolescents in the United States is astounding. Especially impressive is the lack of a submissive attitude of the child toward adults or of students toward their professors. The adults too treat the child as their equal, whereas in Germany it appears to be the natural right of the adult to dominate and the duty of the child to obey. The natural relationship between the adult and the child in the United States is not considered as one between a master and a subordinate but as one between two individuals of basically equal rights. Parents seem to treat their children more respectfully. When they ask the child to bring something, they usually ask for it in a polite manner. In a situation in which a German father or a German mother would most probably utter brief commands, parents in the United States will let the child feel that they enjoy its compliance. It is often the case in the United States that one hears a father or mother say "thank you" after such compliant behavior. [1936/1948[117], p. 27]

Despite the tremendous attitudinal and political changes that have occurred in the last 50 years or so, traditional attitudes of the kind described by Lewin still seem to be somewhat alive

---

[117] Kurt Lewin's *Resolving Social Conflicts*. New York: Harper.

in many homes where they have never been the subject of parental reflection. It should be stressed, however, that Erikson's dark and grave picture of the utterly insensitive and authoritarian father of the German family belongs definitely to the past (Erikson, 1963, pp. 253-54)

Still, while it is true, as noted by Grossmann et al. in 1985, that the authoritarian father of the German family belongs definitely to the past, what Erikson wrote[118] is important within the present study of how *Ritter* and *strict Ritter* personalities were shaped, because Erikson did not limit himself to commenting on the Germans, but contrasted them with the French, the Anglo-Saxons and the Americans:

What differentiates—in an unconscious but decisive way— the German father's aloofness and harshness from similar traits in other Western fathers? I think the difference lies in the German father's essential lack of true inner authority - that authority which results from an integration of cultural ideal and educational method. The emphasis here definitely lies on *German* in the sense of Reichs-German. . . .There came to be something of the French chevalier in every Frenchman, of the Anglo-Saxon gentleman in every Englishman, and of the rebellious aristocrat in every American. This something was fused with revolutionary ideals and created the concept of "free man" - a concept which assumes inalienable rights, indispensable self-denial, and unceasing revolutionary watchfulness. . . .The average German father's dominance and harshness was not blended with the tenderness and dignity which comes from participation in an integrating cause. Rather, the average father, either habitually or in decisive moments, came to represent the habits and the ethics of the German top sergeant and petty official who—"dress'd in a little brief authority"—would never be more but was in constant danger of becoming less; and who had sold the birthright of a free man for an official title or a life pension. (1963, pp. 332-34)

---

[118] Most probably written in 1950, the first edition of *Childhood and Society*; 1963 is the second edition.

The Early Making of the Japanese *Strict Ritter*

As discussed by Nitobe Inazo in *Bushido: The Soul of Japan*:

> Valour, fortitude, bravery, fearlessness, courage being the qualities of soul which appeal most easily to juvenile minds, and which can be trained by exercise and example, were, so to speak, the most popular virtues, early emulated among the youth. Stories of military exploits were repeated almost before boys left their mother's breast. Does a little booby cry for any ache? The mother scolds him in this fashion: "What a coward to cry for a trifling pain! What will you do when your arm is cut off in battle? What when you are called upon to commit *hara-kiri?*". . . . *Parents, with sternness sometimes verging on cruelty,* set their children to tasks that called forth all the pluck that was in them. "Bears hurl their cubs down the gorge," they said. Samurai's sons were let down to steep valleys of hardship, and spurred to Sisyphus-like tasks. Occasional deprivation of food or exposure to cold, was considered a highly efficacious test for inuring them to endurance. Children of tender age were sent among utter strangers with some message to deliver, were made to rise before the sun, and before breakfast attend to their reading exercises, walking to their teachers with bare feet in the cold of winter. . . . *In the days when decapitation was public, not only were small boys sent to witness the ghastly scene, but they were made to visit alone the place in the darkness of night and there to leave a mark of their visit on the trunkless head.* (1905/2001, pp. 44-45; my italics)

The next step in the making of the *strict Ritter* was described by Yamamoto:

> When Lord Katsushige was young, he was instructed by his father, Lord Naoshige: "For practice in cutting, execute some men who have been condemned to death." Thus, in the place that is now within the western gate, ten men were lined up, and Katsushige continued to decapitate one after another until he had executed nine of them. When he came to the tenth, he saw that the man was young and healthy and said, "I'm

tired of cutting now. I'll spare this man's life." And the man's life was saved. (ca. 1700/1985, p. 92)

Also, "Yamamoto Kichizaemon was ordered by his father Jin'-emon to cut down a dog at the age of five, and at the age of fifteen he was made to execute a criminal. Everyone, by the time they were fourteen or fifteen, was ordered to do a beheading without fail" (ib., p. 102).

Two brothers, Sakon and Naiki, respectively twenty-four and seventeen years of age, made an effort to kill Iyéyasu in order to avenge their father's wrongs; but before they could enter the camp they were made prisoners. The old general admired the pluck of the youths who dared an attempt on his life and ordered that they should be allowed to die an honourable death. Their little brother Hachimaro, a mere infant of eight summers, was condemned to a similar fate, as the sentence was pronounced on all the male members of the family, and the three were taken to a monastery where it was to be executed. A physician who was present on the occasion has left us a diary, from which the following scene is translated:

"When they were seated in a row for final dispatch, Sakon turned to the youngest and said—'Go thou first, for I wish to be sure that thou doest it aright.' Upon the little one's replying that, as he had never seen *seppuku* performed, he would like to see his brothers do it and then he could follow them, the older brothers smiled between their tears:—'Well said, little fellow! So canst thou well boast of being our father's child.' When they had placed him between them, Sakon thrust the dagger into the left side of his abdomen and said - 'Look brother! Dost understand now? Only, don't push the dagger too far, lest thou fall back. Lean forward, rather, and keep thy knees well composed.' Naiki did likewise and said to the boy— 'Keep thine eyes open or else thou mayst look like a dying woman. If thy dagger feels anything within and thy strength fails, take courage and double thy effort to cut across.' The child looked from one to the other, and, when both had expired, he calmly half denuded himself and followed the example set him on either hand". (Nitobe 1905/2001, pp. 119-20)

Bushido made the sword its emblem of power and prowess. . . . Very early the samurai boy learned to wield it. It was a momentous occasion for him when at the age of five he was apparelled in the paraphernalia of samurai costume, placed upon a *go*-board and initiated into the rights of the military profession, by having thrust into his girdle a real sword instead of the toy dirk with which he had been playing. (ib., p. 127)

However, even Nitobe was conscious of the abuses: "But, ever within reach of the hand, [the sword] presented no small temptation for abuse. Too often did the blade flash forth from its peaceful sheath. The abuse sometimes went so far as to try the acquired steel on some harmless creature's neck" (ib., p. 130).

Moving to times closer to us, James Moloney in *Child Training and Japanese Conformity* of 1954 reported that:

In the development of *ko* (filial piety), the father is proclaimed the titular and revered head of the family, while the mother, in comparison to the father and to the sons, especially the eldest son, is without status. Even the babe in arms cannot escape obeisance to the father. Filial respect and conformity are foisted upon him while he is still an infant: the mother pushes the head of the suckling into a bow as the father enters the room. Later, if he is not duly obsequious, the baby is chided for his infantilism and unfavorably compared with more dutiful children. If this fails, as a last resort the need for obedience is made clear to him by the burning of dried leaves on his skin. One subjection to this moxa cautery usually suffices, but if it does not, the second searing or branding accomplishes the complete riddance of the child's self-assertiveness and full compliance to the institution of filial respect. . . . In the course of the establishment of submissiveness to the father, the male child is permitted to vent his reactionary hostilities upon the female members of his family. He is even permitted to attack and beat his mother. Submissiveness toward the father is transferred to the emperor through the institution of *chu*. In *chu* self-effacing obedience is developed to such an extent that a Japanese, when inducted into imperial military service, becomes one already dead. He no longer has any right to his own life; it now belongs exclusively to the emperor. So far as individual strivings are concerned, the Japanese soldier or sailor must renounce them completely. . . . In fact, the *ko* to the father, the obsequiousness, is developed when the infant is in his precognitive era. The importance of this fact is becoming recognized by an increasing number of psychiatrists and anthropologists. On his visit to Japan in the eighteenth century, Thunberg made some observations regarding Japanese children which might still be remarked today: "I observed everywhere that the chastisement of children was very moderate. I very seldom heard them rebuked or scolded, and hardly ever saw them flogged or beaten, either in private families or on board of the vessels: while in more civilized and enlightened nations, these compliments abound. . . . With respect to courtesy and submission to their superiors, few can be compared to the Japanese. Subordination to government and obedience to their parents are inculcated into children in their early infancy, and in every situation of life they are in this respect instructed by the good example of their elders."[119]

Menpes observed the strict training of the Japanese children:

"The science of deportment occupies quite half the time of the Japanese children's lives, and so early are they trained that even the baby of three, strapped to the back of its sister aged five, will in that awkward position bow to you and behave with perfect propriety and grace. This Japanese baby has already been taught how to walk, how to kneel down, and how to get up again without disarranging a single fold of its kimono. . . . Modesty and reserve are insisted upon in the youth of Japan. A girl is taught that she must talk very little, but listen sympathetically to the conversation of her superiors. If she has a brother, she must look up to him as her master, even although he be younger than herself. She must give way to him in every detail. The baby boy places his tiny foot upon his sister's neck, and she is thenceforth his slave. If he is sad, her one care must be to make him happy. Her ambition is to imitate as nearly as possible the behavior of her

---

[119] Charles Peter Thunberg (1796), *Travels in Europe, Africa, Asia.* London: F. & C. Rivington; (*3*, pp. 124, 252).

mother towards her own lord and master"[120]. . . .The Japanese child, more so the male child, is trained rather than educated to filial respect and to national duty. The concept of duty, and of following duty as the proper role of the Japanese, is constantly alluded to in literature on Japan and the Japanese people. . . . Moreover, as Sansom points out[121], such loyalty as grew up around a leader transformed itself into a personal loyalty, not a loyalty toward the leader's beliefs. In fact, according to Western concepts, the feeling of the Japanese follower for his leader was not loyalty as we know it, but blind identification. (1954/1962, pp. 214-218).

Then, as seen by Koestler in *The Lotus and the Robot* of 1960: "The rigidity is indispensable in a Spartan education aimed at hardening the character against its innate crustal instability. In her autobiography, Mrs. Sugimoto relates a typical lesson in classics with her private teacher:

> Throughout my two-hour lesson he never moved the slightest fraction of an inch except for his hands and his lips. And I sat before him on the matting in an equally correct and unchanging position. Once I moved. It was in the midst of a lesson. For some reason I was restless and swayed my body slightly, allowing my folded knee to slip a trifle from the proper angle. The faintest shade of surprise crossed my instructor's face; then very quietly he closed his book, saying gently but with a stern air: "Little Miss, it is evident that your mental attitude today is not suited for study. You should retire to your room and meditate." My little heart was almost killed with shame. There was nothing I could do. I humbly bowed to the picture of Confucius and then to my teacher, and, backing respectfully from the room, I slowly went to my father to report as I always did, at the close of my lesson. Father was surprised, as the time was not yet up, and his unconscious

---

[120] Mortimer Menpes (1905), *Japan: A record in colour*. London: Charles Black; (pp. 140-141).

[121] G. B. Sansom (1950), *The Western World and Japan*. New York: Alfred A. Knopf; p. 362 and elsewhere.

remark, "How quickly you have done your work!" was like a death knell. The memory of that moment hurts like a bruise to this very day. (Koestler, pp. 198-99; Sugimoto, 1933, pp. 35-36)

A traditional form of correction in Japanese education was moxa—the burning of a cone containing the leaves of a special plant on the child's skin, where it often left a life-long scar. But this was considered as a cure rather than a punishment. . . . Thus the apparent cruelty of Japanese education is really a form of conditioning, which does not exclude love and affection—on the contrary, it is based on the axiomatic conviction that the child in its innermost being wants to be properly reconditioned that way, as the flower welcomes the wire rack to display its petals to best advantage. But the methods and techniques of this conditioning are more radical, and reach into deeper strata of the subconscious than Western pedagogy would ever dream. They transform not only overt comportment, but also the autonomous responses and unconscious controls—as exemplified, for instance, by the peculiarities of Japanese behaviour in war, in sleep, and in mental homes. (Koestler, pp. 199-200)

The early conditioning of the Japanese child penetrates even its sleeping habits:

From the time I can remember I was always careful about lying quiet on my little wooden pillow at night. . . . Samurai daughters were taught never to lose control of mind or body—even in sleep. Boys might stretch themselves into the character *dai*, carelessly outspread; but girls must curve into the modest, dignified character *kinoji*, which means 'spirit of control'. On the other hand, Japanese men and women have an astonishing capacity to fall asleep in any posture and in any surroundings—once more as if turning off a switch. (Koestler, p. 201; Sugimoto, p. 39)

Do Not Look Intelligent!

William Scott Wilson, the translator of Yamamoto Tsunetomo's *Hagakure* of ca. 1700, wrote this on young Yamamoto: "For the following years there were no outstanding incidents in his life, and by the time he was twenty he was still without an official position. It is related that at this juncture someone pointed out to him that his face was 'too intelligent' and warned him that [his feudal lord] Mitsushige disliked such an expression. Tsunetomo states that he spent the next year in front of a mirror trying to correct this fault" (1979, pp. 12-13).[122]

Further Training of Adulthood

- "Last year I [Yamamoto] went to the Kase Execution Grounds to try my hand at beheading, and I found it to be an extremely good feeling. To think that it is unnerving is a symptom of cowardice" (ca. 1700/1983, p. 103).
- "Horie San'emon's misdeed was robbing the Nabeshima warehouse in Edo of its money and fleeing to another province. He was caught and confessed. Thus it was pronounced, 'Because this is a grave crime he should be tortured to death,' and Nakano Daigaku was ordered to be the official who verified the execution. At first all the hairs on his body were burned off and his fingernails were pulled out. His tendons were then cut, he was bored with drills and subjected to various other tortures. Throughout, he did not flinch once, nor did his face change color. In the end his back was split, he was boiled in soy sauce, and his body was bent back in two" (ib., p. 120). Torture and death must have been witnessed by somebody, possibly by many; certainly the story circulated and impressed itself in many minds.
- "A certain son of Mori Monbei got into a fight and returned home wounded. Asked by Monbei, 'What did you do to your

---

[122] While this story is particularly *strict Ritter,* it still reflects a typical attitude of the great lords, including those of the Renaissance: "It is precisely the best men, according to the Neapolitan Stranger [i.e. according to Tasso], who can expect the worst treatment at court, unless they are able to conceal their excellence" (as summarized by Dain Trafton, 1973, p. 9).

opponent?' his son replied, 'I cut him down.' When Monbei asked, 'Did you deliver the coup de grace?' his son replied, 'Indeed I did.' Then Monbei said, 'You have certainly done well, and there is nothing to regret. Now, even if you fled you would have to commit seppuku anyway. When your mood improves, commit seppuku, and rather than die by another's hand, you can die by your father's.' And soon after he performed *kaishaku*[123] for his son" (ib. p. 133). Similarly, what happened was known not only by Yamamoto, and the story was circulated for the benefit of others.

• In volume 1, in the chapter on the German *Ritter*, I discussed the direct involvement of the German lord in the military training of his people whom he knew personally. Similar things are true for the Japanese *strict Ritter*. Nariakira, the daimyo of Satsuma from 1851 to his death in 1858 had a direct involvement in the training of his samurai:

> Nariakira saw the need for a broader, more practical type of education in his domain. To better acquaint his samurai with the outside world, he invited scholars of Dutch learning to lecture at the domain school. . . . He initiated a compulsory program of military drill for all samurai boys and young men above the age of seven. The young boys carried mock wooden guns, but the older boys and young men were armed with guns produced by the local arsenals. He trained the young samurai himself for several hours each afternoon until sunset, and he selected a crack team from among them that he personally led. (Matsukata Reischauer, 1986, p. 41)

Contemporary Training: Again Many Sticks and Few Carrots

The will to work and learn is instilled in subordinates through harsh words from their superiors. Japanese use the word *shittagekirei*. This expression means that if no one bothers to scold you, it's because you are hopeless. So a boss is hard on his subordinates, particularly on the young ones, in

---

[123] The helpful cutting of the head with a stroke of the sword done by a friend or relative, once the incision of the belly has been completed.

the same way that a parent scolds a child in order to help it mature. This is known as the "whip of love," and a boss uses it to help his staff acquire company know-how. The closer the relationship between boss and subordinate, the more he may use it. (Kagawa, 1997, pp.175-77)

Accordingly, "one thing that Westerners working in Japanese companies find hard to tolerate is that Japanese seldom if ever praise their work. Even worse, they may get criticism despite all their effort.... Westerners at Japanese companies are almost never praised. If their boss does say something, it is usually negative. They become insecure and hurt, and a vicious cycle ensues" (ib., pp. 175, 177).

5. Similarities Between the Japanese *Strict Ritter* and the German *Ritter*

As expected, there are many similarities between the Japanese *strict Ritter* and the German plain *Ritter*. A similar cause (partial Unity of Power) produces similar results which can easily be detected, once we make the needed adjustments for the obvious differences between the two culture.

The first major similarity, and clearly the result of the partial Unity of Power, is the primary importance given, in both Japan and Germany, to the virtue of *Treue*/Fidelity, as discussed in detail in chapter 25 of volume 1.

Moving to the other characteristics of the *Ritter*, listed in Table 6 of volume 1, it is impressive to see how many of them pertain equally to the Japanese *strict Ritter*, such as: courage, hard work, discipline in following orders or in setting an example, energy and endurance, perfectionism and pedantry, heroism, pride, arrogance, hate of compromise, will to power, superhumanism, ferocity and cruelty, a certain love for pomp and uniforms, love of the romantic. This last point of "love of the romantic," together with "ferocity and cruelty," is praised by Nitobe in *Bushido: The Soul of Japan*:

It passes current among us as a piece of authentic history, that as Ota Dokan, the great builder of the castle of Tokyo, was pierced through with a spear, his assassin, knowing the poetical predilection of his victim, accompanied his thrust with this couplet:

"Ah! how in moments like these
Our heart doth grudge the light of life";
whereupon the expiring hero, not one whit daunted by the mortal
wound in his side, added the lines:
"Had not in hours of peace,
It learned to lightly look on life." (1905/2001, p. 46).

Admirably romantic, and very Japanese, especially that philosophy of life of the Ota Dokan couplet, a philosophy of life very common in Japan for centuries, when evil followed ceaselessly on evil,
and when the only consolation came from the teaching of Buddhism
"that everything we desire is illusory and inconstant and that to desire,
to cling to, to love things of this world can only bring sorrow and
endless reincarnation in this sorrowful world. One can gradually
liberate oneself from illusions and clingings, gain more and more
insight into the real nature of things, and eventually escape from the
wheel of rebirth" (Wills, 2001, pp. 162-163). The Buddha, indeed, had
said: "The world is full of suffering. Birth is suffering, old age is
suffering, sickness and death is suffering, to be separated from a
beloved one is suffering. In fact life that is not free from desire and
passion is always involved with distress. This is called the Truth of
Suffering" (ca. 528 BC/1993, p. 74).

In his attempt to explain the complexity of the Japanese personality Fosco Maraini spoke of two basic elements: pacific and warlike:

If Japanese history is looked at more carefully, it will be
seen that it does not consist of the exclusive predominance of
one aspect over the other, but of a predominance of co-exis-
tent elements in ever-changing relationship. The conclusion is
that both aspects, the fundamentally pacific aspect, that of refinement in the art of living and enthusiasm for knowledge
and beauty, and the fundamentally warlike aspect, an extreme
refinement in barbarism and a terrifying enthusiasm for an ideal
absorbed to the point of complete identification with it, form
part of the complex Japanese personality revealed to us through
the centuries. (1960, p. 269)

Many scholars have observed this same contrast for Germany,
and were astonished that the land of Bach and Goethe could have

perpetrated so many horrendous crimes.[124] The answer is the same in both cases: the partial unity of power—immersed in a world of culture (be it Greco-Roman-Judeo-Christian; be it Sino-Korean-Buddhist-Confucian)—loves, protects, develops culture, and fosters the arts[125].

---

[124] "*Doch wie war das möglich: Im Land der Kultur wurden Kinder von ihren Erziehern mit einem Rohrstock geprügelt. Da konnte etwas nicht stimmen. . . . Ich meine die Angst—vor dem deutschen Rohrstock, dem deutschen Konzentrationlager, der deutschen Gaskammer, kurz: vor der deutschen Barbarei. Und die deutsche Kultur, die mir das Fräulein Laura so nachdrücklich und schwärmerisch angekundigt hatte? Auch sie liess nicht lange auf sich warten. Ziemlich schnell geriet ich in den Bann der deutschen Literatur, der deutschen Musik*" (Reich-Ranicki, 1999, pp. 30-31).

(But how was it possible: In the Land of Culture, children were beaten with the rod by their educators. That made no sense. . . . I mean the fear of the German rod, of the German concentration camp, of the German gas chamber: basically, fear of German barbarism. And the German culture of which Miss Laura had told me with so much emphasis and enthusiasm? That, too, did not wait long to manifest itself. Quickly, I came under the spell of German literature and of German music).

[125] See chapter 21 of volume 1 "Central UP May Give Freedom and Favors to some Talented People and Thereby Foster Creativity." What is said there about Louis XIV, Lorenzo de Medici, and Augustus, is valid for many German princes and Japanese daimyo; regarding the latter, see in particular *Japan: The Shaping of Daimyo Culture 1185-1868*, edited by Shimizu Yoshiaki (1988) from which I report the following by Martin Collcutt:

Daimyo were warriors by training and vocation. War was their metier. To succeed they had to be ruthless, cunning, callous, and aggressive. Even when, in the early seventeenth century, conditions of peace and order replaced endemic warfare and the daimyo turned their attention from fighting to governing, they continued to think of their lineages as military houses (*buke*). But few daimyo could survive and prosper simply as illiterate, boorish ruffians. As early as the twelfth century, warrior leaders like Taira Kiyomori (1118-1181) or Minamoto Yoritomo were finding that their newfound political power and the territories they had acquired called for the exercise of administration, and that the social distinction and political power conferred by victory in war, attainment of office, and possession of territory had to be legitimated—not least in their own eyes—by the acquisition and exercise of the arts of peace (*bun*), which included administration, scholarship, poetry, painting, and the study of the Chinese and Japanese classics. And what may first have been assumed as a convenient veneer, or borrowed cultural credential, to dignify naked military power, soon became a consuming interest in its own right—so much so that in much of Japanese warrior culture we can detect both complementarity and tension between the demands of *bu* [warrior tradition] and the appeal of *bun* [civilian arts]. (p. 5)

Similarly, in Europe, in the Feudal North:

The French or Flemish noble exercised a dictatorial paternalism beneath which everything depended from him and the officers of his court. The self-sufficiency of the medieval community which had had to find an outlet of reaction in the Crusades was, in the fourteenth and fifteenth centuries, applied to the court itself. Each noble not only surrounded himself with a household of courtiers and politicians, military men and clergy, *but it became necessary for him to emphasize the traditional authority of his dynasty by becoming the fountainhead of learning and the arts. . . .* Nowhere does this social change reveal itself more clearly than in the status of the artist. No longer the manly and intelligent artisan of the age of the cathedral builders, he becomes a skillful valet, fit for all kinds of services, "adding saddlery to painting and secret commissions to works of real art; a man who ranks in the prince's household with the fool, the minstrel and the tailor". (Taylor, 1948, pp. 46-47)

Yet as soon as things go wrong the lord wants to and must win, and there will be no restrictions he will accept, and his *Ritter* and *strict Ritter* will act accordingly.

There is another interesting *Ritter* similarity between Japanese and Germans: both see themselves as especially unique. Every nation, every people sees itself as special and unique, and that, in part, is true; but the Japanese and the Germans have often seen themselves as especially unique. Starting with Japan:

> The Japanese concept of their difference from other peoples is not so much a matter of superiority, that is, of quality, but a difference in kind. They see themselves as being different not because they are better or worse than others but simply because they are different. In essence it is a deeply racist concept, almost as though Japanese were a different species of animal from the rest of humanity. Conditions as they existed only a little over a century ago lent credence to this feeling. All the people in the world who spoke the distinctive Japanese language and lived in the distinctive Japanese way were to be found in the sharply drawn and isolated Japanese national unit, and, except for a handful of Ainu and still fewer Chinese, Korean, and Dutch traders, there were no other people of any sort in Japan. (Reischauer, 1976, p. 411)

Moving to Germany, Blackbourn & Eley (1984) wrote:

> By and large, those who talked before 1945 about a German *Sonderweg* [Special Way] were more often inclined to endow this with a positive value. In the first half of the last century, for example, while the early German national movement was partly stimulated by aping France, it was also strongly informed by a sense of difference from, and superiority to, the ideas of the French Revolution. Later, after unification, there was a widespread tendency, especially among the academic and professional *Bildungsbürgertum,* to exalt the particular German combination of political, economic, military, and educational institutions: monarchy and industrial success, university and army. Complacent assumptions about the supposed importance of "spiritual" rather than merely "materialist" values in the new Germany were equally apparent [see Thomas

Mann's *Reflections of a Nonpolitical Man*]. Where such institutions and values were praised, Germany's special superiority was very often defined *vis-à-vis* England. (p. 3)

6. Kabuki Constricted and Constricting

In October 2001, I saw a presentation of *Meiboku Sendai Hagi (The Troubles in the Date Clan)* in the Kabuki Theatre in Tokyo. Citing from the program notes of the Kabuki-za:

> "This play is about the attempt to take over one of the most famous samurai households in the Edo period, the Date clan ruling Sendai, a scandal that caused a sensation in its day.

> Scene 1: The Hanamizu Bridge
> The samurai lord Yorikane (Fukusuke) has fallen in love with a courtesan and has neglected responsibilities, causing high-ranking retainers to plot the takeover of his domain. Returning from the pleasure quarters, he is attacked at Hanamizu Bridge, but is able to escape thanks to the help of a sumo wrestler retainer (Yajuro).

> Scene 2: Masaoka's Chambers and Below the Floor
> Yorikane has been removed from office, but now the titular head of the clan is his young son, a very vulnerable target to the forces trying to take over the clan. Masaoka (Tamasaburo), the boy's nurse is desperately afraid that he will be poisoned. She refuses to let anyone see him who might try to assassinate him and attempts to keep him safe in the women's quarters where men are forbidden. She even fixes his meal in her quarters using her delicate tea ceremony implements to cook rice. The plotting faction does not give up, though, and sends poison in the form of candy as a present from the shogun. Masaoka's son sacrifices his life for the young lord by eating the poisoned candy, and when he is killed, Masaoka thinks only of protecting her lord. Her fierce devotion to duty convinces the plotters that she is on their side. Masaoka's actions help save the young lord, and only when she is alone can she grieve for her son."

This scene 2 of *The Troubles in the Date Clan* brings to mind Act 6 of the Kabuki play *The Mystery of Calligraphy*: the one entitled "The Village School (Terakoya)". *Terakoya* was summarized by Nitobe Inazo who related it as something that had truly happened:

The story is of one of the greatest characters of our history, [Sugawara] Michizané, who, falling a victim to jealousy and calumny, is exiled from the capital. Not content with this, his unrelenting enemies [chiefly Fujiwara Shibei] are now bent upon the extinction of his family. Strict search for his son—not yet grown—reveals the fact of his being secreted in a village school kept by one Genzo, a former vassal of Michizané. When orders are dispatched to the schoolmaster to deliver the head of the juvenile offender on a certain day, his first idea is to find a suitable substitute for it. He ponders over his school-list, scrutinizes with careful eyes all the boys, as they stroll into the classroom, but none among the children born of the soil bears the least resemblance to his protégé [Sugawara Kan Shusai]. His despair, however, is but for a moment; for, behold, a new scholar is announced - a comely boy of the same age as his master's son, escorted by a mother of noble mien.

No less conscious of the resemblance between infant lord and infant retainer, were the mother and the boy himself [Kotaro, son of Matsuo]. In the privacy of home both had laid themselves upon the altar; the one his life - the other her heart, yet without sign to the outer world. Unwitting of what had passed between them, it is the teacher from whom comes the suggestion.

Here, then, is the scapegoat! - The rest of the narrative may be briefly told. On the day appointed, arrives [Matsuo] the officer commissioned to identify and receive the head of the youth. Will he be deceived by the false head? Poor Genzo's hand is on the hilt of the sword, ready to strike a blow either at the man or at himself, should the examination defeat his scheme. The officer takes up the gruesome object before him, goes calmly over each feature, and in a deliberate, business-like tone, pronounces it genuine. - That evening in a lonely home awaits the mother [of Kotaro] we saw in the school. Does she know the fate of her child? It is not for his return that she watches with eagerness for the opening of the wicket. Her father-in-law has been for a long time a recipient of Michizané's bounties, but since his banishment, circumstances have forced her husband [Matsuo] to follow the service of the enemy of his family's benefactor. He himself could not be untrue to his own cruel master; but his son could serve the cause of the grandsire's lord. As one acquainted with the exile's family, it was he who had been entrusted with the task of identifying the boy's head. Now the day's—yea, the life's—hard work is done, he returns home and as he crosses its threshold, he accosts his wife, saying: "Rejoice, my wife, our darling son has proved of service to his lord!"

"What an atrocious story!" I hear my readers exclaim." Parents deliberately sacrificing their own innocent child to save the life of another man's!" But this child was a conscious and willing victim: it is a story of vicarious death. (1905/2001, pp. 88-90)

Both stories deal with the killing of young people, about as young as Hidetsugu's children murdered on orders of Toyotomo Hideyoshi, and Hideyori's son murdered at the order of Tokugawa Ieyasu. The fact that the young boy Kotaro is assumed to die willingly to spare young Kan Shusai goes in parallel with the seppuku of the eight year old Hachimaro at the order of Tokugawa Ieyasu: It is nothing but pure brainwashing by the unity of power which has convinced everybody that a daimyo's life is worth more than countless normal lives.

No, Nitobe! The problem is not one of vicarious death, but of no death at all.

Something is fundamentally wrong in a system of so much oppression and ferocity, in which not only the very justified and generous protester Sogoro is crucified but also his wife and four sons. Something is fundamentally wrong in forcing people to apostatize by hanging them day after day in a pit, and forcing priests to apostatize in order to spare the torture perpetrated on their followers. Plainly, the UP is wrong and evil: the partial UP of the German model and the strict partial UP of the Japanese.

However, *horribile dictu*, my reading of the Kabuki plays is totally unorthodox. I was not following what was happening on the stage—the proper Japanese way. I was paying attention to the story and not to the acting! The general introduction to the Kabuki—heard in English over the leased earphones—had told me clearly that the

Kabuki is a theatre of *presentation* not of *representation* as in the West.

In a theatre of presentation, the emphasis is on the actors, on acting, on music, and costumes, and not on the story which is already perfectly known by the public. People go to the Kabuki not for a new interpretation of a known story, but to see how each scene, how each key moment is acted, and acted differently from a prior version with different actors. The theatre of presentation wants to make people think on the basis of the emotions that the acting, costumes and music evoke; whereas the theatre of representation wants to represent something outside of the theatre, and to evoke emotions from the story or ideas which are represented on the scene.

Accordingly, Samuel Leiter spoke of "performance-dominated theater":

The best way to develop a firm grasp of Kabuki's fundamental qualities is to study the same play over and over again, not on the page but on the stage. *The theatergoer wishing to delve into the heart of Kabuki is urged to attend the same production of a play as many times within its month-long run as possible.* Gradually, the finer points in the staging will become clear. At first, one's attention will be mainly concentrated on the intricacies of the plot and character relationships. *Repeated visits, however, will change the focus to those aural and visual elements that compose the mise-en-scène and which, in this performance-dominated theater, take precedence over the play's existence as 'dramatic literature'.* Constant attention to the performance will bring out all the nuances established by the many actors of the past whose interpretive inventions live on in ever more polished form in the artistry of today's performers. When the spectator has become as familiar as he can with the approach of one set of actors he should then see the same play as done by others. This procedure will help him to perceive the fascinating differences in the traditions as they have been transmitted down the years in the various acting families. These differences are often subtle, yet they may also be rather bold. Exposure to them is a prerequisite for full enjoyment and appreciation of Kabuki technique. Only when the spectator can distinguish between the variances in tradition or the difference in the execution of the same tradition will he be in a position to adequately judge the quality of a performance. (1979, p. xvi)

In his introduction to *The Kabuki Handbook* Faubion Bowers (1956) seems at first to take a Western approach to Kabuki:

People usually make two general remarks about Kabuki. One remark—made by Westerners—is that the story really doesn't matter because Kabuki is a spectacle. The other remark—this is what Japanese like to tell you—is that the stories are nonsense. Without setting myself either in judgment on or apart from such large numbers of people, I do feel a fundamental disagreement with both views, even though I know that each has some substantial truth in it.

Kabuki is essentially theatre and, no matter how glamorous or dazzling it may be to look at, or how synthesized with music, dancing, decor and effects, it is primarily and basically the telling of a story. Whatever poetic or scenic flights Kabuki may indulge in, everything depends on the narrative. And too, regardless of the conventions which set Kabuki so strikingly apart from Western theatre, it is still, like all other theatre, the enactment of a plot and the unfolding of a series of affecting situations. These stories which underlie Kabuki, while being nonsense in a way (the Japanese say *nonsensu*, really meaning "illogical", "inconsistent"), still have meaning, emotion, and, often, historical fact behind them. (p. xi)

Obviously a story is needed as the skeleton on which to hang acting, costumes, and music. Obviously one must know the story reasonably well. Yet, when the Japanese call "nonsense" this kind of theatre, they say clearly that their real interest is not in the story, and that when discussing the performance with their friends, they will not discuss the story for its moral or social or psychological or political implications, but they will discuss how actor X played scene Y, not how actor X gave a new political interpretation to the story. Basically, the Japanese public is interested in how actor X rendered the emotions of Matsuo in recognizing that the head was that of his own son, not in how actor X was able to convey his disgust for a system in which one's lord, in this case Fujiwara Shihei, had to destroy all descendants of Sugawara Michizane in order to be sure that, in the future, none of them would return the courtesy and kill all Fujiwaras: It is pure law of the jungle, but so improved that retainers will, on their own initiative, sacrifice their sons, as Matsuo did with his to save a Sugawara boy who, in turn, might be able to test similarly the devotion of the retainers of the Fujiwara clan in the next round of butchery.

In the past, why run the risk of saying something that, if it was overheard by a spy, would bring one into deep trouble? Why say something critical of the society depicted in the play when this will certainly be interpreted as a criticism of the present government? No, the play has to be nonsensical by definition, it has to be a ballet, as stressed by Samuel Leiter in his introduction to the program of the 1982 tour in America of The Grand Kabuki: "One of the most valuable things a student of Kabuki can learn is the variations in the *kata*[126] associated with the leading actors. This allows for an appreciation of Kabuki that is much like that associated with the performance of classical opera or ballet roles, and, to a far lesser extent, with the principal characters in Shakespeare's plays" (pp. 9-10).

Within this UP world of the *kata*, there was no way by which Kabuki could produce a Beaumarchais who would more than hint at the ideals of *liberté, egalité, et fraternité.*

His *The Marriage of Figaro* was written by 1778 but the assault on the social order was considerably more outrageous than in his earlier plays—or in anyone else's earlier play— and the censorship authorities refused permission to perform it until 1784: the première on the 27th of April was perhaps the greatest triumph in the history of the French theater. The combination of gaiety and sedition, of daring and charm, was irresistible. (At one point [act 3] the Count reproaches Figaro for his detestable reputation. Figaro has a ready answer: "And suppose I am better than my reputation? Can many aristocrats say as much?" (Rosen, 1988, p. 8)

---

[126]*Kata*, or 'form' refers to all aspects of a production, from the costumes, wigs, and makeup, to the music, sets, and properties. Most often, it is used with reference to the differences in the acting interpretations of the leading roles.

Throughout the play, Figaro does not lose any opportunity to criticize aristocrats, and, in the very last scene, he has some harsh words for their manner of dispensing justice. Eighteenth-century audiences did not fail to see the far-reaching social and political implications of the *Marriage* amid its joyfulness. Most representative of them is the Baronne d'Oberkirch, who was angry with herself for having been amused by it. She writes: ". . . . nobility showed a great want of tact in applauding it, which was nothing less than giving themselves a slap in the face. They laughed at their own expense, and what was worse they made others laugh too. They will repent it yet. . . ." Judging the work in retrospect, Napoleon thought that it portrayed "the Revolution in action." Even today Beaumarchais's play is viewed as a vivid illustration of the class struggle. (Sungolowsky, 1974, p. 99)

Something else is instructive in understanding Japan while remaining within the magic world of Kabuki: the history of its name.

The establishment of the Tokugawa order did not happen without protest among the *samurai* themselves and without the appearance of opposition groups, among which the *kabuki mono*[127] provide a most interesting occurrence—very much like the British 'punk' phenomenon of the seventies and early eighties. They acquire a special meaning in the context of the study of *kabuki's* background, because they explain the general association that both audiences and government had with the word *kabuki* at the beginning of the Tokugawa era. The verb *kabuku,* used since the middle ages with the meaning of 'to slant,' or 'to tilt,' had acquired, by the beginning of the Tokugawa era, a slang usage for any anti-establishment action that defied the conventions and the proper rules of behavior. The *kabuki mono* were therefore people who expressed their anti-conformism through a series of protests against the established order, which ranged from highly unusual ways of dressing to shocking hairdos and extravagantly decorated, enormous swords, and up to four-foot-long tobacco pipes. Like today's

---

[127] "Kabuki literally means 'crooked,' or 'deviant and licentious,' and 'mono' signifies 'a person.'" (Ikegami, 1995, p. 205).

motorcycle gangs they would roam the streets and oftentimes engage in acts of violence and riots, flaunting their revolt against all conventions and decency. . . . The bulk of the *kabuki mono* was formed of masterless *samurai*, but youngsters of important samurai families, even of *daimyo,* had joined the gangs, in some cases giving a definite political color to violent actions with potential revolutionary implications, and warning of allegiance to traditional Tokugawa enemies. . . . To the Tokugawa regime *kabuki* meant subversion and heresy, something immoral and dangerous, but in the folk mentality the daring and sometimes heroic behavior of a few major *kabuki mono* leaders became the stuff of legend which was celebrated in songs, tales, and on the stages of the very first *kabuki* shows, while their eccentric fashions became popular all over Japan, even in the remotest villages. (Ortolani, 1995, pp. 164-65)

Yes, "their eccentric fashions became popular all over Japan, even in the remotest villages," but nothing more, nothing to compare with the ideological ferment generated by Beaumarchais, which among others provided the material for Mozart's *Le nozze di Figaro*. With Mozart too, there are no doubts who the villains are, who are abusing their power, and it is not the commoners, but the aristocrats.[128]

In order for Kabuki to have produced a Beaumarchais, it should have been a theater of *representation*, where the ideas dominate over the acting, over scenery and music, and not—as it is—a theatre of *presentation* with its opposite priorities, but that was not possible in Tokugawa Japan (as well as for much of post-Tokugawa Japan). Indeed, "Probably in no other epoch or place in the world has the theater been the object of so many decrees of the supreme authority, of

---

[128] Ikegami Eiko, in *The Taming of the Samurai*, reproduced a 1604 picture with the following caption: "A fight between *kabuki mono* (deviant men) during a Toyokuni festival of 1604. The young man on the left is portrayed with his torso half-naked and an extraordinary long sword with a red sheath slung at his waist. The following words are inscribed on the red sheath: 'I am a man twenty-three years old! I have lived too long! I will not restrain myself!' These are clearly words of a frustrated would-be hero in the era of unification" (1995, p. 194e). "We know from several other pictures and an actual sword sheath surviving from this period that the *kabuki mono* appeared to like this phrase, and they inscribed it on their belongings as a written symbol of their lifestyle" (ib., p. 206). However, as just said, these young unrestrained men could do little to improve society for lack of a valid understanding of the evils of their strict Ritter society.

abolitions, restrictions, and regulations affecting every detail" (ib., p. 163).

Moving back to *The Troubles in the Date Clan,* already its very beginning showed how the Kabuki has been constricted by the partial UP of daimyo and shogun, and how, in turn, it constricted its public.

Scene 1 starts with the arrival of the palanquin of lord Yorikane which isattacked by six or seven swordsmen. Two of them stab at the palanquin from one side while Yorikane emerges unscathed from the other side. This surprises and scares the attackers but only for a short moment. From here on, for about half of scene 1, we see the swordsmen attempting to cut down Yorikane, only to be repulsed by either a sharp look of his, or a gestures of his fan. Yorikane—acted by the *onnagata* female specialist Fukusuke, and dressed in a long robe—has nothing of the warrior in him, and he even looks effeminate (acted, I assume on purpose, by an *onnagata*), and yet he is constantly successful in repulsing his attackers with nothing more than a look or a brief gesture. He can even order one attacker to serve him as a bench on which to rest for a while, and order another to bring him a stone as a footstool. The whole is a clear manifestation of the intrinsic superiority of the lord, even when he neglects his responsibilities with long visits to the pleasure quarters. In comparison with him, everybody else on the scene is a midget, even a master swordsman acting in conjunction with other swordsmen.

Clearly, here, the Kabuki has accepted the notion of the innate superiority of the lord; and at the same time, this notion is passed on to the audience who will be confirmed in their respect for authority. Certainly, in a world used to avoiding eye contact, trained never to look directly at a superior, the idea of having Yorikane repel his attacker by a simple sharp look seems right, and represents the true power of a Japanese lord, boss, or person of higher rank.[129]

---

[129] *Caveat:* In no way should the above be read as a criticism of Kabuki which is a wonderful form of entertainment and great art. I am in no way suggesting to go to the Kabuki with a Western mentality. What might be done, in the future, by the readers of this book, is to devote some of their attention to the *strict Ritter* elements of a play (and nearly all plays include *Ritter* elements). There should be no danger in so doing, as no listener of a Mozart opera has ever been disturbed by Da Ponte/Mozart's critique of the aristocracy. As they say in Texas: "A real cowboy can walk and chew gum at the same time."

7. Flexible Immutability

Koestler's and Patrick Smith's Comments

For Koestler in his *The Lotus and the Robot* of 1960,

> to change the metaphor: Japan absorbed Western science and technology like a sponge; but Western culture and the Western way of life were skin-grafts from an alien donor which, though eagerly accepted, never took. . . . The least successful grafts were those in art and philosophy. They imported, together with machine tools and railway engines, German metaphysics, French scepticism and Russian nihilism; a Bismarkian form of government, with the French system of prefectures; Darwin and Beethoven, Chekhov and Rodin, K. Marx and H. Spencer, with polite impartiality, but somehow these component parts proved more difficult to assemble than cameras and motor-cars. . . .
>
> Though the graft never took, it prevented the growth of natural tissue. Tradition survived—stubbornly rather than triumphantly - but it ceased to develop. The Meiji era was one of rapid material progress and spiritual stagnation. The evolution of poetry and drama, of painting and music, architecture and interior decoration, came by and large to a standstill. Haiku and No, flower arrangement and tea ceremony, became more and more self-conscious rituals - fossil pleasures embedded in petrified aestheticism. To the young they had little to offer. (pp. 178-87)

In essence, there was technical flexibility, but ontological immutability, and little relation between the two.

Patrick Smith is well on target:

> They adopted the technological ways of the West,. . . .*[but] Japan rejected the idea that people were the makers of their own history, autonomous agents of reason and judgement.* Such a proposition was blocked at the border like a contaminated vegetable or an uncensored foreign newspaper. In short, Japan did not become modern so much as a consumer of the modern. (1998, p. 52; my italics)

What Smith said takes its proper place within the present book, on the GAM/DP Theory of Personality and Creativity, as soon as we replace "Japan," with "The Japanese partial Unity of Power" (be it of the daimyo/shogun/emperor or nowadays of the state bureaucracy/ industrial concerns), and we add—after "rejected"—"in order to preserve their power and all the corresponding benefits."

In a *ritter world*, and more significantly in a *strict ritter world*, the first techniques adopted from foreigners, enemies or allies, are military: new weapons, new tactics and strategies. Accordingly the daimyo wasted no time in learning from the Portuguese first how to use muskets and arquebuses, then how to manufacture them:

> In 1543 or 1542, a Chinese junk containing three Portu-guese traders was blown of course by a typhoon, and driven on the shores of Tanegashima Island. . . . the three travellers were the first Europeans to set foot in Japan. Although their appearance and strange dress aroused curiosity, what really excited the Japanese were the firearms they carried. . . . These were exceedingly warlike times, and the needs of the moment had lifted Japanese technology to the level where it could cope with the innovation. Both psychologically and technologically the arquebuses arrived at exactly the right time. After a month of lessons *the Lord of Tanegashima purchased the two speci-mens for a colossal sum of money, and gave the guns to his master swordsmith to copy.* The latter was puzzled by certain technical problems, such as how to close the end of the barrel, but when a Portuguese vessel called in a few months later he exchanged his daughter for a series of lessons in gunmaking, and soon his workshop was turning out home-produced imita-tions as good as the originals. The technique soon spread. (Turnbull, 1977, pp. 137-39; my italics to stress the UP origin of the initiative)

[The gun then helped to settle the battles of the Japanese civil wars.] So well had the Japanese taken to it that they learned to make their own and improved on European models. Indeed, at one point in the late sixteenth century the Japanese may well have been manufacturing more muskets than any single

European nation. [However, once the civil wars were settled, and the nation united under a single government], the guns no longer served a useful purpose. On the contrary, they could only make trouble. Worse yet, the gun was an equalizer. With it, the merest commoner could slay the finest samurai swordsman. One couldn't have that. So, no guns. But the skills that went into making guns were pertinent to a whole range of machinery production and work with metals: screw fasteners, mechanical clocks, eventually rickshaws and bicycles. One Japanese scholar [Sawada Taira] has argued that these guns were "the roots of Meiji technology". (Landes, 1998, p. 358)

Know-how, but not Assimilated Knowledge

The speed and thoroughness with which the Japanese can master a new technology is impressive, while the opposite is true in the intellectual world. In the world of technology, *L'occhio del padrone ingrassa il cavallo* (The eye of the owner fattens the horse); and the Japanese master has very sharp eyes, but only for what benefits him; which new ideas do not.

On the other side of the coin, "from his ironic description of what was presumably a strongly traditional society Maruyama [Masao] concludes that, to the Japanese mind, history has usually meant a mere accumulation of recollections. That is, Japanese history has not experienced the dialectic principle, no conscious opposition to what has gone before" (Arima, 1969, p. 5).

Teaching methods, textbooks, and curricula, from ethics and history to morning exercise routines, are decided by the Education Ministry. All stress the dictation of knowledge to the neglect of the student's ability to manage knowledge—that is, *kyo* at the expense of the *iku*. *Pupils are taught not to think* but to accumulate immense piles of disparate facts that can be repeated on command but cannot be connected. This is not an accident or a lapse. *Rote learning is the child's next lesson in dependence. To think is an act of autonomy; to memorize the given is to rely upon authority.* (Smith, 1998, pp. 78-79; my italics)

This situation, combined with the strict training in obedience, explains "the confusion the Japanese typically feel in the face of the unplanned" (ib., p. 74), for instance when faced with an unexpected question. "The Japanese learn to perform only when the script is written. Put them in a situation requiring a flexible response—when the next thought, the next statement, the next act is up to them—and they become unhinged" (ib., p. 74).

"The Japanese normally learn by rote, advancing simply by repeating what they are told. . . . 'While there is no one who cannot read or write due to nine years of compulsory education, the system is preventing the growth of free, individual personalities.' This appraisal of Japanese schools is notable only for who delivered it: Kunio Hatoyama, a career bureaucrat serving, in the summer of 1992, as education minister. Why, after more than a century of education wars, would the general in command of the castle take the position of the insurgents?" (Smith, 1998, pp. 74, 95). Probably because the general realized that the flexibility given him by technological know-how enabled him to win some battles, yet lose the war.

Moving to the industrial and commercial world, we hear criticisms as strict as those, reported above, of Minister Kunio Hatoyama on the school: "A growing number of disillusioned Japanese are recognizing that *the company claim to being a family is a sham. Tear away the facade, they say, and what you find is a feudal system. And they are right.* The same martial values that reshaped the family have been imposed on men in the workplace. The martial emblems are everywhere: in the uniforms, the salutes at the entrance, the ranks of the hierarchy, and the fight-to-the-death mentality, which, I'm sorry to say, is all too literal. Thus, whatever private feelings of independence the worker may harbor, his life, for all practical purposes, belongs to the company. Soldiers may grumble, but they may not disobey" (Naff, 1994, p. 113; my italics).

What we have here is *flexible immutability*: the immutable martial values and respect for authority, the same emphasis on fidelity and total dedication, but flexibly applied to business. Wealth, honor, and power now belong to the financial and academic daimyo.

Without real DP in Japan, without, in particular, a few *wars of the scripts* (see chapter 1 of volume 1) no lofty ideas will be digested properly, assimilated, managed, and overcome dialectically. The system will remain *flexibly immutable*.

8. What if Japan had not been United, but had Evolved into a Confederation?

As noted by William Johnston, the original Christian

> missionary effort was initiated in the Sengoku Period [1490-1600] when Japan, torn by strife among the warring daimyos, had no strong central government. The distressful situation of the country, however, was not without advantages for the missionaries who, when persecuted in one fief, could quickly shake the dust off their feet and betake themselves elsewhere. But unification was close at hand; and Japan was soon to be welded into that solid monolith which was eventually to break out over Asia in 1940. The architects of unity (Nobunaga, Hideyoshi and Ieyasu) were all on intimate terms with the Portuguese Jesuits, motivated partly by desire for trade with the black ships from Macao, partly (in the case of Nobunaga and Hideyoshi) by a deep dislike of Buddhism, and partly by the fascination of these cultured foreigners with whom they could converse without fear of betrayal and loss of prestige. Be that as it may, from 1570 until 1614 the missionaries held such a privileged position at the court of the Bakufu that their letters and reports are now the chief source of information for a period of history about which Japanese sources say little. (1978, pp. 3-4)

These comments on how quickly the missionaries could betake themselves elsewhere in case of trouble, bring to mind a similar observation by Joel Mokyr on the scientific and technological development of the West:

> In China's past, technological progress had typically been absorbed by the political status quo, without disturbing the existing order. Radical technological changes threatening the balance of power were carefully avoided. The difference between China and Europe was that in Europe the power of any social group to sabotage an innovation it deemed detrimental to its interests was far smaller. First, in Europe technological change was essentially a matter of private initiative; the role of rulers was usually secondary and passive. Few significant

contributions to nonmilitary technology were initiated by the state in Europe before (or during) the Industrial Revolution. There was a market for ideas, and the government entered these markets as just another customer or, more rarely, another supplier. Second, whenever a European government chose to take an actively hostile attitude toward innovation and the nonconformism that bred it, it had to face the consequences in terms of its relative status in the economic (and thus, eventually, political) hierarchy. Moreover, the possibilities of migration within Europe allowed creative and original thinkers to find a haven if their place of birth was insufficiently tolerant, so that in the long run, reactionary societies lost out in the competition for wealth and power. (1990, p. 233)

In Japan, the DP of a less unitary state might have permitted not only a continuation of technological development, of scientific discovery, and most importantly of major philosophical, social, and political ideas. Under the influence of Christianity, a fair amount of the strictness in the Japanese character might have been eliminated and replaced by equivalent doses of "Thou shalt love thy neighbour as thyself" and "Behave like the Good Samaritan." The idea of such a development is not far fetched considering the well deserved praise that Maraini gave to pre-Tokugawa Japan: "With Ieyasu a new age begins; a heroic, luminous age, *rich in infinite possibilities,* had ended; its successor was meaner and pettier, dominated by fear and suspicion, spying and bureaucracy. Once Ieyasu had gathered power completely into his own hands, his only thought was how to preserve it for his descendants" (1960, p. 325; my italics).

Obviously, what happened, happened; yet a discussion of what could reasonably have happened could sharpen a discussion of the Japanese personality by placing matters in a proper set of comparisons and contrasts.

9. A critique of Arima Tatsuo's *The Failure of Freedom: A Portrait of Modern Japanese Intellectuals*

Arima Tatsuo has written a fascinating book on the dominant modes of thought of the Japanese intellectual of the Taisho era (1912-1926). Yet it is a flawed book—with all due respect—because of his wrong understanding of Japan, his wrong understanding of the history of the evolution of the West, and correspondingly of his wrong critique of the intellectuals of the Taisho era.

Arima has not been able to free himself from the main Japanese scripts[130] notwithstanding his studies at Harvard University (his book evolved from his doctoral dissertation presented to Harvard's Department of Government).

Arima's Main Thoughts

Arima's preface sets the problem:

> This book deals with the dominant modes of thought in prewar Japan, primarily in the Taisho era (1912-1926), and with the intellectuals' failure to grasp the simple fact that such ideas as freedom and emancipation—which many of them enthusiastically espoused—are basically political and social categories. I have tried to explain some of the reasons why these so-called Taisho intellectuals could not see the virtues of a constitutional form of government, however clumsily inaugurated it may have been in Japan. (1969, p. vii)

Then, in chapter 1 he said:

> Once the changes heralded by the Meiji Restoration were set in motion, not a single institution, ideology, or religion seriously raised a voice in opposition. Maruyama Masao refers to this as the absence of tradition. From his ironic description of what was presumably a strongly traditional society, Maruyama concludes that, to the Japanese mind, history has usually meant a mere accumulation of recollections. That is, Japanese history has not experienced the dialectical principle, no conscious opposition to what has gone before. The negation of the past has not been necessary, for there has been no tyranny of the past as in the West, where Christianity and the Church stood as a bulwark against change, frustrating the

---

[130] Arima was probably a *dedicated personality*. According to the GAM theory, the only effective way to be free from old scripts is to not have them from the beginning, to not have assimilated them during youth, as discussed in volume 1. On the contrary, Natsume Soseki, Mishima Yukio, and Endo Shusaku, were powerful *challenged personalities*.

individual's social emancipation or his freedom of thought. Before a nation-state could assert itself in Europe, the idea of the Universal Church had to be disposed of. Secularization in general entailed the expansion of the liberty of conscience, and this meant that the individual consciousness had to confront directly the Christian dogmas it was in the process of rejecting. Again and again such active confrontations took place, on the intellectual level and on the level of social institutions. And these two levels were closely related. Filmer and Locke, the Leviathan and the Thomistic concept of politics, or Bodin and Althusius were real alternatives for thought and action. It cannot be overemphasized that Japan did not undergo any such experience, either with respect to ideologies or with respect to such institutions as the family or the monarchy. *Since these ideologies and institutions had all the flexibility of the undefined as well as the tenacity of the functional,* there was no reason to apotheosize any one of them in order to kill it. How then was the Japanese intellectual to make the kind of break with convention that would symbolize his emancipation? A number of alternatives suggested themselves. One involved a total flight from society on religious or aesthetic grounds, placing the ultimate hope of the individual outside society, either in eschatological anticipation or in artistic creation. (ib., pp. 5-6; my italics).

Critique of Arima's Thoughts on Japan

For Arima "the negation of the past has not been necessary, for there has been no tyranny of the past as in the West . . . .". This can be read in two ways, either: Japan has not suffered of the tyranny of the past, or: Japan has suffered a tyranny of the past different from that of the West. If it is the second case, we must be clear on what this tyranny consists of, apart from not being the same as suffered by the West.

Later we are told that ideologies and such institutions as the family or the monarchy must be killed. But why? Why, should both be killed if Japan did not suffer of a tyranny of the past?For Arima, the Japanese ideologies and institutions have all the flexibility of the undefined as well as the tenacity of the functional. Flexibility in what? If they are basically flexible, there should be no problem. If they are truly functional, there should, again, be no problem. A country with flexible and functional ideologies and institutions is an ideal country.

Nobody can ask for better. But if so, why kill institutions and family there? Similarly why should a Japanese take "a total flight from [such a flexible and functional] society, on religious or aesthetic grounds"?

At page vii, Arima spoke of a desire for freedom and emancipation. Freedom from what, emancipation from what? Freedom from tyranny, emancipation from tyranny should have been the answer. But which tyranny if there is no tyranny of the past, and one lives under flexible and functional ideologies and institutions?

The truth, as reported in many books on Japan, and in this chapter, is that there was tyranny, for centuries, by the shogun all over Japan, by the daimyo over their principalities, by the samurai over peasants, artisans, and merchants. There was, and still is, a mighty tyranny of the past, of tradition, of history as a mere accumulation of recollections. When Sogoro was crucified with his wife and four children because he had "treated public authority lightly" wasn't this tyranny of the worse kind? (And it was psychological tyranny also, because that story told people never to try to redress a tort, never to try to avoid dying of hunger because of excessive taxes). When Lord Asano had to commit suicide (for a minor error, far more the fault of the system than of himself), when the severest punishments were inflicted on his house: confiscation of property, extinction of the family name, when all his retainers—some three hundred—were thrown into poverty, made into destitute ronin, didn't all this happen because of the tyranny of the shogun and the tyranny of tradition?

While on one side the story of the 47 ronin is a paean in honor of absolute fidelity, on the other it is a story of needless killing. And if everybody in Japan uncritically loves this story, isn't it an indication of a strong tyranny of tradition? Wouldn't it be better to trade this tradition for one which praises the Parable of the Good Samaritan, i.e., a story of unselfish help? As we know, this parable is at the root of the creation of the Red Cross and Red Crescent International organization which unselfishly help others on a huge international scale, with no restrictions as to race, nationality, gender, and religion.

With the Japanese tradition of tyranny, Arima's demand that the Taisho intellectuals should have related their ideas of freedom and emancipation to political and social categories is to demand the impossible; the un-natural.

"From his ironic description of what was presumably a strongly traditional society Maruyama [Masao] concludes that, to the Japanese mind, history has usually meant a mere accumulation of recollections.

That is, Japanese history has not experienced the dialectic principle, no conscious opposition to what has gone before" (ib., 1969, p. 5).

But why did Japan not experience the dialectic principle? Why did Japan lack a conscious opposition to what had gone before? Was it because the Japanese did not need it, or because they were constantly prevented from doing so?

In a *samuraized world* (Smith, 1998, p. 191)—in a world which owed everything to the samurai, who were not only the flower of the nation, but its root as well (Nitobe, 1905/2001, p. 150), in a world in which the best people entrusted matters of good and evil to the lord (Yamamoto, c. 1700/1983, p. 20), in an world in which the samurai's condition consisted first in seriously devoting soul and body to one's master (ib., p. 66, my italics)—there was no possibility for any antithesis. The lord was the law, and not a thesis, because the lord not only could not bear a shade of antithesis, but not even the presence of an intelligent face (ib., p. 13).

The will of the lord had, indeed, "all the flexibility of the undefined as well as the tenacity of the functional" (Arima, 1969, p. 5): *undefined* because the lord's will was conditioned, day by day, by the plans and actions of his opponents, or by the opportunities which suddenly opened up to him for acquiring more land, wealth or glory; and *functional* because everything had to be tailored to his profit, with nothing wasted.

Critique of Arima's Thoughts on the West

To the readers of my books (and many books on the Middle Ages), I need not say that Arima's understanding of Christianity and the Church—as a bulwark against change, frustrating the individual's social emancipation or his freedom of thought—is wrong: it lacks historical, developmental, interactional, and dialectical perspective. For centuries, Christianity and the Church were the main force of social emancipation and freedom of thought, and the authentic West with its DP would be inconceivable without the Church (see chapters 11 and 23 of volume 1).

Yes, by itself, the Church was often UP, but luckily a UP dialectically opposed by the imperial or royal UP, and the result was the beginning of the Western DP and of the *visitor personality*. Today, the successor of the medieval DP is the DP of the First Amendment to the American Constitution which built a wall of separation between

Church and State, according to the lapidary definition of Thomas Jefferson. Luckily, that wall remains porous permitting a constant lively dialectic on such vital subjects as justice, fairness, charity, marriage, education, euthanasia, assistance to the poor, the meaning of life.

The real danger for humanity was never the Universal Church (of say the Catholic type which could be corrected by an unarmed St. Francis of Assisi or defeated by an un armed Martin Luther), but the Universal State of the Chinese, German, Russian, or Japanese type. It was when the State defeated the Church's Ten Commandments, and erased the memory of the Good Samaritan, that we got *La Terreur*, and the Nazi and Communist extermination and concentration camps. On this, Arima should read Levi's *Survival in Auschwitz*, Klemperer's *I will bear witness: A diary of the Nazi Years*, Reich-Ranicki's *Mein Leben*, Solzhenitsyn's *The Gulag Archipelago*. Yes, there was the Spanish Inquisition, the burning alive of Michael Servetus and Giordano Bruno, the forced recanting of Galileo Galilei, the kidnapping of Edgar Mortara, but these crimes pale in comparison with those perpetrated by the State.

Far be it from me to whitewash the Church of its crimes: left alone it would have evolved into a Church-State as bad as a State-Church. However the great DP that began at Canossa in 1077 led to a *visitor critical attitude* reflected—a long time before the Renaissance—in the poem by the Sienese poet Cecco Angiolieri (ca. 1260-1312; discussed in chapter 13, vol. 1) in which he made fun at the same time of pope and emperor:

> If I were pope, I would be merry and would cheat all Christians;
>
> If I were emperor, what would I do? I would chop off everybody's head.[131]

Where in all the Japanese literature can one find the equivalent of Cecco Angiolieri poking fun, at the same time, at both emperor and shogun?

No, Arima, in Western history the State was never better than the Church. Eliminate the Church, as was done during the French Revolu-

---

[131] What Cecco said in fun was later said seriously by Lord Acton: "Power tends to corrupt and absolute power corrupts absolutely."It corrupted emperors, kings, popes, daimyos and shoguns

tion and in Communist Russia, drastically reduce the power of the Church as in Nazi Germany, and you have evil on top of evil. Every form of UP is evil, be it by the church, by the state, the emperor, the shogun, the daimyo. Proof of this can be found in Japan: Who has been there the "bulwark against change, frustrating the individual's social emancipation or his freedom of thought"? Was it the Church, or was it the lay system of shogun-daimyo-samurai?

Ikegami's Correct Thoughts on Japan Versus the West

Also Ikegami Eiko, in his *The Taming of the Samurai* of 1995, felt the need to contrast Japan with the West, and he did it, with great understanding, in a section entitled "Logic of the Shogunate's Legitimacy":

The ability to keep the peace mattered at the formal level of legitimating the Tokugawa shogunate. In order to build a consensus supporting their domination, Western rulers from the Middle Ages through the early modern period usually attempted to legitimate their position by defining the sovereign's role as the guardian of justice[132] and the defender of the orthodox faith. The Western Church played an important part in conferring legitimacy on a regime's authority in this process.[133] In a simi-

---

[132] This, as noted by Strayer (1970), was reinforced by the *Investiture Controversy* "a tendency which already existed: the tendency to consider the lay ruler primarily as a guarantor and a distributor of justice. The Gregorian reformers might believe that the Church defined what justice was, but even they admitted that in normal conditions it was the duty of secular rulers to see that justice was dispensed to the people. It was even more important for kings to emphasize this function. If they no longer shared responsibility for the guidance and governance of the Church, if they were no longer 'bishops for external affairs,' then their only excuse for existence was to enforce justice" (p. 23).

[133] The coronation of Pepin III, the father of Charlemagne, by the Pope in 751, as the first king of the Carolingian dynasty is a clear example of this intervention by the Church. The year before, Pepin—mayor of the palace, and the de facto ruler of the Franks—had sent two envoys to Pope Zacharias with a letter asking: "Is it wise to have kings who hold no power of control?" The Pope answered: "It is better to have a king able to govern. By apostolic authority I bid that you be crowned King of the Franks." The Merovingian King Childeric III was deposed and sent to a monastery, and Pepin was anointed as king at Soissons. Norman Cantor wrote: "By Frankish law there was no way that the Carolingian mayor of the palace could take [the royal title] away from him [the Merovingian king]. He needed ecclesiastical support, particularly papal authority, to usurp the French crown" (1993, p. 174).

In Japan, the lack of a similarly independent ecclesiastical authority made it impossible—among other reasons, but of lesser importance—for a shogun to make himself emperor.

lar manner, by 1600, Japan had already developed a well-established political institution to legitimize the samurai regime: the imperial court with its traditional authority gave the *de facto* ruler of the country *de jure* recognition as the overlord of the samurai with the authority to govern the country. *Upon closer examination, however, this legitimation of the samurai ruler was not mediated by a notion of justice or other overarching abstractions to justify the overlord's power. The emperor's court itself, though its traditional authority was supported by ancient mythology, had never claimed to represent either moral truth or justice.* (pp. 155-56; my italics) . . . .

The absence of a concentrated transcendental religious power meant that the Tokugawa shoguns had no reliable form of legitimation other than formal recognition from the emperor's court. The drawback was that the imperial authority in Japan then did not have a spiritual authority comparable to that of the Christian Church; the emperor simply lacked moral influence over the population at large. . . . In order to understand the unique development of Japan's warrior culture, we must consider this relationship of Japanese feudalism with religious institutions. In Europe, the Church attempted, though not always very successfully, to transform the violence of pre-Christian warrior cultures into an ideal of Christian knighthood. . . . . In Japan, neither the medieval nor the Tokugawa samurai had this forceful experience. There was no *organized* intervention by a religious-ideological power representing transcendental values that institutionally challenged samurai practices in any fundamental fashion. Even though they had the desire, the religious traditions of Japan did not have a sufficient institutional basis in most situations to enforce their values on the samurai population in general" (pp. 189-90).

Fascinating, in relation to the DP theory, are Ikegami's thoughts on the role played by the *War of Supremacy* (between Church and State) in the development of the West, and on the lack of a similar positive influence in Japan:

The great difference in the relationships between religious power and secular feudal power in Europe and Japan respectively must be acknowledged. . . . . Japanese feudalism developed without a supportive religious power comparable to the institutional strength of Christianity. . . . Buddhism, the dominant religion of Japan, never developed a powerful *single institutional* center equivalent to the Catholic Church, which claimed a monopoly of orthodox faith. In terms of ideological content, Japanese religious institutions usually did not generate a power of normative monopoly, thereby claiming superiority to the sovereign's political jurisdiction. Unlike the medieval Church, which asserted the existence of universal standards of truth and justice that were greater than the secular sovereignty of any one European country, the medieval Japanese Buddhist temples did not establish normative and transcendental values to which the secular authority should, in theory, be subject.

Joseph Strayer has argued that, in contrast to the Japanese situation, the role of the state in Europe was first clearly defined through its functional differentiation from the Church, during the period of what was called the *Gregorian Reformation* and the *Investiture Controversy (1075-1122)*. During this process, which is sometimes called the "Papal Revolution," the Roman Catholic Church gained both autonomy and considerable control over secular forces by asserting its supremacy over the laity. This authority included the claim that justice should always be defined by the Church in its capacity as the guardian of ultimate truth. Unexpectedly, the Church's institutional victory required a corresponding redefinition of the state's role, since the Church could not perform all political functions. It then became the duty of secular rulers to dispense justice to the people. In short, "the Gregorian concept of the Church almost demanded the invention of the concept of the State"[134]. (ib., pp. 186-87)

This said, let me add a caveat to Strayer's argument. Based on my studies, the Investiture Controversy should be praised less for "the invention of the concept of the State" than for "the invention of the *visitor personality*." In this understanding I am not alone. Colin Morris noted in his *The Discovery of the Individual 1050-1200* that "there is a

---

[134] Joseph Strayer, *On the Medieval Origins of the Modern State*, 1970. Princeton, NJ: Princeton University Press, p. 22.

rapid rise in individualism and humanism from about 1080 to 1150" (1972, p. 7), and Alfred Crosby wrote in his *The Measure of Reality* that between 1250 and 1350 there came in the West not so much in theory as in actual application, a marked shift "from qualitative perception to, or at least toward, quantification perception" (1997, p. 49).

Less than a socio-political invention, the *visitor personality* (as discussed in chapter 11 of volume 1) is a transformation of the way people think and feel. It is the mental development of people who had to chose between Power A (the Emperor) and Power B (the Pope) when confronted by their demands and offers, and by their propaganda: each claiming to possess the truth and the right to command *urbis et orbis*. At the end of the *war of the scripts*, the *visitors* existed: they had refused the claims of both powers A and B, and were constantly developing new dialectical syntheses.[135]

---

[135] The text by Strayer, quoted by Ikegami, is important and deserves to be quoted in extenso first, then commented: "Like all victories, the victory of the Church in the Investiture Conflict had unforeseen consequences. By asserting its unique character, by separating itself so clearly from lay governments, the Church unwittingly sharpened concepts about the nature of secular authority. Definitions and arguments might vary, but the most ardent Gregorian had to admit that the Church could not perform all political functions, that lay rulers were necessary and had a sphere in which they should operate. They might be subject to the guidance and correction of the Church, but they were not a part of the administrative structure of the Church. They headed another kind of organization, for which there was as yet no generic term. In short, the Gregorian concept of the Church almost demanded the invention of the concept of the State. It demanded it so strongly that modern writers find it exceedingly difficult to avoid describing the Investiture Conflict as a struggle of Church and State" (ib., p. 22).

Yet, expanding on the above, the State, once invented, had the tendency to grow and to turn first against the Church, then (as UP) against everybody like the nameless monster created by Dr. Frankenstein who ultimately turned to evil. Left alone, each— Church and State—will turn to evil, more so the State because of its control of the army, the police, and the ultimate weapon, money. All this, instead, is not the case with the other invention of those times: the *visitor personality* who is capable of siding with one or the other of these powers, or with neither of them. For instance, Henri Dunant, the founder of the Red Cross, Alfred Nobel, the founder of the prizes that bear his name and distribute his money, and Pierre de Coubertin, the founder of the modern Olympic Games, were neither on the side of the State nor of the Church, and as such were the creators of great supra-national entities.

Karl Popper said something important in *The Poverty of Historicism* which confirms my emphasis on the *visitor personality*: "You cannot construct foolproof institutions, that is to say, institutions whose functioning does not very largely depend upon persons: institutions, at best, can reduce the uncertainty of the personal element, by assisting those who work for the aims for which the institutions are designed, and on whose personal initiative and knowledge success largely depends. Institutions are like fortresses. They must be well designed *and* properly manned" (1957/1961, p. 66; italics in the original). Replace the *visitors* with *insulars* or *skeptics*, or with *ritter* and *strict ritter*, and the state will do evil.

Moving to Japan, the problem was not the invention of the concept of the State (the Japanese mastered this concept a long time ago, probably too well) but the lack of the dialectical invention of the *Japanese visitor personality(ies)*[136].

Nishida Kitaro

Following his introductory comments (reported in the main above) Arima had a section entitled "Nishida Kitaro: The epistemological character of Taisho Japan." In it, Arima said that

no one made a more profound attempt to emancipate the self and to actualize his individual aspirations beyond society than Nishida Kitaro (1870-1945). Unanimously, histories of Japanese philosophy single him out as modern Japan's most creative philosopher. His metaphysical system reveals many intellectual elements which he shared with less articulate Japanese. . . . In 1899 he wrote to his closest friend: "What do you think is the means by which we might attain what you name the unity of thought? I believe the method of Zen is the shortest way to attain this end. If we could not get to this unity of thought through Zen . . . . no other means would do. Therefore, regardless of the actual outcome, I intend to discipline myself in the ways of Zen throughout my life." His diary and correspondence show how persistently Nishida meditated in Zen temples. "It has been already a few years since I started to sit at Zen. Progress is slow. I have gained nothing. I feel fully ashamed of myself." Again he writes: "Although I sit (Zen terminology indicating meditation), with the recurrence of such miscellaneous thoughts as the wish to be a college professor or to go abroad to study, etc. . . . . somehow I cannot purify myself." The intellectual's effort to free his inner self from the anxieties of social life is nowhere better and more honestly stated than in these writings of Nishida Kitaro. . . . This category of pure experience is the essence of existence. "In order

---

[136]There is no one single type of visitor personality. We are dealing, as said in chapter 25 of volume 1, with a Wittgensteinian "family resemblance," in which no characteristic is mandatorily needed, but only a high aggregate of them is required.

to comprehend the essence of existence and the genuine nature of the universe, we have to proceed from knowledge which cannot be questioned, knowledge which is free from all artificial hypothesis . . . . Science, for example, is based on hypothetical knowledge, and does not purport to be, or to attain, the profoundest explanation of real existence". (Arima, 1969, pp. 7-8)

Basically, in the above, we encounter a set of aims which the unity of power loves completely:

a) comprehend the essence of existence and the genuine nature of the universe, and proceed from knowledge which cannot be questioned; and

b) despise science, because it does not purport to be, or attain, the profoundest explanation of real existence.

If Mondino de Luzzi, Galileo and Newton had spent their best energies in comprehending the essence of existence we would have no science; and if Dante, Boccaccio, the authors of the Magna Carta, and Lord Acton had tried to comprehend the genuine nature of the universe, they would not have criticized the power of popes and kings: such criticisms would have been far below their lofty contemplations, nothing but petty grievances of petty people.

Luckily, science is not "based on hypothetical knowledge." Instead, "the essence of the scientific method is the insistence that all propositions be subjected to an empirical test. Only after this has been done does the scientist decide to accept or reject a proposition" (Cozby, 1981, p. 5).Similarly, "the scientific enterprise is based on the belief that there are consistencies or laws that can be observed through empirical investigation. . . . The corner stone of the scientific method is its commitment to putting ideas to an empirical test" (Weiten, 1989, pp. 34, 36). It is a very modest program, but the only one which gives truth as correspondence of statements with facts, i.e. a statement is true if and only if it corresponds to the facts. On the other hand, it is this modest program—one empirical test after the other, one empirical consistency or law after the other—that has given us strongly verified and perfectly integrated truths, which have forced the mightiest powers on earth to change their minds, and bow to science.

It was science that went to the popes and told them, "Your Holiness has to change his mind: the earth is not at the center of the universe, but is only a humble satellite of the sun; forget geocentrism and move to heliocentrism." And the popes—surrounded by many *visitor personalities*—accepted.

It was science that said: "The universe was not created in seven days, it was not created a few thousand years ago, but it began at least 10 billion years ago. Also, man is not a special creature—in between angels and animals—but an animal (even if a very clever one to begin with and then increasingly culturally enriched) strictly related to gorillas, orangutans, and monkeys". And again the popes, after some struggle, agreed, because what science said was true.

To the papacy's honor, it was no less than His Holiness Pope John Paul II who said that ". . . . *Western Civilization which is marked by a positive approach to the world, and which developed thanks to the achievement of science and technology*, two branches of knowledge rooted both in the ancient Greek philosophical tradition and in Judeo-Christian Revelation" (1955, p. 88; my italics to stress both the Western "positive approach to the world" and "the achievement of science and technology").

Back to Nishida Kitaro, no thinker who thought he had discovered "the essence of existence and the genuine nature of the universe" would have achieved any reduction of the power of popes and emperors. In such esoteric matters as the "essence of existence" everybody is entitled to say that he or she knows, given that there is no way to validly contrast one essence with another, no way to test them for truth. So, no *supremo* will ever object if his best intellectuals devote themselves completely to the search for the "essence of existence," and leave him free to control the "inferior world of reality."

Uchimura Kanzo

Arima's next chapter is entitled "Uchimura Kanzo: The politics of spiritual despair."

Here we read that for Uchimura:

man's most virtuous concern is patriotism: "My Christianity is patriotic. . . . Patriotism means that one believes in the divine mission of the nation and devotes one's entire self in behalf of the mission. . . . The Japanese should not be merely satisfied with imitating the West but we shall have to add to what the Europeans have created." This sentiment of personal identification with the ends of the Japanese nation was not confined to Uchimura. Even Christian socialists related their ideals to the needs of Japan rather than to those of the individual. . . . In 1916, however, he wrote: "Now that Christianity is dying in Europe and America because of their materialism, they cannot revive it; God is calling upon Japan to contribute its best to His service." This nationalistic concern with Japan held on tenaciously in Uchimura's thinking throughout his life. Like earlier samurai converts, he felt that since the old, traditional ideologies had lost their vigor, Christianity was the only religion that could give direction to Japan and retain the best elements of Japanese asceticism. (ib., pp. 19-20)

Here, again, we are on dangerous UP ground, because the religion of Uchimura renders to Caesar not only the things which are Caesar's but also those which are God's: "My Christianity is patriotic. . . . Patriotism means that one believes in the divine mission of the nation and devotes one's entire self in behalf of the mission." However, the Christianity of Jesus (and of St. Paul, St. Francis of Assisi, and many other great saints) never believed in the divine mission of any nation!

10. "Japan as Swamp" Revisited

In the words of Richard Schuchert: "Christianity has not flourished in Japan, even though the long history of this island country is a story of importing foreign ideas and ways: the Japanese writing system, Buddhist religion and Confucian ethics, industrial technology, democracy, etc. Yet always the people have maintained their distinctive Japanese character. Creatively they adapt whatever is adopted from abroad. Christianity, however, has not been adopted. Why not? Joseph Kitagawa, a noted Christian scholar, is of this opinion:

In sharp contrast to Confucianism and Buddhism . . . . Christianity has tended to reject not only all the rival religious systems but also the values and meanings of the cultural and historical experience of the Japanese. . . . Christianity tends to make Japanese Christians *uprooted*—but not necessarily *lib-*

erated—from their social, cultural, and spiritual traditions and surroundings. (1978, p. 4; italics by Schuchert)

I disagree. Firstly, "the Japanese writing system, Buddhist religion and Confucian ethics, industrial technology, [and] democracy" were not persecuted by burning, decapitation, hanging in the pit, and the psychological torture of key leaders by hanging their followers in a pit.

Secondly, until the persecutions switched into high gear, conversions to Christianity in Japan were high in both quantity and quality. Before the persecutions, "there were about 300,000 Christians in Japan (whose total population was about twenty million) in addition to colleges, seminaries, hospitals and a growing local clergy. 'It would be difficult', writes Boxer, 'if not impossible, to find another highly civilized pagan country where Christianity had made such a mark, not merely in numbers but in influence'" (Johnston, 1978, p. 6). Those Japanese had no problem integrating their past scripts with the new ones.

Thirdly, we should not forget that many things changed between the end of the sixteenth century and the second half of the twentieth century. The intellectual and civilizing power of Christianity is not what it once was. In that time, Europe has gone through the Enlightenment, the French Revolution, the Industrial Revolution; through Marxism, Communism, and the Russian Revolution; through the Scientific Revolution with such giants as Galileo, Newton, Darwin, and Einstein; as well as through the Nazis and the Holocaust. All these developments affected Christianity and made it less modern, definitely not as modern as it was in Japan at the end of the sixteenth century, before the persecutions, when Toyotomo Hideyoshi used to stroll "through the gilded halls of Juraku palace wearing a rosary and Portuguese dress" (Boxer, 1951, p. 153). Today, Christianity may tend "to make Japanese Christians *uprooted* but not necessarily *liberated*," but that was not the case in the sixteenth century.

Fourthly, the problem, as I see it, is not to become liberated from the old social, cultural, and spiritual traditions and surroundings, but to dialectically grow into a *Japanese visitor personality* under full DP (political, economic, cultural). Under DP, creativity blooms and new solutions are discovered, presented and discussed.

As presented in chapter 6 of volume 1 "Creativity via a Detour Abroad," the greatest authors, the best "authentic national writers" had immersed themselves, in their youth, in extensive foreign reading: proof of the importance for creativity of a major *war of the scripts* (national and foreign), and proof also of the vitality of the old (national) scripts when leavened by the new (foreign) scripts. Clearly, nobody can say a priori how the old will be used, but it can be used extensively, and with very good results. It has been done elsewhere, it can be done in Japan. So, there is no ontological swamp, but only a number of old limitations and strictures which can be overcome.

11. Behind the Smiling Mask

"Early in 1893 [Lafcadio] Hearn wrote to Chamberlain concerning his cook: 'My cook wears a smiling, healthy, rather pleasing face. He is a good-looking young man. Whenever I used to think of him I thought of the smile. . . . One day I looked through a little hole in the shoji and saw him alone. The face was not the same face. It was thin and drawn and showed queer lines worn by old hardship. I thought: 'He will look just like that when he is dead.' I went in and the man was all changed—young and happy again—nor have I ever seen that look of trouble in his face since. But I knew when he is alone he wears it. He never shows his real face to me; he wears the mask of happiness as an etiquette. . . ." (Richie, 1997, p. 145).

Alessandro Valignano had already made a similar observation, three hundred years before, in his *Sumario* of 1580:

[The Japanese] have such control over their anger and impatience that it is almost a miracle to witness any quarrel or insulting words in Japan, whether with one another or with foreigners; in such wise that even if they are killed, they do not revile thereat, neither do they ever complain or grumble about bad luck. On the other hand, they are the most false and treacherous people of any known in the world; for from childhood they are taught never to reveal their hearts, and they regard this as prudence and the contrary as folly, to such a degree that those who lightly reveal their mind are looked upon as nitwits, and are contemptuously termed single-hearted men. Even fathers and sons never reveal their true thought to each other, because there can be no mutual confidence between them in word or deed; for when they are most determined to do evil to someone, the more outward compliments they pay him. Thus when they wish to kill somebody, just when they are about to do so, they show him more politeness and kind words, in order the better to effect their intention; and in truth they cannot live with one another in any other way. . . . Among other things, they are accustomed never to discuss affairs of moment face to face, but always through an intermediary; so much so, that even fathers and sons never ask nor discuss any question of importance with each other, nor counsel nor warn each other save through a third person; all of which renders very slow and difficult the dispatch of any weighty business with them. (1962, p. 287-88)

Have things changed since the times of Hearn? Not much. As noted by Patrick Smith:

The first thing we discover about them, ironically, is that they are accustomed to hiding—from themselves as well as others. Every Japanese wears a mask, or so each one is taught. And within their masks the Japanese have learned to live close to one another by living far apart. But beneath the placid, unchanging surface of Japan's oddly vacant, undecided present are countless conflicts, tensions, crosscurrents, and anxieties. They have always been there. They have merely become more apparent now, as if a lid were lifted, or a mask partially removed. . . . For the group is a kind of fiction in Japan. It is within the group that the Japanese put on their masks. To assume a mask is to assume a role—a public, designated role in the group. The masks of the Japanese are also masks of sameness. By wearing them, the Japanese signify to themselves that there are no differences among them, and that having no differences is part of what it means to be Japanese. . . . Then as now, it was not individuality that was missing so much as public individuality, the open manifestation of the self, the self unmasked within the group. In the same way, the Japanese did not live without their own history—no more, at least, than anyone else in a feudal society. Their history was merely hidden by the society that preferred them to remain nameless. There is a vast chasm between the simplicity arriving foreigners often find in Japan and the furtive, unrevealed complexity that lies within. (1998, pp. 35-36, 38-39)

Moving to a different point of view, according to Nitobe: "*What Japan was she owed to the samurai. They were not only the flower of the nation, but its root as well.* All the gracious gifts of Heaven flowed through them. Though they kept themselves socially aloof from the populace, they set a moral standard for them and guided them by their example" (1905/2001, p. 150; my italics).

May be, may be not: "Loyalty can be a fine thing, but Japan's notion of loyalty, loyalty that admits of no questions, led it into a world war, after all. Hard work, by the same token, has historically been a matter of desperate necessity. *As to respect for authority, it is better understood as obsequiousness bred of fear.* A clear picture of the past leads to a fundamental point about the Japanese, an understanding that changes everything. *Once we recognize the conflict beneath the surface, we understand that group identity had more to do with coercion and power than with tradition and culture*" (Smith, 1998, p. 51; my italics). In other words, there is no smiling behind the mask.

12. Conclusion and Recommendation

Arima's own "Conclusion" began as follows:

Natsume Soseki once described the experience of modern Japanese intellectuals in search of meaning as a "hell of loneliness." In *Kojin (Passers-by* [or *The Wayfarer*]) he wrote: "I have no other course for my future but to become insane, to die, or to embrace religion." *The three choices were the alternatives to existing in a hostile society.* The intellectuals were heirs to the legacy of the revolutionary restoration. Deep in their hearts they were trapped by the historical paradox that modern Japan was born not so much of the victory of the new forces over the old as of the skillful self-transformation of the old forces themselves. To reject parts of the new Japanese society, then, often meant to reject the whole of it. Whatever solution they sought, be it independence, freedom, or emancipation, they tended to locate it elsewhere than in their own society, for they found it difficult to recognize such ideals as social categories. (pp. 214-15; my italics)

But was it their fault? Or was it the fault of the high power above them which could easily tolerate thousands of philosophical meditations in Zen temples, but did not tolerate the least interference in the social realm, as was the case with poor Sogoro who had demanded only a mild tax relief?

Basically, all intellectuals were instructed to behave like the three monkeys of Nikko: See no (social) evil, hear no (social) evil, and definitely do not speak of past and present social evil. Before an intellectual would have been able to relate ideals to social categories, he—or some previous thinkers—had to have some power over persons and events, but this was rarely the case under so much oppressive power.

The opposite was true in the West, under division of power, when, for instance, the Church, in the Middle Ages, could preach and impose the *Truce of God* and the *Peace of God*:

"One thing bishops demanded of the nobility—that the nobility's fighting be constrained, organized, and regulated, and that the warrior class refrain from indiscriminate violence. A prime effort in this direction was the *Truce of God* movement, which tried to get the nobility to swear they would not fight on certain days and in certain places and would recognize the ecclesiastics as umpires of legitimate violence" (Cantor, 1995, p. 89). And, in general, the effort succeeded.

As stressed by Latourette, "One other action of the Council of Clermont [of 1095 presided over by Pope Urban II] requires special note, not because it was new but because it is illustrative of a persistent attempt by the Church to bring society to a closer approximation to Christian standards. That was to enforce the *Peace of God*. The *Peace of God* and the *Truce of God* were efforts by the ecclesiastical authorities to reduce the destructiveness of the wars between feudal lords which were chronic during these centuries" (1953, pp. 474-75).[137]

Similar things are true for the contribution by one of the greatest saints of Christianity, Francis of Assisi, a shining product of the DP

---

[137] Here, certainly, the Church did not stand "as a bulwark against change" (as seen by Arima); and Japan would have greatly profited from a similar effort by the Christian Church. Instead, much of *samurai Japan* was the product of the unmitigated "destructiveness of the wars between feudal lords": unmitigated for the lack of a Christian church which had been exterminated by horrible persecutions.

between popes and emperors. Under this DP[138], he and his friars were active in promoting both the *Truce of God* and the *Peace of God*. "Thomas of Spalato, who had heard Francis preach, said that the key to his appeal was his unceasing emphasis on the importance of peace 'for indeed, everything he said was directed towards the extinction of enmity, and re-establishing the brotherhood of peace'. In preaching peace, he was speaking for, as well as to, the poor, to whom the constant wars and threats of war of the times meant nothing but additional burdens in a life already all but intolerably hard" (Holland Smith, 1972, p. 164-65).

On the contrary,

> the kind of statism that produced Japanese victories in the Russo-Japanese War in 1904-5 also produced the suppression of civil liberties and socialist thought in the 1911 Kotoku Shusui affair. Those who questioned the policies of an increasingly autocratic government were forced in turn to examine themselves, in order to think through the implications of their own divergent responses to what was perceived as an increasingly autocratic attitude on the part of government authorities. The suppression of individual rights, as it were, brought to many a stronger awareness of the need to define the necessities of their own spiritual existence. A generation found itself asking where the uniqueness of an individual might lie. Further, did that uniqueness constitute his or her freedom, and if so, how could it be manifested, particularly in relation to a society that, officially at least, seemed increasingly suspicious of individual choice? (Rimer, 1990, p. 4)

Once more we encounter the near impossibility for the Japanese intellectuals, up to recent times, to think in terms of social solutions different from those imposed by the Japanese autocratic government. Natsume/Arima's "existing in a hostile society" says it better than anything else. Indeed, all this chapter has been the discussion of a "hostile society."

---

[138] A first element of DP (Church and State) and pertaining power by the Church was already evident in the West when St. Ambrose in 390 (as discussed in chapter 12 of volume 1) imposed public penance on Emperor Theodosius for having punished a riot in Thessalonica by a massacre of its citizens.

- Hostile to the "lower classes greatly oppressed by the arrogant daimyo and samurai, who lost no opportunity of grinding the faces of the poor" (Boxer, 1951, p. 234);
- Hostile to practically everybody, as described in the previously reported comments by Patrick Smith:

> There was a sort of federalist settlement between the shoguns and the daimyo, but otherwise the era was marked by merciless exploitation, purposeful depriva-tion, paranoic police controls, coercion, more or less constant official violence—and more or less constant popular resistance to all of these things. In its terror and totality, its nightmarish bureaucracy and manipu-lation of knowledge, Edo Japan is usefully compared with the later Soviet Union. In its violent dream of Ori-ental agrarianism it suggests the Cambodia of the Khmer Rouge. . . . It suggests a society dedicated to the com-plete eradication of individual judgment in the name of spirit. The extent of such a society's malevolence could be limited only by the instruments of violence avail-able to it. (1998, pp. 49, 191-92)

- Hostile through the legal sanction given by the Tokugawa sys-tem "to a number of monstrous class privileges; samurai, for instance, enjoyed the right of *kirisute gomen* ('killing and going away'), of which they sometimes took advantage at the expense of wretched peasants or artisans who failed to bow to them with sufficient respect. Another inevitable consequence was the pro-liferation of the notorious *metsuké*, who were originally 'cen-sors', but quickly developed into spies. By means of them the government was kept secretly informed of what both daimyo and people were thinking, doing, and saying, and this with an efficiency which has not been exceeded elsewhere even in our own day" (Maraini, 1960., p. 362-63).
- Hostile to Lord Asano, Lord Kira, the 47 ronin; hostile to young Tokugawa Ieyasu first, then to all those he oppressed and killed;
- Hostile to Sogoro, his wife and four children, and all the peas-ants; hostile to young Kotaro and his parents, to Masoaka and her young son; hostile to all women, to everybody who looked intelligent, to all those Christians hung for days in the pit.
- Hostile to all those who dare look other people in the eye.

When Kotaro was beheaded to save Kan Shusai, what assurances had Genzo and Matsuo that Kan Shusai would be a just, fair and generous leader when he grew up? When young Lord Katsushige went into his training of cutting heads, was he sure that those, on whom he was practicing his martial arts, were criminals? Or were they simply poor people who had done no worse than Sogoro? And Horie San'emon who robbed the Nabeshima warehouse in Edo, did he deserve to have all his hairs burned off, his fingernails pulled out, his tendons cut, his back split, his body bored with drills and boiled in soy sauce? Is this punishment or ugly sadism?

Something is wrong with Yamamoto's *scripts*: with those of a man who goes to the execution grounds to try his hand at beheading, and finds it to be "an extremely good feeling."[139] It is a hostile society which sends its children at night to carve their mark on the skull of the beheaded, and which brings Yamamoto to report that: "If you cut a face lengthwise, urinate on it, and trample on it with straw sandals, it is said the skin will come off. This was heard by the priest Gyojaku when he was in Kyoto. It is information to be treasured" (ca. 1700/

---

[139] It is not that the West has not perpetrated many cruelties. Yet with the centuries these cruelties have been sharply condemned thanks to increasing levels of division of power. Even the Nazi horrors lasted only twelve years, and the worst Nazi leaders—after a long and reasonably fair trial—were hanged. (Proof of the honesty of the trial is that the intelligence of Admiral Dönitz's lawyer saved his client's life). Yes, the West perpetrated many cruelties, but its DP allowed its religious leaders to publicly humiliate two emperors (Henry IV and Frederick I Barbarossa), and its commoners to publicly decapitate two kings (Charles I and Louis XVI). The consequence of this kind of action (combined with the *Truce of God* and the *Peace of God*) was that cruelties—committed by either party—were seen by most people for what they were: cruelties to be condemned and avoided. Year after year the DP that began at Canossa in 1077 brought—in the main—positive changes, and continues to do so.

All this must be considered when trying to understand the success of the West, and its vitality and creativity which are still high (contrary to Barzun's *From Dawn to Decadence 500 Years of Western Cultural Life*; see my critique in chapter 5 of volume 2), and must be included in every comparison of Japan with the West.

Far be it from me to defend the West in everything. Let me remind the reader of who my heroes are: not Augustus, Lorenzo de Medici, Louis XIV, and Napoleon; not Jean Calvin, Clement VIII, Urban VIII, and Pius IX, but the Good Samaritan, Henri Dunant, Lord Acton, Baden Powell, and Chiara Lubich.

246 ♦ The GAM/DP Theory of Personality and Creativity

1985, p. 141). Treasured for what? For being able, one day, to do it in person on the face of an enemy or of a protesting farmer?[140]

Which conclusions should then be drawn from this analysis?

Volume 1 of *The GAM/DP Theory of Personality and Creativity* has three concluding chapters:

1. *The New Volunteerism as the Ultimate Division of Power,*
2. *Lord Acton's Law of Power, and its Four Corollaries,* and
3. *The Role of the Intellectuals,*

I see no reason why not to propose these same conclusions to the Japanese, given that I believe that the GAM/DP theory is right, valid both cross-culturally and cross-historically.

However, in the case of Japan, I would invert the order and start with *The Role of the Intellectuals,* follow with *Lord Acton's Law of Power, and its Four Corollaries,* and conclude with *The New Volunteerism as the Ultimate Division of Power.* I feel the need to begin with the intellectuals in order to clarify many aspects of the Japanese ways of thinking and behaving; and by intellectuals I mean all men and women who love Japan.

What is needed—within the framework of the present interpretation—is, first of all, a long debate—say of ten years, not less[141]—on *Japan, the hostile society. Was Japan a hostile society? Is Japan still a*

---

[140] Moving closer to our times, Fosco Maraini—after having reported that Valignani, in the sixteenth century had written: "'[The samurai] are ready to kill those subject to them on the slightest of pretexts, and think no more of cutting a man in half than of doing so to a dog; many of them, chancing to meet some unfortunate, will cut him in half solely to test the edge of their *katana,*'"—added that "many centuries are needed to change deep-seated national characteristics. In Japan today the strong still exploit the weak if there is no intervention from above to stop them; from below nobody lifts a finger, but everybody bows and accepts; it is sufficient for the strong to raise his voice. A Japanese lorry-driver in charge of a huge vehicle loaded with badly secured sacks, bearing down on you like an avalanche on the wrong side of the road to avoid potholes, is in reality nothing but a poor devil who for a brief hour feels himself to be a *daimyo,* a prince; his behaviour is easy to explain, but hard to forgive" (1960, p. 124).

[141] In the first five years there will probably be more denials than criticisms. If anybody had asked the cook of Lafcadio Hearn if he was happy or unhappy, and if he was living in a friendly or hostile society, he would have certainly answered: "most happy, with nothing better in life than to serve Mr. Hearn." Because of this, I recommend that the debate be based more on "know the others," than "know thyself."

hostile society? These are questions that can and must be formulated in a thousand different ways, each specific to a given condition or social/gender group, each specific to a set of ideas or scripts. Such a debate should start among historians, sociologists, philosophers, psychologists, educators, politicians, and then expand with the participation of every journalist and radio/TV commentator; a debate which, finally, should involve everybody. Such a debate should avoid proposing solutions, because too early AN emphasis on specific programs will severely distort the analysis. After ten years one may begin to envision solutions, many of which will then appear obvious to people used to thinking in new ways.

If there should be a guiding line for many of these debates, this could be the following (drawn from section 2 of my conclusions, the one *entitled "Lord Acton's Law of Power, and its Four Corollaries"*):

De omnibus dubitandum, maxime de Caesaris

Have your doubts, especially of the lord, of anybody in power, of all bureaucrats.

13. From *Strict Ritter*, not to *Visitor* but to *Insular* and *Skeptic*?

Okami, in Particular that of the Educational System

Okami refers to the idea of the organization, or those at the top of the power structure. In the feudal period, opposition to the *okami* was strictly forbidden, and carried a stiff penalty. Even after Japan's transition from a feudal country to a modern one, *okami* remained. What this means is that nearly all the influential government officers and ministers who guided Japan's modernization were former samurai—the highest status in the feudal age. Under their strong direction, Japan was reborn as a modern country. Even after the nation's class system was abolished, they monopolized the political stage. Japan today is a democracy and no longer has a class system. However, the old tradition of *okami* persists, having been translated into a blind respect for and obedience to government ministry bureaucrats. A sign of Japan's continuing elitism can be seen in the prestige of Tokyo University—the former Imperial University—which is a veritable production factory of future bureaucrats.

Numerous scandals have recently tarnished the government ministries' carefully cultivated image of functioning for the country's best interests, above the muck and mire of politics. Increasing numbers of people have started to question bureaucratic authority, although they still usually end up docilely following the *okami's* directives. The education system is probably the most obvious example of this continued obedience to a system that has raised many doubts. As long as the centrally regulated education and exam system exist, real reform will not be possible—even if schools try to create a liberal atmosphere which values individuality. (Kagawa, 1997, pp. 201, 203)

In turn, the *okami* of the educational system created the "entrance exam hell", the "burnt student", and his *kyoiku mama* as discussed by Clayton Naff (1994):

> By far the most debilitating aspect of being a housewife was having to become a *kyoiku mama*, or "education mother", so as to steer one's son through the vast competition that every year produces a few lucky winners who gain admission to prestigious colleges—and millions of despairing losers. Under the banner of educational egalitarianism, the government policy made a woman's status depend entirely on her success in guiding her children through the fires of what came to be called "entrance exam hell" . . . . Manipulation is the only tool the *kyoiku mama* possesses. She is expected to make her child feel highly dependent and then use her love as a motivational lash, tirelessly driving the youngster through the countless hours of mind-numbing study required for entry to a desirable kindergarten, primary school, junior high, high school, and, ultimately, university. Once a boy—it is chiefly boys who are the focus of this effort—begins school, the *kyoiku mama* encourages him to abandon all other responsibilities or pursuits. His life becomes her preoccupation. She cooks his meals, washes his clothes, cleans his room, helps him with his homework, and drills him on material for his exams. As he reaches puberty, she struggles to discourage him from all outside interests, including dating, until he has won acceptance to college. Of course, not all mothers or children adhere to this pattern, but it is common enough to stand as representative. . . . In the eighties, this stress worsened as the competition intensified. The struggle to beat out millions of other youngsters for

a seat in one of the top universities now started before kindergarten. (pp. 85-87)

Of the many sharp sketches of reality drawn by Naff on the basis of his life in Japan, two are important for the present discussion: the first of his sister-in-law Megumi (Naff married a Japanese girl), the second on his daughter Maya:

> She failed the entrance exams to college. This is by no means rare, and reflects nothing on her intelligence. To pass the exams requires an almost inconceivable amount of memorization. The student must have a command of such arcana as the succession of thirteenth-century Chinese kings and the chief industrial products of Pennsylvania. . . . Eventually, on a retry, Megumi passed and entered a junior college. But along the way, she got fed up with studying and living at home. (ib., p. 96)

More telling of the debilitating power of the *okami* of the educational system is the following:

> In fact, Maya, a bright and cheerful child, if I say so myself, had become something of a favorite in the nursery. All the same, the head teacher warned us against placing her in public school: "We like her, but this is just a nursery. *She's too independent, too questioning to get along in a regular school.*" We got the point. Public nurseries are governed by the Ministry of Health and Welfare, and as such have no curricula. They are expressly noneducational institutions. But the public schools fall under the jurisdiction of the arch-conservative Education Ministry. I had interviewed an Education Ministry bureaucrat who freely admitted that Japan's education system was designed to turn out good, compliant workers. *We had seen the uniformed kindergartners in our neighborhood marching about the yard, shouting in unison like a squad of tiny soldiers.* (ib., p. 286; my italics)

These last comments bring to mind the 1885 comments by Arinori Mori, Japan's first education minister, as reported by Patrick

Smith: "Education in Japan is not intended to create people accomplished in the techniques of the arts and sciences, but rather to manufacture the persons required by the State" (1998, p. 71). Specifically on the *exam hell*:

> Savage competition and force-fed information without the cultivation of critical thought go far to explain the character of Japanese graduates. The system's demands—years in exam hell, every other student an adversary—*produce not exploring intellects but the narrow, machinelike people we assume the Japanese to be by nature. Wholly focused on achieving the highest possible place in the hierarchy, they are unable to form healthy ties with equals—horizontal relationships. They are indifferent to most public issues because they are unnaturally inward-looking and (by official design) ignorant of large patches of their own history. Outside of a few conventional settings—karaoke bars are one—they display little sense of autonomy.* (ib., p. 79; my italics)

Exam hell was bad enough at Meiji's end. A student's place in society, the course of his entire adult life, was decided by a test. But it got even worse after 1945. . . . There are many thousands of high school graduates, called *ronin* (after wandering samurai without masters), who failed the entrance exams and wait to retake them. *As everyone in Japan knows, most matriculated students do little during their university years because their place in society is more or less fixed no matter what they accomplish.* The companies they join will finish the task of turning them into *shakai-jin*, social beings. *So their university years are not an education so much as a reward for surviving exam hell,* a last fling at attenuated freedom. [142]

Cram schools, called *juku*, are another oddity. They are a parallel systems at least as important as the schools that award diplomas. Seventy percent of primary and middle school students attend *juku* or (in some cases) have private tutors; for

---

[142] "What is learned for examinations is mostly useless information. Most people quickly forget what they learned after entering college and becoming an adult member of society" (Kagawa, 1997, p. 205).

high school students the figure is 80 percent. (ib., pp. 88-89; my italics)

There was also an unexpected negative impact on the fair sex, and by ricochet on men.

Those Cute Japanese Women

"Why do Japanese women act so cute?" asked Kagawa Hiroshi. "This," he continued, "is another aspect of women in Japan that Westerners have a hard time accepting. Full grown adult Japanese women sometimes speak and act like children.They often decorate their apartments with stuffed animals, or burst out into hysterics in public. . . . But why do Japanese men seem to want cute, childlike women? In the parade of advertisements and comics, these images stand out over images of strong, independent female beauty.

The source of such images may lie in the Japanese school system. In order to get into a good university, Japanese children must study extremely hard. Parents support these children materially and emotionally, and the entire family cooperates to help them improve their grades in school. Children born and raised in this post-war era of prosperity were generally overprotected kids who focused on getting good grades. These children have now become the majority of the adult population. However, many kids who did well in school and survived 'examination hell' to get into good universities remain emotionally immature as adults. This tendency is especially common among men, and they usually want a child-like woman rather than a woman who is more emotionally mature than they are.

Even now, most major Japanese companies and central government agencies prefer to hire graduates of famous universities. Most employees of powerful companies and central government agencies are comprised of such men, though there are countless other men who did not do so well in the 'examination war.' In Japan, debate about the examination wars has been going on for decades. As yet, no one has been able to overhaul the system. Those whose job it is to reform it are themselves products of it, so it is hard for them to implement reforms which negate their own values. Such is the contradictory background of the Japanese penchant for cutesy women, which has its origins in the period of post-war prosperity" (1997, pp. 195, 197).

The above—on the Japanese educational system and on the cute Japanese women—brings to mind the imperial-mandarin world discussed in chapter 7 of volume 2 *Did the Mandarins Kill the Chinese Civilization?* There, on the educational system, I reported how the system of Imperial government that developed in China was organized around a centralized bureaucratic structure composed—at least in part—of people initially selected on the basis of their knowledge of the classics. Each year up to 30,000 students would gather at the local provincial capital, and take a five day test:

> The students' future careers, social status and even prosperity of their family depended on the results of this examination. The pressure was enormous. Even to be able to sit for the first of three levels of examinations, the student would have had to spend at least six years studying the Confucian classics and memorizing long texts, which he would be expected to quote accurately. . . . . [from those who passed the highest level test] would be chosen the officials who administered the provincial and central organs of government. (Merson, 1990, p. 30)

This sounds Japanese, or, more correctly, what is reported on Japan brings to mind China and its mandarins.

On the second point, in that same chapter, I reported Patricia Ebrey's explanation of why upper-class Chinese men did not want their women to be active and capable:

> From poetry, we know of men's attraction to languid women, especially unhappy beauties longing for absent men. For women to be smaller, softer, more stationary, and more languid would of course enhance the image of men as larger, harder, more active. Because the ideal upper-class man was by Sung times a relatively subdued and refined figure, he might

seem effeminate unless women could be made even more delicate, reticent, and stationary. (1993, p. 41)

This too sounds Japanese, or more correctly the Japanese love for cutesy and childlike women seems Chinese. The same causes (UP in China, and now, possibly, more UP in Japan than in the old times of the partial UP of emperor-shogun-daimyo) bring similar results.

It is always difficult to understand the present situation, especially when dealing with *flexible-immutable people*. That was Barzini's problem with Germany as discussed at the beginning of chapter 25 of volume 1:

> Every time I was there on a journalistic mission, I saw a startling new country, only vaguely resembling what I had seen before or what I had read about. . . . I was aware there must have been a constant basic Germany, whose virtues and vices practically went unchanged from one metamorphosis to the next, from one regime to its successor, from one political, philosophic, or aesthetic fashion to another. But it was difficult. . . . It is still difficult for foreigners, and for the Germans themselves. What is the shape of Proteus when caught unaware at rest? (1983, pp. 69-71).

Notwithstanding that difficulty, I asked, at the end of that chapter, if the Germans were not now in the process of evolving from *ritter* to *skeptics*, and not—as desirable—from *ritter* to *visitor*. Rudolf Augstein, the editor-publisher of the influential weekly *Der Spiegel* had said it clearly (and he is not alone in this): "*Ja, ich bin ein Zyniker und ein Skeptiker, natürlich*" [Yes, I am a cynic, and a skeptic, obviously] (1992, p. 45).

The same question applies to Japan: Are they evolving from *strict-ritter* to a blend of modern *skeptics* and old *insulars* after the Chinese model?

14. More on the Recommendation

As indicated above, Japan needs, as a top priority, the direct involvement of its intellectuals. Paraphrasing Alain Peyrefitte on the French (1981, pp. 286, 302), I will say that the psychotherapy of the Japanese must begin with that of their intellectual elite. If it rejects this, what hope is there that the great mass of Japanese people may someday know themselves better and so be cured? The only revolutions that count are those of the mind. It's a mental revolution that the Japanese need and that this book proposes.

In many respects, I am putting more weight on the Japanese intellectuals by not prescribing a detailed cure as did Peyrefitte for the French, but by asking only questions. On the other hand, these questions derive from a general theory of personality and creativity, and as such they propose a valid broad field of inquiry, of comparisons and contrasts. Basically, as with France, there is the need in Japan for a careful inquiry, and a broad debate afterwards.

In summary, the basic two questions remain:

1. *Was Japan (and is it still in part) a hostile society?*
2. *Is Japan evolving toward insularity and skepticism and not toward having a visitor personality?*

In such an inquiry, the voices which will say that Japan is not a hostile society (definitely not more so than other countries) are as important as those that will say that it was and still is a hostile society (more than many other countries). What is needed is a long dialogue over many years, in which—as said in the poem *Ithaca* by Cavafy— what counts is the journey not the arrival: "To arrive there is your ultimate goal. But do not hurry the voyage at all. It is better to let it last for long years." What counts is less the conclusion (yes, or no, or midway), but the mental growth by all participants in the debate: their training in facing two major stories, in listening carefully to the arguments of each side, and making a choice to favor this position, or that, or a totally different one.

There is always the possibility of a refusal of such a debate on the excuse that it would be *lèse-majesté*, that it would diminish the country in the eyes of both its people and the foreigners, or that it would be the purest absurdity in such a friendly/paternal society. In such a case, I let others conclude.

Appendix I

A *Strict Ritter* Passion for Apologies

The Profuse Apologies

In an article of 1956, the Japanese literary critic Hyoye Murakami concluded, on the basis of his European travels, that in Europe, particularly in Germany, there was no ethic of responsibility, as demonstrated specifically by the lack of those profuse apologies that Japanese would offer when told they had committed a mistake. As discussed approvingly by Eichiro Ishida:

> A modern ethic of responsibility based on the individual con-
> science developed in the West in modern times. We have been
> accustomed to thinking that in Japan the awakening of indi-
> vidualism has been delayed, and that, accordingly, an ethic of
> responsibility has not been established, but Murakami began to
> wonder if the reverse might not be true. For instance, in Europe,
> even if an accident occurs through a man's own carelessness,
> he will never acknowledge it. He will argue any other cause but
> his own carelessness, putting forward even the most preposter-
> ous reasons. Japanese trading companies in Germany employ-
> ing many Germans unanimously hold that this is their most un-
> pleasant trait. . . . According to Murakami, as for the relation
> between the actions of Europeans and their code of ethics or
> sense of sin, it is very doubtful whether they feel any guilt after
> committing an offense. Immediately, like a reflex action, an in-
> ner voice urges them to defend themselves. Self-defense and
> personal survival are the primary issues. *In the case of the Japa-*

nese, however, loyalty to the group to which they belong calls forth a deep consciousness of sin. Also among the Japanese, the maintenance of a psychological balance between two factors, namely, that the other party was at fault but that one's own carelessness should also be considered, provides an important method of resolving disputes. However, Europeans carry out matters in an "all or nothing" fashion. Murakami explains that there is a great difference in the way of thinking and feeling about the essence of responsibility. (Ishida, 1974, pp. 125-26; my italics)

Also Kagawa Hiroshi dealt with this same subject in his *The Inscrutable Japanese* by devoting a whole section to "Why do Japanese apologize so much?", followed by another entitled "Why can't Japanese insist that they are right?" He wrote:

Foreigners are often puzzled by why Japanese apologize so much. From an American point of view, apologizing means you've made a mistake. In extreme cases it means defeat. Japanese, on the other hand, feel that Americans rarely apologize and that they always justify themselves, even when they are wrong. Apologizing is very basic for Japanese. Sometimes they begin a conversation by apologizing for the bad weather, or for the problems another person may be having. . . . Japanese who are dealing with superiors or customers usually don't argue with what someone says to them. Rather, they say '*gomen nasai*' ('I'm sorry') when they get a warning from their boss or receive a complaint from a client, even if they are not at fault. In Japan, if you argue back at someone, you run the risk of it being taken as a character assault. Most people choose to apologize first, instead of arguing back and being antagonistic. If necessary, they explain things at a later opportunity. If you argue back at that moment, the person will think, "Oh, he's a narrow-minded person who makes excuses."

I once heard this comment from a Japanese who works with Americans: "Dealing with Americans is so difficult. They've got ten to twenty excuses for anything I point out to them." Americans believe it is a natural human right to justify themselves if necessary. They see nothing wrong with explaining or defending their actions if they feel they are not to blame. (1997, pp. 51-55)

Kagawa understood correctly the contrast between the two mentalities, while Murakami misunderstood it completely: It is natural, just and correct for *visitor personalities* and *plain Ritter* to justify themselves if necessary. They see nothing wrong with explaining or defending their actions if they feel they are not to blame. Not only that, but it is their moral duty to do so. Happily they live under division of power, or plain partial unity of power.

As discussed in chapter 11 of volume 1, the *visitors* (and the same is true in part for the *ritter*), in case of trouble, can always resort to Power Holder A, who will surely welcome new supporters in the fight against Power Holder B. In modern times this will mean having recourse to the legislative power if things go wrong with the executive, or appeal for help to the judiciary, one of the political parties, the clergy, or the unions. Visitors know that they can never be harmed too badly, never be crushed because somebody else will come to their aid. The press, for instance, will always welcome a good fight. Consequently, visitors have faith in themselves as persons in control of important aspects in their lives, and in turn this will give them faith in their autonomy. They may therefore take risks, even against the power closest to them. Instead, without recourse against the power above, *insular persons* (and *strict Ritter*) have no freedom of maneuver, they must bend their head and apologize profusely, even when they are right.

Could Lord Asano honestly have explained and defended himself? No. Could Sogoro logically explain and defend himself and save himself and his family? No. Could Hideyori, his wife, and children defend themselves, No. Any explanation that poor Sogoro could have presented would have undermined the "basic sense of continuity and trust between people," it would have endangered "the long-term relationship" so beloved in Japan!

How can one honestly present one's case when it is recommended not to look intelligent, not to look your superior straight in the eye, because that will offend him and undermine his authority? How can one present one's case, if the superior is a priori right?

The *strict Ritter system* has changed its hat but not its brain: now total dedication is owed to the company instead of to the lord. Correspondingly, in a revised *Hagakure* we might read that: "Being an employee is nothing other than being a supporter of one's boss, entrusting matters of good and evil to him[143], and renouncing self-interest. . . . An employee who serves when treated kindly by the company is not a faithful employee. But one who serves when the company is being heartless and unreasonable is an employee. Better, the true employee is the one who will apologize most often."

Back to modern business: when something goes wrong, often the fault is less of the employee but of the system: the result of unclear instructions, or lack of training, or internal complications. Often too, it is in reality the boss trying to pass down the responsibility of his own mistakes. An American or German will have no qualms in pointing to cases of unclear instructions, lack of coordination with other departments or with the customers, something that a Japanese supervisor will interpret as a general unwillingness to apologize.

There is more to this story with important implications for Japan today and tomorrow. As discussed by Kagawa: "It is often said that Japanese convey messages containing unspoken meanings. The proverb 'Say one, know ten'illustrates the belief that if the whole message is given all at once, a person can give the impression of being

---

[143] Fosco Maraini (1960) made three observations which expand our understanding of the Japanese preference for apologies instead of justifications or even criticisms: ". . . . the new [post Heian] order society came to consist of a rigid pattern of personal loyalties, from warrior to vassal, from vassal to lord, from lord to shogun, the supreme commander. There could be no conflict between loyalty to your superior and loyalty to your principles, because the two were identical. Your superior's word made and unmade good and evil" (p. 243). In other words it is your superior that decides that you did something wrong, and it is up to you to apologize at the very minimum. In turn, this strict ritter system could not but favor a development in which "the Japanese, who are artists, a people of intuition and instinct, have a limited critical sense; they tend to love or hate, accept or reject things, including their own civilization, *en bloc*" (ib., p. 284). Again, why have a strong critical sense if this will lead you against your superior? Better not, just apologize and smile.

"The Japanese always tend to succumb to the fascination of a human personality rather to any system of ideas; in resolutely submitting to the guidance of a master they are able with marvelous ease to still the whirlpools of emotion that arise from the paradoxes of the intellect. There is a Japanese word *makaseru*, almost untranslatable in all its implications, meaning to give one's confidence to somebody, implying submission, complete self-dedication to him; it is frequently used to describe the age-old relationship between man and his leader, between sage and acolyte. '*Sensei-ni o-makase shimashita*' (I have left it to my master to decide), said Takeoka-san" (ib., p. 285). Once more we are faced with the same partial UP situation in which the *critical visitor faculties* are left badly under-developed in favor of submission and complete dedication to the lord/master. Automatically in such a condition the paradoxes of the intellect (and of personal and social life) instead of being resolved, one after the other, increase steadily, forcing even more submission to the master.

too pushy or patronizing to the other party. If the listener is smart and can grasp ten things when only one is spoken, it follows that a good speaker should use expressions with implied meanings. By saying one thing, ten things will be communicated" (1997, p. 69). This can easily be a tyrannical communication method in which the onus is all on the listener—the subordinate—who must grasp all ten things when only one was said. First, it binds the subordinate strongly to his superior: it is the subordinate's responsibility to know his boss (and the company) so well that all ten things will always be grasped when only one is spoken. Second, if something goes wrong it can only be the fault of the subordinate who did not grasp all ten things but only seven or eight. In addition, this requirement greatly limits the freedom to move from one company to the other. How long will it take a newcomer— even with plenty of business experience—to learn how to grasp the new ten things when only one was said?

In Europe and America things are different, as well known by Kagawa: "A message needs to be conveyed clearly and logically, and people who can communicate perfectly are respected as intelligent speakers and leaders" (ib., p. 69). "Unfortunately, there are cases in which a Japanese may explain five points to get ten across, thinking that this is enough. But the Westerner may still only understand half of his explanation. Obviously, this leads to problems in business and may give rise to conflict. The American may complain, 'No, what you said isn't what I heard.'. . . .

Japanese should also prepare themselves to be asked 'why?' by foreigners, particularly Americans" (ib., p. 71).

But shouldn't also the Japanese be allowed to ask "why?" from his Japanese boss? Shouldn't also the Japanese be allowed to complain: "No, what you said isn't what I heard"?

My answer to these two questions is "of course", because asking "why?" of a superior is one of the most important aspects of the freedom, courage, sense of initiative of the *visitor personality*, and one of the best ways to reduce the effects of the Law of Power of Lord Acton: "Power tends to corrupt and absolute power corrupts absolutely."

The System is at Fault, not the Individual

According to Murakami: "In the case of the Japanese, however, loyalty to the group to which they belong calls forth a deep consciousness of sin." But does the group really deserve all that loyalty, when we know that *Power tends to corrupt and absolute power corrupts absolutely*, and that *Power asks for a sense of sin and profuse apologies, and absolute power demands seppuku or crucifixion*?

Did the French aristocrats of the end of the eighteenth century deserve the loyalty of Beaumarchais, or did Empress Maria Theresa and Prince-Archbishop Coloredo deserve the loyalty of Mozart, or did Karl Eugen, Duke of Württemberg, deserve the loyalty of Schiller? No. Their system was wrong. Did the shogun deserve the loyalty of Sogoro? No!

Appendix II

Cui bono[144] the Japanese Virtues of Dependence and Self-Effacement?

A Recent Defense of the Japanese Virtue of Dependence and Self-Effacement

A team of five scholars (Rothbaum, Weisz, Pott, Miyake, and Morelli),[145] concluded, in their 2000 article, that the American studies on attachment[146] may have some validity for the West but not for other cultures, specifically not for Japan with its strong attachment to the virtue of dependence and self-effacement. Specifically they wrote:

---

[144] "Who stands to gain?"

[145] In sequence from: Tufts University, University of California-Los Angeles, Tufts University, Hokkaido University, Boston College.

[146] Attachment refers to a close, emotional bond of affection between an infant and its caregiver. Mary Ainsworth (e.g., 1979) has developed a, by now, famous procedure to measure attachment, consisting of seven 3-minute episodes during which infants are observed with their mother, with a stranger, whith the mother and a stranger, and alone. According to the child's behavior during these episodes, it is classified as securely attached, avoidant and insecurely attached, or resistant and insecurely attached. "Securely attached children were generally more socially outgoing with adults and with other children, more cooperative and compliant with their mothers and with strange adults, better able to cope with stress, and more curious than children classified as insecurely attached" (Mussen, Conger, Kagan, & Huston, 1984, pp. 135-36).

Western adults who are securely attached show higher levels of social competence than do adults who are insecurely attached (ambivalent, resistant, or preoccupied). This finding takes on added significance when combined with the attachment theory claim that secure attachments in infancy and adulthood are related (Bowlby, 1979; Hazan & Shaver, 1994). Adults who are securely attached show greater competence in several areas: They have greater comfort with autonomy and greater valuing of it; indeed, attachment theorists refer to securely attached adults as "autonomous." They have a more positive view of self. . . . There is evidence that all of these aspects of "competence," which are associated with security in the West, are seen more negatively by Japanese: *"From [an East Asian] perspective, an assertive, autonomous. . . .person is immature and uncultivated"* (Fiske, Kitayama, Markus, & Nisbett, 1998, p. 923). *In Japan, self-enhancement is less common and less valued, and self-criticism and self-effacement are more common and more valued. People are expected to respectfully and emphatically preserve harmony by avoiding any expression of discord or direct expression of wants, and adherence to values of filial piety makes negative comments about parents inappropriate* (Fiske et al., 1998; Kitayama et al., 1997).

The dissimilarity between Western and Japanese ideas about consequences of security is clearest with regard to independence. There is substantial evidence in the West that secure adults tend to be less dependent: They are less likely to be clingy and to rely on others to meet their needs, less anxious about gaining acceptance from others, have less of a preference for unqualified closeness, and are less likely to experience love as involving union (Bartholomew & Shaver, 1998; Feeney, 1999; Hazan & Shaver, 1994). *In Japan, dependence (i.e., interdependence), seeking of acceptance and commitment, and desire for union are more common and more likely to be associated with competence (Fiske et al., 1998) and presumably with security.*

What counts as social competence varies substantially from one culture to another. Because attachment theorists define competence largely in terms of Western values, they emphasize exploration, autonomy, efficacy, willingness to discuss strong affect and to disagree with partners, sociability with peers and unfamiliar others, and a positive view of self. *In Japan, where preservation of social harmony is particularly valued, social competence often entails dependence, emotional restraint, indirect expression of feelings, a clear differentiation between appropriate behavior with in-group versus out-group members, self-criticism, and self-effacement.* (2000, pp. 1098-99; my italics)

The five authors then concluded as follows:

> If basic assumptions about attachment are not the same for people of different cultures, then it is inevitable that misconceptions about relationships will occur. For example, Americans' assumptions about attachment lead them to view Japanese caregiving practices as misguided, rather than as simply different, because Japanese practices inhibit infant exploration. Similarly, Japanese assumptions about attachment lead them to perceive U.S. relationships as being undermined by individualism and as weaker than, rather than merely different from, their own relationships. Our review points to the fallacy of cultural analyses that pit individualism against relatedness (e.g., Guisinger & Blatt, 1994) and highlights instead the different ways that people around the world think about and engage in close relationships. An awareness of different conceptions of attachment would clarify that relationships in other cultures are not inferior but instead are adaptations to different circumstances. (p. 1101)

At first one may be tempted to agree with the recommendation made by the five authors, and fully accept the Japanese social model as one of the plurality of ideals favored by Isaiah Berlin when he said:

> I came to the conclusion that there is a plurality of ideals, as there is a plurality of cultures and of temperaments. I am not a relativist; I do not say "I like my coffee with milk and you like it without; I am in favor of kindness and you prefer concentration camps"—each of us with his own values, which cannot

be overcome or integrated. This I believe to be false.[147] But I do believe that there is a plurality of values which men can and do seek, and that these values differ. There is not an infinity of them: the number of human values, of values which I can pursue while maintaining my human semblance, my human character, is finite—let us say 74, or perhaps 122, or 26, but finite, whatever it may be. . . . That is why pluralism is not relativism—the multiple values are objective, part of the essence of humanity rather than arbitrary creations of men's subjective fancies. (1998, p. 57)

However, if we put together the various parts I have put in italics above we may begin to feel that things are not correct, and that too much injustice has been swept under the pluralist rug, and that here too we encounter clear manifestations of Japan as a hostile society:

From [an East Asian] perspective, an assertive, autonomous person is immature and uncultivated. In Japan, self-enhancement is less common and less valued, and self-criticism and self-effacement are more common and more valued. People are expected to respectfully and emphatically preserve harmony by avoiding any expression of discord or direct expression of wants, and adherence to values of filial piety makes negative comments about parents inappropriate. In Japan, dependence (i.e., interdependence), seeking of acceptance and commitment, and desire for union are more common and more likely to be associated with competence and presumably with security.

---

[147] In this respect, Berlin could have mentioned the *Universal Declaration of Human Rights* adopted, on December 10, 1948, in Paris, by an unanimous vote of the General Assembly of the United Nations Commission on Human Rights (with the six members of the Soviet bloc, Saudi Arabia and the Union of South Africa abstaining). Article 1 says: "All human beings are born free and equal in dignity and rights. They are endowed with reason and conscience and should act towards one another in a spirit of brotherhood;" Article 2 says: "Everyone is entitled to all the rights and freedoms set forth in this Declaration, without distinction of any kind, such as race, colour, sex, language, religion, political or other opinion, national or social origin, property, birth or other status."

But does lack of assertiveness and autonomy, and lack of direct expression of want bring something good to the people or only to the domineering elite? Who is gaining by all these widespread social virtues?

In Japan, where preservation of social harmony is particularly valued, social competence often entails dependence, emotional restraint, indirect expression of feelings, a clear differentiation between appropriate behavior with in-group versus out-group members, self-criticism, and self-effacement.

However, who is paying most heavily the price of social harmony? And what does social harmony mean under these conditions?

Cui bono?

One cannot meaningfully speak of a plurality of systems independently of the Ciceronian demand of *cui bono?* [who stands to gain?]. Some systems are more *visitor*, others are more *insular*. On one side, democratic systems are *visitor*; on the other, imperial or dictatorial systems are *insular*. *Visitor* systems favor progress, creativity, the priority of the law; they favor fairness and generosity for everybody. *Insular* systems, on the contrary, are there to serve the *supremo*.

So, *cui bono* in Japan? A long string of scholars have given the answer: The Japanese were indoctrinated with the ideals and values convenient to the ruling class, that is, with such virtues as humility, obedience, and loyalty.

a) From Mikiso Hane's *Japan: A historical survey*:

[In the past, specifically during the Tokugawa period of 1603-1867] the peasantry, constituting more than 80 percent of the population, theoretically ranked next to the samurai in the social hierarchy but in reality their status was lower than that of the townspeople. *Like the townspeople, the peasants could not wear swords or use family names. They were bound to the soil and could not change their occupation . . . . The peasant's life was regulated in minute detail by the ruling class. In the samurai's way of thinking, the peasant's raison d'être was to serve the ruling class's economic needs. . . .* In addition to advocating the virtue of industry, the ruling class sought to instill the concept of frugality among the peasants. They were instructed to consume as little food as possible. Millet rather than rice was to be their staple. Smoking, tea-drinking, and above all consumption of sake—for rice was used to produce it—were discouraged. They were also told to utilize barnyard grass and vegetable leaves as food. They were instructed to use only cotton for clothing and to bind their hair with straw instead of ribbons. Their dwellings were to be simple hovels. All forms of recreation and games were forbidden except on special occasions. Any peasant found amusing himself any other time was punished. Wives who idled their time away by such pastimes as flower-viewing and tea-drinking were to be divorced. Many of these admonitions were embodied in the *Bakufu*'s [i.e., Shogunate] edict issued in 1642. . . . In some *han* [feudal fief] the officials were directed to confiscate the peasants' possessions, even their wives and children, if they failed to pay their taxes. Slavery was prohibited but temporary bondage was permitted. Thus, in order to pay their taxes and debts, the peasants frequently sold their family members into temporary servitude. In reality this resulted in permanent enslavement, because the contract could not be dissolved until the debt was repaid, and this the impoverished peasants could seldom do. The brothels of the big cities were filled with daughters of indigent peasants. . . . It was the Bakufu's policy to keep the peasants intimidated. When Ieyasu heard that the peasants were disturbed at the high-handed behavior of the falconers he is said to have remarked, "Let the falconers be as high handed as they please. This will make the peasants think 'if mere falconers act in such a manner how much more overbearing would high officials be?' and they will be afraid to harbor any disloyal thoughts. Willful farmers are the cause of peasant disturbances."

The peasants' mental horizon was limited because each village tended to be isolated from the surrounding areas. Moreover, the ruling authorities deliberately kept the villages insulated from the towns. Their object was to keep the villagers ignorant. "A good peasant is one who does not know the price of grain," was a common saying among the ruling class. It was said that peasants and townspeople should be forbidden from studying. *They were to be indoctrinated with the ideals and values convenient to the ruling class, that is, with such virtues as humility, obedience and loyalty.* (1972, pp. 168-72; my italics)

b) From Perry Anderson's *Lineages of the Absolutist State*:

The becalmed traditionalism of Japanese feudal society, virtually innocent of contrary ideological gusts in the Tokugawa era, furnishes an especially striking contrast [with Europe]. The intellectual stagnation of Japan, amidst its economic effervescence, of course was to a considerable extent due to the deliberate isolation of the country. . . . The adoption of primogeniture within the aristocratic class consolidated the new feudal hierarchy with the countryside. The peasantry below underwent a corresponding degradation, as their mobility was restricted, and their prestations were increased: the petty rural warriors of the *bushi* stratum were in a better position to squeeze the surplus from the direct producers than the absentee *kuge* nobles had been. . . . At the base of the whole feudal system, the peasantry were juridically tied to the soil and forbidden to migrate or exchange their holdings. . . .

[In the cities] *The chonin*[148] *were juridically at the mercy of the nobility whom they supplied with credit, and their gains could arbitrarily be erased by obligatory benevolences and special levies on them. Tokugawa law was 'socially shallow and territorially limited': it covered only the tenryo domains themselves, lacked any real judiciary and was mainly concerned with repression of crime. Civil law was rudimentary, grudgingly administered as 'a matter of grace' in litigation* between private parties by the *Bakufu* authorities. Legal security for capital transactions was thus always precarious.'. . . .

Deprived of foreign trade, commercial capital in Japan was constantly reined in and re-routed towards parasitic dependence on the feudal nobility and its political systems. . . . Industrial technology was archaic, its improvement foreign to *chônin* traditions. The prosperity and vitality of the Japanese merchant class had produced a distinctive urban culture of great

---

[148] The *chônin* class was comprised of the merchants (*shônin*) and artisans (*kônin*).

artistic sophistication, above all in painting and literature. *But it had not generated any growth in scientific knowledge or innovation in political thought. Chônin creativity was confined to the domain of imagination and diversion; it never extended to enquiry or criticism.* (1974, pp. 427-55; my italics)

c) Pro-Daimyo indoctrination, and full praise for absolute fidelity, even to an evil lord

In chapter 25 of volume 1, I compare the German paean of fidelity to the Japanese one and briefly discussed the famous play *Chûshingura* in honor of the radical fidelity and heroism of the 46 ronin of Lord Enya (Asano) who had been forced to commit suicide by the deceits of Moronao (Kira), the court aristocrat and expert in ceremonial. Much of the play centers around Yuranosuke the leader of the 47 ronin. Donald Keene, Professor of Japanese at Columbia University, says in the introduction to his translation of *Chûshingura*:

> Yuranosuke's loyalty is absolute. There is nothing to suggest that he would have been a particle less loyal to Enya Hangan even if the latter had been a cruel or contemptible master. The "debunkers" of traditional history who have asserted that Enya (Asano), far from being a noble Samurai, was avaricious and cruel, only make us marvel all the more at the unswerving loyalty of the forty-six ronin. And if it is true, as these writers claim, that Moronao (Kira), unlike the mean Enya, was unusually generous to the peasants on his lands, building waterworks for their benefit at his own expense, it is further proof that the ronin were uninterested in anything but the claims of loyalty. This fact is deliberately altered by adapters of *Chûshingura* for the films; in order to please modern audiences they insist that Enya *earned* the loyalty of his men by the sterling administration of his fief. The whole point of the play is the unconditional nature of loyalty. (1971, p. 17)

The message is clear, in no way does the daimyo have any responsibility for the common good. That responsibility belongs first to the peasants, then at a distance to the samurai: a Kantian categorical imperative not subject to discussion. And it is so because it is in the interest of the daimyo who for centuries had the power of shaping the Japanese scripts. And part of these scripts is the notion that to sacrifice one's life for a cruel or contemptible master is the highest and most praiseworthy deed. How dreadful of the adapters of *Chūshingura* for modern audiences to insist that Enya *earned* the loyalty of his men by the sterling administration of his fief!! Even today, total loyalty to one's superior must be given uncritically and unconditionally.

Joel Mokyr also had comments on the inward-looking and conservative aspects of the Tokugawa regime which fully match the previously reported remarks by Perry Anderson on the lack in Japan, at that time, of "any growth in scientific knowledge or innovation in political thought":

> It seems that as a general rule, then, the weaker the government, the better it is for innovation. With some notable exceptions, autocratic rulers have tended to be hostile or indifferent to technological change. The instinctive need for stability and the suspicion of nonconformism and shocks usually dominated the possible gains that could be attained from technological progress. Thus both the Ming dynasty in China (1368-1644) and the Tokugawa regime in Japan (1600-1867) set the tone for inward-looking, conservative societies. (ib., pp. 180-81)

Cui bono? From Puerto Rico to Mexico to Japan

Toward the end of their article, the five authors wrote: "What we propose is a new generation of research and theory on attachment, specifically attuned to ways in which the attachment process is tied to the cultural context in which it is embedded. . . . See Harwood, Miller, and Irizarry's (1995) research in Puerto Rico for an excellent example of how such research might be conducted and the enlightening findings it might yield" (p. 1102).

Interestingly, the studies by Harwood, Miller, and Irizzary on Puerto Rico were discussed in my chapter 11 of volume 1, "The Long Term Effect of Power on Creativity" specifically in section 5: Transmission by Cultural Continuity. There I reported how, in Puerto Rico, mothers were asking for such child-characteristics as being quiet, respectful and obedient—traits which permit the child to behave in an adequate and dignified way in a public context. I then related this to the following from Diaz-Guerrero's (1967/1975) on Mexico, where infants "must become model children who will perforce fit into the system of absolute obedience to the parents. This necessary obedience, humility, and respect to the elders and for authority are imposed in a great many ways. Drilling in courtesy is a prevalent one" (p. 10).

It sounds Japanese because the same UP causes produce the same UP results, all over the world: an indoctrination for the sole benefit of the prince, or daimyo, or company boss.

10

The Western Shift to Quantification Perception in the 13th and 14th Centuries as Additional Evidence for the DP Theory

1. Introduction

After the completion of volume 1, I read two books, the first by Alfred Crosby, the second by Carlo Cipolla, which, while taking a different approach from mine, said things which I felt gave additional evidence for the DP side of the GAM/DP theory of personality and creativity as first discussed in my 1992 article *"Personalidad insular versus visitante"*, then in my 1995 article "Long-term effect of power on creativity", and finally in my previous and present books.

2. Crosby

In chapter 11of volume1 I said that I was not alone in seeing a fundamental change in the ethnopsychology of Western Europe during and after the DP *War of Supremacy* between the Papacy and the Empire of 1075-1312. Another who saw the great importance of that same period was Colin Morris who in his *The Discovery of the Individual 1050-1200* of 1972 remarked on the "rapid rise in individualism and humanism from about 1080 to 1150" (p. 7). Similarly, Alfred Crosby had written, in his *The Measure of Reality* of 1997, that between 1250 and 1350, there came in the West not so much in theory as in actual application, a marked shift "from qualitative perception to, or at least toward, quantification perception" (p. 49).

The supporting evidence for the DP theory comes not only from the fact that Crosby noticed the beginning of a major ethnopsychological change toward what I have called the *visitor personality* at about the same time that both Morris and I had found it, but that Crosby listed among the causes for the change a number of factors which can be read as integral parts of that newly developed *division of power*. Crosby, indeed, wrote:

> *The West lacked firmness of political and religious and, speaking in the broadest generality, cultural authority. It was, among the great civilizations, unique in its stubborn resistance to political, religious, and intellectual centralization and standardization.* (p. 53/54; my italics)

In the above, I have highlighted every word because it would be difficult to give a more compact description of the results of the *War of Supremacy* of 1075-1313 between popes and emperors, of which the *Investiture Controversy* of 1075-1122 was the first episode, as discussed in chapters 11 and 23 of volume 1, and my prior articles.[149]

Crosby continued:

> Western Europe was a warren of jurisdictions—kingdoms, dukedoms, baronies, bishoprics, communes, guilds, universities, and more—a compost of checks and balances. No au-

---

[149] In this context, I gladly pay homage to Helmut Koenigsberger, who in a letter of January 2, 1998 to the editor of the *Times Literary Supplement* wrote "Both John North and William A. Therivel (Letters, December 19) have made valid points about the reason for the greater effectiveness of Western European society as against other advanced civilizations. . . . The conflict arose in the West when the head of the Church, the Pope, and the emperor were geographically separated, in the fifth century. *When, from the eleventh to the thirteenth centuries*, each claimed ultimate authority, their supporters were driven to justify their position rationally. They were on both sides the intellectual leaders of Europe. *From this long-term tension and from the intellectual response to it spread the habit of rational argument in other fields, from politics and theology to mathematics, and this at the very time of the foundation of the universities in the West*" (p. 15, my italics).

thority, *not even the vicar of Christ on earth, had effective political, religious, or intellectual jurisdiction*[150]. . . . [In contrast] The political and religious aristocracies of Asia and North Africa always ultimately united to keep the nouveau riche down. In the West, on the other hand, merchants and bankers even managed to establish their own family dynasties and to insinuate themselves into political prominence; most famous, of course, were the Medici[151], but there were also the Fuggers and a goodly number of lesser lineages of wealth and influence. Money changers were the yeast that the lump—peasant, priest, or noble—never could evict or sterilize, and that quickened and even recruited among the traditional classes.

The elites of palace and cathedral [at first emperors and popes] could not suppress the bourgeoisie because they lacked confidence that they could fulfill their own ambitions without access to the wealth and the skills of this cocky meritocracy. Before the upper classes could convert their scorn and nascent fear into effective policy, the merchants had created a civilization in which others could achieve their own satisfactions only by buying the services of and granting privileges to those who lived by counting. The West was intellectually as well as socially unsolidified. . . . [Also, in parallel,] the first half of the twelfth century was the heroic period of Western higher education, a time in which students spontaneously gathered around masters like the radically rationalistic Peter Abelard, even following them from town to town if necessary. (ib., pp.54-59, my italics)

---

[150] However, without soldiers, how could the Pope have effective political jurisdiction? It is extraordinary that those unarmed popes had any jurisdiction at all. We must not forget that under the Byzantine emperors, the patriarchs of Constantinople had minimal jurisdiction (see chapter 14 of volume 1), and so did the popes under Charlemagne (see chapter 11 of volume 2) who saw himself as the ruler Chosen by God, and the pope as his chaplain responsible for turning the prayer wheel according to Arnold's vivid image (1997, p. 81). Lacking effective political jurisdiction (Thanks be to God), the popes then lacked effective religious or intellectual jurisdiction (once more, Thanks be to God).

[151] Who, in turn, went after the unity of power, like everybody else: "By the second half of the fifteenth century, the Medici had stifled all political action in Florence save that of conspiracy" (Gay, 1966, *1*, p. 267).

So, also Crosby noticed the division of power of the West, in contrast with the unity of power of the Far-East, East and South: a division of power which led to the "West's distinctive intellectual accomplishment [of bringing] mathematics and measurement together and to hold them to the task of making sense of a sensorial perceivable reality" (ib., p. 17).

But why was there division of power in the West? Why could the merchants do more in the West than in the East? Why was there, in the West "a rapid rise in individualism and humanism from about 1080 to 1150"? My answer was given, first in my 1992 and 1995 articles, then in chapter 11 of volume 1 where I wrote that: "Thanks to the continuous fights between popes and emperors from 1075 to 1330, the cities could gradually free themselves from the domination of their masters, the German emperors. In the absence of kings and emperors these cities could develop their "modern' commercial and political institutions:

> Europe's. . . .towns were marked by an unparalleled freedom. They had developed as autonomous worlds and according to their own propensities. . . . In the financial sphere, the towns organized taxation, finances, public credit, customs and excise. They invented public loans. . . .They organized industry and guilds; they invented long-distance trade, bills of exchange, the first forms of trading companies and accountancy. (Braudel, 1979, pp. 509-12)

These towns, in the words of Carlo Cipolla, were:

> to the people of Europe *from the eleventh to the thirteenth centuries* what America was to Europeans in the nineteenth century. The town was 'the frontier', a new and dynamic world where people felt they could break their ties with an unpleasant past, where people hoped they would find opportunities for economic and social success, where sclerotic traditional institutions and discriminations no longer counted, and where there would be ample reward for initiative, daring, and industriousness. . . . Towns had existed in ancient Egypt, as in the classical world of Greece and Rome. In the Middle Ages, towns existed in China as well as in the Byzantine Empire. But the cities of Medieval and Renaissance Europe had something

essentially different from the towns of other areas and other times. In towns of the classical world, as in the towns of China and the Byzantine Empire, the merchants, the professionals, and the craftsmen never acquired a socially prominent position. (1976, pp. 142-44; my italics)

These Chinese and Byzantine merchants and professionals did not acquire a prominent position because of the heavy hand of the unity of power, as was discussed in detail, for instance, in Chapter 12 of volume 1 "The Low Creativity and High Unity of Power of the Byzantine Civilization", and in chapter 7 of volume 2 "Did the Mandarins Kill the Chinese Civilization?".

Moving to the real actors in this extraordinary play, there grew, in the West, individualism and a passion for quantification because more people participated in decision making, arguing for the way they saw things, arguing for their own interests, presenting facts, presenting numbers in favor of their position, and all this in the absence of fear of antagonizing the Great Lord, be he emperor or pope, be he king or cardinal. In open discussions, among free people, the best way to convince others is by proving one's case with numbers, be it the number of people who will profit by the construction of a new bridge or be it the loss of revenues that the city will suffer from curtailing the number of days of the yearly fair. "Indeed, the very engine of communal life was impelled by the urge to elaborate collective norms. The effects were felt in many areas of associative life, with prohibitions against cartels and monopolistic practices" (Becker, 1981, p. 166).

Similar comments were made by Daniel Waley: "One presupposition was constant intervention by the commune in every aspect of social and economic activity. This was connected with the confident belief that problems were soluble. Discussion in council could find solutions which could be enforced by legislation. If experience showed that this was not the correct solution then another would be tested" (1988, p. 59). But how much discussion could take place in front of the Great Lord or his Council? Very little indeed, as illustrated in chapter 7 vol. 2, on China, where I reported how a single imprudent word was enough to ruin the life of historian Ssu-ma Ch'ien (147-87? B.C.). That imprudent word was 'merit' said in front of the imperial council: the merit of general Li Ling who had been accused of being responsible for the loss of a great and bloody battle which so saddened the emperor. Because of his attempt to remind the council of the past loyalty and virtues of Li Ling, Ch'ien was thrown into prison, accused of defaming the Emperor for which the penalty was death. "Ch'ien begged a reprieve so that he could finish compiling his history. The Emperor, reluctant to lose so expert and energetic an Astrologer Royal, graciously ordered that instead of being executed, Ch'ien should be castrated" (Boorstin, 1983, p. 561). It does not need many similar gracious orders to freeze everybody's voice, with a corresponding loss of individualism and passion for quantification.

3. Cipolla

In the words of Carlo Cipolla (1994):

Paper was invented in China, and its manufacture spread to the Muslim empire in the course of the eighth century, probably after the Arabs conquered the city of Samarkand in AD 753. In about AD 793 the first paper factory was set up in Baghdad and by AD 1000 bound books made of paper circulated widely in different parts of the Muslim Empire. *The Byzantines, typically conservative, never learned how to manufacture paper.* The Europeans learned the technique during the thirteenth century. The appearance of the first paper factories at Játiva[152] and at Fabriano[153] represented the transplantation into Europe of an idea born elsewhere. But while the production of paper outside Europe remained at the level of manual production, it is typical that, in the West, the pulp was processed by machines driven by water mills. [Paper mills appeared in Italy, at Bologna before 1200, and at Fabriano in 1276]. . . . *One of the original features of western technological development after the twelfth century was the increasing emphasis placed on the mechanical aspects of technology. There was a real passion for the mechanization of all productive processes.* In the Forez by 1251, there existed a mill to grind mustard, and by the end of the Middle Ages mechanical clockwork had been successfully applied to the roasting of

---

[152] At Játiva in the province of Valencia (at that time part of the Islamic empire of the Almoravids).

[153] In central Italy, 25 miles north of Assisi.

meats. The basic reason for this attitude is not easy to grasp. One may argue that the shortage of labor brought about by repeated epidemics favored the adoption of labor-saving devices, but a phenomenon by its nature so complex can scarcely be reduced to naive and simplistic determinism. Necessity explains nothing; the crucial question is why some groups respond in a particular way to needs or wants which in other groups remain unformulated and unfilled. (pp. 150-51, my italics).

Not only do I agree with Cipolla that necessity explains nothing, and neither do the repeated epidemics because the passion for mechanization was already evident before the great epidemics[154], but I see his comment as an additional piece of evidence for the DP theory, in the sense that *this passion for mechanization* goes in parallel with Crosby's *passion for quantification,* and that both evolved thanks to the DP born as a consequence of the *War of Supremacy,* and did not evolve under the UP of the Byzantine emperors.

Basically, we have a whole string of similar extraordinary pieces of development, all at about the same time, and the same place (chiefly in Italy). We have the rapid rise in individualism and humanism from about 1080 to 1150 discussed by Colin Morris, the "invention" of human dissection—first the famous one by Mondino de Luzzi in Bologna in 1315, discussed in chapter 13 of volume 1, and the then widespread use of clocks as discussed in section 5 "The DP Use of the Clock and Other Democratic Technology by the West, and not by Byzantium" of chapter 12 of volume 1.

A passion for mechanization goes hand in glove with a passion for quantification: the investment in the machine must be justified by the savings in production costs, and the higher quantities produced in

---

[154] The first round of the Black Death ravaged Europe in 1347-1351, followed by reoccurrences in 1361-63, 1369-71, 1374-75, 1390, and 1400; however, as reported by Jean Gimpel in his *The Medieval Machine: The Industrial Revolution of the Middle Ages,* for instance: "A twelfth-century report on the use of waterpower in a Cistercian monastery (that of Clairvaux in France) shows how far mechanization had become a major factor in European economy. The importance of this report, this great hymn to technology, is that it could have been written 742 times over; for that was the number of Cistertian monasteries in the twelfth century, and the report would have held true for practically every one of them" (1977, p. 3).

less time. In turn it takes individualism to start major new things without the blessing and prodding of those higher up who rarely favor the development of democratic technologies as discussed in the above-mentioned section 5. To start a paper factory may not demand all the courage and initiative of a Mondino de Luzzi, yet still plenty, given the times.

I see a convergence of the results of studies by different scholars, each praising a different aspect of the same great mental revolution. And part of the revolution was that extraordinary DP poem by Cecco Angiolieri (born in Siena before 1260) that I never tire to repeat:

If I were pope, I would be jocund
and would cheat all Christians;
If I were emperor, I know what I would do,
I would chop off everybody's head.

On the other hand, and not to be forgotten, the DP theory is universal (which I have tried to prove one chapter after the other) and what is said above should, *mutatis mutandis* (the necessary changes being made), be useful for other places and other times.

11

The Liberating Power
of the English Bible
under DP

Introduction

The complete title of this chapter should be: "The strong long-term civic liberating power of the vernacular Bible (in English) in a DP climate versus the weak long-term civic liberating power of the vernacular Bible (in German) in a UP climate." This chapter therefore studies the contrasting long term civic developments fostered by the same text, the Bible, when translated, at about the same time, in vernacular (German and English) from the original Greek (New Testament) and Hebrew (Old Testament).[155] The emphasis is on "civic" and "long-term".

It is with much interest that I read *The English Bible and the Seventeenth-century Revolution* by Christopher Hill (1994). The first of the five reviewers's quotes on the back cover reads:

---

[155] Luther's translation of the New Testament was published in 1522, and his complete translation of the Bible was published in 1534. On the English side, while the Tyndale translations are of 1525-26 (N.T.) and 1526-1535 (O.T.), the real popular Bible in English was the Geneva translation of 1560, finally superseded by the King James or Authorized Version of 1611.

What caused the English civil war? What brought Charles I to the scaffold?[156] Answer to both questions: the Bible. To sustain this provocative thesis, Christopher Hill's new book maps English intellectual history from the Reformation to 1660, showing how scripture dominated every department of thought from sexual relations to political theory.

— John Carey, in the *Sunday Times*

However, the answer to both questions is incomplete. The answer should have been: "the Bible in a DP climate," because Germany also had its vernacular Bible at that same time, but there the Bible did not have the same civic impact. Under the UP of the German princes, the Bible had a strong religious and linguistic/literary impact but a weak civic influence.

Mine is in no way a criticism of Christopher Hill. In his discussion of the English events, he had no reasons to dwell on the high level of DP in Britain (and its low level in Germany). So, the present chapter is devoted to the high level of DP in Britain and low level of DP in Germany and how these different conditions determined how the vernacular Bible was read and used.

For Britain my presentation will cover both the results discussed by Hill and some references to the high level of DP of Britain at that time; for Germany I will only discuss the high level of UP there given that it is difficult to discuss what did not happen in the civic domain.[157] This chapter therefore is a story of Two Cities: the British DP city of the *visitor* versus the German partial-UP city of the *ritter*.

---

[156] "Charles I, King of Great Britain and Ireland from 1625 to 1649, by attempting to impose his authoritarian rule on a people with growing aspirations for political and religious liberty brought about a civil war that ended with his execution by his subjects" (Ashley, 1978a, p. 52).

[157] There are major differences between the *English Civil War* of 1642-51 between King Charles I and Parliament (a true civil war), and the *Thirty Years' War* of 1618-48 that engaged the Austrian Habsburgs and the German princes, in which so many non-German interests played a major role, e.g. the struggle of Catholic France against the encirclement by the Catholic Habsburg powers (Austria and Spain) and the efforts of the Protestant Dutch Republic to preserve its independence from Spain. There was also a major participation in the war by the armies of King Christian IV of Denmark and of King Gustavus II Adolphus of Sweden.

In England (1560 to 1660)

In the words of Hill (1994) "The availability of the Bible in English was a great stimulus to learning to read; and this in its turn assisted the development of cheap printing and the distribution of books. It was a cultural revolution of unprecedented proportions, whose consequences are difficult to over-estimate. Direct access to the sacred text gave a sense of assurance to laymen which they had previously lacked, and so fortified long-standing criticisms of the church and its clergy" (Hill, 1994, p. 11).[158]

"Ivan Roots's epigram that the Reformation started in the ale-houses of England, expresses a necessary truth. Where else could ordinary people meet for discussion? The printing explosion during the relative freedom from censorship of Edward VI's reign enabled protestantism and religious discussion to establish themselves in England" (ib., p. 15).

Division of Power

Before moving further with Hill's book, the following from Maurice Ashley should give evidence of the high level of DP enjoyed by Great Britain already at the beginning of Charles's reign in 1625:

When his first Parliament met in June, trouble immediately arose because of the general distrust of Buckingham, who had retained his ascendancy over the new king. The Spanish war was proving a failure and Charles offered Parliament no explanations of his foreign policy or its costs. Moreover, the Puritans, who advocated extemporaneous prayer and preaching in the Church of England, predominated in the House of Commons, whereas the sympathies of the King were with what came to be known as the High Church Party, which stressed the value of the prayer book and the maintenance of ritual.

---

[158] "Scholars estimate that by 1640, one-quarter to one third of Englishmen, perhaps even 40 percent, were voting in elections for Parliament. Then there was the evidence of petition signing. . . . All of which argues for a considerable public political awareness. . . . Roughly a quarter of England's two million households owned a Bible—the most influential indictment of pharisees, courtiers, and tyrants ever printed [provided one is allowed to notice it]" (Phillips, 1999, pp. 47-48).

Thus antagonism soon arose between the new king and the Commons, and Parliament refused to vote him the right to levy tonnage and poundage (customs duties) except on conditions that increased its powers, though this right had been granted to previous monarchs for life.

The second Parliament of the reign, meeting in February 1626, proved even more critical of the King's government, though some of the former leaders of the Commons were kept away because Charles had ingeniously appointed them sheriffs in their counties. The failure of a naval expedition against the Spanish port of Cádiz in the previous autumn was blamed on Buckingham and the Commons tried to impeach him for treason. To prevent this, Charles dissolved Parliament in June. Largely through the incompetence of Buckingham, the country now became involved in a war with France as well as with Spain and, in desperate need of funds, the King imposed a forced loan, which his judges declared illegal. (1978a, pp. 52-53)

The reader will remember what I wrote in chapter 12 of volume 2: "Yes, Henry VIII was able to avenge his 'most noble progenitor' [Henry II, flogged at Canterbury in 1174 for the murder of Thomas Becket], but at the cost of giving much power to Parliament, i.e., of increasing substantially the division of power: more division than existed before between king and church."

Back to Hill:

The Bible was no longer the secret sacred book of the educated élite. Most boys and girls learnt to read via the Bible. It was no longer a mystery accessible only to university-educated Latin speakers; . . . .*I speak of "the Biblical Revolution" in two senses. First to emphasize that the language of the Bible was used to express political and ultimately revolutionary opposition to Charles I's government, and to maintain morale during the civil war;* and secondly because the political revolution and its consequences shattered the universal acceptance of the Bible as an infallible text whose pronouncements were to be followed implicitly. . . . The Bible gave confidence and reassurance to men and women who badly needed it. . . .*The*

Bible was of especial use as a yardstick by which to measure and criticize existing institutions and practices. If they could not be found in the Bible they were suspect. The silences of the Bible became almost as weighty as its text." (ib., p. 39, 41; my italics)

And the institution which was most criticized was King Charles himself: "The Man of Blood," so called for *Numbers 35:33* which says that "Blood defileth the land, and the land cannot be cleansed but by the death of him who caused it to be shed." This sentence, indeed, "was cited by the prosecutor at the King's trial, when he called for the land to be purified by the blood of him who had caused the bloodshed" (ib., p. 324). "The sentence of death was read on January 27 [1649]; his execution was ordered as tyrant, traitor, murderer, and public enemy. The sentence was carried out on a scaffold erected outside the banqueting hall of Whitehall on the morning of Tuesday, January 30" (Ashley, 1978a, p. 54).

Most admirable for its increase of the DP:

What was novel in the 1640s was the fact that the unpriviliged, men without the university degree which conferred gentility, now had access to the printing press. . . .*Popular interpretations of the New Testament could overrule the conventionally accepted status and subordination of a hierarchical society.* This was indeed revolutionary. . . What for our purpose is important in this period of English history is the emergence of [*visitor*] radical/critical social attitudes. All serious English political theory dates from this period — Hobbes and Harrington, Levellers, Milton and Winstantley. . . . We look forward to the Royal Society, Newton, and Locke. (Hill, 1994, pp. 178, 415, 422; my italics)

The following is also very *visitor*:

[Later] the Bible lost its universal power once it had been demonstrated that you could prove anything from it, and that there was no means of deciding once the authority of the church could not be enforced. . . . *Fragmentation—both intellectual*

and of congregations was one of the most important conse-
quences of the religious toleration. . . . The breaking of the
absolute authority of the Bible in all spheres is one of the many
triumphs of the human spirit, parallel to (and connected with)
the decline of hell in the seventeenth century. (ib., pp. 428,
430; my italics).

In Germany

In Germany, the Luther Bible had far less civic impact than in
England because of the German *Ritter ethnopsychology* and the
corresponding *Ritter* approach that Luther took toward the authority of
the princes.

At first Luther was moderate and said that

"to burn heretics is against the will of the spirit.". . . . [How-
ever] this early moderation did not survive Luther's increasing dependence on the princes. Once his teaching became established as a state religion, all other forms of Christianity had
to be eliminated, at least in their open expression. . . . By 1527
he had passed to positive, rather than defensive intervention
to ensure uniformity by organizing state ecclesiastical visita-
tions, and in 1529 he went further still to deny "freedom of
conscience": "Even if people do not believe, they should be
driven to the sermon, because of the ten commandments, in
order to learn at least the outward work of obedience." Two
years later he agreed that Anabaptists and other Protestant ex-
tremists "should be done to death by the civil authority".
(Johnson, 1976, pp. 288-89)

The "territorial church," in which the territorial ruler acted
as the highest bishop (*summus episcopus*), became the normal
type of the visible Lutheran Church. . . .Thus the Lutheran
churches became a branch of the state administration; not only
were the mass of church members excluded from taking an
active rule in church affairs but the ministers were supervised
and dependent on the prince and his nearest advisers. . . . Yet
Luther's ideas lent the state a halo that it had not had before.

The state's responsibility for Church organization, in addition to the physical welfare of its subjects, and the submission of the individual to political authority had never been carried to such extremes before.[159] The Lutheran state was an authoritarian state *(Obrigkeitsstaat)* and, within limits, even a "Christian state". (Holborn, 1959/1982, pp. 187, 193)

"But what was to happen in Protestant states went far beyond anything done in Catholic territories, which after all retained the old hierarchy and continued to some extent under papal jurisdiction; also the monastic orders had links and obediences beyond the territories. When the *Landeskirchentum* had fully matured, the Protestant ruler controlled his subject both in his secular and his ecclesiastical role, directly in the former, indirectly through the consistory *(Konsistorium)* in the latter" (Eyck, 1998, p. 302).

Also: "Education became the specialty of Melanchthon, known as *praeceptor Germaniae.* Melanchthon was also the prime author of a

---

[159] For a DP contrast—and as a follow-up of the quote on Charles I—let me report the following on the early political years of Oliver Cromwell: "Though in 1628 [at the age of 29] he had been elected a member of Parliament for the borough of Huntingdon, King Charles I dissolved this Parliament in 1629 and did not call another for 11 years. During the interval, country gentlemen like Cromwell accumulated grievances. . . . When in November 1640 Cromwell was again returned by Cambridge to what was to be known as the Long Parliament, which sat until 1653, his public career begun. [He] had already become known in the Parliament of 1628-29 as a fiery and somewhat uncouth Puritan, who had launched an attack on Charles I's bishops. He believed that the individual Christian could establish direct contact with God through prayer and that the principal duty of the clergy was to inspire the laity by preaching. Thus he had contributed out of his own pocket to the support of itinerant Protestant preachers or 'lecturers' and openly showed his dislike of his local bishop at Ely, the leader of the High Church party, which stood for the importance of ritual and episcopal authority. He criticized the bishop in the House of Commons and was appointed a member of a committee to investigate other complaints against him. Cromwell, in fact, distrusted the whole hierarchy of the Church of England, though he was never opposed to a state church. He therefore advocated abolishing the institution of the episcopate and the banning of a set ritual as prescribed in *The Book of Common Prayer*" (Ashley, 1978b, p. 292).

Karl Marx too had seen the link between the English Bible and the seventeenth-century revolution, when he wrote in his *The Eighteenth Brumaire of Louis Bonaparte* of 1852 that: "Cromwell and the English people had borrowed speech, passions and illusions from the Old Testament for their bourgeois revolution. When the real aim had been achieved, when the bourgeois transformation of English society had been accomplished, Locke supplanted Habakkuk" (1963, p. 17).

theological constitution for a Lutheran church, the Confession of Augsburg submitted to the emperor and the assembled princes at an imperial diet in 1530. Extensive powers in the fields of religion and morals were given to, or appropriated by, the secular authorities, princes, and self-governing cities. Soon it proved expedient to compel people to go to church and to punish deviants and heretics, even to kill them" (Collinson, 1993, p. 271).

Lastly, let me report a second time (the first time was in chapter 25 of volume1 "The *Ritter* (Knight/Warrior) *Personality* of the Germans—Are the Germans the *Last of the Medievals?*") the following by Heiko Oberman in his discussion of Frederick the Wise, Luther's lord and protector:

> Here we meet a late medieval German prince who was by no means an absolute ruler. Yet he had such a sure and strong sense of duty that neither the Roman curia nor the imperial court nor even a Doctor Luther could shake his understanding of the temporal welfare and eternal salvation of his subjects. In the battle between the factions, Frederick was the complete Christian prince, acting in the interests of his subjects' welfare and salvation. The supreme ecclesiastical authority of the German prince was not a result of the Reformation, as often claimed: it preceded the Reformation and provided the cradle for its early emergence and ultimate survival. (1982/1992, p. 20)[160]

So, between this direct authority of the princes, and their indirect authority through their churches, there was no room for an independent reading of the Bible, not even in the translation by Luther. Correspondingly, Germany did not gain those benefits which England attained. As discussed in chapter 25 of volume 1, it was England, and not Germany, which followed its *Sonderweg*.

Canossa, Legnano, and Runnymede prepared the way for the English Bible and its civic influence. In Germany, instead, the undi-

---

[160] Dr. Luther was no less medieval than his prince: "In the economic sphere Luther was as conservative in the same sense as in the theological. In both he charged the Church of his day with innovation and summoned his contemporaries to return to the New Testament and to the early Middle Ages" (Bainton, 1950, p. 236).

minished UP of the German princes (even if it protected Luther against Rome and Madrid, and backed his translation of the Bible) kept a strict control of their Lutheran *Landeskirchen*, including the way in which the Bible was read and not read.

The DP/UP Difference Between Britain and Germany Continued

The sharp contrast, during the 18th century, between DP-*visitor* Great Britain and partial-UP *Ritter* Germany continued during the 18th century as well described in the first chapter of Roy Porter's *Enlightenment: Britain and the Creation of the Modern World*. Particularly vivid are, on one side, his comments on Kant and King Frederick the Great of Prussia, and, on the other, the high praise he reports by the French, Italian, and German/Austrian *philosophes* for "Britain's constitutional monarchy and freedom under the law, its open society, its prosperity and religious toleration" (2001, p. 6):[161]

England's avant-garde enjoyed different prospects from those to be expected elsewhere. Activists were not thwarted at every twist and turn by monarchical *fiat, lettres de cachet* or an ossified *status quo* in State, Church and society. Quite the reverse. . . . Predictably, English piety was also esteemed for its emphasis on works not words: "religion in England, in towns, and even in the smallest villages," envied the Abbé Prévost, "finds its expression in hospitals for the sick, homes of refuge for the poor and the aged of both sexes, schools for the education of the children". (ib., pp. 14-15)

While, on the German side:

In *The Dawn*, written in 1880, Nietzsche alluded to "the hostility of the Germans to the Enlightenment." But he hoped

---

[161] Voltaire wrote that "The English are the only people on earth who have been able to prescribe limits to the power of kings by resisting them; and who, by a series of struggles, have at last established that wise Government, where the Prince is all powerful to do good, and at the same time is restrain'd from committing evil"; and Montesquieu marvelled: "I am here in a country which hardly resembles the rest of Europe. This nation is passionately fond of liberty . . . . every individual is independent" (quoted by Porter, 2001, pp. 6, 24).

that the "obscurantist, enthusiastic and atavistic" spirit which caused the German alienation from the West was passing. He was mistaken. The alienation from the West grew deeper. The heritage of Bismarckism with its emotional rejection of western democracy and its overrating of German strength prevented a realistic reappraisal of the political and intellectual world situation. . . . Reliance on Power, a feeling of superiority, and a disregard for moral factors led Germany into the war of 1914 and, in spite of some very great military successes, into defeat. The fall of the Hohenzollern at the end of the war and the proclamation of the undesired Republic did not establish liberal democracy in Germany. . . . The people were untrained in the practice and responsibility of self-government; democracy seemed an importation from the West unsuited to the German mind; German self-confidence was not shaken by the "undeserved" defeat but morbidly increased as a protest against the historical injustice of a lost war; the struggle against the peace treaty of Versailles was regarded as part of a war against the moral and social ideas of the West. (Kohn, 1960, pp. 12-13)

12

Religious DP Precursors of Canossa

This chapter is divided into the following sections:

1. Introduction
2. Religious DP Precursors and Contributors to Canossa
   The Modern Hierarchical Episcopacy
   The Modern Celibacy of the Clergy
   The Church's Control of Marriages
   The Creation of Canon Law
   The Institution of the Peace of God and Truce of God
   A Certain Control by the Church of the Crusaders
   The Creation of the Military Orders
3. "And East is East . . . ."
4. Post-Canossa High Creativity
5. Post-Canossa Heroes (Becket and More) versus Japanese Heroes
   (47 *Ronin*)

1. Introduction

By now, the reader should be familiar with my thoughts on the birth of the Western Civilization—where and when: Canossa, January 1077; and who is who: Pope Gregory VII and Emperor Henry IV, even if the two hated each other and had no interest in sharing either present or future power neither present nor future. Yet, while the precursors of imperial power are well known, those on the side of the pope are not so. It is therefore with the religious DP precursors of Canossa, and some of the subsequent contributors, that this chapter is concerned.

The main precursors and contributors are the seven listed above, of which the first on the hierarchical episcopacy, and the second on the celibacy of the clergy are the most revolutionary and important ones.

A knowledge of the religious DP precursors of Canossa is important for understanding the long-term success of what otherwise would have been either an impossible event or an oddity without serious consequences. Also, each of these precursors deserves close attention for the unique role they played in the beginnings of the Western civilization and in the process of creativity under DP. Each precursor contributed in making the creativity of the 11th, 12th, and 13th centuries truly admirable.

2. Religious DP Precursors and Contributors to Canossa

The Modern Hierarchical Episcopacy in the West

Of all DP precursors of Canossa, the modern hierarchical episcopacy in the West is the most important. Without it there would have been no papacy: the pope being the bishop of Rome. Without it, none of the other six precursors would have come to life.

This section and the next stress how modern the episcopacy and celibacy of the clergy were, because they were both truly new: deliberately created by the best religious minds of those times in order to overcome the challenges they were facing.

In the first centuries A.D., Christianity was a new religion, not yet burdened with tons of traditions and rules. The founder(s) had left few detailed instructions. In the first centuries, therefore, Christian leaders could be highly innovative without infringing upon deep rooted traditions which simply did not yet exist.[162]

The church began to develop an organizational structure whose main features still endure to the present day in Catholic Christianity. That structure is hierarchical, that is, authority and responsibility within the organization are distributed un-

---

[162] Today, much of what was very innovative, and highly modern at that time, is passé, but that is a different story.

equally among functionaries according to their rank or position. Thus, priests and other ministers among the lower clergy enjoy limited authority over the laity within a small geographical region, called a diocese. The bishop has the right to impose rules on his priests and to discipline or remove those who fail to obey them. The bishop, in turn, is subordinate to a metropolitan or archbishop. . . . . *This hierarchical system emerged as a new stage in the organizational development of the Christian church.* Prior to the fourth century, the structure of the church was far simpler and is better described as collegial, rather than hierarchical. Christianity in that early period was concentrated largely in cities and the entire community of the faithful in each city formed a single unit (usually referred to simply as the church of, say, Ephesus, or Alexandria, or whatever the city's name might be), over which a bishop presided. The bishop was chosen by the members of the local church and he appointed subordinate ministers, such as priests and deacons, to assist him. The bishop, however, remained the sole pastor of all the Christians within his city and was not formally responsible to any higher authority outside of it. *The church adopted the principle of subordination of authority in the fourth century as a consequence of its integration into the administrative system of the Empire, which was already organized as a hierarchical structure.. . . . .*From the reign of Constantine, moreover, the Christian emperors explicitly recognized the jurisdictional authority of bishops and other church officers over issues that involved doctrine and morals and gave their decisions the force of public law. Bishops, in consequence, established their own courts, the *audientia episcopalis*, in order to adjudicate matters that fell under their authority. Canon law thus came to be vested with coercive power, as well as moral authority, and the ecclesiastical hierarchy became in effect an arm of the judicial apparatus of Roman government. (Brundage, 1995, pp. 8-12; my italics)

In the above I have put in italics the points under discussion: Reasonably free to organize itself, the Church adopted the most modern managerial system available at that time, and the most modern for the people and conditions of those times: *the Roman hierarchical system.* It was indeed a Roman aristocrat, Leo, pope from 440 to 461 (later Saint Pope Leo I the Great) who shaped his church according to the best Roman managerial techniques.[163] Leo's letters and sermons also expound his precept of papal primacy in church jurisdiction: Christ granted papal power to St. Peter alone, and that power was passed on by Peter to his successors. Yet, Pope Leo, was not the first Roman aristocrat to develop the modern hierarchic Christianity; St. Ambrose (340-397) bishop of Milan had preceded him:

> Ambrose became the dominant force within the Christian church in the crucial decades of the 370s and 380s. Naturally, he brought the same attitudes of a Roman official to the church and to society. With his bureaucratic cast of mind, he played a large role in moving the church toward a legalistic style of ecclesiastic life and toward the establishment of canon law as a system based on punishment, duty, office, and obligation. He was deeply concerned with obedience, believing that the role of the bishop was like that of a Roman governor. Bishops had already begun to depart from their early role of pius wise men—the spontaneous leaders of the Christian flock—and Ambrose crystallized the new concept that bishops were authoritarian figures quite separate from ordinary laypeople. A bishop dictates, decrees, and pronounces edicts, and the ordinary Christian is more apt to fear than to love him. Ambrose himself (not Jesus) became the model and prototype for the average medieval churchman; most medieval bishops were aristocratic, efficient, legalistic administrators who concentrated on obedience and tax collection. (Cantor, 1993, p. 71)

However, left in isolation, this text by Norman Cantor is misleading: Ambrose was no martinet, no drill sergeant, no dictator, no grand

---

[163] Not only in Rome, but also in what then became France: "As the structure of the Roman Empire disintegrated, invasions multiplied, wars and disorder increased, and life and property became progressively unsafe, the Church stepped into the breach and took over some of the functions for which society had been accustomed to look to the state. It emerged as the protector of the weak, the poor, the widows, and the orphans. That was notably the case in Gaul. *Here in the fifth and sixth centuries the bishops were largely recruited from the Gallo-Roman aristocracy. Drawn as they were from the wealthy, educated, Latinized provincials, they stood for the old order,* but it was on order of comparative justice and stability in a day of an approach towards anarchy" (Latourette, 1953, p. 336, my italics).

inquisitor. He was a scholar, a first-class pastor, a man of profound religiosity:

> Sermons were Ambrose's main literary output. They were acclaimed as masterpieces of Latin eloquence, and they remain a quarry for students of the transmission of Greek philosophy and theology in the West. By such sermons Ambrose gained his most notable convert, Augustine, afterward bishop of Hippo in North Africa and destined, like Ambrose, to be revered as a doctor (teacher) of the church. Augustine went to Milan as a skeptical professor of rhetoric in 384; when he left, in 388, he had been baptized by Ambrose and was indebted to Ambrose's Catholic Neoplatonism, which provided a philosophical base that eventually transformed Christian theology. . . . In Milan, Ambrose "bewitched" the populace by introducing new Eastern melodies and by composing beautiful hymns. . . . He spared no pains in instructing candidates for Baptism. He denounced social abuses and frequently secured pardon for condemned men. He advocated the most austere asceticism: noble families were reluctant to let their daughters attend the sermons in which he urged upon them the crowning virtue of virginity. . . . Ambrose's reputation after his death, in 397, was unchallenged. For Augustine, he was the model bishop. (Brown, 1978, pp. 657-658)

The strict disciplinarian of Cantor would never have converted Augustine. John Burnaby in his pages on St. Augustine said it clearly: "The bishop of Milan was Ambrose, the most eminent Christian churchman of the day. Augustine was introduced to Ambrose, but never came to know him well. He went to hear him preach, however, and this, his first contact with the mind of a Christian intellectual, was enough to shake Augustine's prejudice against Catholic teaching" (1978, p. 365). Later, Augustine's mother, Monica arrived in Milan:

> Ambrose and his celebrated church became a focal point in Monica's life in Milan. At first she thought to continue her African custom "to make meal-cakes and bread and wine to the shrines of the saints on the memorial days," but Ambrose put a stop to it. Surprisingly, she continued to be "greatly devoted to Ambrose" and the bishop reciprocated. "He would

break out in praise of her, congratulating me on having such a mother." Augustine describes a dramatic, hair-raising experience in Milan: "It was only a year, or not much more, since Justina, the mother of the boy emperor Valentinian, had been persecuting your devoted servant Ambrose in the interests of heresy into which the Arians had seduced her. In those days your faithful people used to keep watch in the church, ready to die with their bishop, your servant. My mother, your handmaid, was there with them, taking a leading part in the anxious time of vigilance and living a life of constant prayer." Yea, Monica was in her element, and she loved it. (Smith, 1980, pp. 46)

Would people like Monica be ready to die for an "aristocratic, efficient, legalistic administrators who concentrated on obedience and tax collection"? No. However, if we combine in one person both aspects of St. Ambrose, the highly religious, pius, wise man, and the modern church organizer and leader, then we get the kind of people who will be capable of giving trouble to emperors and kings. Indeed, St. Ambrose was already able to humiliate emperor Theodosius as discussed in chapter 12 of volume 1.[164]

It is the combination of several factors (e.g., a brand new monotheistic religion preaching love and charity[165], a religion of the Books

---

[164] Again, had he been only the legislator and disciplinarian described by Cantor, he would never have had the charisma to win over the emperor.

[165] Here, instead of referring the reader to what I reported before from Rodney Stark, I prefer to quote him a second time, otherwise my praise for the modern episcopacy, as pre-DP of Canossa, would lack foundations. Those Roman managerial techniques were essential, but only when superimposed on something more essential: "To anyone raised in a Judeo-Christian or Islamic culture, the pagan gods seem almost trivial. Each is but one of a host of gods and godlings of very limited scope, power, and concern. Moreover, they seem quite morally deficient. They do terrible things to one another, and sometimes they play ugly pranks on humans. But, for the most part, they appear to pay little attention to things 'down below'. The simple phrase 'For God so loves the world . . . .' would have puzzled an educated pagan, and the notion that the gods care how we treat one another would have been dismissed as patently absurd. . . . Indeed, as E. A. Judge has noted in detail, classical philosophers regarded mercy and pity as pathological emotions—defects of character to be avoided by all rational men. Since mercy involves providing *unearned help* or relief, it was contrary to justice. . . . This was the moral climate in which Christianity taught that mercy is one of the primary virtues—that a merciful God requires humans to be merciful. Moreover, the corollary that *because* God loves humanity, Christians may not please God unless they *love one another* was something entirely new" (1997, pp. 211-12).

but without detailed instruction by the founder, the best modern Roman managerial techniques) which led to the development of a kind of episcopacy capable of paving the way to Canossa.

There is another interpretation of the events which must be integrated with the previous one:

In the long-range perspective, however, the policy of the fourth-century Christian emperors toward the Christian church was fortunate for the survival of Western civilization, for in the fifth century the Roman state in the West disintegrated before the onslaught of the invading Germanic peoples. By the fourth decade of the fifth century, the Roman emperor in the West had no power outside Italy, and the barbarian kingdoms began to emerge in Western Europe. In the seventh decade of the fifth century, there was no ruler left in Italy who even called himself by the grandiose but now empty, title of Roman emperor. *If the Christian emperors of the fourth century had not unified, protected, and favored the Christian church to the extent that it became a state within a state, the church might not have been strong enough to withstand the barbarian invasions of the fifth century.* And thanks to the Christian Roman emperors, the church in the fifth century was still a strong-enough institution to begin the conversion of the barbarian peoples and their education in the Christian Latin culture. The Christian Roman empire in the fourth century had built up the power of the Christian church, and now the church was to supplant the Roman state. . . . As the Roman state disintegrated in the fifth century, the attention of men in the West came more and more to be directed to the only institution that could provide some unity and leadership to religion and education—the bishopric of Rome, the acknowledged leader of the Christian church in the West. The first pope who seems to have perceived the great role in western civilization that the bishopric of Rome could possibly attain as a result of the disintegration of the Roman Empire was Pope Leo I, usually called St. Leo the Great [400-461; pope 440-461]. . . . As a scion of the Italian aristocracy, Leo could not conceive of the end of the empire, although there were many indications in his day that imperial authority was sliding to extinction. *Yet half-consciously the pope worked to make the Roman episcopate the successor to the Roman state in the West.*

The way for this transformation of leadership in the West from the Roman state to the see of Rome was prepared not only by Leo's activities, but even more by the success with which he vindicated the claim of the Roman see to theoretical supremacy in the church. It was a claim that was to prevail in Europe through all the vicissitudes of the early medieval papacy and that constituted a direct challenge to the pretensions of the Byzantine emperor. . . . We can look back over the whole period between the death of Constantine and the end of the pontificate of Leo the Great and see that, *unintentionally, the Christian Roman emperors had laid the foundation for the power of the medieval papacy.* (Cantor, 1993, pp. 62-65; my italics)

The Modern Celibacy of the Clergy

Gérard [Bishop of Cambrai-Arras, in the book he ordered to be written after 1024] was not nearly so concerned about lay marriage as he was about clerical celibacy. . . .*For at the beginning of the eleventh century, amid the great turmoil from which new powers were emerging, the prelates' great preoccupation was to try to save the monopoly, privileges, and immunities of the servants of God.* Their policy was based on the general belief that the men charged with sacrifice, the mediators who interceded with the unseen powers, must keep well away from women. *If the clerics were to claim that the spiritual was superior to the temporal, if they were to preserve the hierarchy that subordinated the laity to the clergy, they had to establish a sexual distinction between men, with some of them consigned to perpetual chastity.* . . . So Gérard of Cambrai's declarations helped to pave the way for Church reform and the struggle against the Nicolaites[166], which was essentially

---

[166] "*Nicolaitism* referred to an obscure sectarian group mentioned in the New Testament (Apocalypse 2:6) and denounced by patristic writers as heretics who were given to sexual promiscuity. The eleventh-century reformers referred indiscriminately to married clergymen, to clerics who kept concubines or frequented prostitutes, and in general to all monks, priests, or other members of the clergy who were in any way sexually active as Nicolaites" (Brundage, 1995, p. 35-36). George Duby (1983) stressed that it was "the bitterness of the struggle against Nicolaitism, which caused the Church as a whole to close ranks under the leadership of the pope" (p. 119-20).

the fight against married priests[167]. . . . Many heads of great families agreed with those who advocated clerical celibacy: they feared competition from clerical dynasties and were glad to see obstacles put in the way of their continuation. Above all, having gone to the trouble to stow away so many young men in cathedral chapters so as to limit the expansion of their families they did not now want them allowed to beget legitimate children. (Duby, 1983, p. 116)

At that time, this idea of the superiority of the clerics—if they were celibate and if they abstained from sex—was more revolutionary than the papal doctrine of the *Two Swords*[168]. While this doctrine roamed on the high intellectual plateaus, and was subject to countless debates, the notion of the chastity of the clergy, and its practice by the majority of its members, meant a sharp and personally felt difference at all levels of society, even in the villages where the priest could claim superiority to the squire because of his celibacy and therefore his special relation with God.

---

[167] Very important also, "Nicolaism (clerical marriage) was not only a moral issue, in the narrow sense, but also a social and political and economic issue. Marriage brought the priesthood within the clan and the feudal structure" (Berman, 1983, p. 91). If the church wanted to separate itself from the lay world, it had to have its members celibate.

[168] "As it had developed by 1300, the doctrine of the two swords provided the most concise statement of the ideology of universal papal sovereignty. As vicar of Christ, and possessing plentitude of power, the pope was not only the wielder of the spiritual or ecclesiastical sword and thus the supreme authority in spiritual jurisdiction on earth, but also the possessor of the secular sword, the channel for the transmission of secular authority by commission or concession to the princes. Although unable to use the secular sword himself, except in extraordinary circumstances such as the government of the papal territories in central Italy, or (as was claimed) when the imperial throne was vacant, the pope was nevertheless seen as the ultimate repository under Christ of power in both church and state. . . . The first known writer who explicitly used the two swords to represent the rival jurisdictions of church and state was Gottschalk of Aachen, when supporting Emperor Henry IV against Pope Gregory VII. . . . Gottschalk used the two-sword analogy in terms based on the differentiation of spiritual and secular authority set forth by Pope Gelasius I (492-496) in his statement *Duo sunt quippe* [Two are certainly]" (Swanson, 1983, p. 233). The origin of the image of the two swords goes back to a short passage in the Gospel of Luke: "And they [some disciples, at the end of the Last Supper] said, Lord, behold, here are two swords. And he said unto them. It is enough" (22:38).

By proclaiming *urbi et orbi* (to the city and the world) the superiority of the clergy (no marriage, sexual purity—at least strongly demanded, and punished in case of infraction), the popes could stress the superiority of the religious sword over the lay sword. The emperor, even as *rex et sacerdos*, had a spouse, and often concubines and bastard offsprings. He had to marry to have children who would continue the dynasty (their absence always meant trouble). But now, through marriage the emperor was placing himself on the side of the weaklings, of the less pure and less holy. A married *sacerdos* was now an oxymoron: the king could only be *rex*. With one stroke, through the celibacy of the clergy, the superiority of the emperor was endangered, and this before Canossa. Even the Canon Law, discussed hereafter, would have remained secondary without the clergy separating itself from the lay people through celibacy.

The Church's Control of Marriages

To these [just discussed] demands for chastity were added the Church's bid for control over marriage contracts. As marriage became more and more a matter of ethics, with emphasis gradually shifting to its spiritual aspect, it fell increasingly under the influence of the priests. When the priests forbade clandestine unions, they received the support of the heads of families. . . . Yet, as the reform went on, ecclesiastical authority grew more and more pervasive, until finally it broke with Carolingian tradition and went so far as to set itself up as sole arbiter in the matter of marriage. (Duby, 1983, p. 119)

The prelates, asked to promote the values of marriage, seized the opportunity to emphasize two rules. First, "the evangelical law concerning one sole wife,". . . . Secondly, a stricter emphasis was laid on the prohibition of taking to wife a cousin within the seventh degree of consanguinity, or blood kinship. (ib., p. 35)

This sacralization of marriage and related strict rules were a wonderful opportunity for the Church to meddle in royal affairs and impose its will. In so doing, the Church had the vivid example of St. John the Baptist who had sternly reproached his direct ruler, Herod Antipas tetrarch of Galilee and Perea, for his unlawful second marriage with Herodias, as narrated in the Gospel of Mark: " For John had

said unto Herod, It is not lawful for thee to have thy brother's wife."
(6:17-19)

Important for the study of the growth of the division of power, this control of marriages by the Church, especially those of the royalty, brought forth a repeat of Canossa, this time with the humiliation of King Philip I of France (r. 1060-1108):

> Philip, growing old, was more and more uneasy under the anathema. In 1096 he pretended to yield and "abjure adultery". Pope Urban II immediately pardoned him. But, when it turned out that Bertrade had not left the royal bedchamber, in 1099 the zealous cardinals summoned the bishops to Poitiers, where they renewed the king's excommunication. . . . But at last, with the passage of time, the business came to an end. . . Since it was necessary to go through the motions of recognizing the superior authority of the papacy, pontifical letters were read out. The bishops of Orleans and Paris asked Philip if he was ready to "abjure the sin of carnal and illicit copulation." In the presence of the abbots of Saint-Denis, Saint-Germain-des-Prés, Saint-Magloire, and Etampes, the king, barefoot and dressed as a penitent [like Henry IV at Canossa], swore on oath: "I will never again have relations or converse with this woman except in the presence of trustworthy persons." Bertrade made a similar promise. So the anathema was lifted. (Duby, 1983, p. 12-13)

Contributing to the DP, King Philip did what he wanted: he and Bertrade "continued to live together and in 1106 were given a warm welcome in Angers by Count Fouque [the first husband of Bertrade] in Anjou" (ib., p. 13).

Neither the Church nor the Crown had full power, and the people knew it. The story stuck in people's mind, and just that knowledge was an essential part of the division of power, a division of power that George Duby had stressed in his book of 1978 *Medieval Marriage: Two Models from Twelfth-Century France*. The two models, or sets of attitudes to marriage being "that of the French kings of the eleventh and twelfth centuries, and that of the clergy of the early medieval church" (Brooke, 1991, p. 120).

In the end, given that "the aristocratic societies of western Europe were increasingly concerned with the effective passage of landed estates and kingdoms by hereditary succession. . . . in the marriage market and the marriage games of medieval catholic Europe, the Church and the Papacy acted as umpires, and were blessed and cursed accordingly" (ib., 142-43). Both these blessings and curses contributed to the increase of the division of power.

The Creation of Canon Law

Early in that conflict [the Investiture Controversy] advocates of reform concluded that canon law must play a key role in their strategy. The abolition of simony and Nicolaitism, they reasoned, must not only be grounded on legal prohibitions of the practices they abhorred, but must also be enforced by legal processes. They believed that the abuses they fought reflected structural weaknesses in the church's legal system, for they could not have taken root had adequate monitoring and enforcement mechanisms been in place. (Brundage, 1995, pp. 36-37)

The issues that brought the largest numbers of people into personal contact with canonical courts at the local level had to do with marriage, family, and sexual behaviour. The exclusive competence of church courts to deal with these matters was well established by the tenth century and was only rarely challenged thereafter. (ib., p. 72)

Medieval canon law was thus a good deal more than simply a set of religious regulations with which pious persons might choose to comply. Rather, *the canons embodied a system of law often parallel to, sometimes in conflict with, and occasionally victorious over, the competing civil jurisdictions of kings and princes.* Canon law offered litigants in many civil controversies an alternative forum in which to air their disputes and seek relief from wrongs. . . . For all its limitations and shortcomings, however, medieval canon law played a central role in medieval political, economic and social life. It was also a significant element in the intellectual ferment of the high Middle Ages. Canonists devised new solutions to problems, old and new, originated fresh approaches to the analysis of institutions, and contributed novel ideas to what has since become the common stock of Western traditions. *Canonists, in short, formed one major creative component of the intellectual as well as the practical life of the European Middle Ages.* (ib., pp 177-79, my italics to stress the DP inherent in the two judicial systems, and the derived high creativity)

The Institution of the Peace of God and Truce of God

The Peace of God was supposed to protect non-combatants, and the Truce of God to prevent hostilities at certain times. In 989, the Council of Charroux pronounced that anyone who robbed churches or attacked an unarmed member of the clergy or stole from peasants would be excommunicated. The order was soon extended to include merchants, and in addition prohibited certain acts such as destroying vineyards or mills. The Truce of God began modestly by reviving one of the capitularies of Charlemagne, which had forbidden the prosecution of blood-feuds on Sundays. . . . The intention was that lords and knights should enter into a pact in which they would swear a formal oath to observe these restrictions. In practice, of course, they frequently refused to do so. They regarded the legislation as unwarrantable interference in their own affairs and there were many, including even some members of the clergy, who criticized the Church for assuming a task which clearly related more to secular than to spiritual matters. *It was a bold move for the Church to try to subject knights directly to its own authority, going over the head of secular authorities and by-passing secular law-enforcement,* such as it was. But this was the beginning of a period which saw the Church claiming to assert ultimate temporal as well as spiritual authority in Christendom and becoming increasingly involved in the struggle for political power. *The movement for the reform of secular authority by the Church, which produced the Peace and Truce of God, was merely a tentative first step towards the revolutionary views put forward by Pope Gregory VII.* (Hopkins, 1996. 79; my italics)

Authored by Abbot Odilo of Cluny (994-1049), the Truce of God suspended warfare at first from Saturday noon until early Monday morning, and later from Wednesday evening until Monday morning as well as during Lent and Advent and on various saints' days. The efforts of Cluny and the church generally to exempt certain classes of people from military service and from attack on their person or property, and to restrict fighting to certain times, could be only partly successful in an age of violence and anarchy such as the tenth and eleventh centuries. *The importance of the peace movement for the future, however, and especially for the future of the Western legal tradition, was enormous*, for the experience of collective oath-taking by groups in the name of peace played a crucial role in the founding of cities in the late eleventh century and thereafter, in the formation of guilds within cities, and in the promulgation of legislation by dukes, kings, and emperors through the so-called ducal or royal peace and through the "land peace" *(pax terrae, Landfriede)*. (Berman, 1983, p.90; my italics)

The movement of peace thus appears as an attempt to alleviate the decline of the royal authority which had hitherto combined spiritual and worldly elements. The result was to bring the spiritual power of bishops face to face with the temporal power of dukes and counts. The confrontation led to a stricter separation of laymen from clergy and monks both socially and in the eyes of the law. This tendency was of great significance in that the *restauratio pacis* [restoration of the peace] conveniently dovetailed into wider aspirations. It took its place in the reaction against the Carolingian order in which church and Christianity had been intimately merged in the person of the king. The movement of reaction was a vehicle for Gregorian ideas. (Duby, 1977, p. 126)

A Certain Control by the Church of the Crusaders[169]

The papal leadership in launching the Crusades, starting with Pope Urban II (r. 1088-1099) is well known. Of the many resulting

---

[169] Strictly, this is a post-Canossa effect, as well as the next point on the Military Orders. However coming so soon after Canossa—Pope Urban II's famous sermon in France was in 1095, less than twenty years after Canossa—they both deserve to be included here.

forms of division of power between clergy and laity, let me mention the following for its brevity and clarity:

> *[The Crusaders] had temporary clerical status, so were subject only to ecclesiastical jurisdiction.* They did not have to pay any taxes, or pay off any debts, or incur any interest on their debts, or perform any ordinary feudal military service, while they were away on crusade. The Church also promised to protect a crusader'sproperty and family against usurping claimants. (Hopkins, 1996, p. 84; my italics)

Here we encounter a parallel of what was discussed in chapter 7 of volume 2 on the dual allegiance of the prelates who served as prime ministers (e.g., cardinals Cisneros, Wolsey, Richelieu). A crusader with his clerical status (even if temporary and partial) had automatically a double allegiance to his feudal lord, and to the church, thereby weakening the power of each, especially of the first.

It is important for the study of the development of the division of power, that partial allegiance to the church was not the same as the dual set of lay obligations (to one's liege lord and to the king or emperor). It was an allegiance to totally different worlds which promoted, in every intelligent mind, the dialectics of church versus state, pope versus emperor, afterlife in Paradise or Hell versus the present life, the dialectics of local truths versus universal ones.

The Creation of the Military Orders

That thousands of knights and men at arms should mount an expedition overseas at the express bidding of the Church was remarkable enough, but out of this strange wedding between warriors and churchmen came an even stranger offspring: the military orders—knights who were also monks. They lived under a monastic rule, which included the usual injunctions to poverty, chastity and obedience. . . . This separated them from the dynastic concerns which preoccupied so many of their secular counterparts and, though many of the military orders became extremely wealthy, they were prohibited from participating in the more frivolous activities of knightly life, such as tournaments or dancing. In that sense they were out of the mainstream of medieval knighthood, but they developed its military aspect to a high degree, particularly in training and discipline, the construction and defence of castles, and the tactics of siege warfare. (Hopkins, 1996, p. 86)

3. "And East is East. . . ."[170]

However Christian Byzantium moved in a totally different way than the West:

[In the Byzantine empire, great importance was given to *solidarity*] which rested on two bases. First, there was a loyalty to the person and mystique of the emperor, the visible symbol of the Christian state. Second, the monks and holy men formed the essential link that bound all classes together, despite every type of social tension and injustice, in a realm believed somehow to be a dim reflection of the divine polity. In touch with the unseen world they exactly fitted this belief. The East never accepted the *Two Cities theory* of human society nor its corollary, the *Two Swords theory* of the relations between church and state[171]. At all levels, Byzantine society consolidated around the person of the emperor. The Cappadocians, for instance, while strongly critical of the emperor Valens's Arianizing policy, had no doubt that the emperors had been entrusted by God with sovereignty over the world, and like stars, filled the world with the light of peace and piety. In moments of enthusiasm, Theodosius II or Marcian would be hailed by Eastern bishops as "priest" as well as ruler. . . . In this Christ-oriented society the emperor was God's vice-gerent and "imitator of the Heavenly Emperor," leading his subjects to both material and spiritual salvation. In return, he could expect loyalty from them, and he received it. . . . *Eastern mo-*

---

[170] This is the title of the last chapter of W.H.C. Frend's book *The Rise of Christianity*.

[171] Specifically, "This doctrine represented a view far removed from that of the Syrian and indeed the great majority of Eastern bishops. It symbolized the difference of outlook that prevailed between Eastern and Western Christianity in the Christian empire" (Frend, 1984, p. 536); "In the eastern part of the empire it never achieved ascendancy. But in the west, the dualism of church and government became accepted doctrine, and it is within this context that the heritage of Rome became bequeathed to medieval Europe" (Friedrich, 1973, p. 619).

nasticism was also a consolidating force that turned popular feeling toward the emperor. Without the monks, loyalty would have been difficult if not impossible to sustain in the face of the gross abuse in taxation, oppression by patrons, money-lenders, and soldiers, and threats from brigands and external enemies that the Eastern provincials suffered. (Frend, 1984, pp. 745-746; my italics)

Never, indeed, would the Eastern monks—shaped by the imperial UP—dream of initiatives like those taken first by Cluniac[172], then by Cistertia monks[173], as discussed in section 3, chapter 12 of volume 1, "In Praise of the Technological and Scientific Contributions by the Benedictines and Cistercian Monks."

A similar observation to Frend's statement that, "Eastern monasticism was also a consolidating force that turned popular feeling toward the emperor", was made by Michael Angold (2001) on how Emperor Arcadius (395-408) dismissed John Chrysostom, patriarch of Constantinople, when the Patriarch refused to go along with the Emperor's plans to make Constantinople a court of appeals for cases from other Churches.

The implication was that the church of Constantinople was claiming primacy over the church at large. Chrysostom defied imperial wishes and very properly declined the commission on the ground that he would be exceeding his powers. He immediately forfeited the support of the imperial court, which saw his actions as betrayal of trust. *Thanks to the support of the monks, the imperial will prevailed. The monks were now*

---

[172] "As early as the tenth century a few monastic houses successfully resisted attempts to bring them under the control of lay interests. The Burgundian monastery of Cluny (founded in 909) was prominent among the reformed religious communities and soon attracted others to the cause. Monasteries independent of lay control became centres from which more ambitious and far-reaching reform ideas began to flow" (Brundage, 1995, p. 34).

[173] "The Cistercians, who were ardent supporters of papal policy, were known for their agricultural expertise, managerial skill, and colonizing zeal. They were particularly adept in the development of implements useful in clearing wilderness areas" (Berman, 1983, p. 101).

instrumental in having Chrysostom removed from office. They drove him into exile. (pp. 11-12, my italics)

This attitude of the Byzantine monks—in contrast with that of Benedictines and Cistercian—goes along with the profound dislike for technology by the Greek Orthodox Church reported in section 5, chapter 12 of volume 1. "The DP Use of the Clock and Other Democratic Technology by the West, and not by Byzantium". There I reported the following—now slightly expanded—from Gimpel:

> In the Greek Orthodox Church, there was no acceptance of new technology and no readiness whatsoever to compromise with new ideas. A remarkable demonstration of the strict observance of tradition in the Orthodox Church is given by the fact that until the twentieth century orthodox priests never allowed a mechanical clock to be installed in an Orthodox church. For them it would have been blasphemy; for them the mathematical division of time into hours, minutes, and seconds had no relationship with the eternity of time. But the Church of Rome had no such objection to clocks being installed on the facades or towers of their churches, and today there are tens of thousands of mechanical church clocks in western Europe. . . . That they adopted our way of measuring time so late has, at least in the majority of Eastern countries, handicapped their economic and industrial development. (1977, pp 169-70)

The pro-imperial attitude of the Byzantine monks, as described by Frend, and by Angold, should be labelled *insular,* according to the following aspects of the *insular personality* in table 5 of volume 1: "Belief in the infallibility of leaders and supremos", "Conservative and less creative (especially in philosophy, religion, politics, science)." Indeed, the *insular,* far more than the *visitor,* will be on the side of the emperor, especially one who is Head of the Church, High Priest of the Empire, who is Emperor by the Grace of God, who is Equal to the Apostles and God on earth, the True imitation of Christ (as discussed in chapter 14 of volume 1). This *insular* love and respect for the supremo, be he emperor or king or pharaoh—which reminds one of the Spanish *"Del rey abajo ninguno* [Beside the king nobody]" discussed in chapter 6 of volume 2—has its logic in the dream that there is at the summit of society a person to whom one may go to ask for justice against abuses. This is very difficult because the king is surrounded by evil counsellors (see chapter 6, this volume), but from time to time the king hears the truth and renders justice even to the most humble of his people. The king, therefore, is the great Father who must be protected against the courtiers around him,[174] including for Byzantium the patriarch of Constantinople (who probably, like most bishops, may have annoyed the monks on occasion).

There are many ways to study the contrast between West and East, yet at the end we come to the same conclusion that the West was formed by the division of power (at first between popes and emperors, i.e. between church and state), and that the Christian East—sadly—was formed by the unity of power of its emperors. In this respect,

> it is highly significant that the power of the monarch (Basileus) to punish and exploit his subjects to an unlimited degree was never questioned in Byzantium; it was simply accepted as the natural order of things. It is quite impossible to imagine anything like Magna Carta—a legal compromise between the monarch and his vassals—in a Byzantine setting. The 'individualism' of the Byzantine aristocrat was the individualism of the lackey looking for a career and a chance to enrich himself, devoid of personal dignity, cringing before his superiors and ready to demean himself for a gratuity. (Gurevich, 1972/1985, p. 191)

---

[174] The simpler the people, the more ignorant they are, and the more they will be on the side of the king, even pardoning him every extravagance, luxury, marital affair—even liking him more because of these extravagances and luxuries—as was the case with Ludwig II of Bavaria, the *Dream King* or *Mad King*. In his last days, "the peasants, who adored their King, were ready and eager to rescue him under an armed guard—for the Chasseurs were still loyal to him—across the Austrian border. Their emissaries, Osterholzer and Weber, came to Ludwig and implored him to give his consent: he had only to say the word and they would come for him. But the king would not agree . . . .He would not help himself; he would not allow others to help him: he was lost" (Blunt, 1973, p. 221).

4. Post-Canossa High Creativity

While working at this chapter, I came across two short texts in praise of the high creativity of the West in the early Middle Ages, plus one in direct praise of the creativogenicity of the Investiture Controversy. These three, especially when read together, give evidence that the great DP which began at Canossa in 1077 (and was prepared by the "progenitors" discussed in this chapter) bore wonderful fruit:

The High Creativity of the 13th Century

The thirteenth century was an age of spectacular innovation in nearly every department of Western life. The century witnessed the birth and flowering of the mendicant religious orders[175], the first appearance of universities, the development of scholastic theology and philosophy, the burgeoning of sophisticated poetry in the vernacular languages, and the invention or improvement of numerous scientific, technical, and mechanical devices. It also produced massive amounts of new law and new legal doctrines nearly everywhere in the Latin West. (Brundage, 1995, p. 164)

The High Creativity of the 11th and 12th Centuries

Maitland called the twelfth century "a legal century." It was more than that: it was *the* legal century, the century in which the Western legal tradition was formed. The great revolutionary events that inaugurated that tradition, however, and the

---

[175] "The emergence of the mendicant orders was associated with the growth of cities in Western Europe. By the thirteenth century that part of the world was beginning to move out of the almost exclusively agricultural economy which had followed the decline of the Roman Empire and the disappearance of the urban civilization which had characterized that realm. Cities were once more appearing. It was to deepening the religious life of the populace of the cities and towns that the friars devoted much of their energy. Most of the earlier monasteries had chosen solitude and centres remote from the contaminating influences of the world. In contrast, the mendicant orders sought the places where men congregated and endeavored to bring the Gospel to them there. The older monasteries were associated with a prevailing rural and feudal milieu. The mendicant orders flourished in the rapidly growing urban populations" (Latourette, 1953, p. 428).

first great legal achievements, occurred not in the twelfth but in the last decades of the eleventh century—the *Dictates* of Pope Gregory VII and the centralizing administrative measures of the Norman rulers of Sicily, England and Normandy, the scholarly achievements of the great canon lawyer Ivo of Chartres (1040-1116) and of the great Roman lawyer Irnerius (about 1060-1125). (Berman, 1983, p.120)

The High Creativity Brought by the *Investiture Controversy* (and by Canossa as its Key Event)

The great changes that took place in the life of the Western Church and in the relations between the ecclesiastical and the secular authorities during the eleventh and the first part of the twelfth century have traditionally been called the Hildebrand Reform or the Gregorian Reform. . . . [Even the principal slogan of the papal reformers "the freedom of the church"[176]] does not adequately convey the full dimensions of the revolutionary transformation, which many leading historians have considered the first major turning point in European history, and which some have recognized as the beginning of the modern age.[177] What was involved ultimately was, in Peter Brown's words, "the disengagement of the two spheres of the sacred and the profane," from which stemmed a release of energy and creativity analogous to a process of nuclear fission. (Berman, 1983, p. 87-88)

---

[176] That that freedom was badly needed can be seen, for instance, by the following from Berman (1983): "Some historians argue that Pope Leo III made Charlemagne emperor, but it is closer to the truth to say that Charlemagne made Leo pope; and in 813 Charlemagne crowned his own son emperor without benefit of clergy. In fact, later German emperors required the pope, on his election, to swear an oath of loyalty to the emperor. Of the twenty-five popes who held office during the hundred years prior to 1059 (when a church synod for the first time prohibited lay investiture), twenty-one were directly appointed by emperors and five were dismissed by emperors" (p. 91).

[177]Refers the reader to more than three pages (pp. 574-78) of notes on eighteen historians, the first being Eugen Rosenstock-Huessy (1931, 1938) who pioneered "The concept of the Papal Revolution as a fundamental break in the historical continuity of the church, and as the first of the great revolutions of Western Europe" ib., p. 574

5. Post-Canossa Heroes (Becket and More) versus Japanese Heroes (47 *Ronin*)

In both the West and Japan, not everyone agreed with the *supremo*, whether he was king or shogun. Thomas Becket did not agree with his king, neither did Thomas More, and both paid for their convictions with their lives; so did the *47 ronin* in Japan. Yet the two groups: Becket and More, and the 47 ronin differed much in the values for which they fought.

Thomas Becket, chancellor of England under Henry II and subsequent archbishop of Canterbury, baffled his contemporaries and has set historians at variance by his sudden change from a devoted servant of the King into an obstinate opponent of his policy, from a worldly clerk into an austere archbishop. The drama of his long quarrel with Henry, which ended with his murder in the Canterbury Cathedral, one of the most familiar and arresting episodes in English history, remains an issue on which the judgment of the historians are divided. . . . Within a few days after Thomas' death, his tomb became a goal of pilgrimage, and he was canonized by Alexander III in 1173. In 1174 Henry did penance at Canterbury and was absolved. For almost four centuries, Becket's shrine was one of the most famous in Europe. Thomas was portrayed in illuminations and sculpture, and churches were dedicated to him throughout western Christendom. (Knowles, 1978, pp. 786-87).[178]

Thomas More is the eminent humanist and statesman, chancellor of England, who was beheaded for refusing to accept King Henry VIII as head of the Church of England. He is recognized as a saint by the Roman Catholic Church (canonized in 1935).

Both cases served to increase the DP between the lay and religious scripts, because of the constant debate over their personalities, and the never-resolved judgment on their motivations. An example of this is the recent study by John Guy, his *Thomas More* (2000). In the words of the reviewer, Alexandra Walsham: "We all think we know Thomas More the distinguished statesman and humanist who placed

---

[178]For a continuation of this story under Henry VIII see chapter 12 of volume 2.

his conscience above allegiance to his king and chose death rather than swearing an oath in vain. . . . The great virtue of John Guy's book is his candid admission that it is ultimately impossible to get beneath More's skin and penetrate his mind" (2001, p. 34).

In Japan things were different on several accounts: Allegiance problems are all lay problems, not state versus religion, not king versus church; and the hero handles his problems differently, often by committing a heroic suicide. As described by Ruth Benedict (1946):

[In Japan] the hero is caught in a conflict of 'giri[179] against human feelings', 'chu against ko', 'giri against gimu.' A hero fails because he is allowing his human feelings to obscure his obligations of giri. He is cornered and sacrifices his family. The conflicts so portrayed are still between obligations both of which are in themselves binding. They are both 'good.'. . . . This way of viewing the hero's life is in great contrast to the Western view. Our heroes are good precisely in that they have 'chosen the better part,' and are pitted against opponents who are bad. 'Virtue triumphs,' as we say. There should be a happy ending. The good should be rewarded. The Japanese, how-ever, have an insatiable appetite for the story of the 'flagrant case' of the hero who finally settles incompatible debts to the world and to his name by choosing death as a solution. Such tales would in many cultures be stories teaching resignation to a bitter fate. But in Japan that is exactly what they are not. They are tales of initiative and ruthless determination. The heroes put forth every effort to pay some one obligation in-cumbent upon them, and, in so doing, they flout another obli-gation. But in the end they settle with the 'circle' they flouted. The true national epic of Japan is the *Tale of the Forty-Seven Ronin*. . . . The graves of the forty-seven have been for genera-tions a favorite pilgrimage where thousands went to pay trib-ute. They left their visiting cards, too, and the ground around the graves was often white with them. The theme of the *Forty-*

---

[179]*Giri*-to-the-world includes duties to one's liege lord, and one's extended family. *Giri*-to-one's-name (the Japanese version of the German *die Ehre*) includes one's duty to 'clear' one's reputation of insult or imputation of failure. *Chu* is the duty to the Emperor, the law, to Japan. *Ko* is the duty to parents and ancestors (by implication, to descendants). *Gimu* includes chu, ko, and *nimmu* (duty to one's work). From Benedict, 1946, p. 116.

Seven Ronin centers around giri to one's lord. As the Japanese see it, it portrays the conflicts of giri with chu, of giri with righteousness—in which giri is of course virtuously triumphant—and of 'merely giri' with limitless giri. . . . The forty-seven heroes offer up everything to it, their reputations, their fathers, their wives, their sisters, their righteousness (gi). Finally they offer up to chu their own lives, dying by their own hands. (pp. 198-200)

Their giri was paid. They had still to pay their chu. Only in their death could the two coincide. They had broken the State rule against undeclared vendetta but they were not in revolt against chu. Whatever was demanded of them in the name of chu they must fulfill. The Shogunate ruled that the forty-seven should commit seppuku. As fifth-grade children's Japanese Readers say: Since they acted to avenge their lord, their unswerving giri had to be regarded as an example for ages eternal. . . . Therefore the Shogunate after deliberation commanded seppuku, a plan which killed two birds with one stone. That is, in killing themselves with their own hands the ronin paid the supreme debt both to giri and to gimu. (ib., p. 205)

Expanding on the comparison and contrast, none of the many versions of *the Tale of the Forty-Seven Ronin* (as far as I know) portrays the suicide of the 47 ronin, nor has any imagined what were their last words. In the long exposition by Sakae Shioya, we read that "the committing of *seppuku* by the loyalists is taken here to follow as a matter of course, but it is well that the actual performance of it is deftly avoided so as not to damp the triumphal effect that has been worked up to so high pitch" (1956, p. 224).

In the case of Thomas More, instead, we know his last words:

He was brief in asking the people to pray for him. Roper[180] says that he told them to bear witness with him that he should "now there suffer death in and for the faith of the Holy Catholic Church." A pamphlet called the *Paris News Letter* carried the report of the trial and execution to the Continent; *it adds the eloquent detail that More said he died the*

---

[180] William Roper (1556/1963). *Life of Saint Thomas More*, p. 50.

king's good servant but God's first. (Marius, 1985, p. 514; my italics)

It would be difficult to summarize more efficiently the great DP between state and church than those words by More: "[being] the king's good servant but God's first". They are the perfect equivalent of the famous saying attributed to Aristotle: *Amicus Plato, sed magis amica veritas*[181] .[182]

---

[181] Plato is dear to me, but dearer still is truth.

[182] In the case of Thomas Becket, "His last words were an acceptance in defense of the church of Christ" (Knowles, 1978, p. 787). Specifically: "Thomas attempted no further resistance. Bowing his head, he joined his hands in prayer and said firmly and loudly: "I commend myself and my church to God and the Blessed Mary, to St. Denis and St. Alphege." (Winston, 1967, p. 365).

13

The Italian *Riconquista* (951-1369) and the Making of the *Visitor*

1. Introduction

> No entiendo cómo se puede llamar reconquista a una cosa *que dura ocho siglos*[183] (José Ortega y Gasset, 1964, p.140).
>
> (I do not understand how you can call Reconquest something which lasts eight centuries.)

Ortega y Gasset could have said the same for the four centuries of the Italian *Riconquista*.[184] Yet for centuries Spain was dominated by Arabs and Moors, and then they were not there anymore; for centuries Italy was dominated by the German emperors, their soldiers and Italian allies, and then they were not there anymore. Neither the Arabs/Moors nor the Germans disappeared willingly: they fought long and hard, but their rule came to an end. There was therefore a Spanish *Reconquista* and an Italian *Riconquista*, provided that we see things in

---

[183] From the defeat of the Moors in the Battle of Covadonga (718) by Pelayo, first Christian King of Asturias, to the reconquest of Granada (1492) by Isabel of Castile and Ferdinand of Aragon.

[184] From the invasion of Italy by Emperor Otto I (951) to the second—and failed—expedition to Italy of Emperor Charles IV (1368-69).

a broad context, especially for the least understood of the two, the *Riconquista*. Here the Italians were trying, at the same time, to free themselves from two mighty masters: the German emperors and the Roman popes, and they could do so only by shifting allegiances and alliances which brought more bloody battles among themselves than against the Germans and the popes.

Definitely, the Italian *Riconquista* was no linear affair, but neither was the Spanish *Reconquista*: "Although later ages considered the Cid a great fighter for the Cross, what strikes the student of his history is the fact that he lived intimately with the Moslems all his life, was fluent in Arabic, and often served them as willingly as he did his Christian masters" (Ramsey, 1973, p. 65). In parallel, there are different interpretations of what the *Reconquista* truly was. The one favored by Ramsey is the new and unconventional interpretation by Jaime Vicens Vives (1910-60), who "maintains that the real motivating force of the early Reconquest was livelihood, the need for more land, for more adequate sources of food. 'What the Christian cared about was to resettle, to conquer better lands and make them fertile for his children, creating a new spiritual climate which was impossible in the steep lands of the North.' Later, of course, religious and political factors enter in, but never completely cancel out the fact that the search for the basic necessities of life had much to do with determining the causes and aspects of the recovery of the Moslem lands. This interpretation has led Vicens Vives to make an extremely interesting and significant distinction between the *military* Reconquest mentioned in all history books—very fast and vigorous after 1212; and what he called the *slow* Reconquest which was based on the resettlement of populations and internal colonization of southern Spain from about 1230 to 1609!" (ib., p. 51).

Mine too is a new, unconventional interpretation of the Italian *Riconquista* which I present briefly in sections 2 and 3. I will also discuss an intrinsic feature of the *Riconquista*, which contributed significantly to the making of the Western *visitor personality*, i.e., the opposed religious positions of the Guelphs (partisans of the Papacy, and therefore religiously *orthodox*) and the Ghibellines (partisans of the Empire, and therefore considere heretics by the Church). This contrast was ceaselessly confused and obscured by local internecine fights and changes of allegiance by the key actors, yet it remained dialectically creativogenic because it was open to debates and personal choices, even if only by a limited, yet influential, number of people. While being a Christian or Mohammedan in Spain was practically never a matter of choice, in Italy—within the obvious restrictions of family or district allegiances—there was room for personal choices which will be discussed through the writings of Dante and Bartolo da Sassoferrato.

2. The Fundamental Importance of the Italian Riconquista for the Free World

Before proceeding, let me explain, through the words of Leopold von Ranke, why I consider the *Riconquista* so important for Europe and the free World —more so than the *Reconquista*. Ranke, the leading German historian of the 19th century, said in his discussion of the encounter, at Chiavenna before the battle of Legnano of 1176, between Emperor Frederick I *Barbarossa* and his cousin Henry of Brunswick *the Lion*:

> *Auf ihrer Vereinigung beruhte die Zukunft des deutschen Reiches, der Welt. Mit vereinter Macht konnten sie die Herrschaft der Deutschen über Italien und das Papsttum herstellen, aber sie verstanden sich nicht. . . . In dem wichtigsten, entscheidensten Moment brach ihre Feindschaft aus und bewirkte, dass das Kaisertum seine Oberhoheit über die Welt nicht behaupten konnte. (1881-88/1921, 7, p. 119)[185]*

At few other times was Western Civilization so much in danger. A victory by Emperor Frederick Barbarossa at Legnano would have easily led to a UP domination of Germany over Europe. With imperial control of the papacy, there would have been no Magna Carta, no Humanism-Reformation-Enlightenment-science, no liberty, no democracy.

---

[185] From their cooperation depended the future of the German empire, of the World. With combined power they could have establish the domination of the Germans over Italy and the Papacy, but they could not agree. . . . At the most important decisive moment, their enmity surfaced and caused the failure of the sovereignty of the Empire over the World.

3. Germanophobia

Every reconquest demands a certain amount of dislike or hatred of the foreign oppressor. Such xenophobia was there, in both the Reconquista and the Riconquista.

In the case of the *Riconquista*, it was clearly Germanophobia as shown in the following examples:

- The German historian Wolfgang Menzel wrote in his *History of Germany*, in the section devoted to Otto I's conquest of Italy in 951 and his conflict with Margrave Berengar of Ivrea:

> Whilst these events were taking place in Germany, more particularly since the death of Ludolf [Otto's eldest son], by whom he had been narrowly watched, Berengar aimed at the independent sovereignty of Italy, in which *he was upheld by the majority of the people, whose national pride ill brooked the despotic rule of either the clergy or the Germans.*" (1882, *1*, p. 336, my italics)

- In the words of Benjamin Arnold, in his *Medieval Germany 500-1300*:

> Some Italians bewailed the advent of the Germans as a disaster, and viewed the achievement of Otto the Great as a foreign conquest. Percy Ernst Schramm drew attention to the way the chronicler Benedict of Monte Soratte[186] relied upon the classical image of Rome's greatness to bewail its submission to Otto I and Otto II as barbarian despoilers:

> > Woe to Rome oppressed and trampled upon by so many peoples, taken prisoner by the Saxon king, your townsfolk ruled by the sword, and your strength all gone. They carry off your gold and silver by the sack-

---

[186] Monte Soratte is a mountain of Latium, 20 miles north of Rome. Its monastery of Sant'Andrea is now famous for the *Chronicon* of its monk Benedict.

ful . . . . At the height of your power you triumphed over the peoples, threw the world into the dust, and throttled the kings of the earth. You held the scepter and the highest authority, now you are thoroughly pillaged and plundered by the Saxon kings. (1997, p. 87)

- Cippo Perelli, in his introductory paper for the 1993 cycle of conferences on *The Middle Ages and the Battle of Legnano*, made it clear that every interpretation of the wars between Emperor Barbarossa and the Italian Communes has to begin with the *"scontro tra germanicità e italianità, una contrapposizione totale, netta"*[187] (p.1)

- Franco Cardini has entitled the XVth chapter of his history of the Lombard League: *"Federico, il tedesco"* (Frederick, the German), because, after his excommunication in 1159 by Pope Alexander III:

    non era più Federico, col favore della divina clemenza imperatore dei Romani. Era Fridericus Theutonicus, "Federico il tedesco": lo scomunicato, la bestia feroce, il nemico della Chiesa.[188] (1991, p. 93)

- In *Cambridge Medieval History*, Balzani (1929) wrote that:

    [at the Battle of Legnano of 1176] the defeat of the Germans was complete and great their slaughter. The exultant Milanese wrote to their brethern of Bologna: "Glorious has been our triumph over our enemies. Their slain are innumerable as well as those drowned and taken prisoners. We have in our hands the shield, banner, cross, and lance of the Emperor, and have found in his coffers much gold and silver, while the booty taken from the enemy is of great value, *but we do not*

---

[187] "collision between Germanicity and Italianicity [between what is German and what is Italian], a total and sharp contrast."

[188] He was no longer Frederick, Emperor of the Romans through the favor of the divine clemency. He was *Fridericus Theutonicus*, Federico the German, the excommunicated, the fierce beast, the enemy of the Church.

consider these things ours, but the common property of the Pope and the Italians.

[Further on, in 1177, in their letter to the Pope, the Lombards wrote:] "Let your Holiness know, and let it be known to the imperial power that we, *so long as the honour of Italy is safe-guarded*, are willing to accept peace and favour from the Emperor provided our liberties remain intact." (pp. 446-47, 449; my italics)

• In his biography of Frederick I, the German historian Rudoph Wahl commented as follows on the immediate consequence of the Emperor's defeat at Legnano:

> *Unbeschreiblicher Jubel erfüllte Mailands Mauern, als die Sieger heimkehrten. Mit der verhassten Herrschaft der Deutschen sollte es nun für alle Zeiten eine Ende haben. . . . Ein einziger Siegesruf schwoll durch die Lombardei: In wenigen Wochen werden die letzen Deutschen davongejagt sein, schon rüsten die Mailänder zum Vernichtungschlag, der Freiheitsgedanke im unlösbaren Bunde mit der Heiligen Kirche hat endgültig triumphiert, das "gottlose Volk der Deutschen" sinkt in den Staub (1941/1950, p. 351, 355; highlighted in the original).*[189]

• "In Italy a strong reaction against the German domination had followed immediately on Henry VI's death [1197]. *Everywhere the German officials were attacked and driven out, the German garrisons were expelled from their fortresses.* The Papacy was not slow to take advantage of these general rebellions. Celestine III in his last days had begun the work of annexation which his successor Innocent III carried on with great energy. . . . In Lom-

---

[189] Undescribable exultation filled the walls of Milan when the victors returned home. Finally there would be an end for all times of the hated German domination. . . . A single shout of victory surged through Lombardy: In a few weeks the last Germans would be expelled. Already the Milanese are arming themselves for the deadly blow. The ideal of liberty, *in indissoluble union, with the Holy Church has finally triumphed, the 'impious nation of the Germans'* falls in the dust."; my italics, highlighted in the original].

bardy and Tuscany anti-imperialist leagues were revived under papal influence. *But though they were anxious enough to throw off German domination, to cast out German officials, they were not prepared to submit to papal domination or papal officials in their place*[190]" (Poole, 1929, p. 52; my italics).

- In 1344-45 Petrarch wrote "one of the greatest of his canzoni, *Italia mia* (*Rime*, CXXVIII). Its noble summons to Italian unity and its bitter hostility to the Teuton[191]have spoken vibrantly to every Italian heart, through centuries of division and subjection, through the Risorgimento and the two World Wars. It is the great classic of Italian patriotism. It runs, in summary, thus :

My Italy, I grieve for the mortal wounds in your beautiful body. Christ, take pity on her, suffering such a cruel war for so slight a cause! Melt the hard hearts, and let me proclaim thy truth! What are these foreign swords doing here? Why is our green land soiled with barbarian blood? Lords of Italy, you compass your own destruction! *Nature built the Alps as a barrier against German rage, but short-sighted interest has brought this plague upon us! Heaven is angry; the predators*

---

[190] This is the point I mentioned in the introduction which renders the Italian situation so complicated and in part hides the Germanophobia; being free of the UP of the German emperors and their Italian allies, without falling under the UP of the popes and their allies.

[191] The notorious "Duke" Werner von Urslingen, the *condottiere* of a band known as *The Great Company*: "He had inscribed on his doublet, in silver letters, the words: 'Duke Werner, the enemy of pity, of mercy, and of God.' He was also the enemy of humanity. He developed a technique: the Great Company would invade an unsuspecting region, rob, burn, rape, and kill; then it would threaten the capital city with attack, unless it would pay an enormous ransom. Thus he obtained vast sums from Siena, Perugia, Florence, and Bologna. In 1343 the Great Company worked its ravaging way to the gates of Parma. Having by that time all the booty it could transport, it was persuaded by bribes to return to Germany" (Bishop, 1963, p. 233). The Duke of Urslingen retired "beyond the Alps laden with booty amid the execration of the towns and villages they left drenched with blood. In 1354 and the following years, the territory of Siena was wasted by pitiless and starving mercenaries; and the kingdom of Naples was put to fire and sword by Conrad of Wolfort (Corrado Lupo, 'Wolf'), by Conrad of Landau (the Count of Lando) [these two Germans, at least from their names], and by Fra Moriale (Montréal) from Narbonne" (Caggese, 1932, p. 51).

are let loose among the flocks![192] Italy's divisions are laying
waste the world's fairest land; and we are paying foreigners to
shed our own blood! Don't you realize German duplicity?
Noble Latin stock, cast off these oppressions and the superstition of German invincibility! (quoted by Bishop, 1963, p. 233;
my italics)

4. But Wasn't the Spanish Reconquista also a Religious War, While the Italian Riconquista was Only a National War?

As anticipated in the introduction, the answer to the title question
is "no", because the *Riconquista* was also a war of religious liberation
fought by the Church, the popes in particular, against the
Caesaropapism of the German emperors.

On several occasions, Emperor Charlemagne (see chapter 11 of
volume 2) instructed and commanded his people on strictly religious
matters, and demanded that the popes stick with turning the prayer
wheels, leaving the rest to him. Then, Emperor Frederick Barbarossa
(see chapter 23 of volume 1) managed to have Charlemagne canonized
in 1165 by "his pope" Paschal III. At this point the logic was perfect
for the caesaropapism of Barbarossa, given that his ancestor, Saint
Charlemagne had practiced it abundantly. The canonization of
Charlemagne was a stroke of imperial genius. A German imperial
victory over the papacy would have step-wise evolved in a repeat of
what Norman Cantor described: "Over the first two centuries A.D.,
however the ruling family transformed the Roman state into an imperial, oriental-state monarchy. By the third century, the emperor had
come to resemble the ancient pharaohs (1993, p. 7).

---

[192] The section in italics corresponds to the following original:

Ben provvide natura al nostro stato,

quando de l'Alpi schermo

pose fra noi e la tedesca rabbia:

ma 'l desir cieco e 'incontr'al suo ben fermo

s'è poi tanto ingegnato ,

ch'al corpo sano ha procurato scabbia.

Or dentro ad una gabbia

fiere selvagge e mansuete gregge

s'annidan sì, che sempre il miglior geme (v. 33-40).

322 ✦ *The GAM / DP Theory of Personality and Creativity*

5. Ideological Guelphs, Ideological Ghibellines

During the struggles between Emperor Frederick II and the papacy, the *parte Guelfa* in Florence came to mean the papal party, the *parte Ghibellina* the imperial.[193] Generally in use in Tuscany by the middle of the 13th century, the names spread from there to the rest of Italy.

In Dante's *Inferno,* the VIth circle is devoted to the punishment of the heretics, whom he describes in Cantos IX and X. There he is addressed by Farinata degli Uberti for many years the Ghibelline leader of Florence. In 1283, posthumously, the Inquisition declared Farinata heretic *"perché il fine degli eretici era in sostanza una lotta contro la Chiesa romana e la lotta dei ghibellini era contro l'ingerenza politica della Chiesa*[194]*"* (Bosco & Reggio, 1979, p. 153). Further on, Dante encounters another heretic in a burning tomb: the Ghibelline par excellence, the Emperor Frederick II, the grandson of Barbarossa. *"La Chiesa e tutti i guelfi lo accusarono di eresia per ragioni politiche, ma certe sue manifestazioni esteriori contribuirono a rafforzare tale fama*[195]*"* (ib., p. 161).

Readers of the *Divine Comedy*, depending on their political allegiance were pleased, or greatly displeased with what they read, specifically for what the Church did, mainly for political reasons. The readers of Dante had to make up their minds, agree or disagree, and not on petty matters. If the reader disagreed, then he, himself, would

---

[193] "At one moment the historic antagonism of Empire and Church seems to be the sufficient explanation of the conflicting terms. [The student of the Italian Middle Ages] sees *the militant Papacy allying itself with every Italian movement that seems to oppose the age-long struggle of the kings in Germany to treat the Peninsula as an appanage of Teutonic power* and to justify themselves by a continuous appeal to their 'imperial' rights. From the time of Frederic Barbarossa down, whenever this great universal issue is uppermost the names Guelph and Ghibelline are used to designate the conflicting parties" (Emerton, 1964, p. 256).

[194] "because the goal of the heretics was in essence a fight against the Roman Church, and the fight of the Ghibellines was against the political interference of the Church." A Catholic writer (or one who is more on the side of the popes than Bosco and Reggio), would have given a more theological and less partisan explanation of what the Church did and Dante "found" in Hell. The same applies to the next quote. On the other hand few commentators are better qualified, in general, than Umberto Bosco and Giovanni Reggio, to guide the reader through the extremely rich text by Dante.

[195] "The Church and all the Guelphs accused him of heresy for political reasons, but certainly some of his external manifestations contributed to reinforce that fame."

be moving on an heretical path. If the reader agreed, he might be in a difficult position later when the popes changed local allegiances.

The important thing for me is to show that the *Riconquista* was not only an economic, political and military endeavor but also a religious one with profound influence on the birth of the *visitor ethnopsychology*.

Not long after, in 1324-1328, similar debates involved King Louis IV (emperor from 1328) of the House of Wittelsbach. First Pope John XXII took

advantage of the contest for the crown of Germany to appoint Robert of Naples imperial vicar in Italy *vacante imperio* (in the absence of a Holy Roman emperor) *and to threaten the Italian Ghibellines with heresy proceedings.* When Louis' own imperial vicar forced the Pope and Robert to raise the siege of Milan, *the heresy proceedings were extended to Louis himself, who was excommunicated in March 1324. This interdiction, never lifted, exposed Louis' adherents to a conflict of conscience while providing his enemies with a convenient excuse for dis-obedience.* In the eyes of the Curia and of his other enemies, he was thenceforth merely *Ludovicus Bavarus, Louis the Ba-varian,* by which name he lives on in history. . . .

When Duke Leopold died in February 1326, Louis boldly opposed the Pope in Italy itself. Supported by the Ghibellines, he accepted the iron crown of Lombardy in Milan (May 31, 1327) and the imperial crown in Rome (January 11, 1328), offered by the representatives of the Roman populace. This unusual move could be considered an emergency measure be-cause the Pope had refused to crown the designated emperor, declaring him a heretic on purely political grounds. *Louis let himself be persuaded to depose the Pope formally by a decree of April 18, 1328, and to countenance the appointment of an antipope* whose incompetence furnished John XXII with an easy triumph. Moreover, Louis' forces were insufficient to sub-jugate Robert of Naples or to institute a stable order in Italy, for which he lacked the necessary prerequisite of a firm hold on Germany. Turning to the north again, he celebrated Christ-mas of 1329 in Trent, whence he had departed for Italy in February 1327. (Lieberich, 1978, p. 117, my italics)

The making of the *visitor personality* from the ideological divide under study, can be seen at work in *De Guelphis*, a treatise, of circa 1340, on the Guelphs and Ghibellines by Bartolo da Sassoferrato the most celebrated jurist of the fourteenth and fifteenth centuries. In *De Guelphis*, Bartolo first discussed the original sense, then the contemporary sense of the two terms:

1. If the words Guelph and Ghibelline are taken in their original sense, no person can be a Guelph in one place and a Ghibelline in another. The reason is this: Those [now] repudiated loyalties, whether to Church or to Empire, are universal and uniform in their application to the whole world, and therefore, to say that a person could hold one allegiance in one place and another in another place would be a contradiction of terms. (1340/1964, p. 276)

2. If the words are used in the modern sense a man may be a Guelph in one place and a Ghibelline in another, because party attachments of this sort may refer to a variety of issues. *Suppose that in one place there is a tyrant, who, together with his following, is called a Guelph.* A good citizen will be opposed to this man as a tyrant, and in that place this citizen is a "Ghibelline", but, *in another city not dependent upon the former, where there is a Ghibelline tyrant,* certainly that same good citizen will be opposed to that tyrant and there he will be a "Guelph,". (ib., p. 276-77; my italics)

Thus, a set of *DP visitor thoughts* (who was right, the Pope or the Emperor, or none, and why?) arose in the mind of every intelligent and educated person as soon as he paid attention to the original meaning of those words Guelph and Ghibelline.[196]

---

[196] In this line of thought I am not alone. John Larner in *Italy in the Age of Dante and Petrarch 1216-1380*, for instance, wrote that "for some men the words [Guelph and Ghibelline] may have had real significance. The spiritual authority of the Church could easily promote political loyalty. . . . Adherence to 'the Church' party could carry with it a belief that papal authority was a force for the suppression of heresy, for a just settlement of ecclesiastical 'rights', for the propagation of true religion in the world. The popes, at least, had enough propagandists in the clerical order, whether theologians or popular preachers, who could place such beliefs in persuasive terms before laymen. So too did the imperialists have their loyalty, a belief, older than that of the papalists, in the need for some final secular tribunal, presided over by one who, like the pope, was marked out by Heaven for its purpose, and who was in a broad sense a descendant and continuator of the rule of Caesar and Charlemagne, one who, within the secular world, should be free from any divisive ecclesiastical control" (1980, p. 32).

Very *visitor* also, is Bartolo's subsequent discussion of the change of denomination in order to oppose a local tyrant: the "good citizen" is expected to evaluate first and then change position if needed. And certainly, he is expected to oppose a tyrant!

I hope to have clarified what I said at the beginning of chapter 20 of volume 1, that "something special had happened in Italy and Spain which prepared the way for centuries of wonderful literary creativity: first visitor creativity, then swan song creativity. That something special at the beginning-which Spain and Italy had in common, and which other European nations did not have—was a long *Reconquista*, by the Spaniards against the Moors, and by the Italian against the Germans. There is indeed, in each country, a most memorable battle of liberation: Covadonga of 718 against the Moors, and Legnano of 1176 against the Germans."

Pace Ortega y Gasset, even if the *Reconquista* lasted 800 years, and the *Riconquista* 400 years, they were both highly influential, probably more so than if they had lasted only 10 years. Here, definitely, the importance of the end result, both in Spain and Italy, was in function of the many years needed to accomplish it.

14

UP Corrupts the *Supremo,* Who Then Corrupts Others

This chapter is divided into the following sections:

1. Introduction
2. Alexander the Great's Demand for *Proskynesis*
3. Other Methods, Beside Proskynesis and Crucifixion
   The Medici in Florence
   The Tokugawa Shoguns in Japan
   Louis XIV, XV and XVI in France
   Did the Tokugawa Shoguns Copy Louis XIV?
4. The Making of an Informer

1. Introduction

> Over the first two centuries A.D., the ruling family transformed the Roman state into an imperial, oriental-style monarchy. By the third century, the emperor had come to resemble the ancient pharaoh. (Cantor, 1993, p. 7)

In the study of *insulars* (chapter 11 of volume 1), I dealt with the corruption induced by the unity of power. Here, my discussion is more specific, aimed first at how the *supremo* is corrupted by power, then on how he, in part voluntarily—to expand and solidify his control over society—and in part involuntarily, corrupts those under him: generals, aristocrats, ministers, intellectuals; and finally on how the corruption percolates to the lower strata of society. *The Law of Power of Lord Acton*: "Power tends to corrupt and absolute power corrupts absolutely" does not apply only to the power holder but also to those subordinate to him.

2. Alexander the Great's Demand for *Proskynesis*

Baron Benoist-Méchin made a fascinating (yet perplexing) comparison in his study of Alexander the Great:

Thanks to his encounter with Asia, Alexander's conception of the royal function had deepened. In Greece, where the commanding oligarchies were composed of touchy republicans, every monarch was automatically considered either a tyrant or an usurper. But not in the Orient, where the monarchy was an institution of divine right which placed the sovereign well above the other mortals. He ruled from the summit of a pyramid whose height was proportioned to the extent of his territories. And as the Persian monarchs had never renounced the claim to rule the whole of the earth—as shown by their title of King of Kings—their throne was the "highest" in the world. The horizontal character of the Hellenic republics prevented them from understanding the mighty verticality of the Asiatic monarchies. (1964, pp. 185-86)

Benoist-Méchin must be complimented for drawing such a vivid contrast between the horizontal character of the Hellenic republics and the vertical-pyramidal character of the Asiatic monarchies. He could have added that the crushing weight on the lower strata of the population—the majority— increases with the height of the pyramid, and so does the distance and the alienation of the *supremo* from the people.

However, on an important point I disagree with Benoist-Méchin. I do not believe that the horizontal character of the Hellenic republics prevented them from understanding the mighty verticality of the Asiatic monarchies; on the contrary they understood it very well, and because of this they did not want to have any part of it: they did not want anything which would enslave them to a "[Persian] *Great King who was unaccountable for his actions and could kill or mutilate by whim"* (Vermeule, 1992, p. 41; my italics).

Also, I would never have said that Alexander's vision of the royalty had become more profound thanks to his knowledge of Asia, but that it was in the process of becoming corrupt and despotic. Indeed, in the end, "few men—and fewer women—lamented Alexander's passing [in 323 B.C.]. In Greece and Asia alike he was regarded as a tyrannous aggressor. For 20,000 miles he carried his trail of rapine slaughter, and subjugation; he imposed his will, but little else. When he moved on, rebellion flared up behind him; and when he died, the empire he had carved out at once split apart into anarchic chaos" (Green, 1970, p. 260). His generals were among those who did not regret his death, feeling he had evolved in a tyrant dominating and corrupting them:

> [In 327 B.C.] before the army moved in the direction of India, there were two more incidents that widened the gap between Alexander's conduct and traditional Macedonian attitudes. First, Alexander attempted to introduce the Persian court ceremonial involving *proskynesis*, or obeisance. Just what this entailed is disputed; perhaps it amounted to different things in different context, ranging from an exchange of kisses to total prostration before the ruler in the way a Muslim says his prayers. What is not in doubt is that for Greeks this meant adoration of a living human being, something they considered impious as well as ridiculous. It was the court historian Callisthenes who voiced the feeling of the Greeks. The *proskynesis* experiment was not repeated: Alexander did not in the end insist on it. It is difficult, however, not to connect Callisthenes' role in this affair with his downfall not long after. (Hornblower, 1993, p. 260)

What Alexander did not insist upon was demanded by late Roman emperors and then by the Byzantine emperors: Emperor Diocletian (r. 284-305) "insisted upon the grovelling *adoratio*, the Persian *proskynesis*" (Grant, 2000 p. 81); in Byzantium an ambassador charged to present a message to the emperor first "knelt and made a three fold *proskynesis*. . . . The ceremonies governing the reception of a foreign ambassador originated in Iranian-Hellenistic soil. This is true not only of the *proskynesis* which had to be made to the Emperor but also of the curtains before the imperial throne and the raising of the throne with the baldachino over it. All this goes back to the Achaemenid period. The great relief of the treasury of Xerxes in Persepolis shows an audience given by the Persian Great King Darius and here the *proskynesis* is being made to him as he sits on his throne over which there is a baldachino. Like the Persian Great King, the Greek Emperor was separated from his counsellors by curtains" (Haussig, 1971, pp. 190-91).

The next phase in the corruption transformed Alexander into just what the Greeks were fearing from the Orient: into a *Great King unaccountable for his actions who could kill or mutilate by whim*: In autumn 324 B.C. Hephaestion died in Ecbatana: "The violence and extravagance of the King's grief went beyond all normal bounds. For a day and a night he lay on the body, weeping: no one could comfort him. General mourning was ordered throughout the East. Alexander cut his hair in token of mourning, as Achilles did for Patroclus, and even had the manes and tails of his horses docked. Haephestion's physician was crucified, and the temple of Asclepius in Ecbatana razed to ground" (Green, 1970, pp. 253-54).

3. Other Methods Beside Proskynesis and Crucifixion

The Medici in Florence

Under the title "Lodovico Alamanni: The making of the courtier," Anthony Molho reported a letter by Alamanni, of November 25, 1516, to Lorenzo de Medici, Duke of Urbino, grandson of Lorenzo the Magnificent, which included the following piece of advice:

If, however, the prince so wishes, the young could be easily weaned from that habit [of not removing their hoods when greeting others] *and accustomed to courtesan manners.* In order to do this, the prince should designate all those young men who in our city-either because of their qualities, or those of their father and families-should be kept in high esteem. He should then invite them, one at a time, and tell them that he would be pleased if they were to come and stay with him, and that he would give to all privileges and prerogatives convenient to him. No one would refuse such an invitation, *and as soon as they came he should change their civilian clothes for a courtesan habit . . .* As a result, their full ambition will be channeled toward earning the favour of His Excellency. *They will be most happy for being chosen, paid and cared for, they will feel that they are appreciated, and every man is content where he finds profit and honour.* (Alamanni, 1516/1969, p. 218-219; my italics)

The Tokugawa Shoguns in Japan

As the *sankin kôtai* system[197] took hold, daimyo heirs were born and brought up with their mothers in Edo. In some cases they might not visit the domain until they were young men and had inherited the title of daimyo. They thus grew up sharing the common experience and cultural values of the daimyo residences and the shogunal court in Edo. The domain, which in any case could be rescinded by the Tokugawa, ceased to be home for them and became instead a place of periodic administrative responsibility. Daimyo quickly began to vie culturally in the decoration of their Edo *yashiki*, in bringing local products and craftsmen to Edo, and in employing artists and craftsmen from Kyoto or Edo in their home castles. *The frugality and toughness that had been the mark of warrior leaders in the sixteenth century soon began to give way to refinement and ostentation.* (Collcutt, 1988, p. 35; my italics)

Another century or two in this direction, and Japan would have become fully oriental: there would have been no daimyo capable of defending the emperor, there would have been total UP as in China.

Louis XIV, XV and XVI in France

The nobility surrendered not only its personal life but its political power. In exchange it received the favors of a ubiquitous master who knew the secrets of every family. . . . Hence all was grace for these aristocrats forced to live in foul-smelling, cramped quarters in the palace mezzanine and attics. Family and friends were sacrificed for the privilege of having to watch whatever one said. A century later Manon Phlipon [i.e., Mme Roland de La Platrière] was outraged to see the Arch-

---

[197] That of leaving daimyo family members as hostages in Edo, together with the compulsory alternate-year residence of each daimyo in Edo.

bishop of Paris living close to Versailles so he could "slink off every morning to the *levers* of those Majesties." Attendance being obligatory, the crowds were so large that it was almost impossible to see. (Castan, 1989, p. 420)

> *For, essentially, the palace [of Versailles] is a golden trap in which to catch the princes and the great aristocrats.* Already in 1662, the Court's increasing splendor was doing just that; but, clearly, occasional festivities were not enough. The King's goal was to attract the once dangerous grandees, not for a few weeks, or even months every year, but for good. That, in itself, would sever them from their power bases in the provinces and keep them where they could be watched: the posts were controlled by the government and all interesting mail opened, read, and reported on. Further, the expenses inherent in the ever glamorous life of the Court were likely to put the nobles even deeper in the King's dependence: once their income proved insufficient, they would have to rely on pensions and salaries as a supplement; and that implied being where the King saw and remembered them. . . . *By multiplying the positions around himself, the Queen and the Royal Family, Louis XIV could catch many more great nobles; by exciting constant jealousy between the different officeholders and the different ranks of the aristocracy, he could also ensure that the energies which had once provoked civil wars would be spent in quarreling about the right to a stool or the order of entrance into the royal bedroom.* (Bernier, 1987, p. 164)

The Duke of Saint-Simon wrote in his *Memoirs* of 1740-50:

> [Louis XIV] availed himself of the frequent festivities at Versailles, and his excursions to other places, as a means of making the courtiers assiduous in their attendance and anxious to please him; for he nominated beforehand those who were to take part in them, and could thus gratify some and inflict a snub on others. He was conscious that the substantial favors he had to bestow were not nearly sufficient to produce a continual effect; he had therefore to invent imaginary ones, and no one was so clever in devising petty distinctions and preferences which aroused jealousy and emulation. . . . Not

only did he expect all persons of distinction to be in continual attendance at Court, but he was quick to notice the absence of those of inferior degree; at his *lever*, his *coucher*, his meals, in the gardens of Versailles (the only place where the courtiers in general were allowed to follow him), he used to cast his eyes to right and left; nothing escaped him, he saw everybody. If any one habitually living at Court absented himself he insisted on knowing the reason; those who came there only for flying visits had also to give a satisfactory explanation; any one who seldom or never appeared there was certain to incur his displeasure. If asked to bestow a favour on such persons he would reply haughtily: "I do not know him"; of such as rarely presented themselves he would say, "He is a man I never see"; and from these judgements there was no appeal. (1918, *5*, pp. 272-73)

What Louis XIV demanded was not the *proskynesis* imposed by the Pharaoh, Persian King of Kings, Byzantine emperor, and attempted by Alexander the Great, but, by its frequency, it may have been more demeaning. *Proskynesis* of important officers was demanded at important ceremonies, a few times a year, while Louis XIV often demanded a daily attendance, a daily homage to himself and humiliation of the attendants: "Etiquette became a means of governing. From that time, the nobility ceased to be an important factor in French politics, which in some respects weakened the nation. . . . [Louis XIV's] irremediable error was to have concentrated all the machinery of the state in his own person, thus making of the monarchy a burden beyond human strength" (Erlanger, 1978, p. 122-23).

Beside that irremediable error, there had been the inevitable absolute corruption from his quasi absolute power, as stressed by Erlanger in a comparison with Napoleon:

[The King was not] the incarnation of the *honnête homme*; he might have had some claim if he had been more open and humane, but he seems to have hardened as he grew older: M. d'Orléans, his brother, undertook to make representation to him about the misery of the people. He received the following reply, worthier of a tiger, if they could talk, than of a Christian king: "If four or five thousand of that *canaille* died, who are not of much use on this earth, would France be any the less

France? I pray you not to meddle in what does not concern you".[198] This is not far removed from Napoleon's—"What the hell do a million dead men mean to me?" (1965/1970, p. 274)

Alain Peyrefitte had equivalent comments:

As far as almost all foreign historians are concerned, Louis XIV's master plan was nothing more than the will to force other princes and nations to bend their knee to him. He devastated Flanders, Holland, the Palatinate, the Rhineland, the Aosta Valley; he bombarded Genoa and Brussels; he forced other states to acknowledge the precedence of France's ambassadors; he humiliated Pope Alexander VII; and he broke treaties, giving his word, only to retract it later. What do we see in the medals struck to the glory of Great Louis accoutered as a Roman emperor, in the equestrian statues, in the frescoes covering the ceilings at Versailles? Sovereigns bowed down before the Sun King. He made France respected only by making it hated. (1976/1981, p. 82)

Did the Tokugawa Shoguns Copy Louis XIV?

The implications [for the daimyos] of the elaborate, ceremonial hostage system were profound. In addition to their castles and administrative headquarters in their *han* [feudal fief], each daimyo had to build, maintain, and staff several residences (*yashiki*) in Edo. *Since the daimyo's function in Edo was to attend upon the shogun, or serve in the shogunal government, rigid standards of dress and protocol had to be met, and domains, however poor, had to keep up appearances or risk official displeasure.* The enormous costs of this system, with residences in the domain and in Edo and the expense of a large entourage traveling ceremoniously between the two—it took nearly two months for the Shimazu retinue to reach Edo—all fell on the domains, and most heavily on the peasantry whose job it was to produce the tax rice that supported the

---

[198] *"Un Colonial au temps de Colbert. Mémoires de Robert Challes, écrivain du Roi,* Paris, 1931" (ib. p. 387

whole *baku-han* power structure. In order to meet the huge ceremonial expenses of *sankin kotai*, domain administrations heavily taxed their peasants and even pared down the stipends of their samurai. In many cases they went heavily into debt with Osaka merchants, *pledging future crops against loans to pay* for the expenses of *sankin kotai*. Intentionally, or by design, the Tokugawa had developed an elaborate hostage system that also added dignity to shogunal rule, drained many domains of resources that might otherwise have been turned against the Tokugawa, and—by bringing daimyo households into close proximity with one another in Edo—fostered social competition among daimyo that kept their attention away from thoughts of war. (Collcutt, 1988, p. 34; my italics to stress the similarities with the methods of Louis XIV).

No, the Tokugawa shoguns did not copy Louis XIV, nor did they have any need to do so. Their behavior, like that of Louis XIV, was a natural manifestation of the universal nature of the unity of power.[199] The same is true for their being corrupted by their quasi-absolute power and their corrupting those under them.

4. The Making of an Informer

The eminent Italian novelist Ignazio Silone, described in *Bread and Wine* (1937/1960)how the police transformed Luigi Murica, a poor university student into an informer. Murica's "account of his duplicity in betraying his comrades after physical threats and blackmail by Fascists is a central episode in the novel, and one of the most effective chapters" (Weaver, 2002, p. 36):

> "One morning as I left the house I was arrested by two policemen, taken to the central police station and shut in a room full of other policemen. After some formalities I was slapped and spat upon for an hour. I probably would have preferred to

---

[199] Leaving aside for a moment the distant emperor in Kyoto, and the local power of the daimyo, as Louis XIV could often forget the pope in Rome and the local power of his aristocrats.

be violently beaten rather than slapped and spat on like that. When the door opened and the functionary who was to question me appeared, my face and chest were literally flowing with spit. The functionary reprimanded his subordinates, or at least pretended to, had me washed and dried and taken into his office. He assured me that he was looking benevolently and understandingly at my case. He knew that I lived in a small room, he knew the place where I took coffee and milk at noon and where I had my soup in the evening. He had minute details about my family and on the troubles which made it doubtful that I could continue my studies. On the impulse which had pushed me to the revolutionary groups[200] he could only guess. '. . . . of and by itself that impulse can't be deemed entirely reprehensible, on the contrary . . . . Youth is dreamy and generous by nature. It would be too bad if that were not the case,' he said. 'But the police has the perhaps unpleasant but socially necessary role of closely controlling the generous and dreamy instincts of youth. . . .'" "In other words," interrupted Don Paolo, "that functionary proposed that you work for the police. What did you answer?" "I accepted," he answered. . . . The young man continued in a tired voice. "I got a hundred lire for my room and in exchange I wrote a school composition on 'How a group functions, what is read and what is discussed there.' 'It's really quite good,' he told me. I was proud that he was satisfied with my work. I committed myself to remain in touch with him, for a hundred and fifty lire a month. In this way I could have soup at noon, too, and I could go to the movies every Saturday night." (Silone, 1962, pp. 285-86)

Very sad and tragic, Murica may be in part Silone himself. Recently (1996-2000) "researchers have begun to turn up documents

---

[200] Shortly before, Murica had told Don Paolo how he had joined that small Socialist/Communist cell: "My being a student attracted the sympathy of the others in the group, who were workers and artisans. I was happy too. The purely human pleasure I took in it prevented me from reflecting at first on the importance of what I was doing. In the group we read poorly printed newspapers and pamphlets preaching hate of tyranny and announcing as a certainty, as inevitable and not far off, the advent of the revolution which was to establish fraternity and justice among men" (ib., p. 285).

in police archives which strongly suggest that Silone, in the decade before he became a writer, acted as an informant for the Fascist police. To grasp how disturbing and unlikely a development this is, one has to appreciate the fact that Silone, who died in 1978, has long been regarded not only as an important novelist but also—like Orwell, Camus, and Malraux—as something of a secular saint, a man of rare intellectual and moral courage, who had opposed Fascism from the start and endured years of exile and persecution for his beliefs" (Stille[201], 2000, p. 44).

"In *L'informatore*, Dario Biocca and Mauro Canali [2000] offer an overwhelming body of archival evidence to suggest that, for over ten years between 1919 and 1930, Silone was a regular informant to a Roman police official called Guido Bellone. Writing under the pseudonym Silvestri, Silone gave Bellone written details of individuals, institutions and activities in whatever political circle he found himself in and wherever he traveled around Europe. Indeed, it was his mobility that allowed Biocca and Canali to pin Silvestri down, circumstantially at least, since the date, place and mission of every single report of this highly placed informant coincided with Silone's activities" (Gordon, 2000, p. 11).

> In one [report], for example, the informant told the police about a network of Communist railway workers who helped smuggle party propaganda into Italy; the network was promptly dismantled. From Berlin, he provided information about go-betweens who brought the Communists donations from abroad, giving names, descriptions, and bank information. But the most chilling evidence comes from the period after Silone was made head of the Party's clandestine organization in Italy, in 1927. Bellone's informant, identified here as "T", provided a detailed breakdown of the underground organizations in Italy's main cities, and these groups were systematically rounded up by the police. . . . What remains mysterious is Silone's motive for informing in the first place. He may, however, have left

---

[201] Alexander Stille is the author of the introduction to the 2000 Steerforth Press's re-issue of Silone's Abruzzo trilogy (*Fontamara, Bread and Wine,* and *The Seed Beneath the Snow)*, translated by Erich Mosbacher and revised by Darina Silone, the widow of the novelist.

some clues in *Bread and Wine*. The book's hero is a sick and disillusioned Communist leader who returns to the Abruzzi and eludes the Fascist police by posing as a priest. The Protagonist is clearly an idealized portrait of the author, but Silone may also have represented himself in a second character, a young Communist who confesses to having acted as a police informant. After he is arrested and beaten by the police, the young man, Luigi Murica, is approached by a kindly policeman, who offers to help him in exchange for a little information. Initially, Murica provides only generic reports but then he is pressured by the police to give more detailed information. He compensates for his betrayal by working harder than ever for the cause, and this allows him, temporarily, to function on two levels at the same time. (Stille, 2000, p. 48)

Seen from a different angle, and one which I fully share:

It seems too easy for writers born after World War II, when Fascism was only a horrid memory, to dictate to the dead, to tell them how they should have behaved when the regime controlled every means of public expression. As for Silone, it seems unlikely that his activities will find a satisfactory explanation. "Behind every secret there is another secret," he once wrote. Silone took his enigmas with him in death, leaving his work to speak for him. Concluding his *New Yorker* article, Stille writes: "The recent revelations don't diminish the power of Silone's writing. If anything, his heroic image may have obscured the darkness and complexity of his books." When I read those words, I wasn't at first convinced. I was still in shock as if someone had revealed that, throughout his life, Thoreau had been involved with the slave trade. But as I began to think about writing something on the subject myself, I returned first to *Fontamara*, then to *Bread and Wine* and to *Luca's Street*. Stille was right. Here was the real Silone—a writer who could at the same time make clear moral judgments and be accepting of human weakness—and he spoke to me as he had in my youth. (Weaver, 2002, pp. 36-37)

Not only do I agree with William Weaver, but I feel the need to back his criticism of those who condemn Silone by forgetting the horrors perpetrated by the Fascists. Indeed, his criticism is similar to mine, reported earlier in this volume, of the Jesuit Father Mathy who, in his introduction to Endo's *The Golden Country*, had said that he could not understand how a man of Ferreira's high caliber could apostatize after only five hours in the pit, while other priests had endured the pit until death, which came after two, four, or six days. What shocked me then, as now in Silone's case, is the emphasis on those who were not heroic, or not heroic as some others, while all the emphasis should be placed on the evil of the unity of power and its henchmen which tortured Ferreira, and which arrested, beat, spit upon and then corrupted Luigi Murica (Silone in 1919 was just 19 years old).

Yes, the truth has to be said of both Ferreira and Silone, but only as a springboard for an extensive discussion of the evil of the unity of power, be it that of the shogun, or of the Roman police before and during the Mussolini era (which began in 1922).

On the other hand, while one must discuss the evil perpetrated by the Roman police, and by the Fascists, the real source of that evil is the *supremo* and derived *insular world*, or to be precise, it is the long interacting chain of *supremo/insular mentality* in which it is nearly impossible to decide which came first.

What is important, at any given time—as in the present discussion of Silone—is to study both the particular and how it fits with the general. The particular, here, is the corruption of young Luigi Murica by the "friendly" police officer, even if this is not exactly what happened to Silone himself (something which will probably never be known). Ideally, the next phase of the study would be a biographical study of Guido Bellone, the real police officer to whom Silone sent his reports. Bellone too was corrupted by the *insular world* and its *supremo(s)*.[202]

It is not only that power tends to corrupt, and absolute power corrupts absolutely the power holder, but that the corruption spreads down, like a cancer, to those who have no power. Probably Bellone

---

[202] "*Tutto induce a pensare che il rapporto con Bellone sia stato fondamentale nella complessa vicenda della quale questo libro* [Biocca & Canali, 2000) *si occupa. Silone, infatti, aveva fiducia solo in Bellone e teneva contatti soltanto con lui* [Everything makes one think that the relation with Bellone was fundamental to the complex story which is the subject of this book. Silone, indeed, trusted only Bellone, and had contacts only with him]" (Melograni, 2000, p. 9).

was already corrupted before he had any power, as it happened to Luigi Murica. This general condition explains why, in each of my volumes, I preach the division of power down to each individual, why I preach the *visitor mentality* and derived generous volunteerism by every individual.

15

Much Vanity Under UP

This chapter is divided into the following sections:

1. The *Buddenbrooks Phenomenon*
2. The Vanity of the *Bourgeois Gentilhomme*
3. The UP Recipe for the Sickness of Vanity: "Maintain Proper Station."
4. From Molière's *M. Jourdain* to Flaubert's *Mme. Bovary*
5. Conclusion

1. The *Buddenbrooks Phenomenon*

Not only Louis XIV, and not only Napoleon[203], but practically every *supremo*, every hierarchical structure, promotes and makes use,

---

[203] " A carefully graded system of military awards-ranging from the coverted Cross of the *Légion d'Honneur*(*), swords of honor, monetary grants and nomination to a vacancy in the Imperial Guard for the rank and file, to the award of duchies, princedoms and even thrones to the elect among the leaders—was one aspect of this policy.... Each of the eighteen marshals was evenually given the title of duke and a large grant of lands and hard cash to enable them to keep up the standards of their new stations in life. The first dukedoms were awarded in 1806, but most of these honors dated from 1808.... In the following year after the coronation, princedoms were awarded to the immediate family, and in due course a crop of dukes, counts, barons and knights made their appearance to support the dignity of the Imperial (ex-Consular) Court. At first all the titles bore foreign names, but in 1808 a purely French nobility was created. By 1814 there were 31 dukes, 450 counts, 1500 barons and as many more knights. (Chandler, 1966, pp. 155, 311-12)

(*) "{Those so Honored] received a blue enamel five-pointed star decorated with oak and laurel, which he wore hanging from the buttonhole attached to a red moiré ribbon. The recipient also received a small money award: 250 francs a year, rising to 5,000 francs for grand officers" (Cronin, 1972, p. 206).

pro domo (for his benefit), of the vanity of the people, so much so that one may think that vanity is a specific feature of the people living under the unity of power. Some of this vanity is a feature of what has been called the *Buddenbrooks phenomenon*. As seen by Francis Fukuyama:

> The third phase [in the evolution of a family business] occurs when control passes to the founding entrepreneur's grandchildren. Those businesses that have survived this long tend to disintegrate thereafter. Since the sons often have unequal numbers of children, the grandchildren's shares vary in size. In the case of very successful families, the grandchildren have grown up in very well-to-do surroundings. Unlike the founding entrepreneur, they more readily take their prosperity for granted and are typically less motivated to make the sacrifices needed to keep the business competitive, or else they have developed interests in other types of activities. The gradual decline in entrepreneurial talent from the first generation to the third is not, of course, something that occurs only in Chinese culture. It characterizes family businesses in all societies and has been labeled the *"Buddenbrooks phenomenon"*. There is, indeed, a traditional Irish saying reflecting the rise and fall of family fortunes: "Shirtsleeves to shirtsleeves in three generations". (Fukuyama, 1995, p. 78)

Part of that decline is due to vanity: wanting to be seen to be made of superior stuff, wanting to be considered an aristocrat. This was the case with Thomas Buddenbrook, for whom things began to change when he was elected to the coveted rank of Senator of his city, a position that in his eyes demanded that he live in a fine mansion, which was done the following year with the construction of a building in the Fisher Lane. Was it vanity, and of a dangerous kind? Yes: "The new light and airy house wastes the family's capital on mere appearance" (Apter, 1979, p. 18).

A few years later—and we now come to a key aspect of the *Buddenbrooks phenomenon*—the Senator realized that his past behavior as businessman had been vulgar, and that in the future his dealings, especially with the aristocrats, would have to be different, more refined, as if he were one of them. The change surfaced when his sister came to him proposing a remunerative loan to an aristocrat in financial difficulties, Herr von Maiboom. At that moment, Thomas realized that he had neither the intention, nor the capability anymore, of being tough and rude in any dealings with von Maiboom, as he had been years before, in a similar occasion, with Count Strelitz.

Having related to his sister how he had humiliated Count Strelitz in the course of the negotiations, he added: "I have told you this in order to ask you if you think I should have the right, or the courage, or the inner self-confidence to behave in the same way with Herr von Maiboom?" (1901/1957, pp. 355-56). At first, the Senator had the good sense to realize that he had changed, and that the higher vision he now had of himself prevented him from making money in the old way. However, after some prodding by his sister and by his newly aristocratic vision of himself, he decided to move on, but in a refined way: "[He] wrote a letter to Herr von Maiboom of Pöppenrade—a letter which, as he read it through, his head feeling feverish and heavy, *he thought was the best and most tactful he had ever written.* That was the night of 27 May. The next day he indicated to his sister, treating the affair in a light, semi-humorous way, that he had thought it all over and decided that *he could not just refuse Herr von Maiboom out of hand and leave him at the mercy of the nearest swindler.* On the thirtieth of May he went to Rostock, whence he drove in a hired wagon to the country" (ib., p. 368; my italics) and met Herr von Maiboom. We are not told the details, only that, later, we hear that the Senator lost a lot of money on this deal, most probably because in his negotiations he played the generous aristocrat with the best and most tactful words, victim of the *Buddenbrooks phenomenon.* Victim of his vanity? Yes. Only of vanity? No. Victim of the unity of power of his times? Definitely yes.

Toward the end of his life, Senator Buddenbrook "realizes that his whole life has been meaningless, his entire program of industry artificial and forced, and one day, felled by a mortal stroke, he collapses in the street, where his carefully groomed head lies in a mud puddle" (Brennan, 1942/1963, p. 7). In the words of Victor Lange, "In *Buddenbrooks* Mann tells the story of a declining family whose effectiveness and public esteem are fatally undermined by the corroding impact of modern philosophical pessimism upon successive generations, and their growing fascination with music and art" (Lange, 1975, p. 1). However, if we leave aside the story of the impact of modern philosophical pessimism (not part of the *Buddenbrooks phenomenon*), we are left with a very aristocratic (especially in the past) fascination with music and art, and a corresponding attitude to the making of money in which *Pecunia olet* (money stinks).

We all want to be treated with respect. Yet, especially in the past, that respect was severely limited. Even as late as the times of Senator

Buddenbrook, or of the writing of *Buddenbrooks,* not to be an aristocrat in Europe was a great handicap: "[Proust] could never quite
forgive himself for failing to be born into the nobility; during his late
teens and early twenties [ca. 1885-1895] the best compensation was to
be invited to exclusive salons" (Hayman, 1990, p. 154).

The author of *A 'la recherche du temps perdu* was not the only
one who suffered for not having been born into the nobility; before
him in that same century, all the great artists felt the same way when
they were treated like servants by the aristocracy:

> Wagner's genius as a composer did not prevent his being
> regarded in Dresden, by his King and his Director, as merely a
> servant. . . .[And yet a] new type of artist was springing up -
> men of natural refinement and culture like Chopin and Liszt,
> who felt themselves to be the equals of the aristocrats who pa-
> tronized them, and were galled by the slighting forms this pa-
> tronage sometimes took. Their talents admitted them into the
> richest society; but there they were made to realize that how-
> ever much they might be admired as artists, there could be no
> question of their being accepted as social equals. . . . High soci-
> ety everywhere looked down patronisingly on the man who re-
> ceived his income from trade [as Senator Buddenbrooks], even
> if the trade were that of music. . . .So difficult was it in those
> days for a *grand dame* to admit a mere musician to her com-
> pany on terms of anything like social equality, even when the
> musician was a man of Liszt's fame, culture, and natural breed-
> ing and distinction of manner! Liszt was fully conscious of all
> these hesitations and condescension; *he smarted under them,*
> *and his life-long predilection for the society and the love of*
> *aristocrats was no doubt due in part to the gratified sense they*
> *gave him of a victory won,* of having forced the world to accept
> an exceptional artist at a proper valuation. Admitted as a raw
> boy into the houses of the richest of the Parisian aristocracy, in
> an epoch when not only titles but costume and formal manners
> and etiquette counted far more than to-day, he must have suf-
> fered many a wound to his pride. . . . Liszt's rather overdone
> ceremoniousness in the later years, his tendency to over-insist
> on the formulae of polite address, especially with aristocrats,
> are no doubt to be explained by the fact that these things were
> an acquired, and painfully acquired, language with him, not a
> natural one, and that in his desire to speak the language with

impeccable correctness he was apt at times to become a trifle overpunctilious. (Newman, 1937/1976, *1*, pp. 163-70)

So if Thomas Buddenbrook—like Wagner, Liszt and Chopin, and before them Mozart as discussed in chapter 11 of volume 1—wanted to be something more, in his case more than a grain merchant and an occasional money lender, he had to find a way to upgrade himself, and, having done so, demand to be seen and treated accordingly. He had tried:

> When the Senate sat to appoint its committees, one of the main departments, the administration of the taxes, fell to his lot. But tolls, railways, and other administrative business claimed his time as well; and he presided at hundreds of committees that called into play all the capacities he possessed: he had to summon every ounce of his flexibility, his foresight, his power to charm, in order not to wound the sensibilities of his elders, to defer constantly to them, and yet to keep the reins in his own hands. (1901/1957, pp. 322-23)

However, these tasks were probably worse—in the line of *pecunia olet*—than those he was performing for his own company: the administration of the taxes, i.e. extracting money from the others, most of them poor, or ensuring that money was spent according to the Senate's orders. These tasks were, definitely, not aristocratic.

Buddenbrooks was written in 1901, during the reign of Emperor Wilhelm II, when democracy in Germany still had a bad name as Thomas Mann himself would stress in his *Reflections of a Nonpolitical Man* written in 1915-1917 and published in 1918: "For I am nonpolitical, national, but nonpolitically disposed, like the German of the burgherly culture and the one of romanticism, which knew no other political demand than the highly national one *for emperor and empire*, and which was *so basically undemocratic* that its spiritual influence alone caused the politicians, the members of the German student fraternities, and the revolutionaries of the Paulskirche, to want a hereditary empire, and made them, as Vogt wrote to Herwegh, '*into complete aristocrats*'" (1983, p. 81, my italics). Here was the officially approved way to become a complete aristocrat: Know no political demand other than the wishes of the emperor and empire, and the wars that the emperor commands.

In a letter which Mann wrote on November 25, 1916 to Paul Amann, he said it clearly: "I hate democracy, and with it I hate poli-

tics, for that is the same thing" (quoted by Hayman, 1995, p. 294).[204]
Very *ritter* also, "writing to Samuel Fisher in mid April [of that same
year], Thomas deplored that the prospect that 'democratic progress
will be imposed on us from outside . . . . through defeat'" (ib., p. 293).

Senator Thomas Buddenbrooks tried to become an aristocrat in
the only way that was allowed him (besides being unpolitical), but
failed, less for his fault than for that of the UP.[205]

---

[204] Yes, Thomas Mann, indeed democracy and politics are the same, and so are their
contributions to science as reported by G. E. R. Lloyd, in his *Early Greek Science:
Thales to Aristotle*, in his discussion of the nature of the scientific revolution started by
the Milesian philosophers who flourished around 580 B.C. in Miletus, a harbor city
located at the eastern border of the Greek world, in Asia Minor (in territories now part of
Turkey):

"Their achievement was rather to have rejected supernatural explanations of
natural phenomena and to have instituted the practice of rational criticism and debate in
that context. To understand the background to this development we must refer not only
to economic factors, but also and more especially to the political conditions in Greece at
the time. It is here that the contrast between the Greek world and the great Near Eastern
civilizations is most marked. It is not, however, that Greece was more peaceful and
stable than Lydia, Babylonia and Egypt. On the contrary, the period was one of great
political upheaval throughout the Greek world, and like many other Greek cities Miletus
itself suffered from bitter party strife and was ruled intermittently by tyrants. *Yet whereas
in the Near Eastern super-powers a change of rule usually meant no more than a change
of dynasty, major developments took place in the political and social structure of the
Greek cities.* The seventh and sixth centuries saw the foundation and consolidation of the
institutions of the city state, the development of a new political awareness and indeed a
proliferation of constitutional forms, ranging from tyranny through oligarchy to
democracy. *The citizens of such states as Athens or Corinth or Miletus not only often
participated in the government of their country; they engaged in an active debate on the
whole question of the best type of government*" (1970, pp. 13-14; my italics).

As an interesting aside, "the word 'idiot' comes from the Greek idiotes, a private
person, as distinct from one interested in public affairs" (Abrams, 1962, p. 1801).

[205] There were, in truth, a few but very difficult alternatives, for instance becoming a
monk, or devoting one's life to the arts—both activities welcomed by the unity of power,
especially the second as discussed in chapter 21 of volume 1, "The central unity of
power may give freedom and favors to some talented people and thereby foster high
creativity." Here, part of the difficulty was the obligation to sing the glory of the great
man, as Molière did at the end of *Tartufe*, or serve indiscriminately as Leonardo da Vinci
did under the infamous Cesare Borgia. "Leonardo was with Cesare when the Duchy of
Urbino was taken by characteristic Borgian treachery. Cesare approached his friend, the
Duke of Urbino, and asked for the loan of some artillery for a campaign elsewhere. The
trusting Duke obliged—and immediately had to flee for his life when he found himself
menaced by his own weapons turned against him. If Leonardo was surprised or shocked
by this, he made no note of it. Instead he drew a ground plan of the fortress of Urbino
and of a dovecote whose beauty impressed him" (Wallace, 1967, p. 123).

And there was not only treachery, but also the utmost cruelty: In Rome, "a man
who had been going about the Borgo masked uttering scurrilous language against
[Cesare] was arrested on Cesare's orders and thrown into the Savelli prison, where his
right hand and part of his tongue were cut out and exposed, with the tongue hanging from
the little finger, for two days at the window of the prison" (Bradford, 1976, pp. 165-66).

2. The Vanity of the *Bourgeois Gentilhomme*

> "*Vanity* is the quality or fact of being vain," and to be *vain* means "having or showing an excessive high regard for one's self, looks, possessions, ability, etc.; being conceited" (*Webster's New World Dictionary*, 1988).

At the beginning of the autumn of 1670 the King's Comedians received another summons to Chambord, where the King [Louis XIV] was on a hunting holiday. Once again his Majesty required new entertainment, having this time stipulated beforehand to Molière that it should include 'some sort of Turkish buffoonery'. The reason for this order, which blossomed into superb farcical comedy, is itself entertaining. Some months previously an envoy of the Grand Turk, Mohammed IV, had arrived in Paris to discuss the Cretan question. Candia had recently been taken by the Turks from the Venetians, a number of whose French allies, some of them men of rank, had been killed or captured, and the French Ambassador had been recalled from Constantinople. The envoy Soliman Pasha was, in the phrase of modern diplomacy, given the full treatment. Having been allowed to wait four weeks for an audience at Versailles he was received at length amid a formidable parade of troops and ushered with his escort into a gallery where the King of France sat superb on a high dais, wearing a hat and a suit of clothes blazing with—according to Court rumour—fourteen million francs' worth of diamonds. Monsieur, similarly bedizened, sat beside him. To the mortification of every courtier, and of Louis himself, the show failed to make any impression on the Oriental mind except that Soliman Pasha, incensed at the hauteur with which Louis accepted the Sultan's letter of greeting, withdrew in a huff and soon afterwards returned to Constantinople. There exists a painting of the episode, showing the Pasha and his twenty attendant Turks before a dazzling Sun King; all plainly garbed, mediocrely turbaned, and wrapped in imperturbable calm. They had seen displays of precious stones before, and far larger ones. Though the matter rankled at the time, Louis decided to treat it as a joke. Hence the order to Molière. (Lewis, 1959, p. 143)

[Molière] determined to construct his comedy in such a way that the Turkish ceremony should not be a mere adjunct to it [the vanity of the bourgeois], but should spring naturally from it. For this purpose it was essential to create a character so grotesquely vain and credulous that he could be taken in by the extravagant imposture of the Turkish episode. Probably Molière was meditating on the theme of middle class citizens who aped the manners and fashions of nobles, when the royal command reached him. In *L'Ecole des Femmes* he had already touched on the subject, and had represented Arnolphe as assuming the territorial name of M. de La Souche in virtue of a small piece of land which was attached to his house. This sort of vanity was evidently common in France in Molière's day as indeed it is in most countries and most ages.

> Se croire un personnage est fort commun en France;
> On y fait l'homme d'importance,
> Et l'on n'est souvent qu'un bourgeois.
> C'est proprement le mal français:
> *La sotte vanité nous est particulière.*[206]
> (La Fontaine, Le Rat et l'Éléphant, viii, 15)[207]

It is this *sotte vanité* which is the dominant trait in M. Jourdain's character. Indeed, it has assumed in him such monstrous proportions that, like some malignant disease, it has

---

[206] "It is quite common in France for people to believe that they are great persons. One behaves as somebody of importance. And yet, most often, one is but a bourgeois. It is truly a French disease; This silly vanity is ours in particular."

[207] In this fable, either La Fontaine is overly strict in his punishment of the rat's vanity, or the rat's name is Figaro, that Figaro who was better than many aristocrats and who had the courage to say so. In the fable, an elephant was carrying in pilgrimage an aristocratic lady (*Une sultane de renom*) together with several of her pets, among them a cat. The rat was surprised that people were so impressed by the heavy mass of the elephant: "*Mais qu'admirez-vous tant en lui, vous autres hommes? Seroit-ce grand corps qui fait peur aux enfants. Nous ne nous prisons pas, tout petits que nous somme,'. . . . Mais le chat, sortant de sa cage, lui fit voir, en moins d'un instant, qu'un rat n'est pas un éléphant*" ['You men, what are you admiring in it? Is it its big body which scares the children? We, we couldn't care less, even as small as we are.'. . . . However, the cat, jumping out of its cage, showed him, in a second, that a rat is not an elephant.'].

vitiated his whole character, blinding his judgment and stifling his natural affections. In the series of inimitable scenes with his music-master and his dancing-master, his fencing-master, his teacher of philosophy, and his tailor, which make up the first two acts, he displays to the full his all-pervading vanity. (Tilley, 1968, pp. 230-31)

However, once we eliminate the obvious exaggerations of the play, who suffered more of *sotte vanité*, M. Jourdain or Louis XIV? If the King had no better idea to impose himself on the Turkish ambassador—who was bringing him an important letter of the Grand Turk—than by having the ambassador wait for four weeks in Versailles, and then by parading his diamonds (a vanity so evident that the Ambassador took pleasure in debunking)[208], why should the others under him do better, including M. Jourdain?

Indeed, under Louis XIV, "*in a situation where the supremacy is based on vanity, both parties, ruler and ruled are obsessed by vanity. . . . The King succeeds in having his absolute superiority recognized by others because he has the means to nourish and sustain their vanity. But he too, in his own way, must constantly be on the watch for any derogation, while pretending of course to be totally unconcerned*" (Gossman, 1969, p. 239; my italics). We are reminded of Hans Christian Andersen's tale of *The Emperor's New Clothes*, in which everybody is fearful of not being fit for his position if he were to admit not to see the new (non-existing clothes), first of all the emperor himself.[209]

---

[208] In section E, chapter 1 of volume 2, "The Magnificent Dukes", I wrote that "quite often the unity of power, especially if inherited, brings with it a passion for magnificence, especially in dress and jewelry, even at the cost of political blunders: When Charles the Bold 'went to Trier in 1473 in the vain expectation of wresting a royal crown from the emperor Frederick III, he fairly dripped with pearls and precious stones, outshining the emperor much as his father had outshone Louis XII a dozen years earlier—with equally negative results. . . . We have seen that when Charles the Bold went to Trier in 1473, he decked himself out with jewels. In this case it proved a psychological mistake, for while the Burgundian despised the modesty of the emperor's following, both numerically and sartorially, the Germans 'despised the pomp and verbiage of said duke, which they attributed to pride'" (Tyler, 1971, pp. 71, 79).

[209] Outstanding coincidence: In my old *Illustrated Treasury of Children's Literature* (edited in 1955 by Margaret Martignoni; New York: Grosset & Dunlap), the Emperor of the story seems to have popped out from a painting of Louis XIV, so clear is the resemblance to the Roi Soleil, big wig included.

"This sort of vanity was evidently common in France in Molière's day[210] as indeed it is in most countries and most ages" wrote Tilley, as reported above. But, why so? Because vanity is a standard vice of the unity of power in which there is no dialogue among the members of the pyramid of power, but only proud commands passed down, and their humble acceptance by those on the lower levels. In turn, one's position, on a given level of the pyramid of power, was made evident by a number of perquisites which were strictly denied to those on the lower levels. Ruth Benedict wrote in *The Chrysanthemum and the Sword* of 1946:

Japan for all its recent Westernization is still an aristocratic society. Every greeting, every contact must indicate the kind and degree of social distance between men. Every time a man says to another 'Eat' or 'Sit down' he uses different words if he is addressing someone familiarly or is speaking to an inferior or to a superior. There is a different 'you' that must be used in each case and the verbs have different stems. The Japanese have, in other words, what is called a 'respect language,' as many other peoples do in the Pacific, and they accompany it with proper bows and kneelings. All such behavior is governed by meticulous rules and conventions; it is not merely necessary to know to whom one bows but it is necessary to know how much one bows. A bow that is right and proper to one host would be resented as an insult by another who stood in a slightly different relationship to the power. And bows range all the way from kneeling with forehead lowered to the hands placed flat upon the floor, to the mere inclination of head and

---

[210] Emmanuel Le Roy Ladurie (2001) made in this respect some important observations: "[Nowadays] few see 'court society' [with its UP] as the remote ancestor of modern bourgeois moderation and contemporary life styles passed down in continuous evolutionary process from the domesticated aristocracy of Versailles to the bourgeois elite that inhabited the wealthier sections of Paris. . . . What [Daniel] Gordon [1994] did was to show that the French elite, and to some extent the lower classes, developed their own style of sociability based on free conversation, egalitarianism, and cordial social relations. . . . The setting in which this took place was not only egalitarian [DP] but, even more significant, apolitical. It included the many salons and academies that sprang into being in the seventeenth and eighteenth centuries. . . . [Norbert] Elias notwithstanding, French sociability did not evolve in the court society of the great palace of the Bourbon, where conversation was inegalitarian, stiff, disciplinary, at times stifling, and pedagogical hierarchical [UP]" (p. 351).

shoulders. One must learn, and learn early, how to suit the obeisance to each particular case. . . . Until the middle of the nineteenth century only noble families and warrior (samurai) families were allowed to use surnames. Surnames were fundamental in the Chinese clan system and without these, or some equivalent, clan organization cannot develop. One of these equivalents in some tribes is keeping a genealogy. But in Japan only the upper classes kept genealogies. (pp. 47-50)

Back to Thomas Buddenbrook's Germany and to M. Jourdain's France, there, one of the few ways to see oneself in a better light was to use one's money in doing some of the things of the higher classes: be it being generous to an aristocrat in debt, or paying for music and fencing lessons because these were signs of nobility. The obvious risk was to be labelled an upstart, a nouveau riche, a social climber, a parvenu, and made fun of, for ones inveterate vanity, like the Bourgeois gentilhomme.

So, La Fontaine was right in making fun of the bourgeois raven who fell victim to the fox who saluted him with that magnificent *Eh! bonjours, monsieur du corbeau*[211]. Yet, we cannot blame the raven for paying attention to how he was saluted, because the way we are addressed plays a role in the vision we have of ourselves, and it played a very important role under UP, as proved by all maneuvers to know if an unknown person encountered in the street or a party was a person of superior or inferior rank to oneself, as just discussed by Ruth Benedict for Japan. Today, in the West, that sounds ridiculous, but only because we live under DP.

Under DP, at any moment, what counts is one's knowledge and capability. Accordingly, vanity disappears (or evolves in milder forms, not rarely useful to society) because it is dangerous to claim more knowledge and capability than one has: one always risks to be told *Hic Rhodus, hic salta*. Under DP, at any moment, one can leave job or place of residence, and move elsewhere, provided one has sufficient know-how to be of use to a new employer or for the beginning of an independent activity, be it as baker or physician. In these new activi-

---

[211] "*Le renard, en se servant de cette façon de parler, fait voir au corbeau qu'il le prend pour un gentilhomme ou un grand seigneur*" [The fox, in so speaking, shows the raven that he considers him a gentleman or a great lord] (Tastu, 1850, p. 36).

ties, claiming to be the Marquis de Carabas, as in the fable of *Puss in Boots*, is of no use.

Sadly, Molière should have made fun of Louis XIV not of poor M. Jourdain, but to do so would have demanded an independence of mind which was not possible under the UP of his time. The progress in DP of the second half of the 18th century was needed before Mozart would be capable of realizing who he was: a thousand times superior to any aristocrats (see section 4 "Mozart, Child of the DP of the Enlightenment", chapter 11 of volume 1).

Interestingly, that understanding of the vices of the aristocrats was already evident to Boccaccio when he wrote *Decameron*. But, sadly, the Renaissance of the *signori* turned the clock back thereby explaining both the pearls of Charles the Bold and the diamonds of Louis XIV.

Basically, under DP, everybody can be a citizen of Missouri, and say: "I come from a state that raises corn and cotton and cockleburs and Democrats, and frothy eloquence neither convinces nor satisfies me. I am from Missouri. You have got to show me." Sadly for Louis XIV, the Turkish ambassador told him about the same: "Those frothy diamonds, and making me wait four weeks, neither convinces nor satisfies me" (leaving aside the fact that any ambassador of Louis XIV to the Sublime Porte would have been treated the same way, or worse).

Yes M. Jourdain was vain, and so was Senator Thomas Buddenbrooks, but the fault was not theirs but that of the UP, of the pyramid of power, of the inevitable effect of the Law of Power of Lord Acton.

3. The UP Recipe for the Sickness of Vanity: "Maintain Proper Station"

Ruth Benedict discovered with pleasure that Japan was practicing the virtues preached by the aristocrat Alexis de Tocqueville:

> In Japan getting rich is under suspicion and maintaining proper station is not. Even today the poor as well as the rich invest their self-respect in observing the conventions of hierarchy. It is a virtue alien to America, and the Frenchman, de Tocqueville, pointed this out in the eighteen-thirties in his book already quoted. Born himself in eighteenth-century France, he knew and loved the aristocratic way of life in spite of his

generous comments about the egalitarian United States. America, he said, in spite of its virtues, lacked true dignity. "True dignity consists in always taking one's proper station, neither too high nor too low. And this is as much within the reach of the peasant as of the prince." De Tocqueville would have understood the Japanese attitude that class differences are not themselves humiliating. (1946, p. 150)

The problem, however, is not that class differences are by themselves humiliating, but that there is no reason to spend all of one's life working, like an animal, for the profit of a useless Japanese daimyo or an equally useless French duke, and that there is no reason not to try to better oneself and one's children. There is no reason to respect the conventions of a hierarchy which give all the fruits of this world to few undeserving aristocrats, be they named Louis XIV or Wilhelm II.

There is more nobility in trying, than in standing pat for the sake of a "true dignity" invented by the UP for its own profit.

4. From Moliere's *M. Jourdain* to Flaubert's *Mme. Bovary*

Flaubert's satire of Emma Bovary and of Monsieur Homais likewise resembles closely the structure of an "open" comedy such as *Le Bourgeois Gentilhomme*. Both, like Jourdain, reject the narrowness and ordinariness of the world in which they are born and aspire to distinctions of which they have read or which they imagine, Emma to the exotic world of literary romance, Homais to the important and impressive world of academic and intellectual honors. Emma longs for a great and poetic love, and Homais longs to be celebrated as a scientist and champion of progress. But as everything Jourdain does reveals what he really is and has never ceased to be, everything Emma and Homais do confirms that they are no different from the very provincials to whom they feel so superior. Emma remains a country doctor's wife, petty and narrowminded. Her great loves are never anything but ordinary acts of adultery, which by the end of her career are scarcely distinguishable from acts of prostitution. (Gossman, 1969, p. 254)

Why couldn't Flaubert have seen something positive in Emma Bovary's and M. Homai's attempts at a more fulfilling life? What is so execrable in rejecting the narrowness and ordinariness of the world in which one is born and aspire to distinctions read or imagined? No! For Flaubert, both must be mocked like M. Jourdain, and both must end miserably like Thomas Buddenbrook.

Not surprisingly, there is affinity between Flaubert and Thomas Mann. As reported in chapter 5 of volume 2, "Flaubert is rather 'apolitical'; because politics, all politics aroused his indignation" (Brombert, 1979, p. 96). Stricter than Mann, Flaubert considers the education of the masses a waste of time "leading only to the reading of newspapers (that 'school for stultification'). [George Sand] believes in universal suffrage, whereas he knows 'I am worth twenty other Croisset voters,' despises the predominance of Numbers, and proposes government by a Mandarinate" (Barnes, 1993, p. 6). "*Prostituer l'art parait à Flaubert la plus ignoble des professions pour la raison précise que l'artiste lui semble le maître homme des hommes*"[212] (Brombert, 1979, pp. 42-43). Thomas Mann would agree, and probably understand why the *maître homme des hommes* saw himself as a true aristocrat when he said "*J'ai la tristesse qu'avaient les patriciens romain au IV siècle*"[213] (ib., p. 91).

5. Conclusion

In the end, I am less concerned with the *Buddenbrooks phenomenon* and its variant of *Shirtsleeves to shirtsleeves in three generations*, than with how the DP helps people to avoid the moving sands of vanity, and rise to a better station through generous volunteerism.

Once more, would we have had the International Red Cross if Henri Dunant had had the "true dignity of maintaining his station," and accordingly had never left Geneva for the battlefield of Solferino? Helping there the wounded was none of his business, as it was none of the Good Samaritan's to help a Jew. To be on the safe side (many readers may not know it, or only in a too concentrated and distant way), let me relate this fundamental parable of the Good Samaritan:

---

[212] To prostitute the arts is for Flaubert the most vile profession, for the precise reason that, for him, the artist is the superior man, teacher of all men.

[213] "I have the gloominess of the Roman patricians of the IVth century."

And Jesus answering [the question of a lawyer who had asked him 'Who is my neighbour'] said, A certain man went down from Jerusalem to Jericho, and fell among thieves, which stripped him of his raiment, and wounded him, and departed, leaving him half dead. And by chance there came down a certain priest that way: and when he saw him, he passed by on the other side. And likewise a Levite, when he was at the place, came and looked on him, and passed by on the other side. But a certain Samaritan, as he journeyed, came where he was: and when he saw him, he had compassion on him, and went to him, and bound up his wounds, pouring in oil and wine, and set him on his own beast, and brought him to an inn, and took care of him. And on the morrow when he departed, he took out two pence, and gave them to the host, and said unto him, Take care of him, and whatsoever thou spendest more, when I come again, I will repay thee. Which now of these three, thinkest thou, was neighbour unto him that fell among the thieves? And he said, He that shewed mercy on him. Then Jesus unto him, Go, and do thou likewise". (Luke, 10:30-39)

Most admirably, the Good Samaritan went twice out of his station, first by helping, and second by helping a Jew: "[early in the parable] the hearers, who thought of their community in terms of Priests, Levites, and Israelites—as perhaps Christians today of bishops, clergy, and lay people—might have been confident that the hero would be an Israelite. Their shock and consternation when the hero turned out to be a hated Samaritan—one publicly cursed in the synagogues and whose evidence was unacceptable in a court of law—can be easily imagined" (Comay and Brownrigg, 1980, p. 399).

Both Henri Dunant and the Good Samaritan lived under DP. Indeed the author of the parable grew up under a very high level of DP: between Jews and Samaritans, between Jewish and Hellenic/ Roman scripts; Aramaic, Hebrew, Greek, Roman languages; the ruling of Pontius Pilate and Herod Antipas; the intellectual and social fights among Sadducees, Pharisees, Herodians, and Essenes; the strong separation of state (Rome/Herod) and church (the Temple and the synagogues). But not so M. Jourdain and Thomas Buddenbrook.

Under UP, what could the successful entrepreneur or professional do, beyond making money, pay heavy taxes, care for the family, and sing the praise of the *supremo*? Play cards, smoke and drink? Yes.

Better, there was the well-paved road of aping the manners and feelings of the upper classes, and losing money in the process, as M. Jourdain and Thomas Buddenbrooks did.

Under, DP the situation is different as pointed out by Tocqueville:

> The Americans make associations to give entertainments, to found seminaries, to build inns, to construct churches, to diffuse books, to send missionaries to the antipodes; in this manner they found hospitals, prisons, and schools. If it is proposed to inculcate some truth or to foster some feeling by the encouragement of a great example, they form a society. Wherever at the head of some new undertaking you see the government in France, or a man of rank in England, in the United States you will be sure to find an association. (1835-40/1987, *2*, p. 106)

What needs to be stressed here is not only the making of associations for this or that cause, but the choice of causes. Under DP it is the individual who first sees a need, and then convinces others to join him/her in solving it. They do not need the concurrence of the king and the money that the king has squeezed from the people. Volunteers use their money, because enough of it remains in their pockets after having paid taxes (even better, they may deduct the money given to non-profit generous causes in their tax declarations).

Andrew Carnegie, the steel industrialist, retired at the age of 66 from business and devoted himself to philanthropy:

> He provided, notably, for a vast number of public libraries in the U.S., Great Britain, and other English-speaking countries; his method was to build and equip, on condition that the local authority provide site and maintenance. He founded the Carnegie Institute of Technology of Carnegie-Mellon University at Pittsburgh (1900) and the Carnegie Institution of Washington, Washington, D.C. (1902). His trust to assist education at Scottish universities brought him election as lord rector of St. Andrews University. He was also a large benefactor of Tuskegee Institute, Tuskegee, Ala., founded by Booker T. Washington. He established large pension funds for Homestead workers (1901) and for U.S. college professors through

the Carnegie Foundation for the Advancement of Teaching, New York City (1905). Other notable contributions were his funds in the U.S. (1904) and the U.K. (1908) for the recognition of heroic deeds. In 1903 he financed the erection of a Temple of Peace at The Hague, The Netherlands, and a Pan-American Palace at Washington, D.C. The Carnegie Corporation of New York, New York City (1911), was liberally endowed for the furtherance of civilization. (*Encyclopaedia Britannica*, 1978, 2, p. 576)

How different would the life of Thomas Buddenbrook have been if, from his early twenties, he had had in mind some important volunteer work for the people of Lübeck, had gradually begun working at it, and included in the endeavor his wife, a large number of friends and acquaintances, and later his son Hanno. Obviously, it would have been a different book, by a different author, and in a different country.

Through volunteerism much of the *Buddenbrooks phenomenon*—as discussed by Thomas Mann—disappears, because wife and son cannot despise the paternal money when it is devoted, in large measure, to generous causes.

Under DP, Thomas Buddenbrook would have been more critical of the aristocrats, and would have paid more attention when his sister told him that "He is a very charming man, Ralf von Maiboom, Thomas; but he is very wild—a hail-fellow-well-met with everybody. He gambles in Rostock, and he gambles in Warnemünde, and his debts are like the sands of the sea" (1901/1957, p. 351). Under DP, where the aristocratic charisma does not exist, there is no reason to condone gambling in Rostock and Warnemünde, and having debts like the sand of the sea. It is up to Mr. Maiboom (and forget the useless and misleading "von") to return to "shirtsleeves." To him pertain—and not to M. Jourdain, Mme Bovary, M. Homais, and Thomas Buddenbrook—the words of the Ecclesiastes: *Vanitas vanitatum, omnis vanitas.*

References

Abrams, M. H. (Gen. Ed.) (1962). *The Norton anthology of English literature. Vol. 2.* New York: Norton.

Ainsworth, Mary D. Salter (1979). Infant-mother attachment. *American Psychologist, 34,* 932-37.

Akdag, Mustafa (1978). Kemal Atatürk. In *Encyclopaedia Britannica* (2, pp. 255-57). Chicago: Encyclopaedia Britannica.

Alamanni, Lodovico (1516/1969). Letter to Lorenzo de Medici, Duke of Urbino. In A. Molho (Ed.), *Social and economic foundations of the Italian Renaissance* (pp. 214-20). New York: John Wiley & Sons.

Albert, Robert S. (1978). Observations, and suggestions regarding giftedness, familial influence and the achievement of eminence. *The Gifted Child Quarterly, 22,* 201-11.

Albert, Robert (1983b). Family position and the attainment of eminence. In R. S. Albert (Ed.), *Genius and eminence: The social psychology of creativity and achievement* (pp. 141-54). Oxford: Pergamon.

Albert, Robert S., & Runco, Mark A. (1986). The achievement of eminence: A model based on a longitudinal study of exceptionally gifted boys and their families. In R. J. Sternberg & J. E. Davidson (Eds.), *Conceptions of giftedness* (pp. 332-57). Cambridge: Cambridge University Press.

Aldred, Cyril (1988). *Akhenaten: King of Egypt.* London: Thames and Hudson.

Amabile, Teresa M. (1990). Within you, without you: The social psychology of creativity, and beyond. In M. A. Runco, & R. S. Albert (Eds.), *Theories of creativity.* Newbury Park, CA: Sage.

Anderson, Perry (1974). *Lineages of the absolutist state.* London: NLB.

Anderson, William (1980). *Dante the maker.* London: Routledge & Kegan Paul.

Angold, Michael (2001). *Byzantium: The bridge from antiquity to the Middle Ages.* London: Weidenfeld & Nicolson.

Apter, T. E. (1978). *Thomas Mann: The devil's advocate.* London: Macmillan

Arima, Tatsuo (1969). *The failure of freedom: A portrait of modern Japanese intellectuals.* Cambridge, MA: Harvard University Press.

Arnold, Benjamin (1997). *Medieval Germany 500-1300.* Toronto: University of Toronto Press.

Ashley, Maurice (1978a). Charles I of Great Britain. In *Encyclopaedia Britannica* (4, pp. 52-54). Chicago: Encyclopaedia Britannica.

Ashley, Maurice (1978b). Oliver Cromwell. In *Encyclopaedia Britannica* (5, pp. 291-95). Chicago: Encyclopaedia Britannica.

Augstein, Rudolf (1992). *Macht und Gegenmacht.* Göttingen: Lamuv.

Bainton, Roland (1950). *Here I stand.* Nashville, TN: Abingdon.

Balazs, Nandor L. (1973). Albert Einstein. In *Encyclopaedia Britannica* (*8*, pp. 95-97). Chicago: Encyclopaedia Britannica.

Balzani, Ugo (1948). Frederick Barbarossa and the Lombard League. In *Cambridge Medieval History* (*5*, pp. 413-53). New York: Macmillan.

Bandura, Albert (1982). The psychology of chance encounters and life paths. *American Psychologist, 37*, 747-55.

Barnes, Julian (1993, June 10). Unlikely friendship [Flaubert—Sand]. *New York Review of Books*, 5-12.

Barnett, Lincoln (1972). Albert Einstein. In B. Mazlich (Ed.), *Makers of modern thought* (pp. 430-57). New York: American Heritage.

Bartolo da Sassoferrato (1340/1964). De Guelphis. In E. Emerton (Ed.), *Humanism and tyranny: Studies in the Italian Trecento*. Gloucester, MA: Peter Smith.

Barzini, Luigi (1983). *The Europeans*. New York: Simon and Schuster.

Barzun, Jacques (2000). *From dawn to decadence 1500 to present: 500 Years of Western cultural life*. New York: HarperCollins.

Beaufre, André (1965). *Introduction à la stratégie*. Paris: Armand Colin.

Beasley, W. G. (1999). *The Japanese experience*. Berkeley: University of California Press.

Becker, Marvin B. (1981). *Medieval Italy: Constraints and creativity*. Bloomington: Indiana University Press.

Benedict, Ruth (1946). *The chrysanthemum and the sword*. Boston: Houghton Mifflin.

Benoist-Méchin, Jacques Gabriel (1964). *Alexandre le Grand ou le rêve dépassé*. Lausanne: Clairefontaine.

Berger, John (1965). *The success and failure of Picasso*. London: Writers and Readers Publishing Cooperative.

Berlin, Isaiah (1998, May 14). The first and the last. *New York Review of Books*, 52-60.

Berman, Harold J. (1983). *Law and revolution: The formation of the Western legal tradition*. Cambridge, MA: Harvard University Press.

Bernier, Olivier (1987). *Louis XIV: A royal life*. New York: Doubleday.

Betts, George T., & Neihart, Maureen (1988). Profiles of the gifted and talented. *Gifted Child Quarterly, 32 (2)*, 248-53.

Beuf, Ann Hill (1990). *Beauty in the beast: Appearance-impaired children in America*. Philadelphia: University of Pennsylvania Press.

Biocca, Dario, & Canali, Mauro (2000). *L'informatore: Silone, i comunisti e la polizia*. Milan: Luni

Bishop, Morris (1963). *Petrarch and his world*. Bloomington: Indiana University Press.

Bjork, Robert A. (2000). Different views of individual differences. *APS Observer, 13 (9)*, 4, 26.

Blackbourn, David, & Eley, Geoff (1984). *The Peculiarities of German history*. Oxford: Oxford University Press.

Bloom, Benjamin S. (1982). The role of gifts and markers in the development of talent. *Exceptional Children, 48*, 510-22.

Bloom. Benjamin S. (Ed.), (1985). *Developing talent in young people*. New York: Balantine.

Blunt, Wilfrid (1973). *The dream king: Ludwig II of Bavaria*. London: Penguin.

Boorstin, Daniel J. (1983). *The discoverers*. New York: Random House.

Bosco, Umberto, & Reggio, Giovanni (1979). Notes. In Dante Alighieri, *La Divina Commedia, Inferno*. Florence: Le Monnier.

Bowers, Faubion (1956). Foreword. In A. S. Halford, & G. M. Halford's *The Kabuki handbook*. Tokyo: Charles S. Tuttle.

Boxer, Charles Ralph (1951). *The Christian century in Japan*. Berkeley: University of California Press.

Boyle, Nicholas (2000). *Goethe: The poet and the age—Vol. 2: Revolution and renunciation, 1790-1803*. Oxford: Oxford University Press.

Bradford, Sarah (1976). *Cesare Borgia*. London: Weidenfeld and Nicolson.

Braudel, Fernand (1979). *The structure of everyday life*. New York: Harper & Row.

Brennan, Joseph Gerard (1962). *Thomas Mann's world*. New York: Russell & Russell.

Brent, Peter (1981). *Charles Darwin: A man of enlarged curiosity*. New York: Harper & Row

Brombert, Victor (1979). *Flaubert*. Paris: Seuil.

Bronowsky, Jacob (1972). Leonardo da Vinci. In B. Mazlish (Ed.), *Makers of modern thought*. New York: American Heritage Publishing.

Brooke, Christopher N. (1991). *The Medieval idea of marriage*. Oxford: Oxford University Press.

Brown, Peter R. L. (1978). Saint Ambrose. In *Encyclopaedia Britannica* (*1*, pp. 657-658). Chicago: Encyclopaedia Britannica.

Brundage, James (1995). *Medieval canon law*. London: Longman.

Buddess, Julian M. (1993). Beethoven. In *Encyclopaedia Britannica* (*14*, pp. 737-43). Chicago: Encyclopaedia Britannica.

Buddha (Siddhartha Gautama) (ca. 528 BC/1993). *The teaching of Buddha*. Tokyo: Society for the Promotion of Buddhism.

Burnaby, John (1978). Saint Augustine of Hippo. In *Encyclopaedia Britannica* (*2*, pp. 364-68). Chicago: Encyclopaedia Britannica.

Burt, Cyril L. (1973). Gifted children. In *Encyclopaedia Britannica* (*10*, pp. 406-07). Chicago: Encyclopaedia Britannica.

Buss, Arnold H., & Plomin, Robert (1984). *Temperament: Early developing personality traits*. Hillsdale, NJ: Lawrence Erlbaum.

Caggese, Romolo (1932). Italy, 1313-1414. In *Cambridge Medieval History* (*7*, pp. 49-77). Cambridge: Cambridge University Press.

Caizzi, Bruno (1962). *Camillo e Adriano Olivetti*. Turin: UTET.

Calvino, Italo (1962/1993). *The road to San Giovanni*. New York: Pantheon.

Cantor, Norman F. (1993). *The civilization of the Middle Ages*. New York: HarperCollins.

Cantor, Norman F. (1995). *Medieval reader*. New York: HarperPerennial.

Cardini, Franco (1991). *La vera storia della Lega Lombarda*. Milan: Arnoldo Mondadori.

Castan, Nicole (1989). The public and the private. In R. Chartier (Ed.), *A history of private life* (*3*, pp. 403-45). Cambridge, MA: Harvard University Press.

Castiglione, Baldesar (c. 1510/1976). *The book of the courtier*. London: Penguin.

Causson, Jean-Louis (1978). Gioacchino Rossini. In *Encyclopedia Britannica* (*15*, pp. 1159-61). Chicago: Encyclopedia Britannica.

Chandler, David (1966). *The campaigns of Napoleon*. New York: Macmillan.

Chaptal, Jean-Antoine (ca. 1825/1962). Portrait de l'empereur. In J. Burnat, G. H. Dumont, & E. Wanty (Eds.), *Le dossier Napoléon* (pp. 177-85). Paris: Editions Gerard.

Charmont, Claude (1970, October 10). Portrait-robot des créateurs performants. *Entreprise*, 115-22.

Cipolla, Carlo (1976). *Before the Industrial Revolution: European society and economy, 1000-1700*. New York: W.W. Norton.

Clark, Ronald W. (1971). *Einstein: The life and times*. New York: World Publishing.

Clemens, Robert J. (1978). Michelangelo. In *Encyclopaedia Britannica (12*, pp. 97-102). Chicago: Encyclopaedia Britannica.

Colcutt, Martin (1988). Daimyo and daimyo culture. In Y. Shimizu (Ed.), *Japan: The shaping of daimyo culture*, (pp. 1-46). New York: George Braziller.

Coleman, Laurence J. (1985). *Schooling the gifted*. Menlo Park, CA: Addison-Wesley.

Coleman, Laurence J., & Cross, Tracy L. (2000). Social-emotional development and the personal experience of giftedness. In K. A. Heller, F. J. Mönks, R. J. Sternberg, & R. F. Subotnik (Eds.), *International handbook of giftedness and talent* (pp. 203-12). Amsterdam: Elsevier.

Collinson, Patrick (1993). The late Medieval church and its Reformation (1400-1600). In J. McManners (Ed.), *The Oxford history of christianity* (pp. 243-76). Oxford: Oxford University Press.

Comay, Joan, & Brownrigg, Ronald (1980). *Who is who in the Bible*. New York: Bonanza.

Cox, Catherine Morris (1926). *Genetic studies of genius: Volume 2, The early mental traits of three hundred geniuses*. Stanford, CA: Stanford University Press.

Cozby, Paul C. (1981). *Methods in behavioral research*. Palo Alto, CA: Mayfield.

Craig, Gordon A. (2000, April 13). Germany's greatest. *The New York Review of Books*, 52-57.

Crankshaw, Edward (1974/1986). *Tolstoy: The making of a novelist*. London: Macmillan.

Crawshay-Williams, Rupert (1978). Bertrand Russell. In *Encyclopaedia Britannica (16*, pp. 34-37). Chicago: Encyclopaedia Britannica.

Cronin, Vincent (1972). *Napoleon Bonaparte: An intimate biography*. New York: William Morrow.

Cropley, Arthur J., & Urban, Klaus, K. (2000). Programs and strategies for nurturing creativity. In K. A. Heller, F. J. Mönks, R. J. Sternberg, & R. F. Subotnik (Eds.), *International handbook of giftedness and talent* (pp. 485-98). Amsterdam: Elsevier.

Crosby, Alfred W. (1997). *The measure of reality*. Cambridge: Cambridge University Press.

Csikszentmihalyi, Mihaly (1988a). Society, culture, and person. A system view of creativity. In R. J. Sternberg (Ed.), *The nature of creativity* (pp. 325-39). New York: Cambridge University Press.

Csikszentmihalyi, Mihaly (1988b). The flow and its significance for human psychology. In M. Csikszentmihalyi & I. Csikszentmihalyi (Eds.), *Optimal experience: Psychological studies of flow in consciousness* (pp. 15-35). Cambridge: Cambridge University Press.

Csikszentmihalyi, Mihaly (1991, April). *The antecedents of intrinsic motivation and creativity in childhood*. Invited address to the biennial meeting of the Society for Research in Child Development, Seattle, WA. (Audio Production magnetic tape #H671).

Csikszentmihalyi, Mihaly (1999). Implications of a system perspective. In R. J. Sternberg (Ed.), *Handbook of creativity* (pp. 313-35). Cambridge: Cambridge University Press.

Csikszentmihalyi, Mihaly, & Wolfe, Rustin (2000). New conceptions and research approaches to creativity: Implications of a Systems Perspective for creativity in education. In K. A. Heller, F. J. Mönks, R. J. Sternberg, & R. F. Subotnik (Eds.), *International handbook of giftedness and talent* (pp. 81-93). Amsterdam: Elsevier.

Dante (tr. 1867/1904). *The divine comedy*, H. W. Longfellow (tr.). Boston: Houghton, Mifflin.

De Bono, Edward (1982). *De Bono's thinking course*. London: British Broadcasting Corporation.

De Conde, Alexander (1978). Alexander Hamilton. In *Encyclopaedia Britannica* (*8*, pp. 584-88). Chicago: Encyclopaedia Britannica

Del Mar, Norman (1986). *Richard Strauss: A critical commentary on his life and work*. Ithaca, NY: Cornell University Press.

Dianin, Serge (1963). *Borodin*. London: Oxford University Press.

Diaz-Guerrero, Rogelio (1967/1975). *Psychology of the Mexican culture: Culture and personality*. Austin, TX: University of Texas Press.

Donaldson, Ian (1996, February 9). The brushers of gentlemen's clothes. *Times Literary Supplement*, 27.

Donington, Robert (1973). Cadenza. In *Encyclopaedia Britannica* (*4*, p. 562). Chicago: Encyclopaedia Britannica.

Drewer, James (1952). *A dictionary of psychology*. London: Penguin.

Drucker, Peter F. (1965). The chief executive's job. In E. Dale (Ed.), *Reading in management* (pp. 78-80). New York: McGraw-Hill.

Duby, Georges (1977). *The chivalrous society*. London: Edward Arnold.

Duby, Georges (1978). *Medieval marriage: Two models from twelfth-century France*. Baltimore: Johns Hopkins University Press.

Duby, Georges (1983). *The knight, the lady and the priest*. London: Allen Lane.

Dworetzky, John P. (1985). *Psychology*. St. Paul, MN: West Publishing.

Ebrey, Patricia B. (1993). *The inner quarters: Marriage and the lives of Chinese women in the Sung Period [960-1279]*. Berkeley: University of California Press.

Edwards, Samuel (1971). *Victor Hugo: A tumultuous life*. New York: David McKay.

Einstein, Alfred (1946). *Mozart: His character, his work*. London: Cassell.

Emerton, Ephraim (1964). *Humanism and tyranny*. Gloucester, MA: Peter Smith.

Emery, Noemie (1982). *Alexander Hamilton: An intimate portrait*. New York: G.P. Putnam's Sons. *Encyclopedia of Catholicism* (1995). San Francisco: HarperSanFrancisco.

Endo, Shusaku (1978). *Silence*. New York: Quartet Books.

Endo, Shusaku (1979). *When I whistle*. London: Peter Owen.

Endo, Shusaku (1989). *The Golden Country*. London: Peter Owen

Erikson, Erik H. (1950/1963). *Childhood and society*. New York: W. W. Norton.

Erlanger, Philippe (1965/1970). *Louis XIV*. New York: Praeger.

Erlanger, Philippe (1978). Louis XIV of France. In *Encyclopaedia Britannica* (*11*, pp. 121-23). Chicago: Encyclopaedia Britannica.

Eyck, Franck (1998). *Religion and politics in German history: From the beginnings to the French revolution*. New York: St. Martin's Press.

Feldhusen, John F. (1987). A conception of giftedness. In R. J. Sternberg, & J. E. Davidson (Eds.), *Conception of giftedness* (pp. 112-27). Cambridge: Cambridge University Press.

Feldhusen, John F., & Jarvan, Fathi A. (2000). Identification of gifted and talented youth for educational programs. In K. A. Heller, F. J. Mönks, R. J. Sternberg, & R. F. Subotnik (Eds.), *International handbook of giftedness and talent* (pp. 271-82). Amsterdam: Elsevier.

Feldman, David Henry (1986). *Nature's gambit: Child prodigies and the development of the human potential*. New York: Basic Books.

Ferguson, Tim, W. (2000, October 9). Noble gestures. *Forbes*, 80-81.

Ferri, Elsa (1976). *Growing up in a one-parent family: A long-term study of child development*. Slough, UK: NFER Publishing.

Ferroni, Giulio (1991). *Storia della letteratura italiana—Il Novecento*. Turin: Einaudi.

Fisher, Robert (1966). Klee, the poet-painter. In R. Fisher (Ed.), *Klee* (pp. 3-13). New York: Tudor Publishing.

Fleming, Thomas (1999). *Duel: Alexander Hamilton, Aaron Burr and the future of America*. New York: Basic Books.

Flexner, James T. (1978). *The young Hamilton*. Boston: Little, Brown.

Fölsing, Albrecht (1993/1998). *Albert Einstein: A biography*. New York: Penguin.

Forkel, Johann Nikolaus (1802/1974). *Johann Sebastian Bach: His life, art and work*. New York: Vienna House.

Frank, Anne (1942-44/1953). *Anne Frank: The diary of a young girl*. New York: Pocket Books.

Freeman, Mark (1989). *Defying the myth of extraordinary artistic abilities*. Paper presented at the biennial meeting of the Society for the Research in Child Development, Kansas City, MO, April, 1989.

Frend, W.H.C. (1984). *The rise of Christianity*. Philadelphia: Fortress.

Friedenthal, Richard (1965). *Goethe: His life and times*. Cleveland: World.

Friedrich, Carl J. (1973). Government. In *Encyclopaedia Britannica* (*10*, pp. 616-23). Chicago: Encyclopaedia Britannica.

Fukuyama, Francis (1995). *Trust*. New York: Free Press.

Gardner, Howard (1993). *Creating minds*. New York: Basic Books.

Gardner, Howard, & Hatch, Thomas (November, 1989). Multiple intelligences go to school. *Educational Researcher*, 4-10.

Gardner, Howard, & Wolf, Constance (1988). The fruits of asynchrony; A psychological examination of creativity. *Adolescent Psychiatry*, *15*, 96-120.

Gay, Peter (1966). *The Enlightenment: An interpretation*. New York: Alfred A. Knopf.

Gay, Peter (1988). *Freud: A life for our time*. New York: W. W. Norton.

Gilot, Françoise, & Lake Carlton (1964). *Life with Picasso*. New York: McGraw-Hill.

Gimpel, Jean (1977). *The medieval machine: The industrial revolution of the Middle Ages*. New York: Penguin.

Glazebrook, Richard T., & Cohen, I. Bernard (1973). Sir Isaac Newton. In *Encyclopaedia Britannica* (*16*, pp. 418-21). Chicago: Encyclopaedia Britannica.

Glueck, Sheldon & Glueck, Eleanor (1950). *Unravelling juvenile delinquency*. Cambridge, MA: Harvard University Press.

Glueck, Sheldon & Glueck, Eleanor (1968). *Delinquents and nondelinquents in perspective*. Cambridge, MA: Harvard University Press.

Goethe, Johann Wolfgang (1795-96/1898). *Wilhelm Meister's Apprenticeship*. London: George Bell.

Goethe, Johann Wolfgang (1811-22/1969). *Dichtung und Wahrheit: The autobiography of Johann Wolfgang von Goethe*. London: Sidgwick & Jackson

Goethe, Johann Wolfgang (1977). *Sämtliche Werke*. Zürich: Artemis; Munich: DTV.

Goleman, Daniel (1980). From 1528 little geniuses and how they grew. *Psychology Today, 13*(2), 28-53.

Gombrich, E. H. (1974). The logic of vanity fair. In P. A. Schilp (Ed.), *The philosophy of Karl Popper* (2, pp. 925-57). La Salle, IL: Open Court.

Gordon, Daniel (1994). *Citizens without sovereignty: Equality and sociability in French thought, 1670-1789.* Princeton, NJ: Princeton University Press.

Gordon, Robert (2000, October 20). Emergency exit: The double life of Iganzio Silone. *Times Literary Supplement,* 11-12.

Gossman, Lionel (1969). *Men and masks: A study of Molière.* Baltimore: Johns Hopkins Press.

Graham, Martha (1991). *Blood memory.* New York: Doubleday.

Grant, Michael (2000). *Constantine the Great: The man and his times.* New York: History Book Club.

Green, Peter (1970). *Alexander the Great.* New York: Praeger.

Grohmann, Will (1954). *Paul Klee.* New York: Harry N. Abrams.

Gross, Miraca U. M. (2000). Issues in the cognitive development of exceptionally and profoundly gifted individuals. In K. A. Heller, F. J. Mönks, R. J. Sternberg, & R. F. Subotnik (Eds.), *International handbook of giftedness and talent* (pp. 179-92). Amsterdam: Elsevier.

Grossmann, Karin; Grossmann, Klaus E.; Spangler, Gottfried; Suess, Gerhard; & Unzer, Lothar (1985). Maternal sensitivity and newborns' orientation responses as related to quality of attachment in Northern Germany. *Monographs of the Society for Research in Child Development, 50*(1-2), 233-56.

Gruber, Howard E. (1981). *Darwin on man: A psychological study of scientific creativity.* Chicago: University of Chicago Press.

Gruber, Howard E. (1986). The self-construction of the extraordinary. In R. J. Sternberg & J. E. Davidson (Eds.), *Conceptions of giftedness* (pp. 247-63). New York: Cambridge University Press.

Guilford, J. P. (1970). Traits of creativity. In P. E. Vernon (Ed.), *Creativity* (pp. 167-88). London: Penguin.

Gumpert, Martin (1938). *Dunant: The story of the Red Cross.* New York: Oxford University Press.

Gurevich, A. J. (1985). *Categories of Medieval culture.* London: Routledge & Kegan Paul.

Guy, John (2000). *Thomas More.* London: Arnold.

Hall, Peter (1998). *Cities in civilization.* London: Weidenfeld & Nicolson.

Hall, Rupert A. (1992). *Isaac Newton: Adventurer in thought.* Oxford: Blackwell.

Hamilton, Nigel (1978). *The Brothers Mann.* London: Secker & Warburg.

Hane, Mikiso (1972). *Japan: A historical survey.* New York: Scribner.

Hare, R. M. (1978, March 16). Conversation with Bryan Magee: R. M. Hare on coloured balloons and moral arguments. *The Listener,* 329-31.

Haste, Helen (1993). Moral creativity and education for citizenship. *Creativity Research Journal, 6,* 153-64.

Haussig, H. W. (1971). *A history of Byzantine civilization.* New York: Praeger.

Hayman, Ronald (1990). *Proust: A biography.* New York: Carroll & Graf.

Hayman, Ronald (1995). *Thomas Mann: A biography.* New York: Scribner.

Herold, J. Christopher (1961). *The mind of Napoleon: A selection from his written and spoken words.* New York: Columbia University Press.

Hibbard, Howard (1974). *Michelangelo.* New York: Harper & Row.

Hill, Christopher (1994). *The English Bible and the Seventeenth-Century revolution.* London: Penguin.

Hill, Forest G. (1973). Philanthropic foundations. In *Encyclopaedia Britannica* (*9*, pp. 654-57). Chicago: Encyclopaedia Britannica.

Hoffmann, Banesh (1972). *Albert Einstein: Creator & rebel.* New York: New American Library.

Hofstadter, Douglas R. (1980). *Gödel, Escher, Bach: An eternal golden braid.* New York: Vintage.

Holborn, Hajo (1959/1982). *A history of modern Germany: The Reformation.* Princeton, NJ: Princeton University Press.

Holland Smith, John (1972). *Francis of Assisi.* New York: Charles Scribner's Sons.

Hollingdale, R. J. (1971). *Thomas Mann: A critical study.* Lewisburg: Bucknell University Press.

Hollo, Anselm (1962). 'Look at his face' A note. In A. Hollo (Ed. and translator), *Some poems by Paul Klee* (pp. 5-6). Lowestoft, UK: Scorpion Press.

Holmes, Frederic L. (1999). Hans Adolf Krebs, 1900-1981, biochemist, discoverer of the urea cycle and the citric acid cycle. In M. A. Runco, & S. R. Pritzker (Eds.), *Encyclopedia of creativity* (*2*, 131-45). San Diego, CA: Academic Press.

Holtzhauer, Helmut (1969). *Goethe-Museum: Werk, Leben und Zeit Goethes in Dokumenten.* Berlin: Aufbau.

Hopkins, Andrea (1996). *Knights.* Markham, Ontario: Fairmount.

Hopkins, Ellice (1983). *Working amongst working men.* London: Kegan Paul, Trench.

Hornblower, Simon (1993). Ancient Greek civilization. In *Encyclopaedia Britannica* (*20*, pp. 218-64). Chicago: Encyclopaedia Britannica.

Hudson, Derek (1977). *Lewis Carrol.* New York: Clarkson N. Potter.

Humble ISD, (1991). *Spice-Wings: Parent handbook.* Humble, TX: HISD.

Hume Brown, P. (1920/1971). *Life of Goethe.* New York: Haskell House.

Hutchings, Arthur (1976). *Mozart: The man, the musician.* New York: Macmillan.

Hutt, Maurice (Ed.) (1972). *Napoleon: Great lives observed.* Englewood Cliffs, NJ: Prentice-Hall.

Ikegami, Eiko (1995). *The taming of the samurai: Honorific individualism and the making of modern Japan.* Cambridge, MA: Harvard University Press.

Ishida, Eiichiro (1974b). *Japanese culture: A study of origins and characteristics.* Honolulu: University Press of Hawaii.

Jahn, Otto (1900). *The life of Mozart.* New York; E.F. Kalmus.

Janson, H. W. (1991). *History of art.* New York: Harry N. Abrams.

Jenkins, Elizabeth (1978). Elizabeth I of England. In *Encyclopaedia Britannica* (*6*, pp. 726-29). Chicago: Encyclopaedia Britannica.

Jericke, Alfred (1964). *Goethe und sein Haus am Frauenplan.* Weimar: Hermann Böhlaus.

Jessop. Thomas E. (1978). David Hume. In *Encyclopaedia Britannica* (*8*, pp. 1191-94). Chicago: Encyclopaedia Britannica.

John Paul II, Pope (1995). *Crossing the threshold of hope.* New York; Alfred A. Knopf.

Johnson, Edgar (1969). Charles Dickens—The dark pilgrimage. In E. W. F. Tomlin (Ed.), *Charles Dickens—1812-1870: A centenary volume* (pp. 41-63). New York: Simon & Schuster.

Johnson, Edgar (1977). *Charles Dickens: His tragedy and triumph.* New York: Viking Press.

Johnson, Paul (1976). *A history of Christianity.* New York: Atheneum.

Johnston, William (1978). Preface. In S. Endo's *Silence* (pp. 1-18). New York: Quartet Books.

Jones, Ernest (1953). *The life and work of Sigmund Freud: Vol. 1—The formative years and the great discoveries 1856-1900.* New York: Basic Books

Kagawa, Hiroshi (1997). *The inscrutable Japanese.* Tokyo: Kodansha International.

Keene, Donald (1971). Introduction. In *Chûshingura: The treasure of loyal retainers*, a puppet play. (pp. 1-26). New York: Columbia University Press.

Kelly, George A. (1963). *A theory of personality.* New York: W. W. Norton.

Kennedy, George (1963). *The art of persuasion in Greece.* Princeton, NJ: Princeton University Press.

Kermode, Frank (2001, April 12). But could she cook? [Review of "Elizabeth I: Collected works"]. *New York Review of Books*, 68-70.

Kincaid, Zoë (1925/1965). *Kabuki.* New York: Benjamin Blom.

Kitson, Michael W. L. (1978). Claude Lorrain. In *Encyclopaedia Britannica* (*4*, pp. 694-96). Chicago: Encyclopaedia Britannica.

Klee, Felix (1960). *Paul Klee: Leben und Werk in Dokumenten.* Zürich: Diogenes.

Klee, Paul (1960). *Paul Klee: Gedichte* (F. Klee, Ed.). Zürich: Die Arche.

Klee, Paul (1962). *Some poems by Paul Klee* (A. Hollo, Ed., and translator). Lowestoft, UK: Scorpion Press.

Klee, Paul (1898-1918/1965). *The diaries of Paul Klee 1898-1918.* (Felix Klee, Ed.). London: Peter Owen.

Knowles, Michael D. (1978). Thomas Becket. In *Encyclopaedia Britannica* (*2*, pp. 786-88). Chicago: Encyclopaedia Britannica.

Koenigsberger, H. G. (1998, January 2). Mathematics in the West. Letter to the *Times Literary Supplement*, 15.

Koestler, Arthur (1960). *The lotus and the robot.* London: Hutchinson

Koestler, Arthur (1961). *Arrow in the blue.* New York: Macmillan.

Kohn, Hans (1960). *The mind of Germany.* New York: Scribner's.

Konopka, Gisela (1966). *The adolescent girl in conflict.* Englewood Cliffs, NJ: Prentice Hall.

Kuhn, Thomas S. (1970). *The structure of scientific revolutions.* Chicago: Chicago University Press.

Kupferberg, Herbert (1972). *The Mendelssohns.* New York: Scribner.

Landes, David S. (1998). *The wealth and poverty of nations: Why some are rich and some poor.* New York: W. W. Norton.

Lange, Victor (1975). Thomas Mann the novelist. In S. Corngod, V. Lange, T. Ziolkowski, *Thomas Mann 1875-1955*. Princeton, NJ: Princeton University Library.

Larner, John (1980). *Italy in the age of Dante and Petrarch 1216-1380.* London: Longman

Latourette, Kenneth S. (1953). *A history of Christianity.* New York: Harper.

Leiter, Samuel L. (1979). *The art of Kabuki: Famous plays in performance.* Berkeley: University of California Press.

Leiter, Samuel L. (1982). Introduction. In the *Grand Kabuki souvenir book* (pp. 5-11). New York: Metropolitan Opera Association and the Japan Society.

Lens, Willy, & Rand, Per (2000). Motivation and cognition: Their role in the development of giftedness. In K. A. Heller, F. J. Mönks, R. J. Sternberg, & R. F. Subotnik (Eds.), *International handbook of giftedness and talent* (pp. 193-202). Amsterdam: Elsevier.

Le Roy Ladurie, Emmanuel (2001). *Saint-Simon and the court of Louis XIV.* Chicago: University of Chicago Press.

Lewin, Kurt (1936/1948). *Resolving social conflicts.* New York: Harper.

Lewis, Wyndham D. B. (1959). *Molière: The comic mask.* New York: Coward McCann.

Lieberich, Heinz (1978). Emperor Louis IV. In *Encyclopaedia Britannica* (*11*, pp 116-18). Chicago: Encyclopaedia Britannica.

Lloyd, G. E. R. (1970). *Early Greek science: Thales to Aristotle.* New York: W. W. Norton.

Lynton, Norbert (1964). *Klee.* London: Spring Books.

Madelin, Louis (1967). *The Consulate and the Empire 1789-1809.* New York: AMS Press.

Mann, Thomas (1901/1957). *Buddenbrooks: The decline of a family.* London: Penguin.

Mann, Thomas (1918/1983). *Reflections of a nonpolitical man.* New York: Frederick Ungar.

Mann, Thomas (1933-43/1978). *Joseph and his brothers.* London: Penguin.

Mann, Thomas (1938/1957). Goethe's Faust. In T. Mann, *Essays by Thomas Mann* (pp. 3-47). New York: Random House.

Mann, Thomas (1945/1955). *Adel des Geistes.* Frankfurt/M: S. Fisher.

Mann, Thomas (1948). Joseph und seine Brüder: Ein Vortrag. In T. Mann, *Neue Studien* (pp. 161-85). Stockholm: Bermann-Fischer.

Manuel, Frank E. (1968). *A portrait of Isaac Newton.* Cambridge, MA: Harvard University Press.

Maraini, Fosco (1960). *Meeting with Japan.* New York: Viking Press.

Marius, Richard (1985). *Thomas More.* New York: Alfred A. Knopf.

Martindale, Colin (2001). Oscillations and analogies: Thomas Young, MD, FRS, Genius. *American Psychologist, 56,* 343-45.

Marx, Karl (1852/1963). *The eighteenth Brumaire of Louis Bonaparte.* New York: International Publishers.

Masten, Ann S., & Coatsworth, J. Douglas (1998). The development of competence in favorable and unfavorable environments: Lessons from research on successful children. *American Psychologist, 53,* 205-20.

Masur, Gerhard S. (1969). *Simón Bolívar.* Albuquerque: University of New Mexico Press.

Masur, Gerhard S. (1978). Simón Bolívar. In *Encyclopaedia Britannica* (*2*, pp. 1205-08). Chicago: Encyclopaedia Britannica.

Mathy, Francis (1989). Introduction. In S. Endo, *The golden country* (pp. 7-14). London: Peter Owen

Matsukata Reischauer, Haru (1986). *Samurai and silk.* Cambridge, MA: Harvard University Press.

Mayo, Charles W. (1970). *Mayo: The story of my family and my career.* London: Hodder and Stoughton.

McCully, Marilyn (2002). Picasso. In *Encyclopaedia Britannica* (*25*, pp. 860-64). Chicago: Encyclopaedia Britannica.

McLellan, David (1973). *Karl Marx: His life and thought.* New York: Harper & Row.

McNeil, Elton B. (1974). *The psychology of being human*. San Francisco: Canfield.

Melograni, Piero (2000). Prefazione. In D. Biocca & M. Canali, *L'Informatore: Silone, i comunisti e la polizia* (pp. 7-11). Milan: Luni.

Menzel, Wolfgang (1882). *History of Germany*. London: George Bell.

Merson, John (1990). *The genius that was China*. Woodstock, NY: Overlook Press.

Michelmore, Peter (1978). Albert Einstein. *In Encyclopaedia Britannica* (6, pp. 510-14). Chicago: Encyclopaedia Britannica.

Miller, Leon K. (1999). The savant-syndrome: Intellectual impairment and exceptional skills. *Psychological Bulletin, 125*, 31-46.

Mokyr, Joel (1990). *The lever of riches: Technological creativity and economic progress*. New York: Oxford University Press.

Moloney, James C. (1954/1962). Child training and Japanese conformity. In B. S. Silberman (Ed.), *Japanese character and Culture* (pp. 214-19). Tucson: University of Arizona Press.

Mönks, Franz J.; Heller, Kurt A.; & Passow, A. Harry (2000). The study of giftedness: Reflections on where we are and where we are going. In K. A. Heller, F. J. Mönks, R. J. Sternberg, & R. F. Subotnik (Eds.), *International handbook of giftedness and talent* (pp. 839-63). Amsterdam: Elsevier.

Mönks, Franz J. & Mason, Emmanuel J. (2000). Developmental psychology and giftedness: Theories and research. In K. A. Heller, F. J. Mönks, R. J. Sternberg, & R. F. Subotnik (Eds.), *International handbook of giftedness and talent* (pp. 141-55). Amsterdam: Elsevier.

Morelock, Martha J., & Feldman, David A. (2000). Prodigies, savants and Williams syndrome: Windows into talent and cognition. In K. A. Heller, F. J. Mönks, R. J. Sternberg, & R. F. Subotnik (Eds.), *International handbook of giftedness and talent* (pp. 227-41). Amsterdam: Elsevier.

Morettini-Bura, Maria Antonietta (1993). *Linee di storia della letteratura italiana—Il Novecento*. Perugia: Università Italiana per Stranieri.

Morgan, Ted (1980). *Maugham*. New York: Simon and Schuster.

Morris, Colin (1972). *The discovery of the individual—1050-1200*. New York: Harper & Row.

Morris, Richard B. (1973). *Seven who shaped our destiny: The founding fathers as revolutionaries*. New York: Harper & Row.

Mozart, W. A. (1965). F. Kerst (Ed.), *Mozart, the man and the artist revealed in his own words*. New York: Dover.

Muller, Joseph-Emile (1976). *Velázquez*. London: Thames and Hudson.

Mussen, Paul H., Conger, John J, Kagan, Jerome, Huston, Aletha C. (1984). *Child development and personality*. New York: Harper & Row.

Naff, Clayton (1994). *About face: How I stumbled onto Japan's social revolution*. New York: Kodansha International.

Nevins, Allan (1954). *Ford: The times, the man, the company*. New York: Scribner.

Newman, Ernest (1937/1976). *The life of Richard Wagner*. Cambridge: Cambridge University Press.

Newton, Eric (1956). *European painting and sculpture*. London: Penguin.

Newton, Eric (1957). Style and vision in art (I, II, III, IV, V). *The Listener*, (March 21, 467-69; March 28, 509-11; April 4, 552-54; April 11, 593-95; April 18, 629-31).

Newton, Eric (1960). *The arts of man*. Greenwich, CT: New York Graphic Society.

Newton, Eric (1962). *The meaning of beauty*. London: Penguin.

Newton, Eric (1964). *The romantic rebellion*. New York: Schocken Books.

Nikiforov, Leonid, A. (1978). Peter I, the Great, of Russia. In *Encyclopaedia Britannica* (*14*, pp. 157-61). Chicago: Encyclopaedia Britannica.

Nitobe, Inazo (1905/2001). *Bushido: The soul of Japan*. New York: ICG Muse.

Oberman, Heiko A. (1982/1992). *Luther: Man between God and the devil*. New York: Doubleday.

O'Connell, D. P. (1968). *Richelieu*. New York: World Publishing.

Ortega y Gasset, José (1921/1964). *España invertebrada*. Madrid: Espasa-Calpe.

Ortolani, Benito (1995). *The Japanese theater*. Princeton, NJ: Princeton University Press.

Padover, Saul K. (1978). *Karl Marx: An intimate biography*. New York: McGraw-Hill.

Park, Robert E. (1928). Human migration and the marginal man. *American Journal of Sociology*, *32*, 881-93.

Pascal, Blaise (1647/1976). *Pensées*. Paris: Mercure de France.

Payne, Robert (1968). *Marx*. New York: Simon and Schuster.

Penrose, Roland (1981). *Picasso: His life and work*. London: Granada.

Perelli, Cippo R. (1993). I tempi di Legnano: La Battaglia del 1176 nel quadro politico dell'Italia padana. In *Il Medioevo e la battaglia di Legnano* (pp. 1-6). Legnano: Sagra del Carroccio.

Peter, Laurence, J. (1972). *The Peter prescription: How to be creative, confident, & competent*. New York: William Morrow.

Peyrefitte, Alain (1976/1981). *The trouble with France [Le Mal Français]*. New York: Alfred A. Knopf.

Phillips, Kevin (1999). *The cousins' wars: Religion, politics, & the triumph of AngloAmerica*. New York: Basic Books.

Piaget, Jean (1952). Autobiography. In E.G. Baring et. al., *History of psychology in autobiography* (*4*, pp. 237-56). Worcester, MA: Clark University Press.

Plant, Margaret (1978). *Paul Klee: Figures and faces*. London: Thames and Hudson.

Policastro, Emma, & Gardner, Howard (1999). From case studies to robust generalization: An approach to the study of creativity. In R. Sternberg (Ed.), *Handbook of creativity*. Cambridge: Cambridge University Press.

Poole, Austin L. (1929). Philip of Swabia and Otto IV. In *Cambridge Medieval History* (*6*, pp. 44-79). Cambridge: Cambridge University Press.

Popper, Karl R. (1961). *The poverty of historicism*. London: Routledge & Kegan Paul.

Porter, Roy (2001). *Enlightenment: Britain and the creation of the modern world*. London: Penguin.

Powell, Colin (1995). *My American journey*. New York: Random House.

Pudney, John (1976). *Lewis Carrol and his world*. London: Thames and Hudson.

Ramsey, John Fraser (1973). *Spain: The rise of the first world power*. University: University of Alabama Press.

Ranke, Leopold von (1881-88/1921). *Weltgeschichte*. Munich: Duncker & Humblot.

Raup. David M. (1986). *The nemesis affair*. New York: W. W. Norton.

Reich-Ranicki, Marcel (1999). *Mein Leben*. Stuttgart: Deutsche Verlags-Anstalt.

Reischauer, Edwin (1976). *The Japanese*. Cambridge, MA: Harvard University Press.

Renzulli, Joseph S. (1986). The three-ring conception of giftedness: A developmental model of creative productivity. In R. J. Sternberg & J. E. Davidson (Eds.), *Conceptions of giftedness* (pp. 53-92). Cambridge: Cambridge University Press.

Richardson, John (1991). *A life of Picasso, I, 1881-1906*. New York: Random House.

Richardson, John (1996). *A life of Picasso, II, 1907-1917.* New York: Random House.

Richie, Donald (1997). Second preface. In Lafcadio Hearn's *Japan: An anthology of his writings on the country and its people.* Tokyo: Charles E. Tuttle.

Rimer, Thomas, J. (1990). *Culture and identity.* Princeton, NJ: Princeton University Press.

Roper, William (1556/1963). *Life of Saint Thomas More.* London: J.M. Dent.

Rosen, Charles (1988, October 27). Inventor of modern Opera. *New York Review of Books,* 8-14.

Rostan, Susan M., Pariser, David, & Gruber, Howard E. (1998). *What if Picasso, Lautrec and Klee were in my art class?* Paper presented at the annual meeting of the American Educational Research Association, San Diego, April 1998.

Rothbaum, Fred, Weisz, John, Pott, Martha, Miyake, Kazuo, & Morelli, Gilda (2000). Attachment and Culture: Security in the United States and Japan. *American Psychologist, 55,* 1093-1104.

Routh, Francis (1975). *Stravinsky.* London: J.M. Dent.

Runco, Mark A. (1991). *Divergent thinking.* Norwood, NJ: Ablex.

Runco, Mark A. (1995). Insight for creativity, expression for impact. *Creativity Research Journal, 8,* 377-90.

Runco, Mark A. (1999). Contrarianism. In M. A. Runco, & S. R. Pritzker (Eds.), *Encyclopedia of creativity (1,* pp. 367-71).

Ryan, Alan (2000, December 15). Misery and mockery: The horrors of Bertrand Russell's family life and his achievements as a liberator (a review of Ray Monk's "Bertrand Russell: The ghost of madness"). *Times Literary Supplement,* 3-4.

Sagar, Keith (1980). *The life of D. H. Lawrence.* London: Eyre Methuen.

Saint-Simon, Duke de (1740-50/1918). *Memoirs of the Duke de Saint-Simon.* London: Stanley Paul

Sakae, Shioya (1956). *Chûshingura: An exposition.* Tokyo: Hokuseido.

Sameroff, Arnold (1975). Transactional models in early social relations. *Human Development, 18,* 65-79.

San Lazzaro, G. di (1957). *Klee: A study of his life and work.* London: Thames and Hudson.

Sansom, George. (1961). *A history of Japan 1334-1615.* Stanford, CA: Stanford University Press.

Schlögel, Hermann A. (1986). *Amenophis IV. Echnaton.* Hamburg: Rowohlt.

Schoon, Ingrid (2000). A lifespan approach to talent development. In K. A. Heller, F. J. Mönks, R. J. Sternberg, & R. F. Subotnik (Eds.), *International handbook of giftedness and talent* (pp. 213-25). Amsterdam: Elsevier.

Schuchert, Richard A. (1978). Translator's preface. In S. Endo, *A life of Jesus* (pp. 3-5). New York: Paulist Press.

Schuldberg, David, & Sass, Louis A. (1999). Schizophrenia. In M. A. Runco, & S. R. Pritzker (Eds.), *Encyclopedia of creativity (2,* pp. 501-14). San Diego, CA: Academic Press.

Scott, Teres Enix (1999). Knowledge. In M. A. Runco, & S. R. Pritzker (Eds.), *Encyclopedia of creativity (2,* pp. 119-29). San Diego, CA: Academic Press.

Shiba, Ryotaro (1998). *The last shogun.* New York: Kodansha International.

Shimizu, Yoshiaki, Ed. (1988). *Japan: The shaping of daimyo culture 1185-1868.* New York: George Braziller.

Siegler, R. S, & Kotovsky, K. (1986). Two levels of giftedness. In R. J. Sternberg & J. E. Davidson (Eds.), *Conceptions of giftedness* (pp. 417-35). Cambridge: Cambridge University Press.

Silone, Ignazio (1937/1962). *Bread and wine*. New York: Atheneum.

Simonton, Dean Keith (1991). Emergence and realization of genius: The lives and works of 120 classical composers. *Journal of Personality and Social Psychology*, *61*, 829-40.

Simonton, Dean Keith (1994). *Greatness: Who makes history and why*. New York: Guilford.

Simonton, Dean Keith (2000). Genius and giftedness: Same or different? In K. A. Heller, F. J. Mönks, R. J. Sternberg, & R. F. Subotnik (Eds.), *International handbook of giftedness and talent* (pp. 111-21). Amsterdam: Elsevier.

Sloane, Kathryn D., & Sosniak, Lauren A. (1985). The development of accomplished sculptors. In B. S. Bloom (Ed.), *Developing talent in young people* (pp. 90-138). New York: Balantine.

Smith, Patrick (1998). *Japan*. New York: Vintage.

Smith, Warren Thomas (1980). *Augustine: His life and thought*. Atlanta, GA: John Knox.

Solomon, Maynard (1995). *Mozart: A life*. New York: HarperCollins.

Sprinthall, Norman A., & Collins, W. Andrew (1984). *Adolescent psychology*. Reading, MA: Addison-Wesley.

Stark, Rodney (1997). *The rise of Christianity*. San Francisco: HarperCollins.

Stepien, William J., Gallagher, Shelagh A., Workman David (1993). Problem-based learning for traditional and interdisciplinary classrooms. *Journal for the education of the gifted*, *16*, 338-57.

Sternberg, Robert J. (1988). *The triarchic mind: A new theory of human intelligence*. New York: Viking.

Sternberg, Robert J., & Lubart, Todd I. (1995). *Defying the crowd: Cultivating creativity in a culture of conformity*. New York: Free Press.

Sternberg, Robert J., & Lubart, Todd I. (1999). The concept of creativity: Prospects and paradigms. In R. J. Sternberg (Ed.), *Handbook of creativity* (pp. 3-15). Cambridge: Cambridge University Press.

Stille, Alexander (2000, May 15). The spy who failed. *The New Yorker*, 44-48.

Strayer, Joseph R. (1970). *On the Medieval origins of the modern state*. Princeton, NJ: Princeton University Press.

Sugimoto, Etsu Inagaki (1933). *A daughter of the samurai*. London: Hurst & Blackett.

Sungolowsky, Joseph (1974). *Beaumarchais*. New York: Twayne

Swanson, R. N. (1983). Doctrine of two swords. In *Dictionary of the Middle Ages* (*12*, pp. 233-35). New York: Charles Scribner's Sons.

Tasso, Torquato (1586/1973). *Il Malpiglio: A dialogue on the court*. Hanover, NH: Darthmouth College.

Tastu, Amable (1850). Notes. In J. de La Fontaine: *Fables*. Paris: Lehuby

Taylor, Alfred E., & Merlan Philip (1973). Plato. In *Encyclopaedia Britannica* (*18*, pp. 20-56). Chicago: Encyclopaedia Britannica.

Taylor, Francis Henry (1948). *The taste of angels*. Boston: Little Brown.

Terman, Lewis, M. (1926). *Genetic studies of genius. Vol. 1 Mental and physical traits of a thousand gifted children*. Stanford, CA: Stanford University Press.

Therivel, William A. (1988). *Personal weltanschauungen and major assistances and misfortunes of life: An empirical approach.* Thesis for the Degree of Master of Psychology. University of Houston.

Therivel, William A. (1990). *Personal weltanschauungen and major assistances and misfortunes of life: An expanded empirical approach.* Dissertation for the Degree of Doctor of Psychology. University of Houston. *Dissertation Abstract International 51,* 05-9024579.

Therivel, William A. (1992). Personalidad insular versus visitante. [Insular versus visitor personality]. In *La Psicología Social en Mexico* (*4,* pp. 380-87). México: Associacíon Mexicana de Psicología Social.

Therivel, William A. (1993). The challenged personality as a precondition for sustained creativity. *Creativity Research Journal, 6,* 413-24.

Therivel, William A. (1995). *Long term effect of power on creativity. Creativity Research Journal, 8,* 173-92.

Therivel, William A. (1998). Creative genius and the GAM theory of personality: Why Mozart and not Salieri? *Journal of Social Behavior and Personality, 13,* 201-34.

Therivel, William A. (1999a). Why are eccentrics not eminently creative? *Creativity Research Journal, 12,* 47-55.

Therivel, William A. (1999b). Why Mozart and not Salieri. *Creativity Research Journal, 12,* 67-76.

Thompson, Lee Anne, & Plomin, Robert (2000). Genetic tools for exploring individual differences in intelligence. In K. A. Heller, F. J. Mönks, R. J. Sternberg, & R. F. Subotnik (Eds.), *International handbook of giftedness and talent* (pp. 157-64). Amsterdam: Elsevier.

Thoreau, Henry David (1854/1975). Walden. In D. F. Flower (Ed.), *Henry David Thoreau: Essays, journals, and poems* (pp. 166-469). Greenwich, CT: Fawcett.

Tilley, Arthur (1921). *Molière.* New York: Russell & Russell.

Tocqueville, Alexis de (1835-40/1987). *Democracy in America.* New York: Alfred A. Knopf.

Tocqueville, Alexis de (1835-40/1988). *Democracy in America.* New York: HarperPerrenial.

Tolstoy, Leo (1876/1965). *Anna Karenina.* New York: Random House.

Torrance, E. P. (1988). The nature of creativity as manifest in its testing. In R. J. Sternberg (Ed.), *The nature of creativity—Contemporary psychological perspectives* (pp. 43-75). Cambridge: Cambridge University Press.

Totman, Conrad (1993). *Tokugawa Ieyasu: Shogun.* Torrance, CA: Heian International.

Toynbee, Arnold J. (1978). Julius Caesar. In *Encyclopaedia Britannica* (*3,* pp. 575-80). Chicago: Encyclopaedia Britannica.

Trafton, Dain A. (1973). Introduction. In T. Tasso, *Il Malpiglio: A dialogue on the court* (pp. 1-3). Hanover, NH: Darthmouth College.

Trotter, Robert J. (1986, August). Profile: Robert J. Sternberg; Three heads are better than one—The triarchic theory. *Psychology Today,* 56-62.

Turnbull, S. R. (1977). *The samurai: A military history.* New York: Macmillan.

Tyler, William, R. (1971). *Dijon and the Valois Dukes of Burgundy.* Norman: University of Oklahoma Press.

Valignano, Alessandro (1580/1962). *Sumario* (selected pages). In B.S. Silberman (Ed.), *Japanese character and culture: A book of selected readings* (pp. 286-88). Tucson: University of Arizona Press.

Vallentin, Antonina (1954). *The drama of Albert Einstein*. Garden City, NY: Doubleday.

Vasari, Giorgio (1550/1967). *Lives of the most eminent painters*. New York: Heritage Press.

Vermeule, Emily (1992, March 26). The world turned upside down. *New York Review of Books*, 40-43.

Wahl, Rudolph (1941/1950). *Kaiser Friedrich Barbarossa*. Munich: F. Bruckmann.

Waley, Daniel (1988). *The Italian city-republics*. London: Longman.

Wallace, Robert (1967). *The world of Leonardo 1452-1519*. New York: Time-Life.

Walsham, Alexandra (2001, April 6). The many Mores. *Times Literary Supplement*, 34.

Wasserman, Jack (1984). *Leonardo*. Norwalk, CN: Easton Press.

Watson, Peter (2000). *A terrible beauty: A history of the people & ideas that shaped the modern mind*. London: Weidenfeld & Nicolson.

Wattenberg, William W. (1973). *The adolescent years*. New York: Harcourt Brace Jovanovich.

Weaver, William (2000, March 14). The mystery of Ignazio Silone. *The New York Review of Books*, 32-37.

Weiss, Beno (1993). *Understanding Calvino*. Columbia: University of South Carolina Press.

Weisberg, Robert W. (1999). Creativity and knowledge: A challenge to theories. In R. J. Sternberg (Ed.), *Handbook of creativity* (pp. 226-50). Cambridge: Cambridge University Press.

Weiten, Wayne (1989). *Psychology: Themes and variations*. Pacific Grove, CA: Brooks/ Cole.

Werner, Eric (1963). *Mendelssohn*. London: Collier-Macmillan

West, D. J. (1967). *The young offender*. London: Penguin.

Westfall, Richard S. (1978). Isaac Newton. In *Encyclopaedia Britannica* (*13*, pp. 16-21). Chicago: Encyclopaedia Britannica.

Westfall, Richard S. (1980). *Never at rest: A biography of Isaac Newton*. Cambridge: Cambridge University Press.

White, Eric W. (1966). *Stravinsky*. Berkeley: University of California Press.

Wills, John E. (2001). *1688: A global history*. London: Granta Books.

Wilson, John, A. (1978). Akhenaton. In *Encyclopaedia Britannica* (*1*, pp. 401-03). Chicago: Encyclopaedia Britannica.

Wilson, Richard (1967). *Thomas Becket*. New York: Alfred A. Knopf.

Wilson, William Scott (1979). Introduction. In T. Yamamoto's (ca. 1700/1979) (pp. 9-16). *Hagakure: The book of the samurai*. Tokyo: Kodansha International.

Winner, Ellen (2000). Giftedness: Current theory and research. *Current Directions in Psychological Science*, *9*, 153-55.

Winner, Ellen, & Martino, Gail (2000). Giftedness in non-academic domains: The case of the visual arts and music. In K. A. Heller, F. J. Mönks, R. J. Sternberg, & R. F. Subotnik (Eds.), *International handbook of giftedness and talent* (pp. 95-110). Amsterdam: Elsevier.

Winston, Richard (1967). *Thomas Becket*. New York: Alfred A. Knopf.

Wood, Alexander, & Oldham, Frank (1954). *Thomas Young, natural philosopher: 1773-1829*. Cambridge: Cambridge University Press.

Yamamoto, Tsunetomo (ca. 1700/1983). *Hagakure: The book of the samurai*. Tokyo: Kodansha International.

Author Index

Subject Index